10th Linguistic Annotation Workshop 2016 (LAW X)

Held in conjunction with ACL 2016

Berlin, Germany
11 August 2016

ISBN: 978-1-5108-2777-6

Printed from e-media with permission by:

Curran Associates, Inc.
57 Morehouse Lane
Red Hook, NY 12571

Some format issues inherent in the e-media version may also appear in this print version.

Printed by Curran Associates, Inc. (2016)

Association for Computational Linguistics
209 N. Eighth Street
Stroudsburg, Pennsylvania 18360

Phone: 1-570-476-8006
Fax: 1-570-476-0860

acl@aclweb.org

Additional copies of this publication are available from:

Curran Associates, Inc.
57 Morehouse Lane
Red Hook, NY 12571 USA
Phone: 845-758-0400
Fax: 845-758-2633
Email: curran@proceedings.com
Web: www.proceedings.com

LAW X

The 10th Linguistic Annotation Workshop held in conjunction with ACL 2016

Workshop Proceedings

August 11, 2016
Berlin, Germany

Introduction to the Workshop

The Linguistic Annotation Workshop (LAW) is organized annually by the Association for Computational Linguistics' Special Interest Group for Annotation (ACL SIGANN). It provides a forum to facilitate the exchange and propagation of research results concerned with the annotation, manipulation, and exploitation of corpora; work towards harmonisation and interoperability from the perspective of the increasingly large number of tools and frameworks for annotated language resources; and work towards a consensus on all issues crucial to the advancement of the field of corpus annotation. The series is now in its tenth year, with these proceedings including papers that were presented at LAW X, held in conjunction with the annual meeting of the Association for Computational Linguistics (ACL) in Berlin, Germany, on August 11, 2016.

In 2016, the LAW celebrates its 10th anniversary – the first workshop took place in 2007 at the ACL in Prague. Since then, the LAW has been held every year, consistently drawing substantial participation (both in terms of paper/poster submissions and participation in the actual workshop) providing evidence that the LAW's overall focus continues to be an important area of interest in the field.

This year's LAW has received 50 submissions, out of which 19 long papers and 2 short papers have been accepted to be presented at the workshop, 7 as talks and 14 as posters. In addition to oral paper presentations, LAW X also features an invited talk by Marie-Catherine de Marneffe and a special theme session both dedicated to this year's special theme "Evaluation of Annotation Quality". The special theme session includes a short tutorial on the advantages of using item-response models by Dirk Hovy as well as a general discussion.

Our thanks go to SIGANN, our organizing committee, for its continuing organization of the LAW workshops, and to the ACL 2016 workshop chairs for their support. Also, we thank the ACL 2016 publication chairs for their help with these proceedings. Most of all, we would like to thank all the authors for submitting their papers to the workshop, and our program committee members for their dedication and their thoughtful reviews. We also thank our sponsor, the Cluster of Excellence "Multimodal Computing and Interaction" (MMCI) at Saarland University.

Special Theme: Evaluation of Annotation Quality

This special theme considers current practice in evaluation of linguistic annotations and its successes and failures by asking questions such as: How are we as a community measuring inter-annotator agreement to date, and are there sounder ways to measure it? How can we estimate the annotation quality of existing resources, and what can be done to document annotated data to help others assess its reliability?

1. How agreement is measured in various (new or existing) annotation projects, and what the different scores tell us in each case.
2. Good acceptance thresholds for different annotation tasks and metrics, and/or how to determine them.
3. Previously proposed but not widely used measures for agreement or annotation quality.
4. Proposals for quantitative or qualitative methods to measure agreement or annotation quality.
5. Proposals for documentation of published resources to support their evaluation, means and methods to achieve community evaluation of linguistically-annotated resources, etc.

Annemarie Friedrich and Katrin Tomanek

Invited Talk: Marie-Catherine de Marneffe

Assessing the Consistency and Use of "Common Sense" and Dependency Annotations

In this talk, I will discuss my work on two types of annotations: "common sense" annotations obtained through crowdsourcing techniques as well as specific linguistic annotations by experts.

First, I will talk about "common sense" annotations gathered on Mechanical Turk. I focus on two datasets, the Internet Argument Corpus, which contains annotation of agreement in online debate (Walker et al., 2012), and the PragBank corpus, which provides veridicality annotations – whether events described in a text are viewed as actual, non-actual or uncertain (de Marneffe et al., 2012). I will review the quality of the annotations of these corpora and how the corpora have been used in research. I will suggest that since judgments of agreement and veridicality are not always categorical, they should be modeled as distributions, in line with Passonneau and Carpenter (2014).

Second, I will turn to annotations of specific linguistic representations, mainly dependency annotations where experts are annotating grammatical relations between words of a sentence, and investigate how we can assess the consistency of these annotations within a corpus. I will present preliminary results of our assessment of how much consistency is found in some of the Universal Dependency corpora using the Boyd et al. (2008)'s technique for identifying errors in dependency annotations.

References:

Adriane Boyd, Markus Dickinson and Detmar Meurers. 2008. *On detecting errors in dependency treebanks*. In Research on Language and Computation 6(2): 113–137.

Marie-Catherine de Marneffe, Christopher D. Manning and Christopher Potts. 2012. *Did it happen? The pragmatic complexity of veridicality assessment.* In Computational Linguistics 38(2): 301-333.

Rebecca J. Passonneau and Bob Carpenter. 2014. *The benefits of a model of annotation.* In Transactions of the Association for Computational Linguistics 2: 311-326.

Marilyn A. Walker, Jean E. Fox Tree, Pranav Anand, Rob Abbott, and Joseph King. 2012. *A corpus for research on deliberation and debate.* In Proceedings of the 8th Language Resources and Evaluation Conference: 812–817.

Bio. Marie-Catherine de Marneffe is an assistant professor in Linguistics at The Ohio State University. She received her PhD from Stanford University in December 2012 under the supervision of Christopher D. Manning. She is developing computational linguistic methods that capture what is conveyed by speakers beyond the literal meaning of the words they say. Primarily she wants to ground meanings in corpus data, and show how such meanings can drive pragmatic inference. She has also worked on Recognizing Textual Entailment and contributed to defining the Stanford Dependencies and the Universal Dependencies representations, which are practical representations of grammatical relations and predicate argument structure. She serves as a member of the NAACL board and the Computational Linguistics editorial board.

Invited Tutorial: Dirk Hovy

How Item-Response Models Can Help us Take the Headache out of Annotation Projects

In annotation projects, we are usually interested in three questions (to varying degrees):

1. how do I aggregate my scores to get the "correct" answer?
2. how much can I trust the annotators?
3. how difficult is the task/individual items?

The traditional approach to answer these has been through inter-annotator agreement (IAA) scores, such as Cohen's Kappa, which can give us weights for each annotator, or simply by raw agreement and majority voting. However, there have been known problems with both Kappa (overestimating chance agreement when one label is prevalent, Feinstein and Cicchetti, 1990) and majority voting (unreliable annotators can swamp the result) that negatively affect questions 1 and 2 (see also Artstein and Poesio, 2008). In addition, neither of these measures tell us how difficult the task is. IAAs are thus only a proxy for the answers we really want.

Recently, Passonneau and Carpenter (2014) have suggested probabilistic item-response models (IRT) as an alternative. These models have several advantages, since thet can directly answer the above questions via

- annotator scores
- distributions over labels
- entropy scores for the task and individual items.

Despite this promise, IRTs are not yet in wide use, possibly because they can seem complex, unintuitive, and complicated to use. In this hands-on tutorial, I want to therefore introduce an available IRT (MACE: Hovy et al., 2013) and show in examples how we can easily get the answers we want from the data, plus a host of other information. The code is freely available, it is easy to use, and it can help us answer all the relevant questions for an annotation task.

References:

Dirk Hovy, Taylor Berg-Kirkpatrick, Ashish Vaswani, and Eduard Hovy. 2013. *Learning Whom to Trust with MACE.* In Proceedings of NAACL HLT.

Rebecca J Passonneau and Bob Carpenter. 2014. *The benefits of a model of annotation.* In Transactions of the Association for Computational Linguistics.

Alvan R. Feinstein and Domenic V. Cicchetti. 1990. *High agreement but low kappa: I. the problems of two paradoxes.* In Journal of Clinical Epidemiology.

Ron Artstein and Massimo Poesio. 2008. *Inter-coder agreement for computational linguistics.* In Computational Linguistics.

Bio. Dirk Hovy is an associate professor in natural language processing at the University of Copenhagen. His research focuses on the interaction of statistical models, language, and demographic factors. He received his PhD in Computer Science from the University of Southern California, and holds an MA in sociolinguistics from the University of Marburg, Germany. Dirk has authored papers on a variety of NLP topics, including semantic and syntactic analysis, domain adaptation, and information extraction. All of these involved annotation at some point, and the associate problems have led to the development of MACE. Outside of research, Dirk enjoys cooking, tango, and leather-crafting, as well as picking up heavy things and putting them back down. You can find an updated biography and more at `http://dirkhovy.com/`.

LAW Co-chairs

Annemarie Friedrich, Saarland University
Katrin Tomanek, OpenTable

Organizing Committee:

Stefanie Dipper, Ruhr University Bochum
Chu-Ren Huang, The Hong Kong Polytechnic University
Nancy Ide, Vassar College
Lori Levin, Carnegie Mellon University
Adam Meyers, New York University
Antonio Pareja-Lora, SIC & ILSA, UCM / ATLAS, UNED
Massimo Poesio, University of Trento
Sameer Pradhan, Cemantix.org and Boulder Learning, Inc.
Ines Rehbein, Leibniz ScienceCampus
Manfred Stede, University of Potsdam
Fei Xia, University of Washington
Nianwen Xue, Brandeis University
Heike Zinsmeister, University of Hamburg

Program Committee:

Adam Meyers, New York University
Alexis Palmer, Heidelberg University
Andreas Witt, Institut für Deutsche Sprache
Ani Nenkova, University of Pennsylvania
Ann Bies, Linguistic Data Consortium
Anna Nedoluzhko, Charles University Prague
Antonio Pareja-Lora, Universidad Complutense de Madrid
Aravind Joshi, University of Pennsylvania
Archna Bhatia, Florida Institute for Human and Machine Cognition
Barbara Plank, University of Groningen
Bonnie Webber, University of Edinburgh
Caroline Sporleder, University of Göttingen
Christian Chiarcos Goethe University Frankfurt
Christiane Fellbaum, Princeton University
Chu-Ren Huang, The Hong Kong Polytechnic University
Collin Baker, University of California, Berkeley
Dirk Hovy, University of Copenhagen
Djamé Seddah, University Paris-Sorbonne
Els Lefever, Ghent University
Fei Xia, University of Washington
Heike Zinsmeister, Hamburg University
Ines Rehbein, Heidelberg University
Joel Tetreault, Yahoo!
James Pustejovsky, Brandeis University
Josef Ruppenhofer, Heidelberg University
Kim Gerdes, University Paris-Sorbonne

Lori Levin, Carnegie Mellon University
Manfred Pinkal, Saarland University
Manfred Stede, University of Potsdam
Markus Dickinson, Indiana University
Martha Palmer, University of Colorado Boulder
Massimo Poesio, University of Essex
Nancy Ide, Vassar College
Nathan Schneider, University of Edinburgh
Nianwen Xue, Brandeis University
Nicoletta Calzolari, Italian National Research Council
Omri Abend, University of Jerusalem
Özlem Çetinoğlu, University of Stuttgart
Sameer Pradhan, Cemantix.org and Boulder Learning, Inc.
Sandra Kübler, Indiana University, Bloomington
Stefanie Dipper, Ruhr University Bochum
Tomaž Erjavec, Jožef Stefan Institute, Ljubljana
Udo Hahn, University of Jena
Valia Kordoni, Humboldt University of Berlin

Invited Speakers:

Marie-Catherine de Marneffe, The Ohio State University
Dirk Hovy, University of Copenhagen

Table of Contents

Workshop Program

9:00 – 10:30	**Session 1: Opening and Invited Talk**
9:00 – 9:10	Opening Remarks
9:10 – 10:05	Invited talk: *Assessing the Consistency and Use of "Common Sense" and Dependency Annotations.* Marie-Catherine de Marneffe
10:05 – 10:30	*Generating Disambiguating Paraphrases for Structurally Ambiguous Sentences* Manjuan Duan, Ethan Hill and Michael White
10:30 – 11:00	**Coffee Break**
11:00 – 12:40	**Session 2: Dependency Annotation and Discourse**
11:00 – 11:25	*Dependency Annotation Choices: Assessing Theoretical and Practical Issues of Universal Dependencies* Kim Gerdes and Sylvain Kahane
11:25 – 11:50	*Conversion from Paninian Karakas to Universal Dependencies for Hindi Dependency Treebank* Juhi Tandon, Himani Chaudhry, Riyaz Ahmad Bhat and Dipti Sharma
11:50 – 12:15	*Different Flavors of GUM: Evaluating Genre and Sentence Type Effects on Multilayer Corpus Annotation Quality* Amir Zeldes and Dan Simonson
12:15 – 12:40	*Annotating the Discourse and Dialogue Structure of SMS Message Conversations* Nianwen Xue, Qishen Su and Sooyoung Jeong
12:40 – 14:00	**Lunch Break**
14:00 – 14:50	**Session 3: Evaluation of Agreement (Special Theme)**
14:00 - 14:25	*Evaluating Inter-Annotator Agreement on Historical Spelling Normalization* Marcel Bollmann, Stefanie Dipper and Florian Petran
14:25 – 14:50	*Filling in the Blanks in Understanding Discourse Adverbials: Consistency, Conflict, and Context-Dependence in a Crowdsourced Elicitation Task* Hannah Rohde, Anna Dickinson, Nathan Schneider, Christopher N. L. Clark, Annie Louis and Bonnie Webber
14:50 – 16:00	**Session 4: Poster Presentations**
14:50 – 15:05	Poster boasters
15:05 – 16:00	Poster presentation and coffee
16:00 – 17:30	**Session 5: Invited Tutorial and Discussion (Special Theme)**
16:00 – 16:30	Invited tutorial: *How Item-Response Models Can Help us Take the Headache out of Annotation Projects.* Dirk Hovy
16:30 – 17:15	Discussion
17:15 – 17:30	Closing remarks: 10 years of LAW

Building a Cross-document Event-Event Relation Corpus

Yu Hong[1,2]**, Tongtao Zhang**[1]**, Tim O'Gorman**[3]**, Sharone Horowit-Hendler**[4]**,**
Heng Ji[1]**, Martha Palmer**[3]
[1]Computer Science Department, Rensselaer Polytechnic Institute
[2]Department of Computer Science, Soochow University
[3]Department of Linguistics, University of Colorado at Boulder
[4]Institute of Reading Development

Abstract

We propose a new task of extracting event-event relations across documents. We present our efforts at designing an annotation schema and building a corpus for this task. Our schema includes five main types of relations: Inheritance, Expansion, Contingency, Comparison and Temporality, along with 21 subtypes. We also lay out the main challenges based on detailed inter-annotator disagreement and error analysis. We hope these resources can serve as a benchmark to encourage research on this new problem.

1 Introduction

The ultimate goal of Information Extraction (IE) is to construct "Information Networks" (Li et al., 2014) from unstructured texts. Most previous IE work focused on constructing entity-centric Information Networks where each node represents an entity and each edge represents a relation. We propose a novel task to construct a new layer of *event-centric Information Networks* across multiple documents, where each node is an event and the edges capture the relations between two events. This task can provide building blocks for many important applications such as event knowledge base population and temporal event tracking (Do et al., 2012). The nodes can be extracted by existing fine-grained event extraction approaches (Ji and Grishman, 2008; Liao and Grishman, 2010; Hong et al., 2011; Li et al., 2013; Li et al., 2014). However, little previous work can be directly exploited to construct the edges.

In this paper we define a comprehensive schema that includes multiple fine-grained event-event relation types. Some types are similar to those in discourse parsing (Soricut and Marcu, 2003). However, event-event relations are fundamentally different from discourse relations: (1) The input consists of structured events instead of unstructured sentences. (2) For cross-document event pairs, there are neither explicit textual clues nor implicit information about the ordering of clauses that might indicate the relation. Following this schema, we annotated a cross-document event-event relation corpus built on top of the Automatic Content Extraction (ACE2005) [1] event annotations. We will define the task (Section 2), describe the annotation schema (Section 3) and present corpus statistics and annotation challenges (Section 4).

2 Task Definition

In an event-event relation schema, events form a crucial foundation because they serve as nodes and are indispensable in event-centric information networks. We follow the definition of events in the ACE guideline [2]:

Event trigger: the main word which most clearly expresses an event occurrence.

Event arguments: the entities, time expressions and values that are involved in an event.

Event mention: a phrase or sentence within which an event is described, including a trigger and a set of arguments.

Event: a set of coreferential event mentions within one document.

We define the event-event relation task as the annotation of all applicable logical relations between two events. For example, as illustrated in Figure 1, the following events are connected by *Condition* and *Temporality* relations:

Event 1: *Media tycoon Barry Diller on Wednesday quit as chief of Vivendi Universal Entertain-*

[1]http://projects.ldc.upenn.edu/ace

[2]https://www.ldc.upenn.edu/sites/www.ldc.upenn.edu/files/english-events-guidelines-v5.4.3.pdf

Proceedings of LAW X – The 10th Linguistic Annotation Workshop, pages 1–6,
Berlin, Germany, August 11, 2016. ©2016 Association for Computational Linguistics

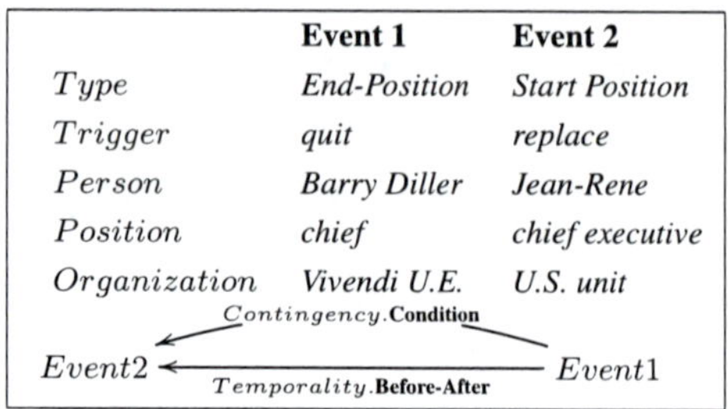

Figure 1: Examples of input and output

ment.

Event 2: *Parent company chairman Jean-Rene Fourtou will replace Diller as chief executive of US unit.*

This example reveals the fact that a successor takes the place only *after the time when (Temporality)* and *under the condition that (Condition)* the predecessor makes room for the successor.

3 Event-Event Relation Schema

Our event-event relation schema includes 5 main ***Types*** – *Inheritance*, *Expansion*, *Contingency*, *Comparison* and *Temporality* – along with 21 ***Subtypes*** as shown in Table 1. Table 1 also demonstrates *Roles*. Events involved in a relation play certain roles. For example, an *Attack* event and an *Injure* event in a *Contingency.Causality* will play *Cause* and *Result* roles respectively. In the following we will present a detailed definition of each subtype.

3.1 Inheritance and Expansion

Inheritance relations include both traditional *Coreference* relations as well as *Subevent* that marks aggregation-to-component relations. *Reemergence* connects recurrent events while *Variation* summarizes the prototype of an event.

Expansion relations include *Confirmation*, which encodes a concept-to-instance or "subset" relation, and *Conjunction* and *Disjunction*, which relate two subevents within a larger event, and mark two subevents as playing similar (*Conjunction*) or dissimilar (*Disjunction*) roles within the larger event. This kind of relation is useful, since a larger event is often not explicitly mentioned.

The combination of these two kinds of relations allow one to build hierarchical representations of parts of an event network, as shown in Figure 2.

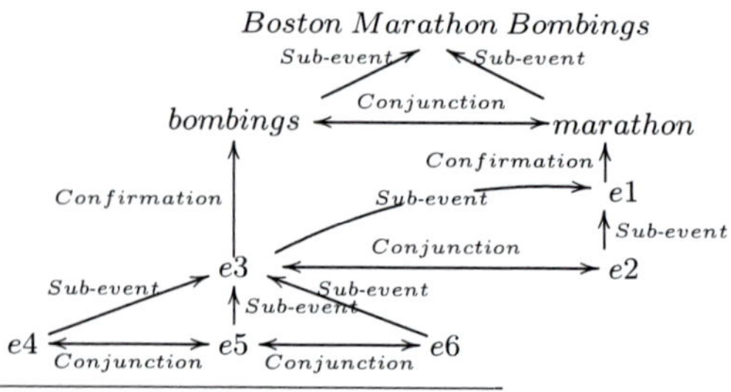

e1 : *117th annual Boston Marathon;*
e2 : *winner crossed the finish line;*
e3 : *explosion near bystanders;*
e4 : 1_{st} *explosion;*
e5 : 2_{nd} *explosion;*
e6 : *the second bomb was placed at the finish line*

Figure 2: A hierarchical event network

3.2 Contingency and Comparison

A ***Contingency*** relation indicates either an event leading to the emergence (*Causality*) or serving as a triggering condition (*Conditional*) of another event.

Comparison relations indicate deeper logical contrasts between relations. *Opposition* indicates a relation in which two events are mutually contradictory, and unlikely to be both true. This has some similarity to *Contrast.Opposition* in the Penn Discourse Treebank (Miltsakaki et al., 2004) or specific annotations of opposition (Feltracco et al., 2015; Takabatake et al., 2015). *Negation* indicates that while two events could both be true, one shows that the other is no longer true. *Competition* shows that two events are contrasting versions of the same underlying "event" (e.g., *retreat* versus *escape in disorder*).

3.3 Temporality

Last but not least, we also define subtypes of *Temporality*, which represents the temporal order of events. *Temporality* has been an active research topic for a long time. We arrange all categories and normalize the subtype names from the previous work to constitute our *Temporality* schema. Figure 3 illustrates the temporal relation subtypes.

In this work, we elaborate the subtypes *Temporality* in comparison with conventional work by introducing *Meet*, *Start* and *Finish*, which emphasizes the existence of time intervals among events.

The correct subtype of the *Temporality* relation has a great impact on the decision of whether the Start-Position and End-Position events have a *Comparison.Opposite* or a *Contingency.Condition*

Types	*Inheritance*	*Expansion*	*Contingency*	*Contingency*	*Temporality*	
Subtypes	**Reemergence**	**Confirmation**	**Comparison**	**Condition**	**Before-After**	**Start**
Roles	Reference	Generalization	Superior	Condition	Before	Included-Start
	Resurgence	Instantiation	Inferior	Emergence	After	Includes
Subtypes	**Sub-event**	**Conjunction**	**Concession**	**Causality**	**Vagueness**	**Overlap**
Roles	Constituent	Homology-1	Not-Achieved	Cause	Vague-1	Partially-Before
	Synthesis	Homology-2	Achieved	Result	Vague-2	Partially-After
Subtypes	**Variation**	**Disjunction**	**Negation**		**Meet**	**Equality**
Roles	Variance	Heterology-1	Negator		Before	Contemporary-1
	Semina	Heterology-2	Initiator		After	Contemporary-2
Subtypes	**Coreference**		**Opposite**		**During**	**Finish**
Roles	Occurrence		Opponent-1		Includes	Includes
	Paraphrasing		Opponent-2		Included-In	Included-Finish

Table 1: Fine-grained event-event relations and roles.

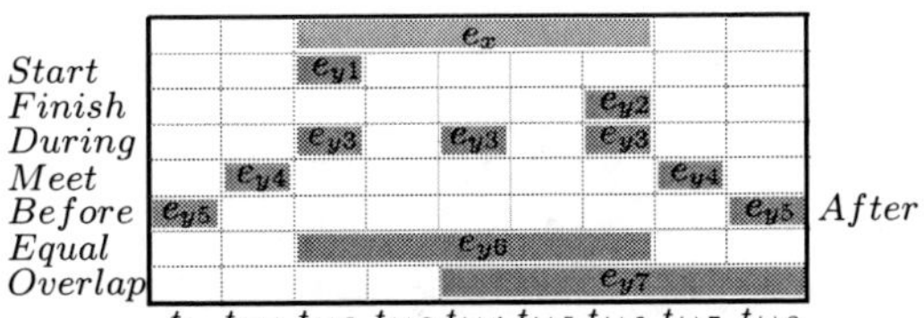

Figure 3: Various temporal relation subtypes between event e_x and event e_{y*} (t is a time interval).

#Topics	**#Documents**	**#Events**	**#Pairs**
Vivendi	3	22	231
Anwar	3	39	741
SARS	2	9	36
MH17	50	196	19,698
Single	67	597	4,904
Total	125	863	25,610

Table 2: Corpus statistics. *Single* denotes topics that only contain one document, and cross-document annotation is not available in those topics. **Pair** indicates the number of pairs consisting of two events from the same topic.

relation, and vice versa.

4 Corpus Annotation

Annotating event-event relations requires an annotator to gain a global view of the overall scenario or topic (e.g., MH17) before exhaustively annotating each event pair. In addition, our relation types are more fine-grained than previous work such as the Richer Event Descriptions (RED) (Ikuta et al., 2014). There are no existing annotation tools to meet these needs, so we developed a new annotation tool to visualize trigger words, arguments and contexts for each event pair to ensure that annotators fully understand documents, background and storyline.

We created an event-event relation corpus based on gold standard events in ACE2005 newswire documents and some additional news documents about *Malaysian Airline 17* (denoted as *MH17*). Table 2 shows the detailed data statistics. Three annotators (*A1* & *A2*: graduate students, *A3*: a linguist) annotate the documents independently. The annotation results from *A1* and *A2* are assessed by *A3* and disagreement among the three annotators is carefully evaluated and *A3* determined the final results.

Table 3 and 4 indicate that this is a very challenging task for annotators. We can see that the major challenge for annotators is the determination of the existence of relations. *Causality* and *Condition* stand as the most challenging types, which require annotators to figure out the storyline of documents and exploit background knowledge. For example, the following two events are from the same document but there are no explicit connectives to indicate the conditional relation between them:

Event 1: *Edward Snowden claimed he was* <u>*trained*</u> *as a secret agent.*

Event 2: *The certification would also have given him some of the skills he needed to* <u>*escape*</u> *scrutiny.*

A1 and A2 also tend to mistakenly label *Sub-*

Annotators	κ Value
A1 and A2	0.1558
A2 and A3	0.1987
A1 and A3	0.1628

Table 3: Stats of Cohen's kappa coefficient.

Transition of Correction	# of Occurrences
unrelated → Condition	142
unrelated → Causality	72
Coreference → unrelated	55
Conjunction → unrelated	48
Causality → unrelated	44

Table 4: Top 5 Error corrections.

event as *Coreference*. Such mistakes happen when the arguments from one event appear as more specific and detailed entities (e.g., *an attack in Baghdad* vs. *an attack in Iraq*). However, when the event network becomes larger and more complicated, errors can be propagated across types, e.g., incorrectly labeled *Sub-event* pairs will also trigger *Conjunction* errors.

Moreover, we have attempted to align the inventory here with other ongoing efforts to annotate within-document event-event relations. Table 5 shows a mapping between a subset of the relations proposed here and those used in the Richer Event Descriptions (RED) (Ikuta et al., 2014). Other similar resources – such as Penn Discourse Treebank (Miltsakaki et al., 2004) – could also be used.

5 Related Work

The proposed schema covers event-event relation types that have been widely studied: (Styler IV et al., 2014; Bethard, 2013; Allen, 1983; Miller et al., 2013; Pustejovsky and Stubbs, 2011; Pustejovsky et al., 2005; UzZaman et al., 2013) also focused on the relation types which are related to *Temporality*. Methods about extracting *Coreference* relations have also been discussed and proposed in (Chen and Ji, 2009; Chen et al., 2009; Bejan and Harabagiu, 2010; Lee et al., 2012; Zhang et al., 2015). (Do et al., 2011; Riaz and Girju, 2013; Mirza and Tonelli, 2014) work on *Causality* relation.

Similar event-event relation schema such as

This work		RED
Inheritance	*Subevent*	***Contains-subevent***
	Coreference	***Identity***
Continency	*Cause*	***Cause***
	Condition	***Precondition***
Comparison	*Opposite*	N/A
	Concession	N/A
Expansion	*Confirmation*	***Set/Member***
Temporality	*Before, After*	***Before***
	During	***Contains***
	Overlap	***Overlap***
	Equality	***Simultaneous***
	Start	***Begins-on***
	Finish	***Ends-on***

Table 5: Mappings to RED (Ikuta et al., 2014)

RED (Ikuta et al., 2014) is in general more coarse-grained and has fewer types and subtypes.

Event-event relations differ from textual entailment (Dagan et al., 2013) or discourse relations (Soricut and Marcu, 2003; Miltsakaki et al., 2004; Radev, 2000), which focus on the relatedness between two sentences, by tackling a full document or multiple documents. We adopted some terminology (e.g., *Causality* and *Expansion*) from the taxonomy of discourse relations (Miltsakaki et al., 2004). We focus on a wider scope of cross-document events with richer and more fine-grained structured event representations.

If we consider each event-event relation instance as a frame (e.g., a contingency/causality event-event relation is similar to the frame causation), the architecture of the Event Networks is also similar to FrameNet (Baker and Sato, 2003) and thus the ontological analysis and constraints in (Ovchinnikova et al., 2010) are also applicable to our task.

6 Conclusions and Future Work

Our work will expand the research venue of IE from entity-centric to event-centric. In the future we will further expand the corpus[3], and compare and integrate with other within-document event-event relation schemas such as RED. We also plan to develop a pilot system using these resources.

[3]The annotated corpus is available at `http://nlp.cs.rpi.edu/data/event_relation.zip`

Acknowledgements

This work was supported by the U.S. ARL NS-CTA No. W911NF-09-2-0053, DARPA DEFT No. FA8750-13-2-0041 and NSF IIS-1523198. The views and conclusions contained in this document are those of the authors and should not be interpreted as representing the official policies, either expressed or implied, of the U.S. Government. The U.S. Government is authorized to reproduce and distribute reprints for Government purposes notwithstanding any copyright notation here on.

References

James F Allen. 1983. Maintaining knowledge about temporal intervals. *Communications of the ACM*, 26(11):832–843.

Collin F. Baker and Hiroaki Sato. 2003. The framenet data and software. In *Proceedings of the Annual Meeting of the Association for Computational Linguistics*.

Cosmin Adrian Bejan and Sanda Harabagiu. 2010. Unsupervised event coreference resolution with rich linguistic features. In *Proceedings of the Annual Meeting of the Association for Computational Linguistics*.

Steven Bethard. 2013. Cleartk-timeml: A minimalist approach to tempeval 2013. In *Proceedings of Joint Conference on Lexical and Computational Semantics*, volume 2, pages 10–14.

Zheng Chen and Heng Ji. 2009. Graph-based event coreference resolution. In *Proceedings of Workshop on Graph-based Methods for Natural Language Processing*.

Zheng Chen, Heng Ji, and Robert Haralick. 2009. A pairwise event coreference model, feature impact and evaluation for event coreference resolution. In *Proceedings of the Workshop on Events in Emerging Text Types*, pages 17–22. Association for Computational Linguistics.

Ido Dagan, Dan Roth, Mark Sammons, and Fabio Massimo Zanzotto. 2013. Recognizing textual entailment: Models and applications. *Synthesis Lectures on Human Language Technologies*, 6(4):1–220.

Quang Do, Yee Seng Chan, and Dan Roth. 2011. Minimally supervised event causality identification. In *Proceedings of Conference on Empirical Methods in Natural Language Processing*.

Quang Xuan Do, Wei Lu, and Dan Roth. 2012. Joint inference for event timeline construction. In *Proceedings of the Joint Conference on Empirical Methods in Natural Language Processing and Computational Natural Language Learning*, pages 677–687.

Anna Feltracco, Elisabetta Jezek, and Bernardo Magnini. 2015. Opposition relations among verb frames. In *Proceedings of the Workshop on EVENTS at the Conference of the North American Chapter of the Association for Computational Linguistics on Human Language*.

Yu Hong, Jianfeng Zhang, Bin Ma, Jian-Min Yao, Guodong Zhou, and Qiaoming Zhu. 2011. Using cross-entity inference to improve event extraction. In *Proceedings of the Annual Meeting of the Association for Computational Linguistics*, pages 1127–1136, Portland, OR, USA.

Rei Ikuta, William F Styler IV, Mariah Hamang, Tim OGorman, and Martha Palmer. 2014. Challenges of adding causation to richer event descriptions. *Proceedings of the Annual Meeting of the Association for Computational Linguistics*.

Heng Ji and Ralph Grishman. 2008. Refining event extraction through cross-document inference. In *Proceedings of the Annual Meeting of the Association for Computational Linguistics*, Columbus, Ohio, USA.

Heeyoung Lee, Marta Recasens, Angel Chang, Mihai Surdeanu, and Dan Jurafsky. 2012. Joint entity and event coreference resolution across documents. In *Proceedings of Conference on Empirical Methods in Natural Language Processing*.

Qi Li, Heng Ji, and Liang Huang. 2013. Joint event extraction via structured prediction with global features. In *Proceedings of the Annual Meeting of the Association for Computational Linguistics*, pages 73–82, Sofia, Bulgaria.

Qi Li, Heng Ji, Yu Hong, and Sujian Li. 2014. Constructing information networks using one single model. In *Proceedings of the Conference on Empirical Methods on Natural Language Processing*.

Shasha Liao and Ralph Grishman. 2010. Using document level cross-event inference to improve event extraction. In *Proceedings of the Annual Meeting of the Association for Computational Linguistics*, pages 789–797, Uppsala, Sweden.

Timothy Miller, Steven Bethard, Dmitriy Dligach, Sameer Pradhan, Chen Lin, and Guergana Savova. 2013. Discovering temporal narrative containers in clinical text. In *Proceedings of the 2013 Workshop on Biomedical Natural Langua ge Processing*.

Eleni Miltsakaki, Rashmi Prasad, Aravind K Joshi, and Bonnie L Webber. 2004. The penn discourse treebank. In *Proceedings of the International Conference on Language Resources and Evaluation*.

Paramita Mirza and Sara Tonelli. 2014. An analysis of causality between events and its relation to temporal information. In *Proceedings of the International Conference on Computational Linguistics*.

Ekaterina Ovchinnikova, Laure Vieu, Alessandro Oltramari, Stefano Borgo, and Theodore Alexandrov. 2010. Data-driven and ontological analysis of framenet for natural language reasoning. In *Proceedings of the International Conference on Language Resources and Evaluation*.

James Pustejovsky and Amber Stubbs. 2011. Increasing informativeness in temporal annotation. In *Proceedings of the 5th Linguistic Annotation Workshop*.

James Pustejovsky, Robert Knippen, Jessica Littman, and Roser Saurí. 2005. Temporal and event information in natural language text. *Language resources and evaluation*, 39(2-3):123–164.

Dragomir Radev. 2000. A common theory of information fusion from multiple text sources, step one: Cross-document structure. In *Proceedings of Special Interest Group on Discourse and Dialogue*.

Mehwish Riaz and Roxana Girju. 2013. Toward a better understanding of causality between verbal events: Extraction and analysis of the causal power of verb-verb associations. In *Proceedings of Special Interest Group on Discourse and Dialogue*.

Radu Soricut and Daniel Marcu. 2003. Sentence level discourse parsing using syntactic and lexical information. In *Proceedings of the Conference of the North American Chapter of the Association for Computational Linguistics on Human Language*, pages 149–156. Association for Computational Linguistics.

William F Styler IV, Steven Bethard, Sean Finan, Martha Palmer, Sameer Pradhan, Piet C de Groen, Brad Erickson, Timothy Miller, Chen Lin, Guergana Savova, et al. 2014. Temporal annotation in the clinical domain. *Transactions of the Association for Computational Linguistics*, 2:143–154.

Yu Takabatake, Hajime Morita, Daisuke Kawahara, Sadao Kurohashi, Ryuichiro Higashinaka, and Yoshihiro Matsuo. 2015. Classification and acquisition of contradictory event pairs using crowdsourcing. In *Proceedings of the Workshop on EVENTS at the Conference of the North American Chapter of the Association for Computational Linguistics on Human Language*.

Naushad UzZaman, Hector Llorens, Leon Derczynski, Marc Verhagen, James F. Allen, and James Pustejovsky. 2013. SemEval-2013 Task 1: TempEval-3: Evaluating Time Expressions, Events, and Temporal Relations. In *Proceedings of the International Workshop on Semantic Evaluation*, pages 1–9.

Tongtao Zhang, Hongzhi Li, Heng Ji, and Shih-Fu Chang. 2015. Cross-document event coreference resolution based on cross-media features. In *Proceedings of Conference on Empirical Methods in Natural Language Processing*.

Annotating *the Little Prince* with Chinese AMRs

Bin Li, Yuan Wen, Lijun Bu, Weiguang Qu
School of Chinese Language and Literature
Nanjing Normal University
Nanjing, China
libin.njnu@gmail.com

Nianwen Xue
Computer Science Department
Brandeis University
Waltham, MA, USA
nwxue@brandeis.edu

Abstract

Abstract Meaning Representation (AMR) is an annotation framework in which the meaning of a full sentence is represented as a rooted, acyclic, directed graph. In this paper, we describe a pilot project in which we develop specifications for the annotation of a Chinese AMR corpus: the Chinese translation of *the Little Prince*. The interagreement smatch score between the two annotators is 0.83. We also propose to integrate alignment into Chinese AMR annotation.

1 Introduction

Abstract Meaning Representation (AMR) is an annotation framework designed to capture the "meaning" of a sentence with a single rooted, acyclic[1], directed graph (Banarescu et al., 2013), departing from previous practices of performing partial semantic annotation that focuses on one component of the sentential meaning at a time. For example, Propbank (Palmer et al., 2005; Xue and Palmer, 2009) and NomBank (Meyers et al., 2004) annotations focus on the predicate-argument structure of verbs and predicative or relational nouns. The annotation is done on a predicate basis and the resulting annotation may not necessarily form a fully connected structure for the entire sentence. The practice was necessary as a first attempt to annotate a key aspect of sentential meaning and contributed to a high-quality corpus that has spurred research in automatic Semantic Role Labeling (SRL) (Gildea and Jurafsky, 2002; Pradhan et al., 2004; Xue and Palmer, 2004; Palmer et al., 2010) and downstream applications. This annotation strategy has been adopted for the predicate-argument structure annotation of other languages as well (Xue and Palmer, 2009; Zaghouani et al., 2012).

As we gain more insights on the sentence meaning from annotating individual meaning components, annotating the meaning for the entire sentence becomes a logical next step. The AMR annotation project is such an attempt, along with other similar efforts such as the Universal Dependency annotation project (Nivre, 2015) and the Semantic Dependency Parsing effort (Oepen et al., 2014).

One salient characteristic of AMR annotation is that it abstracts away from elements of surface syntactic structure such as word order and morpho-syntactic markers. Since word order and morpho-syntactic variations account for much of the cross-linguistic variations, this makes the AMR annotation framework more portable across languages, as the preliminary AMR annotation on Chinese and Czech has demonstrated (Xue et al., 2014).

Another consequence of such "decoupling" from the syntactic structure of a sentence is that the AMR annotation framework gives us more freedom in how we handle cases of syntax-semantic mismatch. Words that do not contribute to the meaning of a sentence (e.g., infinitive "to" in English) are left out of the AMR annotation. In light verb constructions such as "take a bath", since the light verb "take" is semantically impoverished if not vacuous, it is also left out of the AMR annotation. Some discontinuous constructions such as "if... then" can be collapsed into a single relation ":condition".

With this freedom comes responsibility. Since an annotator is free to drop a word or map discontinuous patterns onto single AMR concepts or relations, for the sake of annotation consistency, it is important to provide detailed annotation speci-

[1]Technically, about 0.3% sentences are cyclic in AMR (Banarescu et al., 2015).

Proceedings of LAW X – The 10th Linguistic Annotation Workshop, pages 7–15,
Berlin, Germany, August 11, 2016.

fications for how certain constructions are handled so that they are consistently followed by all annotators.

Since words that "do not carry meaning" are left out of the AMR of a sentence, for purpose of automatic AMR parsing, it is also important to explicitly represent the correspondence between word tokens in the sentence to the concepts and relations in its AMR, that is, the alignment between the input sentence and its AMR presentation. In English AMR annotation (Banarescu et al., 2013), this alignment is performed as a separate step and it is not integrated into AMR annotation itself. For example, to develop a word-to-AMR-concept aligner as the first step of their AMR parser, Flanigan et al. (2014) annotated the alignment between word tokens and AMR concepts and relations for a small corpus which they use as the development set to extract alignment rules. The alignment accuracy of this aligner is about 90%. Pourdamghani et al. (2014) developed an EM-based aligner that yields similar performance without any manual alignment. While these aligners may seem to be very accurate, a 10% error rate in alignment imposes a serious limitation on the overall AMR parsing accuracy.

In this paper we present the Chinese AMR (CAMR) annotation specifications that we use to annotate the Chinese translation of *the Little Prince*, which has 1,562 sentences. The CAMR annotation specifications are adapted from the AMR specification for English (Banarescu et al., 2015). We choose *the Little Prince* for our Chinese AMR annotation experiments because its English translation has already been annotated with AMRs and we can easily compare our AMR annotation with that of the English version for cross-linguistic studies. We also propose an integrated annotation approach in which the alignment step is integrated into the CAMR annotation process so that users of this corpus don't have to create their own alignment. We show that the alignment process shares many of the characteristics of word alignment across languages.

The rest of this paper is organized as follows. In Section 2 we present an overview of the AMR annotation framework and the supporting lexical resources that we use for CAMR annotation. Section 3 describes how we extend AMR to handle Chinese-specific constructions and discourse relations in Chinese. In Section 4, we present results on our CAMR annotation experiments, and analyze sources of disagreement. In Section 5, we describe how we integrate word-to-concept alignment into the CAMR annotation process, and present a few alignment scenarios between word tokens and CAMR concepts. Section 6 gives a brief introduction of related work on the construction of semantic dependency databases. We conclude our paper in Section 7.

2 AMR Overview

In AMR annotation, each sentence is represented as a rooted, directed, acyclic graph in which the nodes are concepts and the edges are relations between the concepts. The backbone of an AMR graph is the predicate-argument structure of verbal or nominal predicates, though syntactic notions such as verbs and nouns are not part of the AMR vocabulary. AMR draws this aspect from the Proposition Bank (Palmer et al., 2005): the core argument roles (Arg0-Arg5) are defined in the PropBank frame files(Bonial et al., 2014), together with the senses of the predicates as different senses of a predicate have different argument structures. In addition, AMR also annotates named entities (person, location, company, etc.), relations between entities, time expressions, polarity and modality.

(1) The boy wants to go to New York.

```
w/want-01
  :arg0 b/boy
  :arg1 g/go-01
    :arg0 b
    :arg1 c/city
      :wiki "New York"
      :name (n/name :op1 "New" :op2 "York")
```

AMR is a graph, not just a tree, because it allows *reentrancy*. This happens when an argument is shared by more than one predicate as in control structures, or when there is coreference. For example, in (1) *boy* serves as the Arg0 of *want.01* as well as Arg0 of *go.01*. This is illustrated by the fact that the same concept ID *b* is used as an argument for both *want.01* and *go.01*.

In CAMR annotation, we generally adopted the vocabulary used for annotating English AMRs (Banarescu et al., 2013). However, we used argument labels and the predicate senses that are defined in the Chinese Proposition Bank (CPB) (Xue and Palmer, 2009), which are very similar in convention to that of the English Proposition Bank. When developing the CAMR annotation specifications, most of our effort is expended on how to annotate some Chinese-specific constructions, which we will describe in detail in Section 3. These constructions are described in syntactic terms and are well recognized in Chinese linguistics.

3 Specifications for CAMR Annotation

When annotating CAMRs for *the Little Prince* corpus, we generally adopt the tagset for the (non-lexical) concepts and relations in the English AMR specifications. In English AMR, there are two types of concepts: *lexical concepts* that are grounded to word tokens in a sentence, and *abstract concepts* that are not linked to a specific lexical item. The former are typically lemmatized forms of word tokens with (e.g., *go.01* in (1)) or without word sense (e.g., *boy* in (1)). The latter are inferred from the context and are not tied to a specific lexical item (e.g., *city* in (1)). In the case of *city*, it can be viewed as a named entity tag for "New York", but not all abstract concepts are named entity tags. There are also labels for numbers, time expressions, dates, as well as concepts that represent discourse relations. We obviously cannot use the lexical concepts in English AMR for CAMR annotation, but we have generally adopted the abstract concepts in AMR. Since Chinese has little inflectional morphology, in most cases the lexical concepts are just the words themselves.

(2)男孩 想 去纽约。
nanhai xiang qu niuyue
boy want go New York
"The boy wants to go to New York."

```
x/想-01
    :arg0 x1/男孩
    :arg1 x2/去-01
        :arg0 x1
        :arg1 x3/city
            :wiki "纽约"
            :name (n/name :op1 "纽约")
```

The AMR relations include semantic roles as well as nominal relations. We use 6 labels for core arguments (Arg0-Arg5, as they are defined in the CPB frame files), and 42 labels for adjunctive arguments and other semantic relations largely taken from the English AMR vocabulary. As shown in (2), the Chinese translation of "The boy wants to go to New York" is annotated similarly to its English counterpart. Notice that *city* is a non-lexical abstract concept that is not an actual word in the sentence.

Even though we use the same annotation conventions and mostly the same vocabulary as used in the English AMR, we still need to specify how to annotate Chinese-specific constructions that are not in English so that these constructions are consistently annotated. Due to the limitation of space, we only describe six such constructions: the number and classifier construction, the serial-verb construction, the headless relative construction, the verb-complement (VC) construction, the split verb construction, and reduplications. We will also discuss how to represent discourse relations in Chinese AMR, an area where there are significant adaptations.

3.1 Number and Classifier Construction

When a number modifies a Chinese noun or verb, it is always followed by a classifier. A classifier can be a measure like 吨, which has an equivalent word in English, "ton". However, there is also another type of classifier which does not have an English equivalent. It serves as a cognitive measure of things and its meaning is hard to represent. The word 只 in (3) is such an example. It is also very idiosyncratic in the type of nouns it can modify. For example 只 can be used to modify sheep/goats or chickens, but not other types of animals such as cows or pigs. They are generally referred to as "individual classifiers" in Chinese linguistics. As AMR is concerned with the abstract meaning, we keep the measure words in the AMR representation but leave out the individual classifiers. Notice that the numbers are also normalized to Arabic numerals.

(3)三 千 只 羊
san qian zhi yang
three thousand CL sheep
"3000 sheep"

```
x/羊
    :quant 3000
```

3.2 Serial-Verb Construction

Serial-verb constructions are very common in Chinese. They are characterized by having several verbs in a sequence, but it is sometimes very hard to determine the grammatical relations between them. For example, one verb can modify another or the two can be semantically equally important as in a coordinate structure. We choose to avoid making this hard decision for now for the sake of consistent annotation and consider these verbs to be in a coordination structure and create a non-lexical "and" concept to connect them.

(4)他 走　过去　说...
ta zou guoqu shuo
he walk over say
"He walked over and said..."

```
a/and
   :op1 x/走-01
      :arg0 x1/他
         :direction x2/过去
   :op2 x3/说-01
         :arg0 x1
```

3.3 Headless Relative Construction

Headless relative constructions are relative constructions without an explicit noun head. Syntactically it is realized as a relative clause followed by 的(DE), a function word that serves multiple purposes, one of which is as the marker of a relative clause. The dropped noun head of the relative clause could play any number of roles with regard to the verb in the relative clause: agent, patient, instrument, location, etc. When annotating the AMR, we use an abstract concept to represent the dropped noun head. In (5), for example, the abstract noun head is a "person", and it is Arg0 of the verb 跳舞(dance).

(5)跳舞　的 走　了。
tiaowu de zou le
dance DE leave COMPLETE
"The person who danced has left."

```
x/走-01
   :arg0 p/person
      :arg0-of x1/跳舞-01
```

3.4 Verb-Complement Construction

A Verb-Complement (VC) construction is composed of a verb followed by another verb that indicates possibility, result, etc. The function word 得(DE) can optionally come between those two words. In AMR annotation, we make the meaning of the construction explicit using abstract concepts or relations. In (6), for example, the VC construction has a modal meaning, represented by "possible", although there isn't one word that specifically means possible. This meaning comes from the VC construction. In (7), there is a causal relationship between the two verbs 跑(pao) and 丢(diu), represented as a "cause" relation between the two verbs.

(6)买　得　起　房子。
mai de qi fangzi
buy DE rise house
"Can buy a house."

```
p/possible
   :arg0 x/买-01
      :arg1 x1/房子
```

(7)它 会　跑　丢　的。
ta hui pao diu de
it will run lost DE
"It will run and then get lost."

```
x/会-02
   :arg0 x1/丢-02
      :arg1 x2/它
      :cause x3/跑-01
         :arg0 x2
```

3.5 Split Verb Construction

A "split verb" is a verb whose two parts can be separated by other linguistic material. 帮忙(help) is a typical example. When it is separated, it takes the form of a verb (帮) followed by an object (忙), separated by some modifiers. Its syntactic representation is quite a paradox: on the one hand, the semantics of the two parts are not separable, and it simply means "help" in its totality. On the other hand, it takes the form of a verb-object construction, and needs to be represented that way. AMR solves this paradox by just representing the entire construction as one concept, 帮忙, regardless of whether it is split or not.

(8)地理学 帮 了 我 很 大 的 忙。
dilixue bang le wo hen da de mang
geography help PAST me very big DE business
"Geography helped me a lot"

```
x/帮忙-01
    :arg0 x1/地理学
    :arg1 x2/我
    :degree x3/大
        :degree x4/很
```

3.6 Reduplications

There are two types of reduplications in Chinese. In the first type of reduplications (9a-9b), the reduplicated form has roughly the same meaning as the root form. The reduplication has either an aspectual meaning that the root form does not have (9a), or has its meaning intensified (9b). For the moment, we do not represent such subtle aspectual meanings or intensification. In the second type, however, the reduplicated form clearly adds meaning to its root form (9c-9d). We annotate their actual meaning by adding an abstract concept. The root form is in brackets in the following examples:

(9a)看看 (看)
kankan (kan)
"take a look"
(9b)干干净净 (干净)
ganganjingjing (ganjing)
"very clean"
(9c)人人 (人)
renren (ren)
"every person"
(9d)他 天天 (天) 跑步。
ta tiantian (tian) paobu
he everyday (day) run
"He runs everyday."

```
x/跑步-01
    :arg0 x1/他
    :frequency x2/rate-entity-91
        :arg3 x3/temporal-quantity :quant 1
            :unit x4/天
```

3.7 Discourse Relations

One of the more significant adaptations to the AMR annotation specifications in CAMR is how discourse relations are annotated. Since for the moment AMR is a sentence-level meaning representation, here we only discuss intra-sentential discourse relations to the exclusion of inter-sentential relations.

(10)他 专心 地 看 着, 随后 又 说:
ta zhuanxin de kan zhe suihou you shuo
he carefully DE watch ASP then also say
"我 不 要 。"
wo bu yao
I not want
"He looked at it carefully, then he said:'I don't want it.' "

```
x/temporal
    :arg1 x2/看-02
        :arg0 x3/他
        :manner x4/专心-01
    :arg2 x5/说-01
        :mod x6/又
        :arg0 x3
        :arg1 x8/要-04 :polarity -
            :arg0 x3
```

In English AMR, discourse relations are represented with a combination of abstract concepts (e.g., *and*, *or*, *contrast.01*) and relations (*:cause*, *:condition*, *:concession*, *:purpose*). In CAMR, we represent discourse relations with 10 concepts defined in the Chinese Discourse TreeBank (CDTB) (Zhou and Xue, 2015). These 10 discourse relations include *and*, *or*, which are also used in English AMR, but they also include *causation*, *condition*, *contrast*, *expansion*, *purpose*, *temporal*, *progression*, *concession*. Some of these discourse relations, e.g., *causation*, *condition*, *purpose*, and *concession* are treated as relations in AMR, and others are not part of the AMR vocabulary (*expansion*, *progression*, and *temporal*). In particular temporal represents the temporal precedence of a sequence of discourse segments while progression means one argument represents a progression from the other, in extent, intensity, scale, etc. As CDTB discourse relations are formally predicates that take two or more discourse segments as their arguments, the argument labels are meaningful as well. (10) is an example of temporal relation.

The arguments are arranged in chronological order, with Arg1 temporally preceding Arg2.

4 Annotation Experiments

We annotated all of the 1562 sentences in the Chinese version of *the Little Prince* following the CAMR specifications. Two linguistic undergraduate students were trained to perform the annotation. Each completed the annotation for all of the 1562 sentences, and the inter-agreement is calculated by Smatch toolkit (Cai and Knight, 2013). The overall Smatch score between the two annotators is 0.83.[2]

We analyzed the annotated data from the two annotators to see to what extent the graph representation of the meaning of a sentence is necessary. Out of the 1,562 sentences of the two annotated files, 576 and 548 of them have non-tree CAMR graphs in Chinese version of *the Little Prince*. This is in comparison with the 663 sentences that have non-tree AMR graphs in the English version, which is sentence-aligned with the Chinese version. The Pearson correlation of the sentences having non-tree graphs is around 0.56, indicating the bilingual semantic representation of the same sentence pair is similar. When one Chinese sentence has a non-tree graph structure, its English translation does too.

We also analyzed the sources of disagreement between the annotators. The causes of disagreement between the annotators are mostly from two sources. The first source of disagreement is that the two annotators have different interpretations of the same sentence. Disagreement also occurs when either or both annotators missed some concepts when annotating long sentences. The annotation tool that they use does not keep track of which words have been covered and which have not, and this contributes to this problem. Another issue with the annotation tool, which may or may not lead to disagreement in annotation, is that the annotator has to constantly shift between Chinese and English input modes to type Chinese characters for lexical concepts and English alphabets for abstract concepts. Motivated by the need to address these shortcomings of the annotation tool, as well as the need to incorporate word-to-concept alignment in the CAMR annotation process, we have redesigned the annotation framework, which we describe in detail in the next section.

[2]The annotation data is available at http://www.cs.brandeis.edu/~clp/camr/camr.html.

5 Integrating Alignment to Annotation

When annotating *the Little Prince*, we followed the English AMR approach in which the concepts in CAMR are not aligned to word tokens in the sentence. Since AMR abstracts away from surface forms of a sentence, there is a non-trivial alignment problem between the AMR concepts and word tokens in a sentence. Some word tokens are considered to be devoid of meaning and are not represented in the AMR. Words that are not represented in AMR include determiners such as "a", "an" and "the", infinitive marker "to". As we have discussed in Section 3, individual measure words are not represented in CAMR. On the other hand, abstract concepts in AMR are not grounded to any specific lexical item and are inferred from the context. In some cases, one word token is analyzed into multiple AMR concepts. For example, the English word "teacher" is represented in a similar way to "person who teaches" in the AMR. In other cases, multiple word tokens in a sentence may represent a single AMR concept. These word tokens do not even have to be contiguous. For example, Chinese parallel discourse connective 因为(because)... 所以(therefore)... is mapped to one single discourse relation concept *causation*. So other than straight-forward one-to-one mappings between word tokens and AMR concepts, there are also complex alignment patterns such as one-to-zero, zero-to-one, one-to-many and many-to-one. In many ways, this is not too different from the word alignment between two languages. As we mentioned briefly above, having this alignment is important to AMR parsing, which is a process of mapping the input sentence to its AMR. Word-to-concept alignment is essential to this process, not unlike the role of word alignment to statistical machine translation.

The word-to-concept alignment is not integrated into the English AMR, mainly out of concern that it will slow down AMR annotation too much and it's too complex to provide annotation to support for this. There was also hope that the alignment can be learned in an unsupervised manner with EM-based algorithms, just like word alignment between different languages can be learned automatically without the need for manual annotation. Although this expectation has been partially met in the work of Pourdamghani et al. (2014), but we argue that an error rate of around 10% is too much of a deficit in the AMR parsing process, especially considering the level of difficulty in syntactic parsing where there is no alignment issue (or where there is perfect alignment between word tokens in the input sentence and terminal nodes in its parser tree).

We propose an annotation approach in which we integrate alignment with Chinese AMR annotation. Its basic idea is to use the index of a word token as the ID of the concept it aligns to in the AMR representation, thus establishing the alignment between the AMR concepts. We develop an annotation tool that allows an annotator to simply input the index of a word token in place of a concept during the annotation process. The tool will automatically retrieve the word token based on its index and generate the concept as well as the concept ID for it. This assumes that the tool does automatic lemmatization, which fortunately is very straightforward for Chinese where there is little inflectional morphology and the concepts are generally the same as their word forms. The tool also allows the annotator to revise the concept, and this is useful when a word does have inflections in a limited number of cases or when the word is misspelled. Words that do not correspond to a concept will of course receive no concept IDs and are not aligned. For abstract concepts that do not correspond to any word token, they are assigned IDs that have a value that is higher than the number of word tokens in the sentence. An example is given below. The IDs for the concepts are prefaced with "x". Note that the *city* concept has an ID of "x5", which does not correspond to any word token in the sentence.

(2)男孩[1] 想[2] 去[3] 纽约[4]。
boy want go New York
"The boy wants to go to New York."

```
x2/想-01
    :arg0 x1/男孩
    :arg1 x3/去-01
        :arg0 x1
        :arg1 x5/city
            :wiki "纽约"
            :name (n/name :op1 x4/"纽约")
```

The annotation tool also keeps track of which words in the sentence have been "covered" by the AMR by highlighting words that the annotator has created concepts for. This is an especially useful feature when annotating long sentences, as it is very easy for the annotator to miss some words.

In addition to one-to-one, one-to-zero, and zero-to-one alignments, there are also one-to-many and many-to-one alignments between word tokens in a sentence and concepts in its AMR. The following is the AMR for Example (8) where one AMR concept is aligned to two word tokens that are also discontinuous. This is a case of split verbs that we discussed in Section 3. The word tokens are "帮...忙" and the AMR concept is simply 帮忙. Its ID is a concatenation of the indices of the two word tokens "x2_x8".

(8)地理学[1] 帮[2] 了[3] 我[4] 很[5] 大[6] 的[7] 忙[8]。
geography help PAST me very big DE business
"Geography helped me a lot."

```
x2_x8/帮忙-01
    :arg0 x1/地理学
    :arg1 x4/我
    :degree x6/大
        :degree x5/很
```

(11) is an example where one word is aligned to multiple concepts. This usually happens when the word has a complicated internal structure and each morpheme corresponds to an AMR concept. Chinese has very little derivational or inflectional morphology, but compounding is a highly productive morphological process.

(11)市场-分析-家[1] 说[2]
shichang-fenxi-jia shuo
market-analyze-expert say
"The market analyst says..."

```
x2/说-01
    :arg0 x1_5/家
        : arg0-of x1_3_4/分析-01
            :arg1 x1_1_2/市场
```

In (11), the compound word 市场分析家(market analyst) has 5 characters and corresponds to three AMR concepts: 市场(market), 分析(analyze) and 家(expert). In this case, we represent the alignment with the character offsets within the compound word. Notice that the character offsets, unlike the word indices, are not prefixed with "x" This is how we differentiate word indices from character offsets. For example, the concept ID for 市场 is "x1_1_2", meaning that it is aligned with the first two characters of the first word. Similarly, 分析 is aligned with the third and fourth character of the first word, and its ID is "x1_3_4". Finally, the ID for the concept 家 is "x1_5", meaning that it is aligned with the fifth character of the first word.

In sum, this new annotation framework integrates word-to-concept alignment to the entire AMR annotation process. It also has the advantage of being able to keep track of word tokens that have been accounted for in the AMR (and those that have not), and helping to address the "missing word" problem in AMR annotation. In CAMR annotation, the annotator needs to switch back and forth between different input methods to input the lexical concepts that are composed of Chinese characters and the abstract concepts that are in English alphabets. The new annotation tool allows the annotator to use word indices and character offsets to input the lexical concepts and thus avoids the need to shift input modes, thus improving annotation efficiency.

6 Related work

Other than the AMR annotation project, other efforts aimed at annotating and parsing the semantic representation of a sentence with a graph structure include the semantic dependency parsing effort of Oepen et al. (2014). The difference is that the work of Oepen et al. (2014) does not abstract away from the surface word order and "semantically empty" words, and as far as we know, does not make use of abstract concepts as AMR does.

There are several efforts for constructing the Chinese semantic dependency resources. Li et al. (2004) reported parsing experiments on a one million word Chinese corpus annotated with semantic dependencies, but their dependency structure is tree-based rather than graph-based. Chen and Ji (2011) described a three thousand sentence corpus annotated with semantic graphs. Corpora annotated with semantic graphs also include those reported in Ding et al. (2014) and Zheng et al. (2014). These semantic resources vary in the types of semantic relations they use, but they all differ from the work we report here in that they define semantic relations between word tokens instead of abstract concepts.

7 Conclusion and Future Work

In this paper, we present our effort in developing specifications as well as an annotation tool for Chinese AMR (CAMR) annotation. We first annotate all 1,562 sentences of the Chinese translation of *the Little Prince* following the English AMR annotation framework while developing annotation guidelines to handle certain Chinese-specific syntactic constructions. We show that while we have achieved consistent annotation, there are shortcomings with this annotation approach. We then develop a new annotation tool and redesigned our annotation framework to address these shortcomings. In the future we plan to annotate additional data with this new framework.

Acknowledgements

We are grateful for the comments of the anoymous reviewers. This work is supported in part by National Natural Science Funds of China(No.61272221, 61170181) and Jiangsu University Philosophy and Social Science Fund(No.2016SJB740004).

References

Laura Banarescu, Claire Bonial, Shu Cai, Madalina Georgescu, Kira Griffitt, Ulf Hermjakob, Kevin Knight, Philipp Koehn, Martha Palmer, and Nathan Schneider. 2013. Abstract meaning representation for sembanking. In *Proceedings of the 7th Linguistic Annotation Workshop and Interoperability with Discourse*, pages 178–186, Sofia, Bulgaria, August.

Laura Banarescu, Claire Bonial, Shu Cai, Madalina Georgescu, Kira Griffitt, Ulf Hermjakob, Kevin Knight, Philipp Koehn, Martha Palmer, and Nathan Schneider. 2015. *Abstract Meaning Representation (AMR) 1.2.2 Specification*. https://github.com/amrisi/amr-guidelines/blob/master/amr.md.

Claire Bonial, Julia Bonn, Kathryn Conger, D. Hwang, Jena, and Martha Palmer. 2014. Propbank: Semantics of new predicate types. In *The 9th edition of the LanguageResources and Evaluation Conference*, pages 3013–3019, Reykjavik, Iceland, May.

Shu Cai and Kevin Knight. 2013. Smatch: an evaluation metric for semantic feature structures. In *Proceedings of the 51st Annual Meeting of the Association for Computational Linguistics (Volume 2: Short Papers)*, pages 748–752, Sofia, Bulgaria, August. Association for Computational Linguistics.

Bo Chen and Donghong Ji. 2011. Chinese semantic parsing based on dependency graph and feature structure. In *International Conference on Electronic and Mechanical Engineering and Information Technology*, volume 4, pages 1731–1734, Aug.

Yu Ding, Yanqiu Shao, Wanxiang Che, and Ting Liu. 2014. Dependency graph based chinese semantic parsing. *Lecture Notes in Computer Science*, 8801:58–69.

Jeffrey Flanigan, Sam Thomson, Jaime Carbonell, Chris Dyer, and Noah A Smith. 2014. A discriminative graph-based parser for the abstract meaning representation. In *Proceedings of the* 52nd *Annual Meeting of the Association for Computational Linguistics*, pages 1426–1436.

Daniel Gildea and Daniel Jurafsky. 2002. Automatic labeling of semantic roles. *Computational Linguistics*, 28(3):245–2883.

Mingqin Li, Juanzi Li, Zuoying Wang, and Lu Dajin. 2004. A statistical model for parsing semantic dependency relations in a chinese sentence. *Chinese Journal of Computers*, 27(12):1679–1687.

Adam Meyers, Ruth Reeves, Catherine Macleod, Rachel Szekely, Veronika Zielinska, Brian Young, and Ralph Grishman. 2004. The nombank project: An interim report. In A. Meyers, editor, *Proceedings of the Workshop Frontiers in Corpus Annotation at HLT-NAACL 2004*, pages 24–31, Boston, Massachusetts, USA, May 2 - May 7.

Joakim Nivre. 2015. Towards a universal grammar for natural language processing. *Computational Linguistics and Intelligent Text Processing*, 9041:3–16.

Stephan Oepen, Marco Kuhlmann, Yusuke Miyao, Daniel Zeman, Dan Flickinger, Jan Hajic, Angelina Ivanova, and Yi Zhang. 2014. Semeval 2014 task 8: Broad-coverage semantic dependency parsing. In *Proceedings of the 8th International Workshop on Semantic Evaluation (SemEval 2014)*, pages 63–72, Dublin, Ireland, August. Association for Computational Linguistics and Dublin City University.

Martha Palmer, Daniel Gildea, and Paul Kingsbury. 2005. The proposition bank: An annotated corpus of semantic roles. *Computational Linguistics*, 31(1):71–105.

Martha Palmer, Daniel Gildea, and Nianwen Xue. 2010. Semantic role labeling. In Graeme Hirst, editor, *Synthesis Lectures on Human Language Technology Series*. Mogan & Claypoole Publishers.

Nima Pourdamghani, Yang Gao, Ulf Hermjakob, and Kevin Knight. 2014. Aligning english strings with abstract meaning representation graphs. In *Proceedings of the 2014 Conference on Empirical Methods in Natural Language Processing (EMNLP)*, pages 425–429, Doha, Qatar, October. Association for Computational Linguistics.

Sameer Pradhan, Wayne Ward, Kadri Hacioglu, James H. Martin, and Daniel Jurafsky. 2004. Shallow semantic parsing using support vector machines. In *Proceedings of the Human Language Technology Conference/North American chapter of the Association of Computational Linguistics (HLT/NAACL)*, Boston, USA.

Nianwen Xue and Martha Palmer. 2004. Shallow semantic parsing using support vector machines. In *Proceedings of 2004 Conference on Empirical Methods in Natural Language Processing*, Barcelona, Spain.

Nianwen Xue and Martha Palmer. 2009. Adding semantic roles to the chinese treebank. *Natural Language Engineering*, 15(1):143–172.

Nianwen Xue, Ondrej Bojar, Jan Hajic, Martha Palmer, Zdenka Uresova, and Xiuhong Zhang. 2014. Not an interlingua, but close: Comparison of english amrs to chinese and czech. In Nicoletta Calzolari, Khalid Choukri, Thierry Declerck, Hrafn Loftsson, Bente Maegaard, Joseph Mariani, Asuncion Moreno, Jan Odijk, and Stelios Piperidis, editors, *Proceedings of the Ninth International Conference on Language Resources and Evaluation (LREC'14)*, pages 1765–1772, Reykjavik, Iceland, May. European Language Resources Association (ELRA).

Wajdi Zaghouani, Abdelati Hawwari, and Mona Diab. 2012. A pilot propbank annotation for quranic arabic. In *Proceedings of the NAACL-HLT 2012 Workshop on Computational Linguistics for Literature*, pages 78–83, Montréal, Canada, June.

Lijuan Zheng, Yanqiu Shao, and Erhong Yang. 2014. Analysis of the non-projective phenomenon in chinese semantic dependency graph. *Journal of Chinese Information Processing*, 28(6):41–47.

Yuping Zhou and Nianwen Xue. 2015. The chinese discourse treebank: a chinese corpus annotated with discourse relations. *Language Resources & Evaluation*, 49(2):1–35.

Converting SynTagRus Dependency Treebank into Penn Treebank Style

Alex Luu, Sophia A. Malamud, Nianwen Xue
Brandeis University
415 South Street, Waltham, Massachusetts USA
alexluu,smalamud,xuen@brandeis.edu

Abstract

This paper presents the conversion of SynTagRus dependency structures into Penn Treebank style phrase structures, whose resulting data will be used to train a statistical constituency parser for Russian and create a large-scale constituency-parsed corpus. The implemented conversion includes various innovative features in order to create phrase structure trees that are closest to Penn Treebank style while optimally preserving information of the original dependency structure annotations. We believe the newly converted phrase structure treebank will be not only an adequate training dataset for our ongoing project but also a valuable resource for traditional and computational linguistic research.

1 Introduction

A treebank is usually created based on either dependency structure (DS) or phrase structure (PS) such that the selected formalism is optimally compatible with the language under consideration. From this perspective, DS formalism is suited for SynTagRus, the first general-purpose treebank (1M words) for Russian, a Slavic language with a relatively free word order (Boguslavsky et al., 2002). In contrast, existing gold standard corpora involving language variation and change such as Penn corpora of historical English (Kroch and Taylor, 2000; Kroch et al., 2004; Kroch et al., 2016) and the corpus of Appalachian English (Tortora et al., in progress) use PS formalism similar to English Penn Treebank (PTB) (Bies et al., 1995). To facilitate the creation of comparable corpora for less-configurational languages, and to enable the use of the wealth of NLP and theoretical research tools, such as CorpusSearch[1] developed for PTB-style corpora, we aim to enrich this formalism to optimally capture the grammatical details of a free word order language like Russian, and to convert SynTagRus DS into this enriched PTB style PS (henceforth, DS-to-PS conversion[2]) without loss of information. Eventually, we will use the newly converted data to train a statistical PS parser for Russian and create a large-scale PS-parsed corpus. In this paper, we report our effort in developing the enriched PS representation and implementing DS-to-PS conversion.

2 Related Work

To the best of our knowledge, Avgustinova and Zhang (2010) is the only prior work addressing the conversion of SynTagRus DS into PS. Within the framework of Head-driven Phrase Structure Grammar (HPSG) the conversion implemented in this work outputs HPSG-conform PS trees via three steps: converting DS into pseudo PS by creating additional constituent nodes that immediately dominate head words and their dependents, annotating the branches of the pseudo PS with HPSG-oriented schemata, and binarizing the pseudo PS. This conversion process is specific to HPSG framework and cannot be straightforwardly manipulated for PTB style PS. Consequently, we follow a more universal DS-to-PS conversion procedure suggested in (Xia, 2008; Bhatt et al., 2011), including the following steps:

1) DS to DS+: removing non-projectivity
2) DS+ to PS+: simple and general conversion
3) PS+ to PS: handling subtleties

In addition, we adopt the approaches of DS+ to PS+ conversion proposed in (Xia and Palmer,

[1] http://corpussearch.sourceforge.net/index.html.

[2] The code for this conversion is available at https://github.com/luutuntin/SynTagRus_DS2PS.

Proceedings of LAW X – The 10th Linguistic Annotation Workshop, pages 16–21,
Berlin, Germany, August 11, 2016. ©2016 Association for Computational Linguistics

2001; Xia et al., 2008), which include simple heuristic rules and take language-specific information as input in defining projections for each syntactic category and attachment levels for each head-dependent pair. Compared with other work on DS-to-PS conversion, (Collins et al., 1999; Aldezabal et al., 2008, a.o.), this approach gives us more flexibility to produce PS that are as close to PTB style as possible while preserving information of the original DS annotations.

An innovation in our proposal is that we use functional tags to represent the extremely fine-grained (and open) list of dependency link types in SynTagRus (Boguslavsky et al., 2002), and utilize this information in the projection rules that create the PS representations.

3 SynTagRus DS-to-PS Conversion

The converted SynTagRus includes 66 dependency link types, 49,420 sentences, 708,480 tokens excluding punctuation marks, 38,311 lemmas, and 1,365 phantom nodes, corresponding to the omitted elements in elliptical constructions.

3.1 Phrase Labeling

We constructed the tag set for our target PS treebank (see Table 1), taking into account language-specific information in SynTagRus.

DS (SynTagRus) POS	DS POS tag (X)	PTB phrase label (XP)
Noun	S	NP
Adjective	A	ADJP
Verb	V	VP
Adverb	ADV	ADVP
Numeral	NUM	QP
Preposition	PR	PP
Conjunction	CONJ	CONJP
Particle	PART	PRT
Exclamation *yes, no*	P	INTJ
Interjection	INTJ	INTJ
uninflected word	NID	NIDP
combining form	COM	*NP modifier*

Table 1: POS tags and phrase labels.

In addition to the phrase labels presented in Table 1, we use two clause labels, *SS* and *SBAR*, corresponding to *S* (simple declarative clause) and *SBAR* (relative/subordinate clause) in PTB, respectively. To handle *wh*-phrases, we assign the *wh*-feature to every word whose lemma belongs to the list of *wh*-lemmas and whose POS tag is not *CONJ*, using functional tag *-WH*.

3.2 DS to DS+

The free word order of Russian causes a large number of non-projective dependency trees in SynTagRus (cf. Bhatt et al. (2011) for Hindi/Urdu). We propose an algorithm (Table 2) that converts non-projective to projective dependency trees, using traces and co-indexation in the form of null elements **NP2P** (see section 3.5 for a converted example). The recursive helper function path(G) in this algorithm generates a specific sequence of all the nodes in a DS graph G such that any dependent node comes before its head. We call this specific order **tree-oriented**.

```
Input: a non-projective DS graph G
DS Graph nonprojective-to-projective(G)
  for (each edge of head i & dependent j in G)
   if is-nonprojective-edge(G, i, j)
     insert a null element headed by i and
                          co-indexed with j into G
  for (each node i in path(G))
   if (i is a null element)
     get the co-indexed node j
     assign head of j to variable h
     while (is-nonprojective-edge(G, h, j))
        assign head of h to h
     make h the new head of j
     remove edge between j and its old head
Output: a projective DS graph G
```

Table 2: DS to DS+ conversion.

3.3 DS+ to PS+

To convert projective dependency graphs (DS+) into the preliminary form of PTB style PS trees (PS+), we decompose the conversion of a complete DS+ (corresponding to a sentence) into a series of conversions for each subgraph of a head node and its (immediate) dependents, which we call a **unit subgraph**. When converting a unit subgraph (Fig. 1), we construct a specific head projection chain for each node in the subgraph, taking into account its POS tag and the dependency links (if any) between it and its head as well as its dependent(s)(see more details in sections 3.3.1 and

3.3.2). In the next step, we attach the root of each dependent's projection chains to the corresponding node in the head's projection chain to form a complete representation of the subgraph.

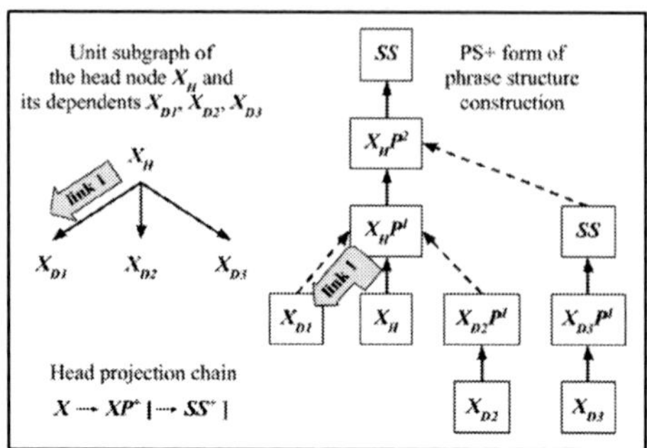

Figure 1: Unit-subgraph DS+ to PS+ conversion.

3.3.1 Head Projection Table

The projection of each node to the phrase level (*X* → *XP*) is defined by the head projection rules (Table 3), based on its POS tag in DS.

DS POS	X → XP
Noun	$S \rightarrow NP$
Adjective	$A \rightarrow ADJP$
Verb	$V \rightarrow VP$
Adverb	$ADV \rightarrow ADVP$
Numeral	$NUM \rightarrow QP$
Preposition	$PR \rightarrow PP$
Conjunction	$CONJ \rightarrow CONJP$
Particle	$PART \rightarrow PRT$
exclamation *yes, no*	$P \rightarrow INTJ$
Interjection	$INTJ \rightarrow INTJ$
uninflected word	$NID \rightarrow NIDP$

Table 3: Head projections at the phrase level.

3.3.2 Link Projection Table

Each syntactic dependency link type, involving a head X_H and a dependent X_D, has its own projection rule. As there are 66 link types in SynTagRus, Table 4 only presents some examples to show the diversity of projection rules that best describe their desired PS construction (e.g. a *relative* link between X_H and X_D will project to X_HP, which is similar to the projection of *link 1* in Figure 1).

Here, we not only reuse as many PTB functional tags (e.g., *PRD* for *predicate* and *SBJ* for *subject*) as possible, but also create new tags that reflect the fine-grained syntactic links in SynTagRus (e.g., *RLT* for *relative* and *EXP* for *expletive*) and therefore are invaluable for implementing different transformations at the PS+ to PS stage.

[3]Tag -PRD is only applied for non-VP predicates

Link type	Link projection
Actant: Predicative	*SS* → X_HP-*PRD*[3] X_DP-*SBJ*
Attributive: Relative	$X_HP \rightarrow X_H$ X_D-*RLT*
Coordinative	X_HP-*CRD* → X_HP X_DP
Auxiliary: Expletive	$X_HP \rightarrow X_H$ X_DP-*EXP*

Table 4: Link projections.

Our treatment of the differentiation between sister and Chomsky adjunction departs from Xia and Palmer (2001) and is similar to the optimization implemented in Xia et al. (2008). This differentiation is needed to produce PS that are close to the trees in PTB. To treat each type of dependency link in SynTagRus appropriately, we directly incorporate the concrete adjunction styles into the projection rules for each link, rather than distinguishing them in the modification table and implementing an additional step to handle Chomsky adjunction structures, as Xia and Palmer (2001) do. For example, in Table 4 the *coordinative* link corresponds to Chomsky adjunction (in which the head node necessarily projects to the phrase level) while the *expletive* link corresponds to sister adjunction (in which the head node does not necessarily project to the phrase level).

3.3.3 Construction of PS+ Trees

We use the algorithm presented in Table 5 for converting DS+ into PS+.

Input: a projective DS graph *G*
Tree DS-toPS(*G*) **for** (each node *i* in *G*) get projection chain *c* of *i* build (non-branching) PS tree for *i* using *c* **for** (each node *i* in path(*G*)) attach dependents' PS trees to *i*'s PS tree return PS tree *T* of the root node
Output: a PS tree *T*

Table 5: DS+ to PS+ conversion.

In order to preserve the linear word order of all nodes in a unit subgraph, the projection chain of the dependent which is linearly farther from the head should not be attached to a lower position in the projection chain of the head. If this violation occurs, we will move up the attachment position of this dependent chain until it is at least equal to those of the dependents which are linearly closer to the head. In other words, we attach it as low as possible as long as this does not cause non-projectivity. Additionally, we insert a null element *, co-indexed with the moved-up node, in the original attachment position of the moved-up node. This null element as well as the null element *NP2P*, which is introduced when eliminating non-projective trees, are descriptive devices for capturing scrambling phenomena in Russian in a theory-neutral manner.

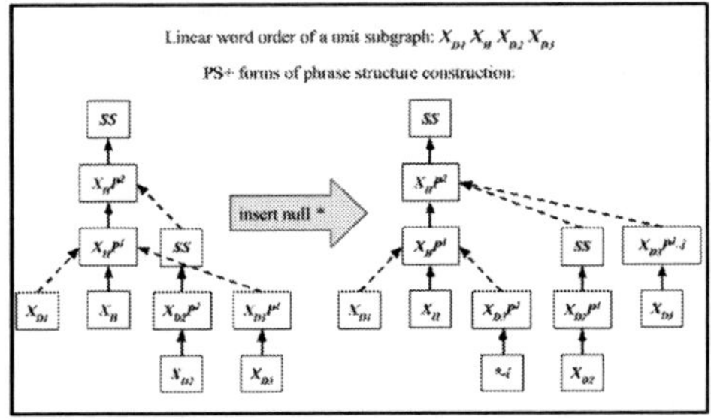

Figure 2: Insertion of null element *.

3.4 PS+ to PS

In this stage we implement the following types of tree transformations:

1) Label replacement, e.g. changing *CONJP* to *SBAR* for subordinative structures

2) *Wh*-movement, e.g. adding null elements **T**, *SBAR* nodes for relative clauses

3) Eliminating intermediate nodes, so that in phrase structure trees, the dependents in formerly non-projective edges c-command their traces null elements **NP2P**

4) Label merging, mainly used for handling coordinative structures

It is worth emphasizing that the resulting PS in PTB style adequately preserve all the enriched information of SynTagRus DS annotation.

3.5 A Converted Example

We examine the sentence in Figure 3, involving several phenomena characteristic of Russian: an impersonal modal *nado* "its necessary" which takes an infinitival phrase as its argument, a scrambled accusative object of the infinitive *knopku* "button.ACC" which participates in

Кнопку	*надо*	*нажимать*	*той*	*же*
Knopku	*nado*	*nažimat'*	*toj*	*že*
Button.ACC	*necessary*	*press.INST*	*that.INF*	*PRT*

рукой,	*которой*	*делается*	*ход.*
rukoj,	*kotoroj*	*delaetsja*	*xod.*
hand.INST,	*which.INST*	*make.3S.SPASS*	*move.NOM.*

It's necessary to press the button with the same hand with which the move is made.

Figure 3: An example sentence.

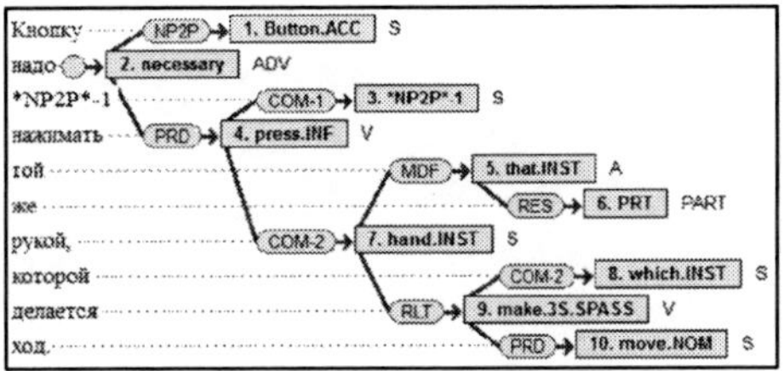

Figure 4: Non-projective SynTagRus DS.

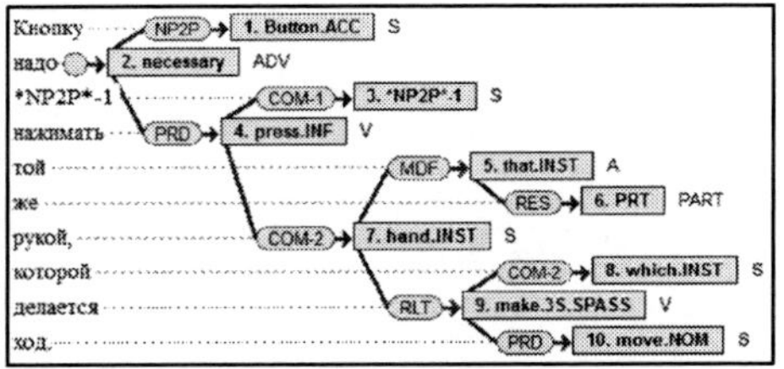

Figure 5: Projective SynTagRus DS+.

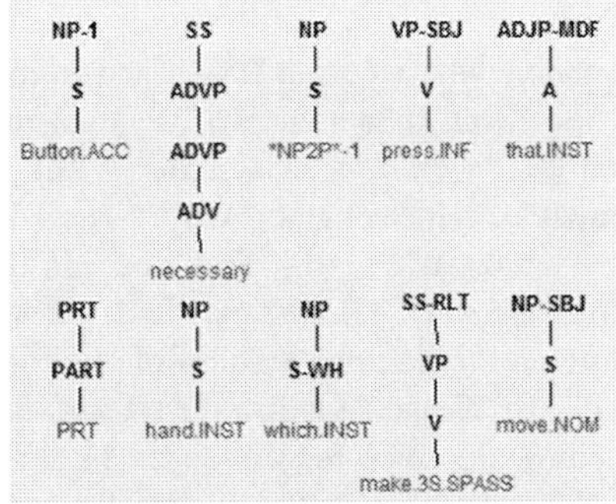

Figure 6: Non-branching PS trees.

a non-projective dependency, and a relative clause containing a *sja*-passive. The original DS of this sentence in SynTagRus, presented in Figure 4, includes the non-projective edge of syntactic link *COM-1* (i.e. *1st completive*) between "button.ACC" and "press.INF". This non-projectivity is resolved by the DS to DS+

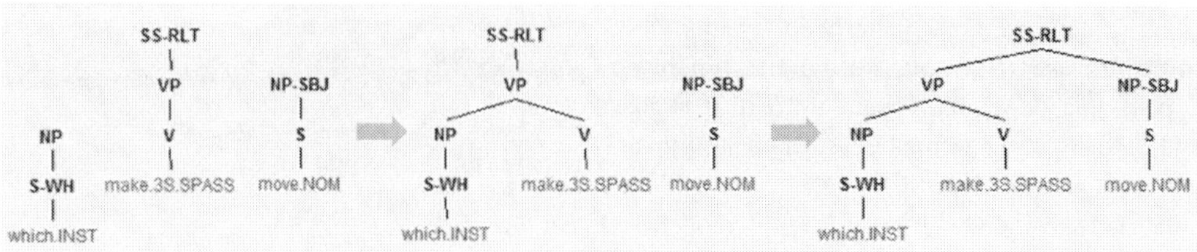

Figure 7: PS+ construction for a unit subgraph.

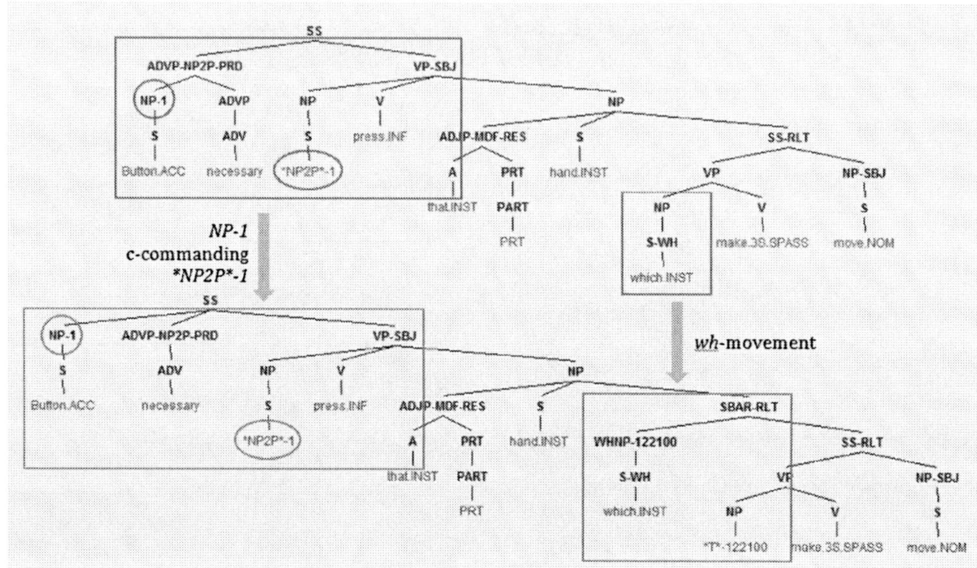

Figure 8: PS+ to PS conversion.

conversion, whose output DS+ is shown in Figure 5. Specifically, "button.ACC" is moved up to attach to "necessary" via general link *NP2P*; meanwhile, null element **NP2P*-1*, co-indexed with "button.ACC" (the first node in DS), is inserted between "necessary" and "press.INF", occupying the original position of "button.ACC" in DS. To create PS+, we first build the non-branching PS trees for all nodes in DS+ (Fig. 6). Next, we construct a PS tree for every unit subgraph in DS+ according to the following tree-oriented order: "move.NOM" → **NP2P*-1* → "PRT" → "that.INST" → "which.INST" → "make.3S.SPASS" → "hand.INST" → "press.INF" → "button.ACC" → "necessary". For example, the construction of PS+ for the unit subgraph headed by "make.3S.SPASS" is presented in Figure 7. Finally, Figure 8 shows the conversion from the PS+, the upper tree, to the PS, the lower tree, which involves such transformations as scrambled constituents c-commanding their traces and *wh*-movement.

4 Conclusions and Future Work

In this paper, we report on a conversion of the SynTagRus DS corpus into PTB style PS, preserving the information contained in the original DS annotations. We are currently working to refine our PS annotation guidelines and manually correct the converted data to create the gold standard for evaluating the implemented conversion. After this evaluation, the newly converted corpus will be distributed under the same noncommercial license as SynTagRus in its original form. We believe that the resulting PS treebank and the enriched PS formalism will be not only an adequate training dataset for automatic parsing of new Russian data, but also a valuable resource for traditional and computational linguistic research.

Acknowledgments

We would like to thank Marie Meteer and the anonymous reviewers for very constructive comments and valuable suggestions. All errors and mistakes are, of course, the responsibility of the authors.

References

Izaskun Aldezabal, Maria Jesùs Aranzabe, Arantza Diaz de Ilarraza, and Enrique Fernández. 2008. From dependencies to constituents in the reference corpus for the processing of Basque. *Procesamiento del Lenguaje Natural*, 41:147–154.

Tania Avgustinova and Yi Zhang. 2010. Conversion of a Russian dependency treebank into HPSG derivations. In *Ninth International Workshop on Treebanks and Linguistic Theories*, page 7.

Rajesh Bhatt, Owen Rambow, and Fei Xia. 2011. Linguistic phenomena, analyses, and representations: Understanding conversion between treebanks. In *IJCNLP*, pages 1234–1242. Citeseer.

Ann Bies, Mark Ferguson, Karen Katz, Robert MacIntyre, Victoria Tredinnick, Grace Kim, Mary Ann Marcinkiewicz, and Britta Schasberger. 1995. Bracketing guidelines for Treebank II style Penn Treebank project. *University of Pennsylvania*, 97:100.

Igor Boguslavsky, Ivan Chardin, Svetlana Grigorieva, Nikolai Grigoriev, Leonid L Iomdin, Leonid Kreidlin, and Nadezhda Frid. 2002. Development of a dependency treebank for Russian and its possible applications in NLP. In *LREC*. Citeseer.

Michael Collins, Lance Ramshaw, Jan Hajič, and Christoph Tillmann. 1999. A statistical parser for Czech. In *Proceedings of the 37th annual meeting of the Association for Computational Linguistics on Computational Linguistics*, pages 505–512. Association for Computational Linguistics.

Anthony Kroch and Ann Taylor. 2000. The Penn-Helsinki parsed corpus of Middle English (PPCME2). *Department of Linguistics, University of Pennsylvania, CD-ROM.*

Anthony Kroch, Beatrice Santorini, and Lauren Delfs. 2004. The Penn-Helsinki parsed corpus of early modern English (PPCEME). *Department of Linguistics, University of Pennsylvania, CD-ROM.*

Anthony Kroch, Beatrice Santorini, and Ariel Diertani. 2016. The penn parsed corpus of modern British English (PPCMBE2). *Department of Linguistics, University of Pennsylvania, CD-ROM.*

Christina Tortora, Beatrice Santorini, and Frances Blanchette. The audio-aligned and parsed corpus of Appalachian English (AAPCAppE). In progress.

Fei Xia and Martha Palmer. 2001. Converting dependency structures to phrase structures. In *Proceedings of the first international conference on Human language technology research*, pages 1–5. Association for Computational Linguistics.

Fei Xia, Owen Rambow, Rajesh Bhatt, Martha Palmer, and Dipti Misra Sharma. 2008. Towards a multi-representational treebank. *LOT Occasional Series*, 12:159–170.

Fia Xia. 2008. General techniques for creating treebanks. Lectures of TCS NLP Winter School, collocated with the Third International Joint Conference on Natural Language Processing, Hyderabad, India.

A Discourse-Annotated Corpus of Conjoined VPs

Bonnie Webber* **Rashmi Prasad†** **Alan Lee♯** **Aravind Joshi♯**
*University of Edinburgh †University of Wisconsin-Milwaukee ♯University of Pennsylvania
Edinburgh UK Milwaukee WI Philadelphia PA
bonnie.webber@ed.ac.uk prasadr@uwm.edu [aleewk, joshi]@seas.upenn.edu

Abstract

English grammars indicate a variety of relations holding between conjoined VPs. VPs conjoined by *and* evince such senses as Result, Temporal Sequence and Concession. Although all these senses are ones associated with discourse relations, conjoined VPs have not been fully included in discourse annotation. Because of the value of discourse-annotated corpora for developing approaches to automated sense recognition, we have added their annotation to the Penn Discourse TreeBank. This paper describes how tokens were identified; how the process of span and sense annotation was modified and extended in order to keep the annotation of intra-sentential multi-clausal structures consistent with the rest of the corpus; and what the resulting corpus looks like, in terms of token frequency and common sense patterns.

1 Introduction

As frequently noted, discourse relations can hold within a sentence (i.e., *intra-sententially*) as well between larger units of text. Interest in automatically recognizing intra-sentential discourse relations (Joty et al., 2015) has recently grown e.g. to support Statistical Machine Translation (Guzmán et al., 2014) or Question Answering (Prasad and Joshi, 2008; Mannem et al., 2010). We have therefore started to expand the annotation of intra-sentential discourse relations in the Penn Discourse TreeBank (Prasad et al., 2008; Prasad et al., 2014), starting with conjoined VPs.

According to English grammar (Huddleston and Pullum, 2002), conjoined VPs can have senses other than simply **Conjunction** (and), **Disjunction** (or), and **Contrast** (but). Huddleson & Pullum note that *X and Y* may, for example, convey:

- **Consequence** (X and therefore Y), as in
  (1) Scopes was convicted and fined $100 ... [wsj_0946]
- **Temporal Sequence** (X and then Y), as in
  (2) Tripoli says Rome kidnapped 5,000 Libyans and deported them as forced labor. [wsj_0990]
- **Concession** (despite X, Y), as in
  (3) Blacks and Hispanics currently make up 38% of the city's population and hold only 25% of the seats on the council. [wsj_1137]
- **Temporal Inclusion** (X while Y), as in
  (4) ...the government can ensure the same flow of resources and reduce the current deficit. [wsj_1131]

Although all of these are senses usually associated with discourse relations, we have found only one corpus in which conjoined VPs have

Proceedings of LAW X – The 10th Linguistic Annotation Workshop, pages 22–31,
Berlin, Germany, August 11, 2016. ©2016 Association for Computational Linguistics

been fully treated as a locus of discourse coherence. This is a ∼53K-word corpus of home repair instructions (Subba and Di Eugenio, 2009) that was annotated according to guidelines in (Kim and Eugenio, 2006). The corpus contains ∼540 conjoined verb phrases and conjoined verbs annotated with either generic senses such as **General:Specific**, **Comparison**, **Restatement**, etc. or senses specific to the domain of instructions, such as **Criterion:act** and **Criterion:wrong-act** (depending on whether the specified action is appropriate or sub-optimal if the criterion holds). In future work, we will consider this sense annotation in more depth.

With respect to the RST Corpus (Carlson et al., 2003), its annotation guidelines[1] call for the segmentation of some but not all coordinated VPs into separate EDUs (Section 2.5.2), with only those segmented into EDUs being annotated with RST relations. With respect to the 2007 SDRT corpus, its annotation manual[2] specifies that coordinated VPs are only treated as separate discourse segments "when they either include a discourse particle or contain discourse structure within (at least one of) the coordinated constituents".

Because of the value of corpora annotated for discourse coherence for developing approaches to automated sense recognition, we decided to expand the Penn Discourse TreeBank (PDTB2) to include discourse relations associated with conjoined VPs and to package up these new annotations, along with some related annotation already in the PDTB2 (see below), for early release of a conjoined VP sub-corpus. This paper thus describes how we identified tokens to be included in the sub-corpus (Section 2); how we modified and extended the process of span and sense annotation used in the PDTB2 in order to produce annotation of intra-sentential multi-clausal structures that was consistent with the rest of the PDTB2 (Sections 3–4); and what the resulting sub-corpus looks like, in terms of inter-annotator agreement prior to adjudication, and then final token frequency and common sense patterns after adjudication was complete (Section 5).

[1] https://www.isi.edu/∼marcu/discourse/tagging-ref-manual.pdf

[2] http://timeml.org/jamesp/annotation_manual.pdf

2 Creating a Corpus of Conjoined VPs

2.1 Identifying Conjoined VPs

We took as our goal, to annotate every token in the Penn Wall Street Journal (WSJ) corpus that was analyzed as a conjoined VP in the Penn Treebank syntactic annotation of the corpus.[3] However, as Maier and colleagues have noted (2012), coordination is not reliably annotated in the PTB (or any other large treebank, for that matter). They note, in particular, that punctuation used to separate elements of a conjoined structure is annotated no differently than punctuation used for other purposes. In response, they have developed an algorithm for enhancing the annotation of punctuation used in conjoined structures.

The two-step process we used for identifying conjoined VPs did not make use of this algorithm *per se*, but something similar, focussed on conjoined VPs:

- Search the PTB parses for all sister VPs separated by a conjunction, conjunction phrase (e.g. *rather than*) or punctuation, and an optional adverbial.

- For each such pair of sisters, pre-annotate the righthand VP as **Arg2** of a potential discourse relation. If a conjunction or conjunction phrase appears between the two sister VPs, the type of the token was taken to be **Explicit** and the conjunction or conjunction phrase was labelled as the connective. If the sister VPs were separated by punctuation, the token type was taken to be **Implicit**. Later, during sense annotation (cf. Section 4), this type could be changed to **AltLex** (alternative lexicalization), if the annotators identified material in either *Arg1* or **Arg2** that made the insertion of an implicit connective seem redundant. In some cases, *Arg1* could be pre-annotated as well.

This process of pre-annotation produced false positives and false negatives, as well as true positives, all of which are informative with respect to understanding what the corpus contains.

2.1.1 False Positives (FPs)

FPs derive from two aspects of PTB analyses. The first involves ambiguous punctuation, as al-

[3] The Penn WSJ Corpus comprises the texts underlying both the Penn TreeBank (PTB) and the PDTB2.

ready noted (Maier et al., 2012), where VPs separated by comma-punctuation are not actually conjoined. The second involves tokens of *argument/adjunct cluster coordination* (Mouret, 2006; Steedman, 1989; Steedman, 2000), also called *non-constituent conjunction*, that are analyzed as conjoined VPs in the Penn TreeBank, but whose righthand conjunct lacks a verb, as in

(5) "I pay a lot to the farmer and **five times the state salary to my employees**," he says [wsj_1146]

where corresponding pairs of direct and indirect objects of *pay* have been coordinated, and

(6) She adopted 12 of assorted races, naming them the Rainbow Tribe, and driving her husband first to despair and **then to Argentina**. [wsj_1327]

where corresponding pairs of adverb and PP have been coordinated. Since they were relatively easy to recognize manually, we decided to simply exclude all such verbless VPs from the corpus.

2.1.2 False Negatives (FNs)

FNs comprise the ~170 sequences that were analyzed in the Penn TreeBank as conjoined S-nodes with null subjects. These were discovered after completing the annotation of pre-annotated conjoined VPs, when we turned our attention to intra-sentential conjoined clauses. The tokens pre-annotated for this task were sister S-nodes separated by a conjunction, conjunction phrase (e.g. *rather than*) or punctuation, and an optional adverbial. Among the pre-annotated sister S-nodes were ones with (co-indexed) null subjects, as was the case with sentences such as the following:

(7) He joined the firm in 1963 and **bought it from the owners the next year**. [wsj_0305]

(8) The company said its directors, management and subsidiaries will remain long-term investors and **won't tender any of their shares under the offer**. [wsj_0308]

(9) The NAM embraces efforts, which both the administration and the medical profession have begun, to measure the effectiveness of medical treatments and **then to draft medical-practice guidelines**. [wsj_0314]

Since these were incorrectly analyzed according to the Penn TreeBank Guidelines (Marcus et al., 1993) and do not actually differ from the tokens already included in the corpus, we decided to include them.

On the other hand, we decided to exclude tokens containing conjoined verbs that should possibly have been analyzed as conjoined VPs, such as *exist and fight* in

```
( (S (RB Then)
   (NP-SBJ (-NONE- *) )
   (VP
     (VP (VB take)
         (NP (DT the) (VBN expected) (NN return) ))
     (CC and)
     (VP (VB subtract)
         (NP (CD one) (JJ standard) (NN deviation) )))
       (. .) ))
```

Figure 1: PTB Parse Tree for Ex. 13, showing its resemblence to the analysis of conjoined VPs

(10) The wonder is not that the resistance has failed to topple the Kabul regime , but that it continues to exist and fight at all. [wsj_2052]

We did not discover such tokens until late in the annotation process, and we lacked the resources to manually review them. It would be possible to return in the future and find and annotate them.

2.1.3 True Positives (TPs)

TPs identified through this pre-annotation process included conjoined tensed VPs (Ex. 11), conjoined adjunct VPs (Ex. 12), and conjoined imperative sentences (Exs. 13–14), which are parsed in the Penn TreeBank as conjoined VPs (Figure 1).

(11) It employs 2,700 people and **has annual revenue of about $370 million**. [wsj_0007]

(12) But many owners plan to practice frugality – crossing out the old code and **writing in the new one** until their stock runs out. [wsj_1270]

(13) Then take the expected return and **subtract one standard deviation**. [wsj_1564]

(14) Be careful boys; **use good judgment**. [wsj_0596]

2.2 Discourse Adverbials

As can be seen from the presence of *then* in Ex. 9, conjoined VPs can themselves contain discourse adverbials. As with all discourse adverbials, ones that appear in **Arg2** of a conjoined VP can link to material elsewhere in the text, as in Ex. 15

(15) Separately, the Federal Energy Regulatory Commission turned down for now a request by Northeast seeking approval of its possible purchase of PS of New Hampshire. Northeast said it *would refile its request* and **still hopes for an expedited review by the FERC** ... [wsj_0013]

While the discourse adverbial *still* shares its **Arg2** with the conjoined VP, its *Arg1* has been taken to be the FERC turning down its request for *approval of its possible purchase of PS of New Hampshire*, which appears in the previous sentence.

Although such adverbials can link to material in previous sentences, the far more common situation (occurring in 229/230 of the VP conjuncts in the Penn *Wall Street Journal Corpus* that contain discourse adverbials) is for such adverbials to link with the first argument *Arg1* of the conjoined VP. When they do, they serve as an explicit signal of one or more discourse relations holding between the two arguments. Among the annotated discourse adverbials from the PDTB2 found in conjoined VPs are *instead, still, then,* etc. – e.g.,

(16) He could develop the beach through a trust, but instead is trying to have his grandson become a naturalized Mexican so his family gains direct control. [wsj_0300]

(17) This year, Mr. Wathen says the firm will be able to service debt and still turn a modest profit [wsj_0305]

(18) In the engine department, several companies displayed experimental models that within a decade could provide power equal to today's engines and yet take up only half the space, ... [wsj_0956]

As such, we decided to add these tokens to the conjoined VP sub-corpus, so that one would be able to compare relations between conjoined VPs signalled with an explicit discourse adverbial with relations between them that were left implicit.

3 Labelling Arguments and their Spans

3.1 Changes to argument labelling

Early in the new annotation task, we realized that if we strictly followed the conventions used earlier in labelling arguments in the PDTB2, some span labels would be inconsistent. Here we describe what we did to overcome the problem in a way that would avoid any inconsistency.

Arguments were labelled in the PDTB2 according to the following two-part convention.

- For spans linked by an explicit discourse connective (called **explicit** relations), **Arg2** was the argument to which the connective was attached syntactically, and the other was *Arg1*. This allowed the arguments to subordinating conjunctions to be labelled consistently, independent of the order in which the arguments appeared. The same was true for coordinating conjunctions, whose argument order is always the same, and for discourse adverbials, whose *Arg1* always precedes the adverbial, even when *Arg1* is embedded in **Arg2**, as in

  (19) **A farmer** who *was kicked by his donkey* **would** nevertheless **not take revenge**.

- For spans linked by adjacency (called **implicit** discourse relations), *Arg1* was always the first (lefthand) span and **Arg2**, the second (righthand) span.

Blindly applying these same conventions *intra-sententially* produced inconsistent labelling because of (1) variability in where an explicit connectives can attach within a sentence; and (2) the ability of marked syntax to replace explicit connectives.

The first problem can be illustrated with paired connectives like *not only ... but also*. Here, both members of the pair may be present (Ex. 20), or just one or the other (Ex. 21 and Ex. 22):

(20) Japan not only outstrips the U.S. in investment flows but also outranks it in trade with most Southeast Asian countries ... [wsj_0043]

(21) The hacker was pawing over the Berkeley files but also using Berkeley and other easily accessible computers as stepping stones ... [wsj_0257]

(22) Not only did Mr. Ortega's comments come in the midst of what was intended as a showcase for the region, it came as Nicaragua is under special international scrutiny ... [wsj_0655]

A labelling convention that requires **Arg2** to be the argument to which the explicit connective attaches will choose a different argument for **Arg2** in Ex. 21 than in Ex. 22, and an arbitrary argument in the case of Ex 20, when semantically, the lefthand argument is playing the same role in all three cases, as is the righthand argument.

The second problem can be illustrated with preposed auxiliaries, which signal that a **Conditional** relation holds between the clause with the preposed auxiliary (as *antecedent*) and the other clause (as *consequent*). As with subordinating clauses, the two clauses can appear in either order:

(23) Had the contest gone a full seven games, ABC could have reaped an extra $10 million in ad sales ... [wsj_0443]

(24) ... they probably would have gotten away with it, had they not felt compelled to add Ms. Collins's signature tune, "Amazing Grace," ... [wsj_0207]

But since there is no explicit connective in either clause, if position is used to label *Arg1* and **Arg2**, the result will again be inconsistent.

A solution that addresses both these issues, while not requiring any change to existing labels in the PDTB 2.0 is the following:

- The arguments to inter-sentential discourse relations remain labelled by their *position*: *Arg1* is first (lefthand) argument and **Arg2**, the second (righthand) argument.

- With intra-sentential coordinating structures, the arguments are also labelled by their *position*: *Arg1* is first argument and **Arg2**, the second one.

- With intra-sentential subordinating structures, *Arg1* and **Arg2** are determined syntactically. The subordinate structure is always labelled **Arg2**, and the structure to which it is subordinate is labelled *Arg1*.

3.2 Changes to span-labelling

In PDTB2 annotation, the arguments to relations are text spans. But the text span(s) that make up an argument are required to subsume *at least one full clause*, including parts of the clause that might not be *relevant* to the relation. While this continues to be the guideline for annotating non-coordinating constructions, for coordinating constructions, the guideline has been changed such that annotators are asked to annotate just the conjuncts, which in the case of conjoined VPs is *not* a whole clause. Thus, in Ex. 7, *Arg1* subsumes only *joined the firm in 1963*, and not the subject *he*. The same goes for Ex. 11.

A second change involves *relevance*: Annotators were told that material that contributes semantically to both arguments of a conjoined VP should be omitted, so that it is not taken to be specific to one argument or the other. The result is that spans in the corpus may not completely match the spans of VPs in the Penn TreeBank. For example, in

(25) UAL ... reversed course and plummeted in off-exchange trading after the 5:00 p.m. EDT announcement. [wsj_1305]

the PTB takes *reversed course* as being conjoined with *plummeted in off-exchange trading after the 5:00 p.m. EDT announcement*, even though both reversing course and plummeting happened *in off-exchange trading after the 5:00 p.m. EDT announcement*. Recognizing this, the annotators changed the second conjunct to *plummeted*.

Annotators were also told that the spans of both arguments should be parallel — both bare infinitives, or to-infinitives, or tensed clauses, etc. So in Ex. 9, since **Arg2** is the to-infinitive *then to draft medical-practice guidelines*, selected as *Arg1* would be the to-infinitive *to measure the effectiveness of medical treatments*.

Also common among conjoined VPs are *attribution phrases* such as *said* and *added* in Ex. 26 and *declare* in Ex. 27. When annotating implicit relations on conjoined VPs, annotators were told to retain only those attributions that contribute to the semantics of the relation (as in Ex. 27, where the **Purpose** of declaring something a pesticide is so that it can be pulled from the marketplace). In Ex. 26, neither *said* nor *added* contribute to the **Concession** relation that is taken to hold, so annotators omitted them from the spans of *Arg1* and **Arg2**.

(26) The company, based in San Francisco, said *it had to shut down a crude-oil pipeline in the Bay area to check for leaks* <u>but</u> added that **its refinery in nearby Richmond, Calif., was undamaged**. [wsj_1884]

(27) Give the EPA more flexibility to *declare a pesticide an imminent hazard* <u>and</u> **pull it from the marketplace**. [wsj_0964]

The final thing to say here about attribution is that where an annotator takes the same relation to hold between attribution phrases as between content of attribution, we ask that the relation be annotated between the latter, indicating the minimal spans that give rise to the particular relational sense.

4 Labelling Relation Senses

4.1 Changes to the Relation Hierarchy

We have extended and simplified the PDTB2 relation hierarchy, producing a new PDTB3 relation hierarchy (Figure 2). Some of the changes (such as restricting Level-3 relations to differences in directionality, eliminating rare and/or difficult-to-annotate senses, and replacing separate senses with features that can be added to a given sense) are meant to simplify annotation (Section 4.1.1). Other changes are additions to the relation hierarchy motivated by the intra-sentential relations we have been annotating, including ones associated with conjoined VPs (Section 4.1.2).

4.1.1 Simplifying the relation hierarchy

Although the hierarchy retains the same four Level-1 relations, relations at Level-3 now only encode *directionality* and so only appear with asymmetric Level-2 relations.[4] Those Level-3 relations in the PDTB2 that did not convey directionality were either moved to Level-2 — **Substitution** (renamed from the PDTB2 **Chosen Alternative**) and **Equivalence** — or eliminated due to their rarity or the difficulty they posed for annotators — in particular, those under the Level-2 relations of **Contrast**, **Condition** and **Alternative** (now renamed **Disjunction**).

With respect to directionality, annotating additional intra-sententential discourse relations has called attention to asymmetric Level-2 relations

[4]A sense relation $\Re$ is *symmetric* iff $\Re$(*Arg1*, **Arg2**) and $\Re$(**Arg2**, *Arg1*) are semantically equivalent. If a relation is not symmetric, it is *asymmetric*.

Level-1	Level-2	Level-3
Temporal	Synchronous	--
	Asynchronous	Precedence
		Succession

Level-1	Level-2	Level-3
Comparison	Contrast	--
	Similarity	--
	Concession $^{+/-\beta, +/-\zeta}$	Arg1-as-denier
		Arg2-as-denier

Level-1	Level-2	Level-3
Contingency	Cause $^{+/-\beta, +/-\zeta}$	Reason
		Result
	Condition $^{+/-\zeta}$	Arg1-as-cond
		Arg2-as-cond
	Negative condition $^{+/-\zeta}$	Arg1-as-negcond
		Arg2-as-negcond
	Purpose	Arg1-as-goal
		Arg2-as-goal

Level-1	Level-2	Level-3
Expansion	Conjunction	--
	Disjunction	--
	Equivalence	--
	Instantiation	--
	Level-of-detail	Arg1-as-detail
		Arg2-as-detail
	Substitution	Arg1-as-subst
		Arg2-as-subst
	Exception	Arg1-as-excpt
		Arg2-as-excpt
	Manner	Arg1-as-manner
		Arg2-as-manner

Figure 2: PDTB3 Relation Hierarchy. Only asymmetric relations are specified further at Level-3, to capture the directionality of the arguments. Superscript symbols on Level-2 senses indicate features for implicit beliefs (+/-β) and speech-acts (+/-ζ) that may or may not be associated with one of the defined arguments of the relation. Features are shown on the relation in the table here only for clarity, but should not be seen as a property of the relation, rather of the arguments.

whose arguments have been found to occur in either order (rather than the single order assumed in the PDTB2). In particular, the argument conveying the condition in **Condition** relations can be either **Arg2** (as was the case throughout the PDTB2) or *Arg1* as in Ex. 28, while the argument conveying the "chosen alternative" (now called "substitute") in **Substitution** relations can be either **Arg2** (as was the case throughout the PDTB2) or *Arg1*, as in Ex. 29. In the case of the rare relation called **Exception**, it was not previously noticed that in some of the tokens so annotated, the exception appeared in **Arg2**, while in the rest, the exception appeared in *Arg1*. The difference is now supported with a distinct Level-3 type in each direction (Exs. 30–31).

(28) **Arg1-as-cond:** *Call Jim Wright's office in downtown Fort Worth, Texas, these days* <u>and</u> **the receptionist still answers the phone, "Speaker Wright's office.** [wsj_0909]

(29) **Arg1-as-subst:** "The primary purpose of a railing is *to contain a vehicle* <u>and</u> **not to provide a scenic view,"** [wsj_0102]

(30) **Arg1-as-excpt:** *Twenty-five years ago the poet Richard Wilbur modernized this 17th-century comedy merely by avoiding "the zounds sort of thing," as he wrote in his introduction.* <u>Otherwise</u>, **the scene remained Celimene's house in 1666**. [wsj_1936]

(31) **Arg2-as-excpt:** *Boston Co. officials declined to comment on Moodys action on the units financial performance this year* <u>except</u> **to deny a published report that outside accountants had discovered evidence of significant accounting errors in the first three quarters results**. [wsj_1103]

Level-2 pragmatic relations have been removed from the PDTB2 and replaced with features that can be attached to a relation token to indicate an inference of *implicit* belief (epistemic knowledge) or of a *speech act* associated with arguments, rather than with the relation itself. Figure 2 shows the relations for which these features have so far been found to be warranted, based on the empirical evidence found during annotation. Ex. 32 shows an implicit **Cause.Result** relation but one where the result **Arg2** argument is the (speaker's/writer's) *belief* that the deadline could be extended. **Arg2** is therefore annotated with a +belief feature because the belief is implicit. Similarly, Ex. 33 shows a **Concession.Arg2-as-denier** relation, but what's being denied (or cancelled) is the speech act associated with **Arg2**, and this is annotated as a feature on **Arg2** because it is implicit.

(32) That deadline *has been extended once* <u>and</u> <u>Implicit=so</u> **could be extended again**. [wsj_2032]

(33) He spends his days *sketching passers-by*, <u>or</u> **trying to**. [wsj_0039]

Also simplifying the PDTB2 hierarchy is removal of the **List** relation, which does not appear semantically distinguishable from **Conjunction**. And the names of two asymmetric PDTB2 relations have been changed to bring out commonalities. In particular, **Restatement** has been renamed **Level-of-detail**, with its **Specification** and **Generalization** subtypes in the PDTB2 now just taken to be directional variants renamed **Arg2-as-detail** and **Arg1-as-detail**, respectively; and the subtypes of **Concession**, opaquely called **Contra-expectation** and **Expectation**, have been renamed to reflect simply a difference in directionality: **Arg1-as-denier** and **Arg2-as-denier**.

4.1.2 Augmenting the relation hierarchy

Additional senses found to be needed for annotating conjoined VPs include **Manner** under **Expansion** (both Level-3 directions), and **Negative_Condition** and **Purpose** under **Contingency** (with both Level-3 directions for each). The new symmetric Level-2 relation of **Similarity** (under **Comparison**) was added because of its obvious omission from the PDTB2 as the complement of the symmetric relation **Contrast**.

Definitions and examples for these new relations are given in Table 1.

Note that the entire PDTB2 is being mapped to senses in the revised relation hierarchy, not just the conjoined VP sub-corpus. Most often, the mapping is simply 1:1. Where the mapping is 1:N or M:N, manual review has been required, with further adjudication to ensure both agreement and consistency. When the PDTB3 is released to the public in September 2017, we will record the frequency with which each PDTB2 sense has been replaced by a specific PDTB3 sense.

4.2 Sense labelling of conjoined VP tokens

The VPs presented to annotators were conjoined either lexically or by punctuation. The annotators were given guidelines for assigning sense relations that depended on the particular configuration involved — specifically:

1. An explicit conjunction can have a single sense, which can be **Conjunction** (Ex. 34), or something else (Ex. 35-36).

   (34) The concept may be simple: Take a bunch of loans, *tie them up in one neat package*, and **sell pieces of the package to investors**. (**Expansion.Conjunction**) [wsj_1635]

   (35) These active suspension systems *electronically sense road conditions* and **adjust a car's ride** (**Contingency.Purpose.Arg2-as-goal**) [wsj_0956]

   (36) Stocks *closed higher in Hong Kong, Manila, Singapore, Sydney and Wellington*, but **were lower in Seoul**. (**Comparison.Contrast**) [wsj 0231]

2. The arguments to an explicit conjunction can also be linked by an additional relation, conveyed implicitly (Ex. 37-38) or by an explicit discourse adverbial. (Such adverbials were taken to have been already annotated in PDTB2.) To indicate an additional implicit relation, annotators created a new annotation token for the same two conjuncts, inserted an appropriate implicit connective and labeled it with the sense(s) they inferred. Argument spans of the explicit and the implicit relation were *not* required to be the same, so annotators could adjust the spans of the new token if needed.

   (37) We've got to *get out of the Detroit mentality* and Implicit=instead **be part of the world mentality**," declares Charles M. Jordan, GM's vice president for design ... (**Expansion.Conjunction, Expansion.Substitution.Arg2-as-subst**) [wsj_0956]

   (38) ... Exxon Corp. *built the plant* but Implicit=then closed it in 1985. (**Comparison.Concession.Arg2-as-denier, Temporal.Asynchronous.Precedence**) [wsj_1748]

3. If inserting an implicit connective was perceived as redundant, appropriate material in **Arg2** could be annotated as *AltLex* (Ex. 39), as done elsewhere in the PDTB2 (Prasad et al., 2010).

   (39) His policies *went beyond his control* **and resulted ... in riots and disturbances**. (**Expansion.Conjunction, Contingency.Cause.Result**) [wsj_0290]

The second guideline above points to a new feature of our discourse annotation: While multiple relations were annotated in the PDTB2 as holding between identical or overlapping argument spans, all were associated with either multiple explicit connectives or multiple inferred relations. What is new in the annotation of conjoined VPs is the possibility of an explicit relation co-occurring with ones that are inferred (implicit relations). We expect to identify more of these in other syntactic contexts.

5 Corpus Characteristics

For annotation, the pre-annotated tokens were divided into 25 batches. After a batch was annotated by two annotators, inter-annotator agreement was calculated (see below), and then adjudication was carried out, for the annotators and authors to reach agreement. Annotated tokens of discourse adverbials in **Arg2** of the conjoined VPs were imported from the PDTB2 (Section 2.2), with sense labels automatically updated to reflect the revised relation hierarchy (Section 4) if there was a 1:1

Similarity: One or more similarities between *Arg1* and **Arg2** are highlighted with respect to what each argument predicates as a whole or to some entities it mentions.	..., *the Straits Times index is up 24% this year*, so investors who bailed out generally did so profitably. Similarly, **Kuala Lumpur's composite index yesterday ended 27.5% above its 1988 close**. [wsj_2230]
Negative Condition: One argument describes a situation presented as unrealized (the antecedent or condition), which if it doesn't occur, would lead to the situation described by the other argument (the consequent).	**Arg1-as-negcond:** In Singapore, a new law requires smokers to *put out their cigarettes before entering restaurants, department stores and sports centers* or **face a $250 fine**. [wsj_0037]
Purpose: One argument presents an action that an agent undertakes with the purpose (intention) of achieving the goal conveyed by the other argument.	**Arg1-as-goal:** She ordered *the foyer done in a different plaid planting*, and Implicit=for that purpose **made the landscape architects study a book on tartans**. [wsj_0984]
Manner: The situation described by one argument presents *how* (i.e., the manner in which) the situation described by other argument has happened or is done.	**Arg1-as-manner:** He argued that program-trading by roughly 15 big institutions is *pushing around the markets* and Implicit=thereby **scaring individual investors**. [wsj_0987]

Table 1: New relations in PDTB3

mapping between a discontinued PDTB2 sense label and its corresponding new PDTB3 label. If there wasn't a 1:1 mapping, the sense label was left empty and the annotation tool would flag the token as requiring a new sense label. The span annotations of each token were also modified to accord with the new span guidelines (Section 3.2).

The corpus comprises 3372 conjoined VPs annotated with a single sense and 1261 annotated with multiple senses. Each discourse relation is recorded as an *annotation token*, with multi-sense conjoined VPs recorded as either two linked annotation tokens (each with one or more senses) or as a single annotation token with multiple senses. In total, the corpus comprises 5894 annotation tokens.

Prior to adjudication, inter-annotator agreement (IAA) on sense annotation (full agreement on one or more senses) was 74%. Partial agreement on at least one sense was 74.3%. IAA on both senses and argument spans was 69.8%. Partial IAA on at least one sense and span was 70.1%. Of the 658 sense disagreements, the most common involved Contrast and Concession.Arg2-as-denier (127/658 =19.3%). We did not consider as disagreements, cases where only one annotator reported an additional inferred sense: On review, the other annotator acknowledged simply not noticing it.

5.1 Single-sense Conjoined VPs

Of the 3372 single-sense relations in the corpus, 2962 are lexically-conjoined VPs (2933 Explicit conjunctions and 29 Explicit adverbials) and 410 are punctuation-conjoined VPs.

Among these single-sense relations, **Expansion.Conjunction** is the most common sense, but other senses occur fairly often as well, as shown in Table 2 for Explicit conjunctions and Table 3 for punctuation-conjoined relations.

The most common single-sense Explicit connectives are *and*, *but* and *or*. While explicit *and* has **Expansion.Conjunction** as its most common sense, its senses still show the kind of variability noted in Section 1, as shown in Table 4. The most common Implicit connectives are *and*, *then* and *or*. Also relatively frequent is the use of *not* as an AltLex with the sense of **Substitution**, as in Ex. 29.

5.2 Multi-sense Conjoined VPs

As noted in Section 4.2, more than one sense may hold between the arguments of a conjoined VP, either through inference or through the presence of an explicit discourse adverbial in **Arg2**.

The corpus contains 214 Explicit adverbials linked to an Explicit conjunction, sharing their arguments. Table 5 shows the distribution of these Explicit conjunction+adverbial pairs and Table 6 their associated sense pairings.

Annotators also inferred multiple senses on conjoined VPs in the absence of an explicit adverbial. In most cases, such inferences are annotated either as a separate Implicit or AltLex tokens linked to a token containing the Explicit conjunction, while multiple senses could also be recorded on a single annotation token. Annotators inferred 53 different Implicit connectives or AltLex text spans in these cases, the most common being *then*, *therefore/as a result*, *thereby* and *instead*. There are 1047 such multi-sense conjoined VPs in the corpus, with the main sense pairings shown in Table 7.

In total, the corpus contains 1261 multi-sense conjoined VPs. In most cases, these multi-sense relations are annotated via the linking of two or

Sense	Frequency
Expansion.Conjunction	2113
Comparison.Concession.Arg2-as-denier	320
Expansion.Disjunction	219
Contingency.Purpose.Arg2-as-goal	106
Comparison.Contrast	93
OTHER	82
TOTAL	**2933**

Table 2: Sense distribution of single-sense lexically-conjoined conjunctions

Sense	Frequency
Expansion.Conjunction	290
Temporal.Asynchronous.Precedence	51
Expansion.Substitution.Arg2-as-subst	14
Expansion.Disjunction	14
Expansion.Equivalence	12
OTHER	29
TOTAL	**410**

Table 3: Sense distribution of single-sense punctuation-conjoined VPs

more tokens, with these links explicitly marked in the annotation files.

6 Future Work

We plan to release the corpus in two forms, for the Linguistic Annotation Workshop in August 2016. For researchers with access to the Penn TreeBank, the corpus will be available as stand-off annotation. For those lacking access to the Penn TreeBank, we will provide a limited version of the corpus containing just those sentences that contain conjoined VPs, with annotation of their spans and senses. While we will be continuing to further enrich the PDTB, the goal of this early release of a corpus of conjoined VPs is to encourage research targetted at shallow discourse parsing of these constructions, given how common they are and how useful recognition of the relations expressed in them might prove.

Acknowledgments

This work has been supported by the National Science Foundation (NSF) under grants RI 1422186 and RI 1421067.

References

Lynn Carlson, Daniel Marcu, and Mary Ellen Okurowski. 2003. Building a discourse-tagged corpus in the framework of Rhetorical Structure The-

Sense	Frequency
Expansion.Conjunction	2032
Contingency.Purpose.Arg2-as-goal	106
Expansion.Manner.Arg2-as-manner	18
Expansion.Substitution.Arg1-as-subst	5
OTHER (4)	8
TOTAL	**2169**

Table 4: Common senses of Explicit *and*

Connective	Frequency
and + then	71
and + thus	18
and + also	15
and + later	11
and + therefore	10
OTHER (e.g. but+also, but+instead)	89
TOTAL	**214**

Table 5: Distribution of Explicit conjunction and adverbial pairs

Sense	Frequency
Conjunction + Precedence	94
Conjunction + Result	44
Conjunction + Conjunction	19
Conjunction + Arg2-as-denier	14
Arg2-as-denier + Precedence	9
OTHER	34
TOTAL	**214**

Table 6: Distribution of sense pairs associated with Explicit conjunction and adverbial pairs

Sense	Frequency
Conjunction + Result	402
Conjunction + Precedence	378
Conjunction + Arg2-as-subst	51
Conjunction + Arg2-as-detail	44
Result + Arg1-as-manner	41
OTHER	131
TOTAL	**1047**

Table 7: Distribution of sense pairs inferred on an explicit conjunction

ory. In Jan van Kuppevelt and Ronnie Smith, editors, *Current Directions in Discourse and Dialogue*, pages 85–112. Kluwer.

Francisco Guzmán, Shafiq Joty, Lluís Màrquez, and Preslav Nakov. 2014. Using discourse structure improves machine translation evaluation. In *Proceedings of the 52nd Annual Meeting of the Association for Computational Linguistics)*, pages 687–698, Baltimore, Maryland, June.

Rodney Huddleston and Geoffrey Pullum. 2002. *The Cambridge Grammar of the English Language*. Cambridge University Press, Cambridge UK.

Shafiq Joty, Giuseppe Carenini, and Raymond Ng. 2015. CODRA: A novel discriminative framework for rhetorical analysis. *Computational Linguistics*, 41:385–435.

Su Nam Kim and Barbara Di Eugenio. 2006. Coding scheme for instructional corpus: Identifying segments, relations and minimal units. Technical report, University of Illinois at Chicago, March.

Wolfgang Maier, Sandra Kübler, Erhard Hinrichs, and Julia Kriwanek. 2012. Annotating coordination in the Penn Treebank. In *Proceedings, 6th Linguistic Annotation Workshop*, pages 166–174, Jeju, Republic of Korea.

Prashanth Mannem, Rashmi Prasad, and Aravind Joshi. 2010. Question generation from paragraphs at UPenn: QGSTEC system description. In *Proceedings, Third Workshop on Question Generation.*

Mitchell Marcus, Beatrice Santorini, and Mary Ann Marcinkiewicz. 1993. Building a large annotated corpus of English: The Penn TreeBank. *Computational Linguistics*, 19(2):313–330.

Francois Mouret. 2006. A phrase structure approach to argument cluster coordination. In Stephan Müller, editor, *Proceedings, 13th International Conference on Head-Driven Phrase Structure Grammar*, pages 247–267.

Rashmi Prasad and Aravind Joshi. 2008. A discourse-based approach to generating why-questions from texts. In *Proceedings, Workshop on Question Generation Shared Task and Evaluation Challenge.*

Rashmi Prasad, Nikhil Dinesh, Alan Lee, Eleni Miltsakaki, Livio Robaldo, Aravind Joshi, and Bonnie Webber. 2008. The Penn Discourse TreeBank 2.0. In *Proceedings, 6th International Conference on Language Resources and Evaluation*, pages 2961–2968, Marrakech, Morocco.

Rashmi Prasad, Aravind Joshi, and Bonnie Webber. 2010. Realization of discourse relations by other means: Alternative lexicalizations. In *Proceedings, International Conf. on Computational Linguistics (COLING).*

Rashmi Prasad, Bonnie Webber, and Aravind Joshi. 2014. Reflections on the Penn Discourse TreeBank, comparable corpora and complementary annotation. *Computational Linguistics*, 40(4):921–950.

Mark Steedman. 1989. Constituency and coordination in combinatory grammar. In M. Baltin and A. Kroch, editors, *Alternative Conceptions of Phrase Structure*, pages 201–231. University of Chicago Press.

Mark Steedman. 2000. *The Syntactic Process*. MIT Press.

Rajen Subba and Barbara Di Eugenio. 2009. An effective Discourse Parser that uses Rich Linguistic Information. In *Proceedings, NAACL-HLT2009*, pages 566–574.

Annotating Spelling Errors in German Texts Produced by Primary School Children

Ronja Laarmann-Quante, Lukas Knichel, Stefanie Dipper and Carina Betken
Ruhr-University Bochum
`laarmann-quante@linguistics.rub.de, lukas.knichel@rub.de, dipper@linguistics.rub.de, carina.betken@rub.de`

Abstract

We present a new multi-layered annotation scheme for orthographic errors in freely written German texts produced by primary school children. The scheme is closely linked to the German graphematic system and defines categories for both general structural word properties and error-related properties. Furthermore, it features multiple layers of information which can be used to evaluate an error. The categories can also be used to investigate properties of correctly-spelled words, and to compare them to the erroneous spellings. For data representation, we propose the XML-format *LearnerXML*.

1 Introduction

Orthographic competence is one of the key skills to be acquired in primary school. In many cases, the systematicity and logic behind the German writing system seems not to play a sufficiently large role in school teaching yet. One area where this becomes apparent is the interpretation of orthographic errors. Well-established instruments of assessing spelling abilities such as the HSP (May, 2013), OLFA (Thomé and Thomé, 2004) or AFRA (Herné and Naumann, 2002) only partly classify errors along graphematic dimensions, as has been criticized before (Eisenberg and Fuhrhop, 2007; Röber, 2011). However, we believe that the German graphematic system and children's orthography acquisition are closely related in that orthography acquisition involves the detection of regularities in the writing system, be it by implicit or explicit learning.[1]

We developed a new annotation scheme which closely follows the graphematic theory by Eisenberg (2006). Its main novelty is that it features multiple layers of annotation to keep apart information that gets mixed up, or is not even available, in other available schemes for German spelling error annotation. Besides error categories, it includes general linguistic information, such as the syllabic and morphological structure of a word.

We further propose *LearnerXML*, an XML-scheme for the representation of our annotations, and the use of *EXMARaLDA*[2] (Schmidt and Wörner, 2009; Schmidt et al., 2011) as a suitable annotation tool.

Our aim is twofold: Firstly, we want to provide a means for constructing detailed and graphematically valid error profiles for individual learners and groups of learners to study the development of orthographic competence. Our annotations allow us to pursue new research questions with regard to the relation of graphemics and orthography acquisition, e.g. whether errors are more frequently related to the prosodical or morphological structure of a word. Secondly, our scheme can also serve as a tool for analyzing the orthographic properties of German words in general. This way we can investigate what kind of spelling phenomena occur in texts children are confronted with (e.g. in children's books or in schoolbooks) and how this relates to the kinds of spelling errors they produce (see also Berkling et al. (2015)).

The paper is organized as follows. Section 2 introduces Eisenberg's (2006) theory of the German graphematic system, section 3 discusses related work. Section 4 presents our annotation scheme, which comprises both annotations of general structural properties of words as well as spe-

[1] Graphemics is about describing properties of the writing system, orthography is about standardizing it (Dürscheid, 2006, p. 126). That means that orthographically correct spellings are determined by convention and form a subset of graphematically possible spellings.

[2] `www.exmaralda.org`

Proceedings of LAW X – The 10th Linguistic Annotation Workshop, pages 32–42,
Berlin, Germany, August 11, 2016.

cific grapheme-related features. Section 5 deals with the data representation in LearnerXML and in EXMARaLDA, followed by figures on inter-annotator agreement in Section 6.[3]

2 Theoretical Background

Our annotation scheme is largely based on the graphematic theory by Eisenberg (2006). He takes *grapheme-phoneme correspondences* (GPCs) as the basic component of the German writing system. For instance, the word <bunt> 'colorful' can be spelled purely phonographically, by following the basic GPC rules set up by Eisenberg (2006). (1) shows the relevant rules.

(1)	/b/	→	<b>	/n/	→	<n>
	/ʊ/	→	<u>	/t/	→	<t>

Simple GPC rules can be overwritten by *syllabic principles*. For instance, *Ruhe* 'quietness' is pronounced [ʀuːə] and according to GPC rules it would be spelled as *<Rue>[4]. The principle of *syllable-separating "h"* inserts <h> to indicate the syllable boundary: <Ru.**h**e>. Other syllabic principles are consonant doubling (<Ka**nn**e> 'pot'), vowel-lengthening <h> (<Ko**h**le> 'coal') and vowel doubling (<S**aa**l> 'hall'). Phonographic and syllabic spellings taken together are called *phonological spellings* by Eisenberg. They make reference to the word's prosodic structure and help determining its pronunciation and prosody given its spelling.

Finally, phonological spelling principles can be overwritten by *morphological principles*, which help recognizing a word's morphological structure. The main principle is that of *morpheme constancy* (MC), which means that a morpheme is always spelled in the same way regardless of its syllabic context. The "reference spelling" of a morpheme usually follows GPC and syllabic principles and is derived from so-called *explicit forms*. These are word forms with a trochaic stress pattern (*stressed-unstressed* as in 'under') or dactylic stress pattern (*stressed-unstressed-unstressed* as in 'memorize'.

For instance, for a monosyllabic word like singular *Hund* [hʊnt] 'dog', the explicit form would be the disyllabic plural form *Hunde* [hʊndə] 'dogs'. For these forms, GPC and syllabic rules would predict the spellings *<Hun**t**> (due to final devoicing) and <Hun**d**e>, respectively. Morpheme constancy states that <Hun**d**> is the correct singular spelling, inheriting the grapheme for the voiced plosive from the explicit form. MC becomes also visible e.g. in spellings of g-spirantization (GPC: *<Köni**ch**>; MC: <Köni**g**> because of <Köni**g**e> 'king/kings') and morphologically-determined <ä>-spellings (GPC: *<R**eu**ber>; MC: <R**äu**ber> 'robber' because of <**rau**ben> '(to) rob'). Another example are inhereted syllabic spellings where there is no actual structural need (<ko**mm**st> because of <ko**mm**en> '(you/to) come').

From the learner's perspective, Eisenberg's taxonomy is a suitable background to interpret errors against: Firstly, it takes GPCs as a basis, which is in accordance both with typical models of orthography acquisition (Siekmann and Thomé, 2012) as well as predominant teaching methods at school such as "Lesen durch Schreiben" ('reading through writing') (Reichen, 2008). Furthermore, the taxonomy clearly groups orthographic phenomena by form and function (e.g. principles that facilitate pronunciation or identification of morphemes), hence errors can be assessed in a graphematically systematical way.

3 Related Work

Error analysis has recently been of particular interest in the area of second language learner data. Here, spelling errors are often only one type of errors analyzed (besides grammatical errors) and not further subclassified (e.g. Rozovskaya and Roth (2010) and Dahlmeier et al. (2013) for English, Reznicek et al. (2012) for German). In contrast, work that is specifically directed at spelling errors often models and annotates causes of errors (e.g. Deorowicz and Ciura (2005), Hovermale and Martin (2008)), or describes the deviations from a rather technical point of view (e.g. edit-distance or single vs. multi-token (Bestgen and Granger, 2011; Flor, 2012)). This is largely language-independent, and a sample application for this kind of annotations is automatic spelling correction.

What is needed for an assessment of the development of spelling competence, however, is an annotation scheme that takes into account the properties and phenomena of the words that are to be

[3]The annotation scheme and the data of the pilot study reported here are available at `https://www.linguistics.ruhr-uni-bochum.de/litkey/Scientific/Corpusanalysis/Resources.html`.

[4]Asterisks mark an orthographically incorrect spelling.

spelled. For English, such annotations have been applied for comparing L1 and L2 learners (Bebout, 1985) and to derive implications for spelling instructions for L1 learners (Arndt and Foorman, 2010). Since annotations which reflect the orthographic properties of the words to be spelled are highly language specific, we focus on the literature on German spelling error annotation in the remainder of this section.

For German, quite a large number of orthographic annotation schemes exist already, many of which are part of well-established tests to assess children's spelling competence. However, their connection to the German graphematic system is often only loose. Some of them, for instance *Hamburger Schreib-Probe* (HSP) (May, 2013) and *Oldenburger Fehleranalyse* (OLFA) (Thomé and Thomé, 2004), are based on orthographic acquisition models and assign errors to phases of acquisition rather than graphematically well-founded categories. Hence, it can often not be assessed how an error relates to the systematics of the German writing system. OLFA, for example, has four designated error categories for *s*-spellings, namely *s for ß*, *ß for s*, *ss for ß* and *ß for ss*. These categories confound different cases, though. For instance, *ß for s* would apply to *<leßen> for <lesen> '(to) read'. This error violates basic GPCs: <lesen> is pronounced [leːzən] and, hence, spelled with <s>. *ß for s* also applies to *<Haußstring> for <Haus> 'house', without violating GPCs this time but morpheme constancy instead.

Similarly, HSP considers <ß> for the phoneme /s/ in <Gießkanne> 'watering can' an element that has to be memorized because the same phoneme can be represented by <s> elsewhere, for example in <Gras> 'grass' (May, 2013, p. 35). This disregards that the morphologically-related verb forms (*gießen* '(to) water' and *grasen* '(to) graze', respectively) make the correct spelling deducible (see also Röber (2011) and Eisenberg and Fuhrhop (2007) for further criticism on the HSP).

Aachener Förderdiagnostische Rechtschreibanalyse (AFRA) (Herné and Naumann, 2002) is a largely graphematically-based scheme but still the categorization of misspelled words is not fully transparent with regard to the German writing system. For instance, *<faren> for <fahren> '(to) drive' and *<Stull> for <Stuhl> 'chair' both fall under "misspelling of a long vowel which is marked by lengthening-h or doubled vowel". Grouping *<faren> and *<Stull> together misses the fact that *<faren> is a graphematically possible spelling for <fahren>, while *<Stull> for <Stuhl> is not, marking the vowel incorrectly as a short vowel.

Thelen (2010) designed an annotation scheme that reflects the graphematic system to a high degree. It takes the syllable as its central unit and codes whether syllable onset, nucleus or coda as well as certain orthographic phenomena (like consonant doubling, marked vowel duration) were spelled correctly. This scheme strictly distinguishes between phonological and morphological spellings. Moreover, the scheme grades whether a misspelling was phonologically plausible. There are also some downsides to this scheme, though. Firstly, overgeneralizations and random uses of phenomena are not differentiated. So for instance, there is no way to mark that *<Buss> for <Bus> 'bus' is a plausible overgeneralization (hypercorrection) of consonant doubling whereas *<Brrot> for <Brot> 'bread' is graphematically not legitimate at all. Secondly, as also Fay (2010) notes, the annotation scheme focuses on marking whether a phenomenon was spelled correctly or not, but many details are not recorded. Fay gives *<Gahbel> and *<Garbel> as misspellings of <Gabel> 'fork' as an example: Both would fall under "false spelling of syllable nucleus", missing the fact that they represent overgeneralizations of two different orthographic phenomena (namely vowel-lengthening <h> and vocalized <r>).

Fay's (2010) aim was also to create a scheme that was both graphematically systematic and learner-oriented (p. 57). However, as its main drawback, this scheme does again not differentiate between structurally-determined phenomena (such as doubled <m> in <kommen>) and morphologically-inherited phenomena (such as doubled <m> in <kommst>).

Except for Thelen's (2010) scheme, which also codes the phonological plausibility of a spelling, the existing schemes are all single-layered and annotate misspellings only with (possibly multiple) error categories.

Our annotation scheme is inspired by Thelen (2010) and Fay (2010), and extends them by defining additional annotation layers and more fine-grained categories. Since the scheme is based on a graphematic theory, it is not purely descriptive but requires interpretation in terms of what orthographic phenomenon is present. This allows for a comprehensive view on the different factors that impact on the interpretation of a spelling error.

4 Annotation Scheme

Our annotation scheme distinguishes between two types of words, the original words produced by the children, and a target word generated by the annotator, which is the word form that the child most probably had in mind.[5] If the original word is correctly spelled, the original and target forms are identical. Otherwise, the target form is the correctly-spelled version of the original form. In our annotations, original and target words are aligned in a way to state exactly which characters correspond to which. Errors are then annotated at the affected character alignments. This allows us to pin down the exact location of an error, and makes it possible to determine its context in terms of surrounding characters, syllables, morphemes, etc.

The annotation scheme consists of two parts. Part I defines general linguistic properties of words, such as syllables and morphemes. Most of them are annotated at the target word. Part II defines error-related categories, which are annotated at the original word.

4.1 Annotation Layers I: General Properties

As we have seen, written words are not single-layered constructs but have structural properties on various levels such as syllables and morphemes, which in turn influence a word's spelling. We believe that in order to fully understand the nature of an orthographic error, one needs access to multiple pieces of information that a spelling carries.

Most of the information relates to the target words, i.e. the correctly-spelled forms of the original words. This is because in the misspelled words, some information can only be extracted clearly with reference to the target word, e.g. *<Schle> appears to be monosyllabic but knowing the target word <Schule> 'school' makes it more probable that the nucleus of the first syllable was simply forgotten. Hence, we evaluate its structures on the basis of the target word.

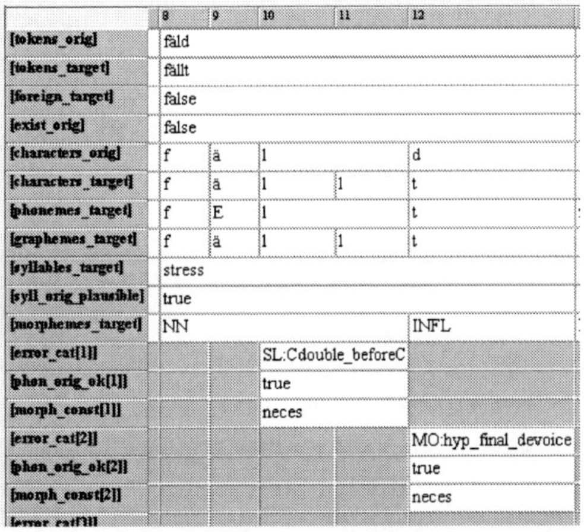

	8	9	10	11	12
[tokens_orig]	fäld				
[tokens_target]	fällt				
[foreign_target]	false				
[exist_orig]	false				
[characters_orig]	f	ä	l		d
[characters_target]	f	ä	l	l	t
[phonemes_target]	f	E	l		t
[graphemes_target]	f	ä	l	l	t
[syllables_target]	stress				
[syll_orig_plausible]	true				
[morphemes_target]	NN				INFL
[error_cat[1]]			SL:Cdouble_beforeC		
[phon_orig_ok[1]]			true		
[morph_const[1]]			neces		
[error_cat[2]]					MO:hyp_final_devoice
[phon_orig_ok[2]]					true
[morph_const[2]]					neces
[error_cat[3]]					

Figure 1: Annotations of the spelling *<fäld> (screenshot of EXMARaLDA)

The layers that our annotation scheme comprises are given in the following (for each layer, it is specified whether the information relates to the original or the target form). An example annotation for the spelling *<fäld> for <fällt> '(he) falls' is given in figure 1, visualized in EXMARaLDA (see sec. 5.2). The text is presented horizontally and each annotation layer corresponds to one tier, arranged vertically.[6]

phonemes (target) Each character (or character sequence) is mapped to a phoneme.

graphemes (target) Each character (or character sequence) is mapped to a grapheme, following Eisenberg's (2006) grapheme definition.

syllables (target) All syllables are classified as stressed, unstressed, or reduced. Knowing in which type of syllable an error occurred can be helpful for its interpretation. For instance, vowels can more easily be misheard in an unstressed syllable than in a stressed syllable, and reduced syllables are often spelled very differently from how

[5]There is exactly one target hypothesis for each original word. Note that our annotation scheme only deals with spelling errors, i.e. grammatical errors such as incorrect inflectional endings are ignored. The target word is therefore usually rather easy to determine (see section 6 for inter-annotator-agreement), in contrast to syntactic target hypotheses (see e.g. Hirschmann et al. (2007)). It is further facilitated by the fact that the texts in our corpus are all descriptions of picture stories, which provide a contextual frame.

[6]In our project, phonemes (represented in SAMPA), graphemes, syllables and morpheme types are determined automatically by means of the web service *G2P* of the Bavarian Archive of Speech Signals (BAS) `https://webapp.phonetik.uni-muenchen.de/BASWebServices/#/services/Grapheme2Phoneme` (Reichel, 2012; Reichel and Kisler, 2014), followed by some heuristic mappings. For aligning phonemes with characters, Levenshtein-based scripts by Marcel Bollmann were used `https://github.com/mbollmann/levenshtein`. We currently work on also automizing the other features.

they are pronounced (see also Fay (2010)).

morphemes (target) All morphemes are differentiated with regard to their morpheme type: for bound morphemes, if it is a derivational or inflectional affix; for free morphemes, its part of speech. The morpheme type can for instance give information about a learner's grammatical skills in relation to orthography by separately assessing the spelling of grammatical morphemes (see also Fay (2010)).

foreign_target (target) For each erroneous word, we indicate whether the target word is a foreign word, because many spelling regularities only apply to the German core vocabulary.

exist_orig (original) For each erroneous spelling, it is determined whether it (by chance or confusion) resulted in an existing word form, a so-called real-word error (e.g. *<feld> 'field' for <fällt> '(she) falls'). Knowing that the learners constructed or retrieved a plausible word form which they might have encountered before can be valuable information to assess their spelling competence.

plausible_orig (original) This feature codes for each syllable whether it is a possible syllable in German. This refers to graphotactics, i.e. permitted character sequences. For example, *<trraurig> (for <traurig> 'sad') is graphotactically not permitted as doubled consonants never occur in a syllable onset. A hypothesis one can test with this feature is that good spellers rarely commit errors which violate graphotactics.

4.2 Annotation Layers II: Error Categories

Our annotation scheme focuses on orthographic errors in single word spelling. As it is designed to be used for freely-written coherent texts, a few phenomena on the textual level are included as well.

We distinguish four classes of error categories: phoneme-grapheme correspondence (PG), syllable (SL), morphology (MO), and phenomena beyond word spelling (e.g. syntax-based) (SN), which is in accordance with Eisenberg's taxonomy and has also been similarly applied by Fay (2010). There are 69 error tags in total; class PG: 19 tags (with 3 subclasses), SL: 32 tags, MO: 6 tags, SN: 8 tags, and 4 tags for 'other systematic errors'. Each error is assigned exactly one tag, i.e. the scheme is designed in a way that only one category is the best fit for a given error. Here are some examples of the phenomena we cover:

PG:repl_unmarked_marked: learner used the ordinary, unmarked GPC-compliant spelling, instead of the marked target grapheme (*<Fogel> for <Vogel> 'bird')[7]

PG:literal: learner used GPC-compliant spelling, ignoring the exceptional spelling of a particular phoneme combination (*<schpielen> for *<spielen> '(to) play')

SL:Cdouble_beforeC: learner ignored consonant doubling before other consonants (*<komt> for <kommt> '(he) comes')

SL:separating_h: learner ignored a syllable-separating <h> (*<Rue> for <Ruhe> 'quietness')

SL:rem_Vlong_short: learner marked a long vowel for a phonetically short vowel (*<Sahnd> for <Sand> 'sand')

MO:final_devoice: learner ignored that final devoicing is not reflected in the spelling (*<Hunt> for <Hund> 'dog')

MO:hyp_final_devoice: learner incorrectly assumed final devoicing (*<räd> for <rät> '(he) guesses')

SN:low_up: learner ignored capitalization (*<hund> for <Hund> 'dog')

SN:merge, SN:split: learner incorrectly spelled words separately (*<zu frieden> for <zufrieden> 'satisfied') or in one word (*<unddann> for <und dann> 'and then')

The categories show that some phenomena get a more detailed analysis than in any other annotation scheme. For instance, with regard to missed consonant doubling, different contexts are explicitly distinguished: (i) between vowels, (ii) between vowel and another consonant (see above: SL:Cdouble_beforeC), and (iii) at the end of a word. The different contexts are motivated by different challenges for the learner: (i) consonant doubling between vowels (e.g. <kommen>, '(to) come') is a pattern that requires knowledge of the word's syllabic structure; a single consonant would result in a different pronunciation of the word (the preceding vowel would be pronounced long). (ii) A doubled consonant before another consonant, however, cannot be motivated by means of the syllable structure and vowel duration alone: The spellings *<komst>

[7]The category label reads as follows: "replace the original unmarked grapheme by a marked target grapheme".

and <kommst> '(you) come' can be pronounced the same way and do not differ in syllable structure. Instead, morpheme constancy is decisive. (iii) Consonant doubling at the end of the word is not regulated in a completely consistent way in the German writing system (compare <Bus/Busse> 'bus/busses' and <Fluss/Flüsse> 'river/rivers'). Such cases must be memorized. Although missed consonant doubling is a very frequent error (see for example Fay (2010)), their appearance in different graphematic contexts has not been studied yet. Having explicit categories for them facilitates the analysis.

Hypercorrection and overuse also play a central role in our scheme. In order to decide, e.g., whether superfluous consonant doubling is a hypercorrection (i.e. graphematically plausible) or just overused, we refer to the pronunciation, i.e. to vowel quality (tense/long vs. lax/short). For instance, *<Buss> for <Bus> 'bus' is regarded a hypercorrection because the fact that there is no doubled consonant in the target can be seen as an exception in the writing system (see above). Similarly, *<kämmpfen> for <kämpfen> '(to) fight' is categorized as a hypercorrection because the doubled consonant was applied after a lax vowel, which is a legitimate location (not affecting pronunciation). In contrast, *<gebben> for <geben> '(to) give' is an overuse of consonant doubling because it was applied after a tense vowel, where it never occurs as it would change the pronunciation (from [geːbən] to [gɛbən]).

There are two further properties stored for each error:

phon_orig_ok (original) This feature assesses for each error whether the incorrect spelling is phonetically sensible (cf. Bebout (1985) for English data). The feature encodes whether the pronunciation is similar in standard German (e.g. *<ier> for <ihr> 'her'), or in some dialect or colloquial register (e.g. *<Kina> for <China> 'China' in Southern German dialects), or not similar (e.g. *<Schle> for <Schule> 'school'). It shows to what extent a learner considers the relation between a word's spelling and its pronunciation.

morph_const (target) Morpheme constancy is, in some way, orthogonal to the other principles. There are clear cases which can only be explained by inheritance via morpheme constancy, such as consonant doubling in <kommst>) '(you) come', from <kommen> '(to) come'. In other cases, however, consonant doubling could be both prosodically determined (<kommend> 'coming') and motivated by morpheme constancy. Finally, in some exceptional cases, morpheme constancy is even violated, as in <Bus/Busse> 'bus/busses'.

The layer codes, for each error, whether reference to morpheme constancy is necessary in order to arrive at the correct spelling, whether it is redundant, whether is violated (i.e. a case of hypercorrection), or irrelevant.

A hypothesis to test is that orthographic phenomena that are determined by morpheme constancy alone are more difficult for learners than those which conform to different principles simultaneously. Another hypothesis would be that cases of hypercorrection occur more frequently with good spellers than bad spellers.

4.3 Using Error Categories for Characterizing Correctly-Spelled Words

Switching the perspective, our error categories can also be used to describe orthographic properties of a target word. For instance, a category label like *SL:Cdouble_interV* can be read as an instruction "apply consonant doubling between vowels to achieve the correct target form". At the same time, it can also be interpreted as "the target form shows consonant doubling". In the second reading, it can be annotated to a correct word form like <kommen> '(to) come'.

In contrast, the category *SL:Vlong_single_h* states "change a single long vowel to one with a vowel-lengthening <h>", or, reformulated for correct words: "the word contains a vowel-lengthening <h>". This category cannot be applied to the word <kommen> as there is no vowel-lengthening <h> in this word.

The set of categories that can be applied to a given correctly-spelled word encodes its orthographic properties and allows us to estimate its orthograpic complexity. We can thus analyze the level of difficulty of children's schoolbooks. Moreover, when applied to a child's text, the categories show which phenomena a child already masters and which of the possible errors it did *not* commit. This knowledge is important if one wants to make statements about a child's spelling competence (see also Fay (2010)).

To give an example, the word <fällt> 'falls' is characterized, among others, by use of the unmarked <f> in the first position (category *PG:repl_marked_unmarked*) and by a double consonant before other consonants (*SL:Cdouble_beforeC*).

We can now apply each category to the word and construct 'error candidates', i.e. incorrectly-spelled words that result from violating the respective error category, showing what the word would look like if this error in fact had occurred. One category may give raise to different error candidates, and several categories could be applied simultaneously. Table 1 lists some examples, also specifying the features *phon_orig_ok* and *morph_const*.[8]

5 Data Representation

5.1 LearnerXML

To represent the annotations, we developed an XML-based representation format called *LearnerXML*. Its main features are that the smallest units are characters, and errors are annotated to alignments between original and target characters. This section describes the format in detail.

Figure 2 shows an example fragment, featuring the misspelling *<fäld> for <fällt> '(he) falls' (see Table 1).

The root element `tokens` contains the individual `tokens` (words), with attributes `orig` (the original token as written by the child), `target` (the corrected version of the original token), and `foreign_target` and `exists_orig` as explained in section 4.1.

`token` elements embed further elements that encode various relevant word properties:

characters_orig, characters_target with sub-elements `char_o`, `char_t`, representing the individual characters in the child's original word and in the target word, respectively. These elements duplicate the information already contained in the token's attributes `orig` and `target`, to provide the basis for character-based alignment of both forms.

characters_aligned with sub-elements `char_a` for individual alignments between original and target character(s). By means of the attributes `o_range` and `t_range`, an alignment element can refer to: (i) one `char_o` and one `char_t`; (ii) a range of `char_o` (e.g. `o3..o5`) and one `char_t` (if several original characters correspond to one target character); (iii) or one `char_o` and a range of `char_t`.

It is also possible that there is no corresponding character that can be aligned. In these cases, `char_a` refers to (iv) only one `char_o` (an erroneous insertion in the child's form) or (v) only one `char_t` (i.e. an erroneous deletion). In cases (iv) and (v), the attributes `t_range` and `o_range`, respectively, are absent.

Ranges are of the form `x1..x3`, indicating the first and last element of the range. Note that no n-to-m correspondences, where $n, m \geq 2$, are allowed, neither are 0-to-n correspondences, where $n \geq 2$ (see annotation in EXMARaLDA in the next section).

phonemes_target with sub-elements `phon` for phonemes that are related to the corresponding characters or character sequences in the target word, as indicated by the `range` attribute. These are given in SAMPA notation as specified under `http://www.phon.ucl.ac.uk/home/sampa/german.htm`.

graphemes_target with sub-elements `gra` for individual graphemes of the target word. Multi-character graphemes have an attribute `type` which explicitly names the grapheme (e.g. `"ch"`).

syllables_target, morphemes_target with sub-elements `syll`, `mor` for individual syllables and morphemes of the target word, respectively, as described in section 4.1.[9]

errors with sub-elements `err`, each corresponding to one orthographic error in the original word. Errors are defined with regard to the alignment units, which connect original and target word fragments. An error annotation can point to one or more aligned characters (e.g. `a1` or `a1..a3`). The other attributes encode the information described in section 4.[10]

5.2 Annotation in EXMARaLDA

In order to visualize LearnerXML and to carry out manual annotations, we import the data into the *Partitur-Editor* of the tool EXMARaLDA (Schmidt and Wörner, 2009; Schmidt et al., 2011),

[8] In case 5, morpheme constancy applies to the inflectional ending *<-d> for <-t>. If the learners realize that the ending is the marking for 3rd person singular present tense, they can deduce the correct form from analogous forms like <sag-t> '(he) says, <lach-t> '(he) laughs', etc.

[9] Morpheme boundaries and types are determined automatically, see section 4.1. We currently do not correct these annotations, hence the incorrect part-of-speech assignment "NN" (noun) to the verbal stem in the example in figure 1.

[10] Right now, we only analyze orthographic errors but if the analysis is extended to e.g. grammatical errors, they can be represented as different `err`-types.

	Category	Error candidate(s)	phon_orig_ok	morph_const
1	PG:repl_marked_unmarked	**v**ällt, **ph**ällt	true	n.a.
2	PG: repl_unmarked_marked	f**e**llt	true	necessary
3	SL:rem_Vlong_short	fä**h**llt	false	n.a.
4	SL:Cdouble_beforeC	fä**l**t	true	necessary
5	MO:hyp_final_devoice	fäll**d**	true	necessary
6	4+5 together	fä**ld**	true/true	nec./nec.

Table 1: Examples of characterizing categories and corresponding error candidates of the word <fällt> '(he) falls'

```
<?xml version="1.0" ?>
<tokens id="test">
   <token id="tok1" orig="fäld" target="fällt"
          foreign_target="false" exist_orig="false">
     <characters_orig>
        <char_o id="o1">f</char_o>
        <char_o id="o2">ä</char_o>
        <char_o id="o3">l</char_o>
        <char_o id="o4">d</char_o>
     </characters_orig>
     <characters_target>
        <char_t id="t1">f</char_t>
        <char_t id="t2">ä</char_t>
        <char_t id="t3">l</char_t>
        <char_t id="t4">l</char_t>
        <char_t id="t5">t</char_t>
     </characters_target>
     <characters_aligned>
        <char_a id="a1" o_range="o1" t_range="t1"/>
        <char_a id="a2" o_range="o2" t_range="t2"/>
        <char_a id="a3" o_range="o3" t_range="t3..t4"/>
        <char_a id="a4" o_range="o4" t_range="t5"/>
     </characters_aligned>
     <phonemes_target>
        <phon_t id="p1" t_range="t1">f</phon_t>
        <phon_t id="p2" t_range="t2">E</phon_t>
        <phon_t id="p3" t_range="t3..t4">l</phon_t>
        <phon_t id="p4" t_range="t5">t</phon_t>
     </phonemes_target>
     <graphemes_target>
        <gra id="g1" range="t1"/>
        <gra id="g2" range="t2"/>
        <gra id="g3" range="t3"/>
        <gra id="g4" range="t4"/>
        <gra id="g5" range="t5"/>
     </graphemes_target>
     <syllables_target>
        <syll id="s1" range="t1..t5" type="stress" plausible_orig ="true"/>
     </syllables_target>
     <morphemes_target>
        <mor id="m1" range="t1..t4" type="NN"/>
        <mor id="m2" range="t5..t5" type="INFL"/>
     </morphemes_target>
     <errors>
        <err range="a3" cat="SL:Cdouble_beforeC" phon_orig_ok="true"
             morph_const="neces"/>
        <err range="a4" cat="MO:hyp_final_devoice" phon_orig_ok="true"
             morph_const="neces"/>
     </errors>
   </token>
</tokens>
```

Figure 2: Example annotation of the misspelling *<fäld> for <fällt> '(he) falls' in LearnerXML

as shown in figure 1. EXMARaLDA allows for character-wise annotation of texts. The smallest units that can be annotated are called *timeline items*, which correspond to characters in our application. On the annotation tiers, timeline items can be merged, and the alignments and the range of each annotation (i.e. the characters an annotation refers to) can be made visible. In figure 1 for instance, "l" at level "characters_orig" (5th row) is aligned with "ll" at level "characters_target (6th row). Similarly, all error-related annotations (rows 12–14 and 15–17) refer to such ranges.

6 Inter-Annotator Agreement

Children's texts are typically handwritten, so before orthographic errors in a child's text can be annotated, those texts have to be transcribed. Furthermore, the intended target words have to be recovered. We conducted a small pilot study to judge how manageable these tasks are.

Four students transcribed 12 freely-written texts produced by German primary school children of grades 2–4. The texts were taken from the corpus by Frieg (2014), for which children had to write down a story that was shown in a sequence of six pictures. The texts of our pilot study contained 951 tokens with 3640 characters in total. We computed pairwise inter-transcriber percent agreement for characters. Average agreement was 98.67% (SD: 0.15).

We then constructed a gold transcription for each text, and the same annotators annotated the target forms. They achieved a word-based average agreement of 96.44% (SD: 1.93).

Finally, we constructed a gold normalization for each text, and three of the annotators annotated the orthographic errors using EXMARaLDA as annotation tool. In this pilot study, only the error category was annotated, the other layers were left aside. We only evaluated annotated misspelled characters or character sequences (possibly overlapping; 295 annotations of 49 different categories in total;). Chance-corrected agreement according to Fleiss' κ was .80.[11]

The evaluation shows that transcribing and constructing target forms was done with high reliability. Error categorization also resulted in an agreement that is commonly considered "substantial".

[11] For computing agreement, we used the software tool R and the package "irr", `https://cran.r-project.org/web/packages/irr/`.

The disagreements do not reveal major systematic difficulties with the annotation scheme, rather individual inattentiveness. For instance, sometimes a category for an underspecified insertion was chosen although a specific category would exist (*PG:ins_C* vs. *SL:Vlong_single_h*), or ignoring a principle and its hypercorrection would be mixed up or an error was completely overlooked.

7 Conclusion

We presented a new multi-layered annotation scheme for orthographic errors in freely written German texts produced by primary school children. Compared to most existing schemes, it is much more closely linked to the German graphematic system. Furthermore, it features multiple layers of information which can be used to evaluate an error. To represent these data, we proposed *LearnerXML*, an XML-format which can be also be transferred to other formats, e.g. to visualize the data in EXMARaLDA.

Our first aim is to get new insights into the interrelation of orthographic errors and the graphemic system. Furthermore, we want to use the annotation scheme to investigate what kind of spelling phenomena occur in texts that children are confronted with, and how this relates to the kinds of spelling errors they produce. For instance, we plan to enrich *childLex*, the German Children's Book Corpus (Schroeder et al., 2014), with information about the orthographic properties of the words.

Hence, our future work is dedicated to a large-scale annotation of errors to pursue research questions such as whether spellings which relate to morpheme constancy are more error prone than spellings which can be derived from a word's pronunciation and prosody. The full corpus that we want to annotate, from which the data of the pilot study is a small extract, consists of around 2000 texts written by primary school children. We are also working on an automation of the categorization process.

Acknowledgments

This research is part of the project *Literacy as the key to social participation: Psycholinguistic perspectives on orthography instruction and literacy acquisition* funded by the Volkswagen Foundation as part of the research initiative "Key Issues for Research and Society". We would also like to thank the anonymous reviewers for their helpful comments.

References

Elissa J. Arndt and Barbara R. Foorman. 2010. Second graders as spellers: What types of errors are they making? *Assessment for Effective Intervention*, 36(1):57–67.

Linda Bebout. 1985. An error analysis of misspellings made by learners of English as a first and as a second language. *Journal of Psycholinguistic Research*, 14(6):569–593.

Kay Berkling, Rémi Lavalley, and Uwe Reichel. 2015. Systematic acquisition of reading and writing: An exploration of structure in didactic elementary texts for German. In *Proceedings of the Int. Conference of the German Society for Computational Linguistics and Language Technology*, pages 67–76, Duisburg/Essen, Germany.

Yves Bestgen and Sylviane Granger. 2011. Categorising spelling errors to assess L2 writing. *International Journal of Continuing Engineering Education and Life Long Learning*, 21(2-3):235–252.

Daniel Dahlmeier, Hwee Tou Ng, and Siew Mei Wu. 2013. Building a large annotated corpus of learner English: The NUS corpus of learner English. In *Proceedings of the Eighth Workshop on Innovative Use of NLP for Building Educational Applications*, pages 22–31.

Sebastian Deorowicz and Marcin G. Ciura. 2005. Correcting spelling errors by modelling their causes. *International Journal of Applied Mathematics and Computer Science*, 15(2):275.

Christa Dürscheid. 2006. *Einführung in die Schriftlinguistik*. Vandenhoeck & Ruprecht, Göttingen, 3rd edition.

Peter Eisenberg and Nanna Fuhrhop. 2007. Schulorthographie und Graphematik. *Zeitschrift für Sprachwissenschaft*, 26:15–41.

Peter Eisenberg. 2006. *Grundriss der deutschen Grammatik Band 1: Das Wort*. J.B. Metzler, Stuttgart, 3rd edition.

Johanna Fay. 2010. *Die Entwicklung der Rechtschreibkompetenz beim Textschreiben: Eine empirische Untersuchung in Klasse 1 bis 4*. Peter Lang, Frankfurt a. M.

Michael Flor. 2012. Four types of context for automatic spelling correction. *TAL*, 53(3):61–99.

Hendrike Frieg. 2014. *Sprachförderung im Regelunterricht der Grundschule: Eine Evaluation der Generativen Textproduktion*. Ph.D. thesis, Ruhr-Universität Bochum.

Karl-Ludwig Herné and Carl Ludwig Naumann. 2002. *Aachener Förderdiagnostische Rechtschreibfehler-Analyse*. Alfa Zentaurus, Aachen, 4th edition.

Hagen Hirschmann, Seanna Doolittle, and Anke Lüdeling. 2007. Syntactic annotation of non-canonical linguistic structures. In *Proceedings of Corpus Linguistics 2007*, Birmingham.

DJ Hovermale and Scott Martin. 2008. Developing an annotation scheme for ELL spelling errors. In *Proceedings of MCLC-5 (Midwest Computational Linguistics Colloquium). East Lansing, MI.*

Peter May. 2013. *Hamburger Schreib-Probe zur Erfassung der grundlegenden Rechtschreibstrategien: Manual/Handbuch Diagnose orthografischer Kompetenz*. vpm, Stuttgart.

Uwe D. Reichel and Thomas Kisler. 2014. Language-independent grapheme-phoneme conversion and word stress assignment as a web service. In Rüdiger Hoffmann, editor, *Elektronische Sprachverarbeitung: Studientexte zur Sprachkommunikation 71*, pages 42–49. TUDpress.

Uwe D. Reichel. 2012. PermA and Balloon: Tools for string alignment and text processing. In *Proceedings of Interspeech*, Portland, Oregon.

Jürgen Reichen. 2008. Lesen durch Schreiben: Lesenlernen ohne Leseunterricht. *Grundschulunterricht Deutsch*, 2:4–8.

Marc Reznicek, Anke Ludeling, Cedric Krummes, Franziska Schwantuschke, Maik Walter, Karin Schmidt, Hagen Hirschmann, and Torsten Andreas. 2012. Das Falko-Handbuch. Korpusaufbau und Annotationen Version 2.01. Technical report, Department of German Studies and Linguistics, Humboldt University, Berlin, Germany.

Christa Röber. 2011. Zur Ermittlung rechtschreiblicher Kompetenz. In Ursula Bredel and Tilo Reißig, editors, *Weiterführender Orthographieerwerb*. Schneider-Verlag Hohengehren, Baltmannsweiler.

Alla Rozovskaya and Dan Roth. 2010. Annotating ESL errors: Challenges and rewards. In *Proceedings of the NAACL HLT 2010 Fifth Workshop on Innovative Use of NLP for Building Educational Applications*, pages 28–36. Association for Computational Linguistics.

Thomas Schmidt and Kai Wörner. 2009. EXMARaLDA: Creating, analysing and sharing spoken language corpora for pragmatic research. *Pragmatics*, 19(4):565–582.

Thomas Schmidt, Kai Wörner, Hanna Hedeland, and Timm Lehmberg. 2011. New and future developments in EXMARaLDA. In Thomas Schmidt and Kai Wörner, editors, *Multilingual Resources and Multilingual Applications. Proceedings of GSCL Conference 2011 Hamburg.*

Sascha Schroeder, Kay-Michael Würzner, Julian Heister, Alexander Geyken, and Reinhold Kliegl. 2014. childLex: A lexical database of German read by children. *Behavior research methods*, pages 1–10.

Katja Siekmann and Günther Thomé. 2012. *Der orthographische Fehler: Grundzüge der orthographischen Fehlerforschung und aktuelle Entwicklungen.* isb-Verlag, Oldenburg.

Tobias Thelen. 2010. *Automatische Analyse orthographischer Leistungen von Schreibanfängern.* Ph.D. thesis, Universität Osnabrück.

Günther Thomé and Dorothea Thomé. 2004. *Oldenburger Fehleranalyse OLFA: Instrument und Handbuch zur Ermittlung der orthographischen Kompetenz aus freien Texten ab Klasse 3 und zur Qualitätssicherung von Fördermaßnahmen.* isb Verlag, Oldenburg.

Supersense tagging with inter-annotator disagreement

Héctor Martínez Alonso[♠] **Anders Johannsen** **Barbara Plank**[♡]
[♡] Center for Language and Cognition, University of Groningen, The Netherlands
[♠] Univ. Paris Diderot, Sorbonne Paris Cit – Alpage, INRIA, France
hector.martinez-alonso@inria.fr, anders@johannsen.com, b.plank@rug.nl

Abstract

Linguistic annotation underlies many successful approaches in Natural Language Processing (NLP), where the annotated corpora are used for training and evaluating supervised learners. The consistency of annotation limits the performance of supervised models, and thus a lot of effort is put into obtaining high-agreement annotated datasets. Recent research has shown that annotation disagreement is not random noise, but carries a systematic signal that can be used for improving the supervised learner. However, prior work was limited in scope, focusing only on part-of-speech tagging in a single language. In this paper we broaden the experiments to a semantic task (supersense tagging) using multiple languages. In particular, we analyse how systematic disagreement is for sense annotation, and we present a preliminary study of whether patterns of disagreements transfer across languages.

1 Introduction

Consistent annotations are important if we wish to train reliable models and perform conclusive evaluation of NLP. The standard practice in annotation efforts is to define annotation guidelines that aim to minimize annotator disagreement. However, in practical annotation projects, perfect agreement is virtually unattainable. Moreover, not all of disagreement should be considered *noise* because some of it is *systematic* (Krippendorff, 2011).

The work of Plank et al. (2014a) shows that the regularity of some disagreement in part-of-speech (POS) annotation can be used to obtain more robust POS taggers. They adjust the training loss of each example according to its possible variation in agreement, providing smaller losses when a classifier training decision makes a misclassification that matches with human disagreement. For example, the loss for predicting a particle instead of an adverb is smaller than the loss for predicting a noun instead of an adverb, because the particle/adverb confusion is fairly common among annotators (Sec. 3).

In this article, we apply the method of Plank et al. (2014a) to a semantic sequence-prediction task, namely supersense tagging (SST). SST is considered a more difficult task than POS tagging, because the semantic classes are more dependent on world knowledge, and the number of supersenses is higher than the number of POS labels. We experiment with different methods to calculate the label-wise agreement (Sec. 3.1), and apply these methods to datasets in two languages, namely English and Danish (Sec. 3.2). Moreover, we also perform cross-linguistic experiments to assess how much of the annotation variation in one language can be applied to another.

2 Variation in supersense annotation

This section provides examples of reasonable disagreement in supersense annotation. We have extracted examples of disagreement from English supersense data (Johannsen et al., 2014), which we later use in our experiments. Tables 1 provides example nominal and verbal expressions, and how they have been annotated by three annotators, namely A_1–A_3.

In the first noun example, *human being* is seen by most as a two-token multiword of N.PERSON, but A_2 emphasizes the biological reading of human being when assigning senses, thus interpreting it as N.ANIMAL.

For *lightning*, we observe a disagreement across two types (N.EVENT and N.PHENOMENON) that

Proceedings of LAW X – The 10th Linguistic Annotation Workshop, pages 43–48,
Berlin, Germany, August 11, 2016. ©2016 Association for Computational Linguistics

	A_1	A_2	A_3
human	B-N.PERSON	B-N.ANIMAL	B-N.PERSON
being	B-N.PERSON	I-N.ANIMAL	I-N.PERSON
October	B-N.COMM.	B-N.COMM.	B-N.TIME
Iron	I-N.COMM.	I-N.COMM.	B-N.LOCATION
Range	I-N.COMM.	I-N.COMM.	I-N.LOCATION
eNews	I-N.COMM.	I-N.COMM.	B-N.COMM.
lightning	B-N.EVENT	B-N.PHEN.	B-N.PHEN.
run	V.POSS.	V.CHANGE	V.CHANGE
stop	V.MOTION	V.STATIVE	V.CHANGE
rewind	V.MOTION	V.COGNITION	V.COGNITION

Table 1: Disagreement examples. The table shows two multi-word sequences and four single words. The labels COMMUNICATION, PHENOMENON, and POSSESSION are abbreviated.

arguably have a hyponymy relation between them (phenomena being a type of event), and we consider this disagreement a consequence of the overlap in the supersense inventory. The word *thunder* shows the same disagreement.

In the case of *October Iron Range eNews*, there is disagreement on the extension of the spans of the multiword. This difference also makes A_3 provide a different semantic type to each of the three multiwords.

Even without span-size disagreements and with a slightly smaller inventory, supersense annotation for verbs is harder than for nouns. For instance, *run* is the main verb of "*He's gonna run out of money*", and even though *run* is prototypically V.MOTION, the three senses provided in Table 1 reflect the meaning of "*run out of*". In the second example, the word *stop* has full disagreement, and it even has two supersenses that seem contradictory, namely V.MOTION and V.STATIVE. This disagreement is a result of the overlap between possible annotations for *stop*.

The case of *rewind* seems more surprising, but it comes from the sentence "*Rewind the 1st time I gave you a bar of chocolate*", where *rewind* is used to mean *remember*. Both A_2 and A_3 have chosen V.COGNITION to give account for the metaphorical meaning of the verb, while A_1 has given the prototypical, literal sense of *rewind*.

3 Method

Our approach is based on the confusion-matrix cost-sensitive learning described in Plank et al. (2014a). We use a soft notion of correctness, so that the cost of making a prediction y' depends not only on whether the correct gold label y is recovered, but also on how often annotators clashed when deciding between between y and y'. The idea is to give the learner more leeway to make mistakes as long as these mistakes are the same as those made by human annotators. The learning algorithm is parameterized with a cost matrix C, where the $C_{i,j}$ is the cost of predicting j when i is the true label.

To obtain the costs, we first calculate the disagreement matrix D for each doubly-annotated dataset. An entry $D_{i,j}$ contains the probability of two annotators providing a conflicting annotation with labels i and j. High-probability entries indicate low agreement. The cost matrix is then $C_{i,j} = 1 - D_{i,j}$. In our experiments we use a structured perceptron with cost-sensitive updates as the learner.

3.1 Factorizations

While disagreement for POS is straightforward, disagreement on supersense labels can be estimated in various ways, because supersense tags contain span, POS and sense information. Supersense tags are similar to named entity tags, but using semantic types from WordNet's lexicographer files. A tag for a content word is of the form {B,I}-{POS}.{SEMANTIC-TYPE}. Function words receive the "other" tag O. Some examples of valid supersense tags are B-NOUN.PERSON, I-NOUN.PERSON or B-VERB.PERCEPTION. We abbreviate the POS block to its initial.

To account for the various kinds of information captured by the supersense tags, we use four different *factorizations*, i.e., four different ways of factoring costs into the model training. Each factorization determines when two tags are considered different in terms of applying a different loss during cost-sensitive training.

1. WHOLETAGS: disagreement over whole tags. That is, all count as disagreement if any of their parts are different, e.g., B-N.PERSON $\neq$ I-N.PERSON
2. JUSTSENSE: disagreement over the supersense, ignoring the BI prefix. That is, e.g., B-N.PERSON = I-N.PERSON, but B-N.COGNITION $\neq$ B-V.COGNITION
3. NOPOS: Only the {SEMANTIC-TYPE} block is compared, disregarding the {B,I}{POS} prefix, e.g., I-N.COGNITION = B-V.COGNITION

4. BIOPREFIX: Only the {B,I} prefix is compared, e.g., B-N.PERSON = B-V.COGNITION

3.2 Data

We use supersense data from two languages, Danish and English. For Danish, we use the SemDax corpus (Pedersen et al., 2016), a collection of supersense-annotated documents of different domains.[1] For English, we use SemCor (Miller et al., 1994) and the Twitter data presented in (Johannsen et al., 2014), RITTER-dev, RITTER-eval, and LOWLANDS. The two first Twitter data sets adds an additional layer of annotation to the corpus first introduced in Ritter et al. (2011). Table 2 provides an overview of all the individual data sets used for our supersense tagging experiments.

lang	data set	sentences	tokens
EN	SEMCOR	20132	434.7k
DA	NEWSWIRE-train	400	7k
EN	RITTER-dev	118	2.2k
EN	RITTER-eval	118	2.3k
EN	LOWLANDS	200	3k
DA	NEWSWIRE	200	3.5k
DA	BLOG	100	1.6k
DA	CHAT	200	2.9k
DA	FORUM	200	4.1k
DA	MAGAZINE	200	3.9k
DA	PARLIAMENT	200	6.2k

Table 2: Supersense tagging data sets, the first two are training data sets.

Tag inventory The English data uses the supersense inventory determined by WordNet's lexicographer files, while the Danish supersense inventory is larger, because it extends some supersenses into subtypes, e.g., N.VEHICLE, N.BUILDING and N.ARTIFACT whereas WordNet only provides N.ARTIFACT; additionally the Danish data set provides four coarse supersenses for adjectives: A.MENTAL, ADJ.PHYS, A.TIME, A.SOCIAL.

Doubly-annotated data Table 3 provides statistics on the doubly-annotated data used to calculate disagreement factorizations, including annotator agreement scores. Note that the English doubly-annotated data is considerably smaller.

[1]https://github.com/coastalcph/semdax

sample	dataset	sents	tokens	labels	A_o	κ
$\mathbb{S}_{EN}$	LOWLANDS	40	0.8k	67	0.88	0.79
$\mathbb{S}_{DA}$	NEWSWIRE	200	3.5k	71	0.68	0.53

Table 3: Statistics on the doubly-annotated data, incl. raw observed agreement A_o and Cohen's κ.

3.3 Model

Supersense tagging is typically cast as a sequential problem like POS tagging, but the class distribution is more skewed with a majority class O. We use the structured perceptron RUNGSTED, which allows cost-sensitive training.[2] We use the same feature representation as Martínez Alonso et al. (2015b), which includes information on word forms, morphology, part of speech and word embeddings. We use 5 epochs for training. All results are expressed in terms of micro-averaged F_1-score, calculated using the official CONLLEVAL.PL script from the NER shared tasks.

4 Experiments

We perform two kinds of experiments: monolingual and cross-language. For the monolingual experiments we use each of the four possible factorizations (Sec. 3.1) to train SST models with different costs on a single language. We evaluate each system against the most-frequent sense baseline (MFS), and against a regular structured perceptron without cost-sensitive training (BASELINE).

The cross-language experiments assess whether some of the disagreement information captured by the factorizations can be used cross-lingually. To study this hypothesis, we run factorized systems using $\mathbb{S}_{DA}$ (Sec. 3.1) on English, and viceversa.

Adapting $\mathbb{S}_{DA}$ to English requires projecting back to the canonical supersense inventory, namely removing the adjective supersenses and treating, e.g., all cases of NOUN.VEHICLE as N.ARTIFACT, before calculating factorizations for the different confusion matrices.

Applying the complementary process—using English disagreement information to train cost-sensitive models for Danish SST—is more involved. We have converted all the Danish data to the English SST inventory to be able to use the coarser inventory of $\mathbb{S}_{EN}$ by projecting the extended senses to their original sense. Modifying the Danish data to harmonize with $\mathbb{S}_{EN}$ has thus

[2]https://github.com/coastalcph/rungsted

lang	dataset	MFS	BASELINE	WHOLETAGS	JUSTSENSE	NOPOS	BIOPREFIX
EN	*Average*	42.51	51.36	**52.31**	**51.72**	51.13	51.13
EN	*SemCor	62.53	65.58	65.57	65.45	64.39	64.47
EN	RITTER-dev	41.54	53.44	**53.95**	52.76	52.51	52.30
EN	RITTER-eval	38.94	49.03	**49.65**	**49.97**	**49.41**	**49.42**
EN	LOWLANDS	27.11	37.38	36.93	**38.71**	**38.22**	**37.33**
DA	*Average*	33.63	40.53	39.95	**40.70**	39.94	39.08
DA	NEWSWIRE-eval	31.47	42.13	**42.21**	**42.78**	41.27	40.93
DA	BLOG	25.57	39.43	35.73	37.50	37.04	38.04
DA	CHAT	36.06	38.18	**39.12**	**38.79**	**39.81**	**38.72**
DA	FORUM	31.08	35.35	34.68	**35.45**	35.15	34.45
DA	MAGAZINE	34.28	41.97	40.91	**42.67**	**42.09**	41.44
DA	PARLIAMENT	38.57	43.04	42.81	42.84	41.32	39.20

Table 4: F_1 scores for English and Danish supersense tagging, with language-wise macro-average.

an effect on the most frequent sense baseline, because the test data is effectively relabeled.

5 Results

Table 4 shows the performance of our system compared to the MFS baseline and the non-regularized baseline that does not use factorizations. Note that our baseline structured perceptron already beats the though MFS baseline. We mark results in bold when another system beats the BASELINE. Some factorizations are more favorable for certain datasets. For instance, all factorizations improve the performance on Ritter-eval, but only WHOLETAGS aids on Ritter-dev. Over all in-language data sets, WHOLETAGS beats the macro-averaged baseline for English. However, the most reliable factorization overall is JUSTSENSE, which beats BASELINE for English and Danish.

For Danish-JUSTSENSE we observe that the adjective supersenses improve (A.MENTAL goes from 0.00 to 16.53 for a support of 15 instances, and A.SOCIAL goes from 48.87 to 56.75 for a support of 169 instances in the training data), but also other senses with much higher support improve, regardless of POS, like N.PERSON (from 49.72 to 52.66 for 951 instances) or V.COMMUNICATION (from 49.66 to 50.31 for 364 instances).

With regard to our cross-lingual investigation, only the direction of using Danish disagreement on English proves promising. Table 5 shows the results of using $\mathbb{S}_{DA}$ when training and testing on English. While JUSTSENSE still helps defeat BASELINE, using NOPOS yields better results in this setup, indicating that coarser information might be the easiest to transfer across languages. Indeed, we find that N.COMMUNICATION goes from 60.63 to 66.60 and V.COMMUNICATION goes from 71.34 to 72.05.

Unfortunately, we have not found the improvements across factorizations to be statistically significant using bootstrap test and $p < 0.05$. Some of the differences in performance for the two languages can spawn from the differences in size of the doubly-annotated sample. In fact, the amount of data in $\mathbb{S}_{DA}$ is much larger than $\mathbb{S}_{EN}$ (200 newswire sentences vs. 40 tweets).

The results indicate that there is supporting evidence that the systematicity of annotator disagreement in supersense annotation can be used for cost-sensitive training, in particular using the JUSTSENSE factorization. Notice that the improvements in Plank et al. (2014a) for tagging reach a maximum of 4 accuracy points over the regular baseline. It would be unrealistic to expect improvements of such a magnitude for SST instead of POS tagging, in particular when evaluating with label-wise micro-averaged F1 instead of accuracy.

6 Related Work

Statistical NLP has been aware of the importance of annotator bias for NLP models (Yarowsky and Florian, 2002). Ratnaparkhi and others (1996) already mentioned that annotator identity was a predictive feature for maximum-entropy POS tagging, thereby including annotator bias as a feature.

dataset	MFS	BASELINE	WHOLETAGS	JUSTSENSE	NOPOS	BIOPREFIX
Average	42.51	51.36	50.86	**51.32**	**52.52**	49.70
SemCor	62.53	65.58	64.56	64.69	**65.69**	65.06
Ritter-dev	41.54	53.44	53.04	53.52	53.42	52.31
Ritter-eval	38.94	49.03	**49.17**	**49.58**	**49.55**	**48.90**
Lowlands	27.11	37.38	38.68	37.50	37.53	32.51

Table 5: F_1s for English using cross-lingual costs calculated from $\mathbb{S}_{DA}$

Instead of training on annotator-specific data, we use disagreement to regularize over individual annotators. Tomuro (2001) has used mismatching annotations between two sense-annotated corpora to find causes of disagreement such as systematic polysemy.

Reidsma and op den Akker (2008) aim at finding ways to integrate subjective and consensual annotation in ensemble classifiers, while more recent studies (Jurgens, 2013; Aroyo and Welty, 2013; Plank et al., 2014b; Lopez de Lacalle and Agirre, 2015; Martínez Alonso et al., 2015a; Martínez Alonso et al., 2015c; Plank et al., 2015) have treated inter-annotator disagreement as potentially informative for NLP. Other research efforts advocate for models of annotator behavior (Passonneau et al., 2010; Passonneau and Carpenter, 2014; Cohn and Specia, 2013).

7 Conclusions

We presented an application of cost-sensitive learning (Plank et al., 2014a) to supersense tagging. Prior work only focused on syntactic tasks and single languages. We evaluate different factorizations of label disagreement, run monolingual experiment on languages, and attempted a cross-lingual regularization experiment.

We identify a consistent factorization (JUSTSENSE) that beats the baseline in both monolingual scenarios and in the cross-lingual scenario of using Danish annotation disagreement to train an English SST model.

We believe that capturing semantic disagreement is even more adequate for cross-lingual studies as semantics is more abstract and should better carry over to other languages. However, our investigation is only preliminary, and we would like to test the approach on further semantic tasks for which doubly-annotated data is available.

References

Lora Aroyo and Chris Welty. 2013. Measuring crowd truth for medical relation extraction. In *2013 AAAI Fall Symposium Series*.

Trevor Cohn and Lucia Specia. 2013. Modelling annotator bias with multi-task Gaussian processes: An application to machine translation quality estimation. In *ACL*.

Anders Johannsen, Dirk Hovy, Héctor Martínez, Barbara Plank, and Anders Søgaard. 2014. More or less supervised supersense tagging of Twitter. In *Lexical and Computational Semantics (*SEM 2014)*.

David Jurgens. 2013. Embracing ambiguity: A comparison of annotation methodologies for crowdsourcing word sense labels. In *HLT-NAACL*, pages 556–562.

Klaus Krippendorff. 2011. Agreement and information in the reliability of coding. *Communication Methods and Measures*, 5(2):93–112.

Oier Lopez de Lacalle and Eneko Agirre. 2015. A methodology for word sense disambiguation at 90% based on large-scale crowdsourcing. In *Lexical and Computational Semantics (*SEM)*.

Héctor Martínez Alonso, Anders Johannsen, Oier de Lopez de Lacalle, and Eneko Agirre. 2015a. Predicting word sense annotation agreement. In *Workshop on Linking Models of Lexical, Sentential and Discourse-level Semantics (LSDSem)*, page 89.

Héctor Martínez Alonso, Anders Johannsen, Sussi Olsen, and Sanni Nimb. 2015b. Supersense tagging for danish. In *Nordic Conference of Computational Linguistics NODALIDA 2015*, page 21.

Héctor Martínez Alonso, Barbara Plank, Arne Skjærholt, and Anders Søgaard. 2015c. Learning to parse with iaa-weighted loss. In *Proceedings of Naacl*. Association for Computational Linguistics.

George A. Miller, Martin Chodorow, Shari Landes, Claudia Leacock, and Robert G. Thomas. 1994. Using a semantic concordance for sense identification. In *Proceedings of the workshop on Human Language Technology*, pages 240–243. Association for Computational Linguistics.

Rebecca J Passonneau and Bob Carpenter. 2014. The benefits of a model of annotation. *TACL*, 2:311–326.

Rebecca J Passonneau, Ansaf Salleb-Aouissi, Vikas Bhardwaj, and Nancy Ide. 2010. Word sense annotation of polysemous words by multiple annotators. In *LREC*.

Bolette Sandford Pedersen, Anna Braasch, Anders Johannsen, Héctor Martínez Alonso, Sanni Nimb, Sussi Olsen, Anders Søgaard, and Nicolai Sørensen. 2016. The semdax corpus–sense annotations with scalable sense inventories. In *LREC*.

Barbara Plank, Dirk Hovy, and Anders Søgaard. 2014a. Learning part-of-speech taggers with inter-annotator agreement loss. In *EACL*.

Barbara Plank, Dirk Hovy, and Anders Søgaard. 2014b. Linguistically debatable or just plain wrong? In *ACL*.

Barbara Plank, Héctor Martínez Alonso, Željko Agić, Danijela Merkler, and Anders Søgaard. 2015. Do dependency parsing metrics correlate with human judgments? In *CoNLL*.

Adwait Ratnaparkhi et al. 1996. A maximum entropy model for part-of-speech tagging. In *Proceedings of the conference on empirical methods in natural language processing*, volume 1, pages 133–142. Philadelphia, USA.

Dennis Reidsma and Rieks op den Akker. 2008. Exploiting 'subjective' annotations. In *Workshop on Human Judgements in Computational Linguistics, COLING*.

Alan Ritter, Sam Clark, Oren Etzioni, et al. 2011. Named entity recognition in tweets: an experimental study. In *Proceedings of EMNLP*.

Noriko Tomuro. 2001. Tree-cut and a lexicon based on systematic polysemy. In *NAACL*.

David Yarowsky and Radu Florian. 2002. Evaluating sense disambiguation across diverse parameter spaces. *Natural Language Engineering*, 8(04):293–310.

Filling in the Blanks in Understanding Discourse Adverbials: Consistency, Conflict, and Context-Dependence in a Crowdsourced Elicitation Task

Hannah Rohde* **Anna Dickinson*** **Nathan Schneider*,†**
Christopher N. L. Clark* **Annie Louis‡** **Bonnie Webber***

*University of Edinburgh, Edinburgh, UK
†Georgetown University, Washington, DC, USA
‡University of Essex, Colchester, UK

{hannah.rohde, bonnie.webber}@ed.ac.uk,
{anna.y.dickinson, chrisclark272}@gmail.com,
nschneid@inf.ed.ac.uk, aplouis@essex.ac.uk

Abstract

The semantic relationship between a sentence and its context may be marked explicitly, or left to inference. Rohde et al. (2015) showed that, contrary to common assumptions, this isn't *exclusive or*: a conjunction can often be inferred alongside an explicit discourse adverbial. Here we broaden the investigation to a larger set of 20 discourse adverbials by eliciting ≈28K conjunction completions via crowdsourcing. Our data replicate and extend Rohde et al.'s findings that discourse adverbials do indeed license inferred conjunctions. Further, the diverse patterns observed for the adverbials include cases in which more than one valid connection can be inferred, each one endorsed by a substantial number of participants; such differences in annotation might otherwise be written off as annotator error or bias, or just a low level of inter-annotator agreement. These results will inform future discourse annotation endeavors by revealing where it is necessary to entertain implicit relations and elicit several judgments to fully characterize discourse relationships.

1 Introduction

Existing work highlights the importance of understanding discourse relations in context, showing a range of phenomena that are sensitive to the semantic connection that holds between two spans of discourse (Hirschberg and Litman, 1987; Kehler and Rohde, 2013). Such connections can be made explicit in text via an overt connective or marked syntax; otherwise they must be inferred. Various contextual cues have been identified that guide the establishment of discourse relations (Hirschberg and Litman, 1987; Kehler, 2002; Webber, 2013).

When it comes to producing resources annotated with discourse relations—e.g., the Penn Discourse Treebank (PDTB; Prasad et al., 2008)—it is commonly assumed that at most a *single* discourse relation holds between two spans of discourse. It may not be simple to identify or infer that relation, but once achieved, the task is taken to be done. But properties of the discourse adverbial **instead** (Webber, 2013) have challenged this assumption. In particular, sentence-initial **instead** supports the inference of another discourse relation, with the specific relation depending on properties of the spans. This can be seen through what coordinating conjunction makes the relation explicit—compare:

(1) I planned to make lasagna. Instead I made hamburgers.
⇒ But instead I made hamburgers

(2) I don't know how to make lasagna. Instead I made hamburgers.
⇒ So instead I made hamburgers

(3) Surprisingly, they ignored the lasagna. Instead they just ate the salad.
⇒ And instead they just ate the salad

While this means that full annotation of **instead** requires asking annotators what additional relation they infer (besides that associated with **instead** itself), one still needs to ask:

- For clauses starting with discourse adverbials other than **instead**, is the relation signalled by the adverbial all there is, or can an additional relation be inferred with the previous text? In the former case, no additional annotation is required; in the latter, it is.

Proceedings of LAW X – The 10th Linguistic Annotation Workshop, pages 49–58,
Berlin, Germany, August 11, 2016.

- If another relation can be inferred, can it be inferred deterministically based on the adverbial alone? If so, no additional work is required, as the relation can be annotated automatically.
- If it can't be inferred based on the discourse adverbial alone (as in the case of **instead**), how should an annotator figure out what it is?
- Could there be different ways of framing the inferred relation, such that annotators may disagree as to its identity, but all still be correct?

This paper addresses these questions using crowdsourced data elicited on 969 passages involving twenty discourse adverbials. We describe our methodology, what we have so far been able to learn, and how *inter-annotator disagreements* have led us to look more deeply into the judgments and what conclusions we can draw from them. Our results demonstrate that inter-annotator disagreement is informative, and need not be treated as annotator bias, inattention, or noise.

2 Background

The current work should be seen against the background of two research areas: Research on multiple co-occurring connectives and research on acquiring useful linguistic judgments from a large number of annotators, whether by crowdsourcing or in-house.

In the PDTB, all explicit connectives in a sentence were separately annotated. Then, *if and only if* a sentence lacked an explicit inter-sentential connective linking it to the previous context, annotators were asked to infer and annotate its relation, if any, to the previous sentence. This reflected the common assumption, noted earlier, that the situation is "either/or" – if a discourse relation is marked, there is nothing to infer.

With respect to research on explicit multiple co-occurring connectives, over 15 years ago, Webber et al. (1999) used them to argue that discourse spans could be related by both adjacency relations and anaphoric relations. Similary, in the context of Catalan and Spanish oral narrative, Cuenca and Marín (2009) used them to argue for different patterns and degrees of discourse cohesion. Oates (2000) considered how multiple discourse connectives should be used in Natural Language Generation, noting that the order in which they occur correlates with the hierarchy of discourse connectives presented in (Knott, 1996), while Fraser (2013) offers an account of the order in which multiple *contrastive* connectives co-occur, in terms of what he calls *general contrastive* discourse markers and *specific contrastive* discourse markers. For Turkish, Zeyrek (2014) has described patterns of multiple co-occuring connectives that signal *contrastive* and/or *concessive* relations.

These efforts have all been directed at explaining the existence of multiple explicit connectives and how they pattern. Closer to the focus of the current paper is work by Rohde et al. (2015), in which judgments were crowdsourced on four adverbials: **after all**, **in fact**, **in general** and **instead**. Rohde et al. found that, given one of these discourse adverbials, naïve participants identified an operative discourse relation—via a conjunction whose presence they endorsed alongside the discourse adverbial. They did so reliably both for explicit passages in which the author's explicit pre-adverbial conjunction had been elided and for implicit passages in which the adverbial originally appeared alone. For Rohde et al.'s four adverbials, the inferred relation could not be predicted entirely on the basis of the adverbial alone. The current study extends Rohde et al.'s work to a larger set of adverbials. We focus on participant judgments on implicit passages since such cases are left largely untreated by existing annotation endeavors as well as current formal accounts.

The other research area that forms the background to the current work is research on acquiring linguistic judgments from a large number of annotators, whether by crowdsourcing or in-house. Here, research has addressed either identifying and correcting for problems arising from judgments from large numbers of unknown, possibly biased and/or inattentive annotators (Hovy et al., 2013; Passonneau and Carpenter, 2014), or identifying benefits that arise from having a large number of annotators (Artstein and Poesio, 2005, 2008). Work in the former area attempts to eliminate judgments that should be treated as noise, while the latter work shows that annotator bias decreases with the number of annotators.

In related research, Poesio and Artstein (2005) reflect on the "true ambiguity" of some pronoun tokens and how the presence of these distinct co-present viable interpretations can be brought to light via a sufficiently large number of annotators. In one example they cite, a boxcar has been attached to a train engine. The next sentence specified what should then be done. Over half their participants interpreted the pronoun *it* in this next sentence as referring to the boxcar, while others interpreted it to refer to the engine. But the situation associated with these two different interpretations was the same in both cases, since the engine and boxcar had effectively become a single moving, functioning unit. This ambiguity would not necessarily have been made apparent or taken to be as significant without the large number of participants.

Lastly, there is new work (Scholman et al., 2016) that tests naïve annotators' ability to infer discourse relations, specifically to distinguish four dimensions along which relations are posited to vary. Their work targets annotator agreement, and shows consistency comparable with expert annotators for two of the four posited dimensions. Unlike their task, which asked participants to make a decision about abstract semantic features, our methodology involves asking participants to consider whether a short passage with an explicit conjunction is a paraphrase of one without that conjunction. Crucially, we will avoid the assumption that there is a single correct answer.

3 Crowdsourcing judgments on discourse adverbials: Methodology

Here we extend the crowdsourcing approach of Rohde et al. (2015) to a larger dataset with many more adverbials. The goal is to learn from participants' endorsements of particular conjunction–adverbial combinations in naturally occurring passages, as to whether additional annotation will be needed.

3.1 Participants

We recruited 28 participants from Amazon Mechanical Turk. All were native English speakers and were paid $88 each for their participation. These 28 individuals were selected from a larger pool who participated in a pre-trial involving 50 annotations. The pre-trial allowed us to identify participants who understood the task, whose responses were in line with the group average, who did not overuse NONE, and who were not outliers in speed.

3.2 Materials

The target passages that participants read were selected from the NY Times Annotated Corpus (Sandhaus, 2008). Passages varied from 9 to 122 words (minimally a sentence and maximally, a short paragraph). They were chosen to be comprehensible as stand-alone excerpts. Each target passage consisted (minimally) of two spans of text, the second beginning with a discourse adverbial, as in examples (1)–(3) and the sample materials shown in (4)–(5).

(4) "Nervous? No, my leg's not shaking," said Griffey, who caused everyone to laugh / _____ indeed his right foot was shaking.

(5) Sellers are usually happy, too / _____ after all / they are the ones leaving with money.

In example (4)'s original form, the author had included an explicit conjunction (*because*). In example (5), the original text contained only the adverbial, meaning that a discourse relation conveyed by a conjunction would have been implicit. Punctuation adjacent to the adverbial was replaced with a slash.

Each passage contained one of the following discourse adverbials after the gap: **actually**, **after all**, **first of all**, **for example**, **for instance**, **however**, **in fact**, **in general**, **in other words**, **indeed**, **instead**, **nevertheless**, **nonetheless**, **on the one hand**, **on the other hand**, **otherwise**, **specifically**, **then**, **therefore**, and **thus**. These represent a sampling of high-frequency adverbials, which belong to a variety of semantic classes and which showed a range of conjunction co-occurrence patterns in counts extracted from the Google Books Ngram Corpus (Michel et al., 2011; Lin et al., 2012).

Half the target passages originally contained a conjunction before the adverbial. For those *explicit passages*, we excised the conjunction and replaced it with a gap. For excerpts that were originally *implicit passages*, we simply inserted a gap before the adverbial. For each of the 20 adverbials, participants saw 25 explicit passages and 25 implicit passages, with the exception of **however**, which appeared in 25 implicit passages and 1 explicit passage (due to the rarity of conjunctions that naturally occur directly before **however**).

The distribution of original (author-chosen) conjunctions in the explicit passages reflected the distribution observed in Google n-gram counts of each adverbials with each of the conjunctions AND, BECAUSE, BUT, OR, SO. These 5 conjunctions appeared in a list of possible response options for participants.

With 20 adverbials and 50 passages per adverbial (26 passages for **however**), this yields a set of 976 passages. Due to presentation errors in 7 passages, the dataset for analysis consists of participant responses to 969 unique passages. The experiment also included 32 catch trials, which were used to check that participants were paying attention and using the experimental interface correctly. The catch trials contained well-known quotes and expressions that had a 'correct' conjunction (e.g., *you can lead a horse to water _____ you can't make it drink*). Some of the catch trials expected the response BEFORE, so this was included as a 6th option in the list of possible conjunction responses.

How much can we learn from participants' selection of a conjunction? All six conjunctions we use are relatively unambiguous: In the PDTB (Prasad et al., 2008), each has a different main sense that it is associated with >90% of the time.[1] More to the point, while 5.9% of the explicit tokens of **and** were assigned a *result* sense, of the 1272 tokens where AND was inserted as an implicit connective, none were labelled with the inferred sense *result*. (97% of the time, when AND was inserted as an implicit connective, it was with an inferred sense of *conjunction* or *list*, as with explicit tokens of AND.) As such, there are grounds for believing that the experiment targeted the participants' inferred relation through choosing a conjunction that realizes it, even if the sense is only a coarse one.

3.3 Procedure

All participants saw all passages. Participants were instructed to fill in the gap with the word of their choice (from the six conjunctions AND, BECAUSE, BEFORE, BUT, OR, SO) that "best reflects the **meaning** of the connection" between the spans. They also had the option of choosing either NONE AT ALL (if they felt that no conjunction was possible) or OTHER WORD OR PHRASE (if they felt that only some option other than the six presented conjunctions was appropriate). The instructions were followed by three practice items.

During pilot testing, it emerged that participants sometimes chose NONE AT ALL when it sounded more fluent and less awkward to them than did an explicit conjunction. To avoid this, we explicitly instructed participants to choose the conjunction that best conveyed the sense of the connection, "even if the resulting text sounds awkward", but then offered them the opportunity to record whether or not they would in fact use the chosen conjunction in that context (recording "I could say it this way" or "It sounds strange here").

[1] OR has the sense *Disjunction* 86.7%, since it is labelled as *Conjunction* when it is in a negative context.

To avoid order effects, passages were pseudo-randomised: Participants never encountered more than three of the same adverbial in a row, and for explicit passages, they never saw excerpts whose original (author-chosen) conjunction was the same more than three times in a row. Also randomized was the list of possible conjunctions from which participants selected their response: The list appeared in a different order for each participant. Cursory examination of a sample of the data fails to show any obvious bias from the order in which the choices were presented.

The task was completed over several weeks. Participants worked at a rate of roughly 85 tokens per hour (making the hourly rate roughly $8/hour). They were not permitted to do more than 100 tokens per day.

4 Results

4.1 Issues addressed by the results

Our crowdsourced data can be used to answer distinct questions: Responses on explicit passages (§4.2) can be used to test whether untrained participants *can* do the task and deliver useful information. Given that the answer is found to be 'yes', responses on implicit passages (§4.3) can be used to answer our fundamental research questions: (1) Do inferrable discourse relations hold in implicit passages containing only a discourse adverbial, and (2) how can individual adverbials best be characterized with respect to inferrable discourse relations?

Assuming that the first question is answered in the affirmative (as was shown by Webber (2013) for **instead**), the two strongest answers to the latter question would be either:

i. **Uniformity across adverbials:** All adverbials co-occur with the same preferred conjunction.
ii. **Uniformity per adverbial:** Each adverbial has a single preferred conjunction, not necessarily the same across adverbials but possibly predictable from the semantic class of the adverbial.

If either was the case, it would be straightforward to obtain additional annotation of discourse adverbials. However, §4.3 will show that conjunctions preferred by participants are neither uniform across adverbials (contra (i)) nor uniform across passages for a particular adverbial (contra (ii)). We can nevertheless use these two types of variability to characterize the adverbials in this study.

§5 will then show that systematic variability in the responses of our untrained annotators reveals cases in which multiple interpretations are inferable—an outcome that, as in (Poesio and Artstein, 2005), only presents itself with the use of multiple annotators. We discuss implications for large-scale annotation frameworks and methods.

4.2 Responses for explicit passages

For each of the 20 adverbials in our study, we elicited responses for 25 *explicit* passages, where the original sentence contained an adverbial preceded by a conjunction. (As already noted, for **however** we elicited responses for only one explicit passage; also, in the case of four explicit passages containing other adverbials, there were errors in presentation.) With 28 participants who saw all of these explicit passages, we have 13,216 analyzable data points.

The results show that conjunctions selected by authors in original texts are indeed recoverable: More than half the time (57%), participants selected the conjunction that the author had used. Moreover, it has been noted that the conjunction AND provides a less specified signal regarding the intended discourse relation (Knott, 1996) than some other conjunctions. For our data, if one considers SO and BUT as compatible with author-chosen AND and allow for such matches in computation of the overall agreement rate, participant selections matched the authors' original conjunction 70% of the time. The confusion matrix for author-chosen and participant-selected conjunctions is shown in table 1.

	AND	BECAUSE	BUT	OR	SO
AND	2686	149	325	159	344
BECAUSE	280	786	176	156	156
BUT	1000	174	2798	179	180
OR	68	41	15	355	28
SO	550	127	129	298	1215
BEFORE	4	2	1	0	1
NONE	248	105	158	108	167
OTHER	8	16	10	5	9

Table 1: Confusion matrix of author conjunctions (columns) and participant responses (rows) in explicit passages

Other cases of divergence in participant selection point to contexts in which normally different conjunctions can convey the same relation. A case in point are passages containing the adverbial **otherwise** (table 2). Here, author OR received an unexpectedly high number of BECAUSE participant responses, and vice versa.

It appears that, with **otherwise**, both BECAUSE and OR can be used to express a reason. This is apparent in passage (6) below, where responses to author OR were split, with 17 participants selecting OR and 11, BECAUSE.

	AND	BECAUSE	BUT	OR	SO
AND	8	2	3	3	0
BECAUSE	31	62	11	95	4
BUT	30	7	157	2	8
OR	27	35	6	133	9
SO	2	0	4	1	3
NONE	14	6	15	18	4

Table 2: Confusion matrix for explicit passages containing **otherwise** (author conjunctions as columns, participant responses as rows)

(6) "The Ravitch camp has had about 25 fundraisers and has scheduled 20 more. Thirty others are in various stages of planning," Ms. Marcus said. "It has to be highly organized _____ otherwise it's total chaos," she added.

These two strong signals are neither noise nor disagreement nor evidence of ambiguity (as in Poesio and Artstein (2005)), but rather different, context-specific ways of conveying the same sense.

Given the number of possible responses on each trial (6 conjunctions, NONE, OTHER) and the different senses that these conjunctions are usually taken to express, our observed levels of agreement are encouraging and suggest that participants can recognize intended concurrent relations and provide meaningful responses in this task.

4.3 Responses for implicit passages

For each of the 20 adverbials in our study, we elicited responses for 25 *implicit* passages, where the original sentence contained an adverbial not preceded by a conjunction (excepting 3 implicit passages with errors in presentation). With 28 participants who saw all implicit passages, we have 13,916 analyzable data points.

To help categorize participants' behavior across adverbials, we visualize each adverbial's response profile as a stacked bar chart, as shown in figure 1 for all 20 adverbials. Every point on the x-axis represents a passage, and passages have been ordered for presentation here to highlight trends for the adverbial.[2] For each passage, bars color-coded by response (chosen conjunction) are sized according to the number of respondents who chose that response, and stacked in a consistent order: first AND (blue) at the bottom, then BECAUSE (green), then BUT (yellow), etc. The y-axis reaches 28 because

[2]In crowdsourcing the data, passages were presented in pseudo-random order (§3.3).

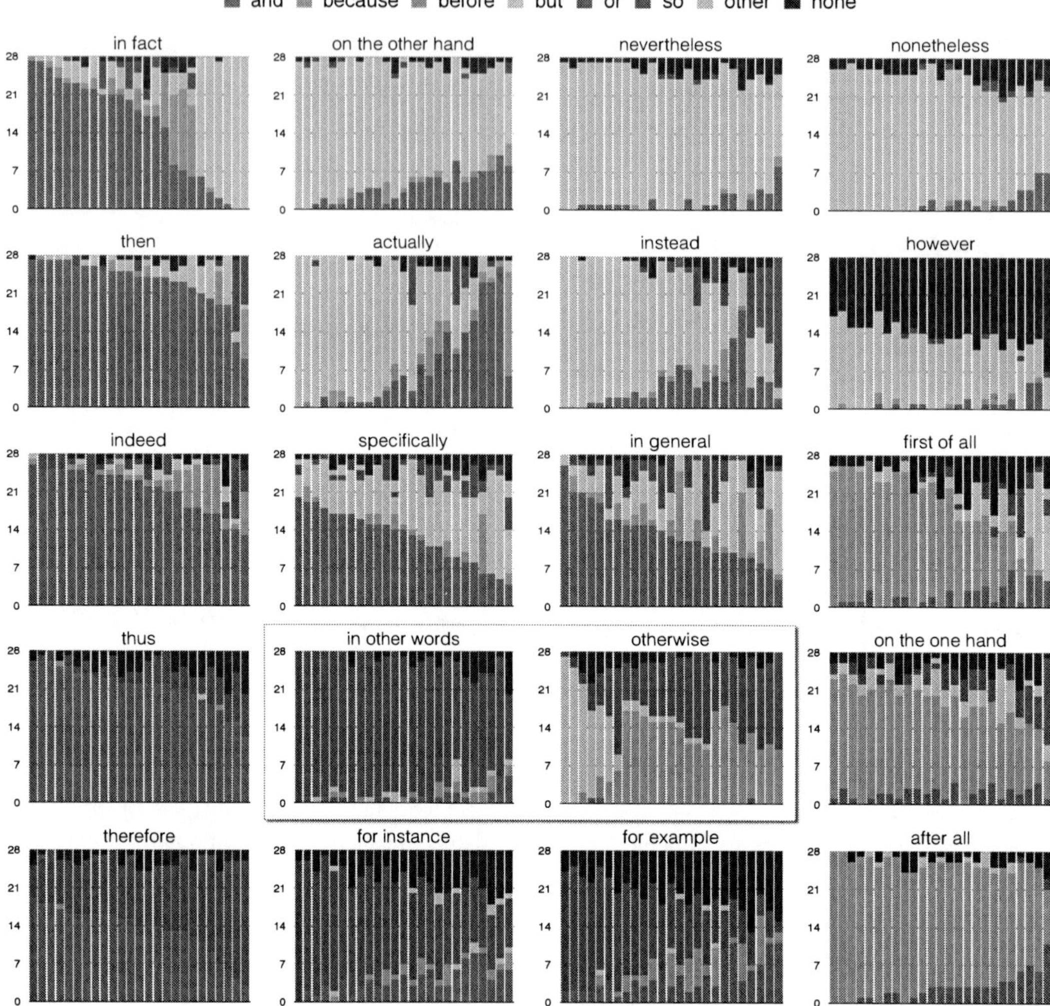

Figure 1: Data for implicit passages. Plots are arranged according to the dominant response(s).

every passage has 28 responses. We have manually arranged the plots so that patterns of dominant responses can be observed; e.g., plots with high concentrations of BUT (shown in yellow) are in the upper portion of the figure.

Comparing even just two of the plots in figure 1 leads us to several observations. Consider **otherwise** and **in other words** (highlighted in the middle of the fourth row of figure 1).

- These two adverbials have markedly different profiles of inserted conjunctions, suggesting different patterns of implied/inferred discourse relations.
- Neither response pattern is totally random; clear trends are observable in each. At the same time, neither adverbial has a single conjunction that is dominant overall. Instead, we see 2 or 3 conjunctions that are most often chosen for passages with the adverbial.
- Neither adverbial has a completely consistent distribution of responses within particular passages. The plot for **in other words** shows an overall preference on most passages for SO, but the degree of competition from BUT and OR (and even BECAUSE and AND) varies depending on the passage. For **otherwise**, some passages favor BUT whereas others are split between BECAUSE and OR responses.

We can also see that several observations in Rohde et al. (2015) regarding their 4 targeted adverbials are replicated here: The preferred conjunctions for **after all** and **in fact** are again BECAUSE and AND/BUT/BECAUSE, respectively; likewise, **in general** has the same dominant preference for AND, although the frequency of alternative conjunctions differs. Rohde et al. reported that **instead** favored SO, but our data show SO second to BUT. This may be taken to underscore the sensitivity of these inferences to the passages in which **instead** appears.

More generally, these plots reveal striking similarities as well as striking differences. With respect to the question of whether a conjunction *can* co-occur with a discourse adverbial even when the author did not use one, the answer is yes: Participants favored the NONE option for only a few adverbials (**however**, **for instance**, **for example**), implying that the conjunctions they endorsed for other adverbials reflect connections they saw in the text and were not merely an artefact of the experiment. Furthermore, with respect to the question of how to characterize individual adverbials, figure 1 shows that neither of the uniformity outcomes listed in §4.1 hold for these data: It is not the case that all adverbials co-occur with the same preferred conjunction, nor does each have a single preferred conjunction or necessarily pattern with other adverbials from the same semantic class.

More specifically, we see that all adverbials have 1–3 frequent responses out of the 8 options. Although none the plots are overwhelmingly dominated by a single conjunction, **nevertheless** and **nonetheless** come closest with their preference for BUT. The responses BEFORE (orange) and OTHER (gray) were very rare. Some pairs of neighboring plots are highly similar, e.g., **nevertheless/ nonetheless** in the upper right, and **for instance/ for example** in the bottom center. This is reassuring as the members of each pair have intuitively similar meanings. That said, even though **actually**, **indeed**, and **in fact** would all be classified as modal stance adverbials (Aijmer and Simon-Vandenbergen, 2007), they elicit different response patterns: **actually** and **in fact** elicit AND, BUT, and BECAUSE with a smattering of SO, while **indeed** elicits AND and BECAUSE.

On the other hand, **instead** exhibits a context-specific pattern of inference: Many **instead** passages elicit a BUT response, but others elicit SO, showing that what drives the choice must be specific to the passage, not the adverbial alone. Likewise for **otherwise**: some passages elicit BUT, but most reflect an explanation, conveyed with either BECAUSE or OR, similar to responses for the ex-

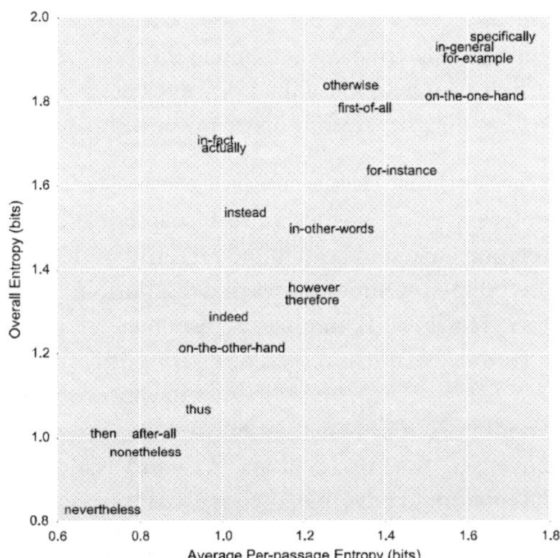

Figure 2: Each adverbial's entropy of responses for implicit passages. The x-axis is mean per-passage entropy; the y-axis is entropy of the distribution aggregating all responses over all passages for the adverbial.

plicit **otherwise** passages (§4.2).

Entropy. An important facet to understand in our data is the extent to which (in)consistency in responses comes from *adverbials* vs. individual *passages*. Qualitatively, we observe from figure 1 that adverbials like **therefore** have a "consistent inconsistency"—i.e., most passages produce responses split evenly between two conjunctions, so the overall response distribution looks a lot like the individual passage distributions.[3] In other cases, like **in fact**, most *passages* have a dominant response, though that response differs across passages.

The within-passage vs. overall (in)consistency can be quantified by **entropy**. Each adverbial is shown in Figure 2 with the x-axis indicating the mean entropy across of the response distribution for each passage, and the y-axis indicating the entropy of the aggregate distribution of responses across passages. The adverbials differ markedly in entropy, with extremes being **nevertheless** and **specifically**. Most adverbials have overall entropy slightly greater than mean per-passage entropy, but a few stand out as having unusually high overall

[3] One might wonder if the split for an adverbial like **therefore** reflects a split between participants who uniformly favored AND and those who uniformly favored SO. However, this does not appear to be the case: No participant chose the same conjunction for all **therefore** passages; likewise for **otherwise** (which yielded a 3-way split). Both adverbials show a cline in strength of preference for each of the dominant conjunctions. **However** was an exception with 5 participants who always responded NONE and 1 who always responded BUT.

entropy given their per-passage entropies: **in fact** and **actually** are most extreme in this regard. These are cases where individual passages are *more* consistent than the overall distribution would suggest.

Implications. Our analysis suggests that, if an annotation effort wishes to fully capture the sense relations taken to hold in the presense of discourse adverbials, it should always use multiple annotators. However, if annotation resources are limited, adverbials in the lower left of figure 2 offer the most consistency, allowing one to get away with fewer annotators. Further, if an effort wants reasonable coverage of sense relations, it should assign more annotators to adverbials whose within-passage entropy accounts in our data for most of the overall entropy (i.e., those close to the diagonal).

5 Characterization of adverbials

The notion that conjunction+adverbial combinations *could* occur has been introduced in prior work (Webber, 2013; Jiang, 2013; Rohde et al., 2015), but the range observed in our dataset is unprecedented. What does this mean for annotation schemes of discourse relations? At the very least, an annotation scheme must include the possibility that, given an adverbial, another relation, signalled by a conjunction, can also be inferred.

Our data suggests how conjunctions and adverbials combine. Although one might expect this to be limited, as §4 shows, the range of combinations far exceeds any limits imposed by *ad hoc* definitions. One might expect that the combinations can be predicted based on the semantic class of the adverbial. However, when we group the adverbials by class, we see mixed results: on the one hand, adverbials that convey exemplification (**for example**, **for instance**) pattern similarly; on the other hand, it is not the case that adverbials that convey resulting states (**thus**, **therefore**) pattern uniformly (participants endorse SO for **therefore** nearly 4 times as often as for **thus**), and our examples of modal stance adverbials (**actually**, **in fact**, **indeed**) show very different distributions.

Contrary to these hypotheses, it appears that the two parts of a conjunction+adverbial combination can contribute in different ways:

i. **Same sense:** The adverbial conveys the same lexical semantics as the conjunction (e.g., SO **thus**, in which both convey the sense that the second argument is the result of the first)

ii. **Separate sense:** The adverbial conveys distinct lexical semantics from the conjunction (e.g., SO **in other words**, in which the result sense conveyed by SO has no overlap with the restatement conveyed by **in other words**)

iii. **Parasitic sense:** The sense conveyed by the adverbial serves that conveyed by the conjunction (e.g., SO **for example**, where SO conveys a result, which is then evidenced by one or more examples)

The combinations we observe suggest that the adverbial contributes meaning, but context determines what that meaning is contributed to. When both adverbial and inferred conjunction convey the same sense, it suffices to consider the discourse relation expressed by the adverbial; otherwise, the the meaning of each must both be considered.

Finally, we turn to annotator disagreement. We define *divergent tokens* as those for which at least 8 participants chose each of two conjunctions from the set BECAUSE, BUT, OR or SO. Since AND can sometimes be taken as underspecified and hence compatible with SO and BUT, it is not included here as a fully independent competitor.

Some *divergent tokens* show annotators connecting the post-gap text to different parts of the context through different conjunctions. In the explicit passage shown in (4), 13 participants chose BECAUSE (the original author's choice) and 11 chose BUT. Closer examination reveals that different choices connect to different parts of the pre-gap context: BECAUSE links "his right foot was shaking" to the subordinate clause ("who caused everyone to laugh"), whereas BUT, like the adverbial **indeed**, links it to the statement "No, my leg's not shaking". In this case, the divergent participant choices demonstrate the disambiguating effect of the conjunction where multiple relations are possible. By removing the conjunction (which performed a different role from the adverbial), relations between the two spans are rendered ambiguous.

Other *divergent tokens* show annotators drawing different interpretations between the same spans. For the passage shown in (7), 15 participants selected BECAUSE, and 11 chose BUT (the original author's choice).

(7) There was a testy moment driving over the George Washington Bridge when the toll-taker charged him $24 for his truck and trailer, ______ after all it was New York.

Here, BUT can be taken to express a concession

with respect to the expectation that bridge tolls are usually a small amount of money (not $24), whereas BECAUSE expresses the reason why the reader should not be surprised why it's so high.

6 Conclusion and future work

We set out to gather further evidence that a semantic relationship between a sentence and its context may both be marked explicitly **and** involve inference. The extensive data we gathered through crowdsourcing judgments (20 adverbials, 50 different passages each, 28 different participants), replicate and extend earlier findings that discourse adverbials do indeed license inferred conjunctions. The patterns we have observed show that selected conjunctions are neither uniform across all 20 adverbials nor uniform within passages for a particular adverbial, but that both types of variability can be used to characterize the adverbials. In some cases, the adverbial and conjunction selected by participants share the same sense; in other cases, they are distinct (or sometimes even parasitic on the other).

Further, the diverse patterns observed for the adverbials include cases in which more than one valid connection can be inferred, each endorsed by a substantial number of participants. This resembles the *true ambiguity* of coreferential pronouns observed earlier by Poesio and Artstein (2005). Without gathering judgments from a substantial number of participants, such differences in annotation might otherwise be written off as annotator error or bias, or just a low level of inter-annotator agreement. Here, they reveal real differences in how people take a piece of text to relate to its context.

A reviewer asks if participant behavior changes over time. Because we ensured that the passages for a given adverbial appeared in a different pseudo-random order for each participant, any performance differences early or late in the token set could yield noise but not overall bias per adverbial. Token order was recorded, so future analysis is possible to test for changes in the overall rate of certain responses over time or the interactions over time between different adverbials, different participants, different conjunction-presentation orders, etc.

To extend our set of analyzed adverbials and to understand the mutual informativity between adverbials and conjunctions, another crowdsourced study with 35 new adverbials is underway, with a complementary study planned that asks participants to fill in an adverbial following a conjunction (i.e., given a conjunction, is an adverbial recoverable?). In addition, we are piloting a new response interface in which participants can select multiple conjunctions, as a means of testing whether individual participants endorse the alternative and sometimes divergent conjunctions observed across participants for a given passage.

Acknowledgments

This work has been supported in part by a grant from the Nuance Foundation. We thank Yangfeng Ji for a helpful suggestion of related work, and anonymous reviewers for their feedback.

References

Karin Aijmer and Anne-Marie Simon-Vandenbergen. 2007. *The Semantic Field of Modal Certainty: A Corpus-Based Study of English Adverbs*. Mouton de Gruyter.

Ron Artstein and Massimo Poesio. 2005. Bias decreases in proportion to the number of annotators. In James Rogers, editor, *Proceedings, 10th Conference on Formal Grammar and 9th Meeting on Mathematics of Language*, pages 139–148. CSLI Publications, Edinburgh, Scotland, UK.

Ron Artstein and Massimo Poesio. 2008. Survey article: Inter-coder agreement for computational linguistics. *Computational Linguistics*, 34:555–596.

Maria-Josep Cuenca and Maria-Josep Marín. 2009. Co-occurrence of discourse markers in Catalan and Spanish oral narrative. *Journal of Pragmatics*, 41(5):899–914.

Bruce Fraser. 2013. Combinations of contrastive discourse markers in English. *International Review of Pragmatics*, 5:318–340.

Julia Hirschberg and Diane Litman. 1987. Now let's talk about *now*: identifying cue phrases intonationally. In *Proceedings, 25th Annual Meeting of the Association for Computational Linguistics*, pages 163–171. Stanford, California, USA.

Dirk Hovy, Taylor Berg-Kirkpatrick, Ashish Vaswani, and Eduard Hovy. 2013. Learning whom to trust with MACE. In *Proceedings, 2013 Conference of the North American Chapter of the Association for Computational Linguistics: Human Language Technologies*, pages 1120–1130. Atlanta, Georgia, USA.

Xi Jiang. 2013. *Predicting the use and interpretation of implicit and explicit discourse connectives*. Ph.D. thesis, Linguistics and English Language (LEL), University of Edinburgh. MSc in English Language.

Andrew Kehler. 2002. *Coherence, Reference and the Theory of Grammar*. CSLI Publications.

Andrew Kehler and Hannah Rohde. 2013. A probabilistic reconciliation of coherence-driven and centering-driven theories of pronoun interpretation. *Theoretical Linguistics*, 39(1–2):1–37.

Alistair Knott. 1996. *A Data-driven Methodology for Motivating a Set of Coherence Relations*. Ph.D. thesis, Department of Artificial Intelligence, University of Edinburgh.

Yuri Lin, Jean-Baptiste Michel, Erez Aiden Lieberman, Jon Orwant, Will Brockman, and Slav Petrov. 2012. Syntactic annotations for the Google Books Ngram Corpus. In *Proceedings, ACL 2012 System Demonstrations*, pages 169–174. Jeju Island, Korea.

Jean-Baptiste Michel, Yuan Kui Shen, Aviva Presser Aiden, Adrian Veres, Matthew K. Gray, The Google Books Team, Joseph P. Pickett, Dale Hoiberg, Dan Clancy, Peter

Norvig, Jon Orwant, Steven Pinker, Martin A. Nowak, and Erez Lieberman Aiden. 2011. Quantitative analysis of culture using millions of digitized books. *Science*, 331(6014):176–182. PMID: 21163965.

Sarah Oates. 2000. Multiple discourse marker occurrence: Creating hierarchies for natural language generation. In *Proceedings, ANLP-NAACL 2000 Student Research Workshop*, pages 41–45. Seattle, Washington, USA.

Rebecca Passonneau and Bob Carpenter. 2014. The benefits of a model of annotation. *Transactions of the Association of Computational Linguistics*, 2(1):311–326.

Massimo Poesio and Ron Artstein. 2005. The reliability of anaphoric annotation, reconsidered: Taking ambiguity into account. In *Proceedings, Workshop on Frontiers in Corpus Annotations II*, pages 76–83. Ann Arbor, Michigan.

Rashmi Prasad, Nikhil Dinesh, Alan Lee, Eleni Miltsakaki, Livio Robaldo, Aravind Joshi, and Bonnie Webber. 2008. The Penn Discourse TreeBank 2.0. In *Proceedings, 6th International Conference on Language Resources and Evaluation*, pages 2961–2968. Marrakech, Morocco.

Hannah Rohde, Anna Dickinson, Chris Clark, Annie Louis, and Bonnie Webber. 2015. Recovering discourse relations: Varying influence of discourse adverbials. In *Proceedings, First Workshop on Linking Computational Models of Lexical, Sentential and Discourse-level Semantics*, pages 22–31. Lisbon, Portugal.

Evan Sandhaus. 2008. New York Times corpus: Corpus overview. LDC catalogue entry LDC2008T19.

Merel C.J. Scholman, Jacqueline Evers-Vermeul, and Ted J.M. Sanders. 2016. A step-wise approach to discourse annotation: Towards a reliable categorization of coherence relations. *Dialogue & Discourse*, 7(2):1–28.

Bonnie Webber. 2013. What excludes an alternative in coherence relations? In *Proceedings, 10th International Conference on Computational Semantics*, pages 276–287. Potsdam, Germany.

Bonnie Webber, Alistair Knott, and Aravind Joshi. 1999. Multiple discourse connectives in a lexicalized grammar for discourse. In *Third International Workshop on Computational Semantics*, pages 309–325. Tilburg, The Netherlands.

Deniz Zeyrek. 2014. On the distribution of contrastive-concessive discourse connectives *ama* ('but/yet') and *fakat* ('but') in written Turkish. In P. Suihkonen and L.J. Whaley, editors, *On Diversity and Complexity of Languages Spoken in Europe and North and Central Asia*.

Comparison of Annotating Methods for Named Entity Corpora

Kanako Komiya[1] **Masaya Suzuki**[1] **Tomoya Iwakura**[2] **Minoru Sasaki**[1] **Hiroyuki Shinnou**[1]
Ibaraki University[1] Fujitsu Laboratories Ltd.[2]
4-12-1 Nakanarusawa, Hitachi-shi, Ibaraki, 316-8511 JAPAN
1-1, Kamikodanaka 4-chome, Nakahara-ku, Kawasaki, Kanagawa, 211-8588 JAPAN
{kanako.komiya.nlp, 13t4038a}@vc.ibaraki.ac.jp,
iwakura.tomoya@jp.fujitsu.com,
{minoru.sasaki.01, hiroyuki.shinnou.0828}@vc.ibaraki.ac.jp

Abstract

We compared two methods to annotate a corpus via non-expert annotators for named entity (NE) recognition task, which are (1) revising the results of the existing NE recognizer and (2) annotating NEs only by hand. We investigated the annotation time, the degrees of agreement, and the performances based on the gold standard. As we have two annotators for one file of each method, we evaluated the two performances, which are the averaged performances over the two annotators and the performances deeming the annotations correct when either of them is correct. The experiments revealed that the semi-automatic annotation was faster and showed better agreements and higher performances on average. However they also indicated that sometimes fully manual annotation should be used for some texts whose genres are far from its training data. In addition, the experiments using the annotated corpora via semi-automatic and fully manual annotation as training data for machine learning indicated that the F-measures sometimes could be better for some texts when we used manual annotation than when we used semi-automatic annotation.

1 Introduction

The crowdsourcing made annotation of the training data cheaper and faster (Snow et al., 2008). Snow et al. evaluated non-expert annotations but they did not discuss the difference in the annotation qualities depending on how to give them the corpus. Therefore, we compared the two methods to annotate a corpus, which are semi-automatic and fully manual annotations, to examine the method to generate high quality corpora by non-experts. We investigate Japanese named entity (NE) recognition task using a corpus that consists of six genres to examine the annotation qualities depending on the genres.

The annotation of NE task is difficult for non-experts because its definition has many rules, and some of them are complicated. Therefore, the semi-automatic annotation seems a good way to decrease the annotation errors. However, sometimes the existing system also can make mistakes, especially on corpora in other genres but newswires, because it is trained only from the newswire corpus. Therefore, we compare the two methods to annotate a corpus, which are the semi-automatic and fully manual annotations and discuss them, from the point of view of time, agreement, and performance based on the gold standard to generate high quality corpora by non-experts. We also discuss the difference in performances according to the genres of the target corpus as we used the multi-genre corpus for analysis.

2 Related Work

Snow et al. (2008) evaluated non-expert annotations through comparing with expert annotations from the point of view of time, quality, and cost. Alex et al. (2010) proposed agile data annotation, which is iterative, and compared it with the traditional linear annotation method. van der Plas et al. (2010) described the method to annotate semantic roles to the French corpus using English template to investigate the cross-lingual validity. Marcus et al. (1993) compared the semi-automatic and fully manual annotations to develop the Penn Treebank on the POS tagging task and the bracketing task. However, as far as we know, there is no paper which compared the semi-automatic and

Proceedings of LAW X – The 10th Linguistic Annotation Workshop, pages 59–67,
Berlin, Germany, August 11, 2016.

fully manual annotations to develop high quality corpora via non-expert annotators.

We investigate the named entity recognition (NER) task. NER involves seeking to locate and classify elements in text into predefined categories, such as the names of people, organizations, and locations, and has been studied for a long time. Information Retrieval and Extraction Exercise (IREX)[1] defined the nine tags including eight types of NEs, i.e., organization, person, artifact, date, time, money, and percent as well as the option tag for shared task of Japanese NER. However, only newswires were used for this task. For the researches of NER, Hashimoto et al. (2008) generated extended NE corpus based on the Balanced Corpus of Contemporary Japanese (BCCWJ) (Maekawa, 2008)[2] . Tokunaga et al. (2015) analyzed the eye-tracking data of annotators of NER task. Sasada et al. (2015) proposed the NE recognizer which is trainable from partially annotated data.

In 2014, researchers analyzed the errors of Japanese NER using the newly tagged NE corpus of BCCWJ, which consists of six genres as Japanese NLP Project Next [3] (Iwakura, 2015; Hirata and Komachi, 2015; Ichihara et al., 2015). Ichihara et al. (2015) investigated the performance of the existing NE recognizer and showed that the errors increased in the genres far from the training data of the NE recognizer. This paper indicates that the semi-automatic annotation can make some errors on the corpus far from the training data.

We evaluate the semi-automatic and fully manual annotations for Japanese NER task, from the point of view of time, agreement, and performance based on the gold standard to generate high quality corpora by non-experts.

3 Comparison of Annotating Method

This paper compared the following two methods to annotate a corpus.

KNP+M Semi-automatic annotation, which is revising the results of the existing NE recognizer: KNP (Sasano and Kurohashi, 2008) [4]

Manual Fully manual annotation, whichi is annotating NEs only by hand

[1]http://nlp.cs.nyu.edu/irex/index-j.html

[2]http://pj.ninjal.ac.jp/corpus_center/bccwj/

[3]https://sites.google.com/site/projectnextnlp/

[4]http://nlp.ist.i.kyoto-u.ac.jp/index.php?KNP

		Method X				
		Tag 1	Tag 2	...	Tag n	Sum
Method Y	Tag 1	a_{11}	a_{21}	...	a_{n1}	a_{01}
	Tag 2	a_{12}	a_{22}	...	a_{n2}	a_{02}
	...	...	...	...	...	...
	Tag n	a_{1n}	a_{2n}	...	a_{nn}	a_{0n}
	Sum	a_{10}	a_{20}	...	a_{n0}	a_{00}

Table 1: The number of tag matching between two annotaters

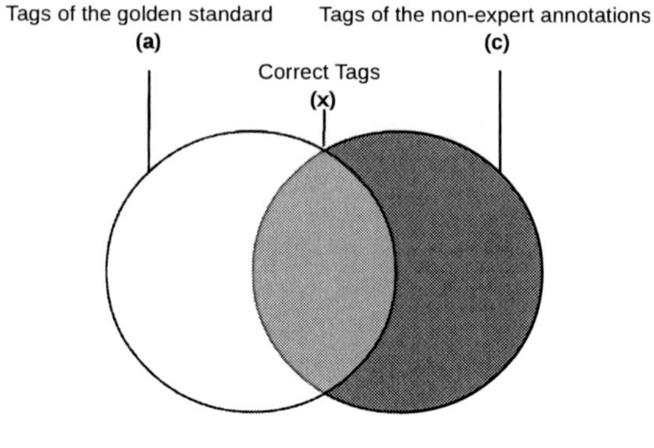

Figure 1: Example of a set of tags

We investigated the annotation time for each text, the observed agreement and Kappa coefficient of annotations, and the precision, the recall, and the F-measure based on the gold standard.

The observed agreement and Kappa coefficient are calculated as equ. (1) and equ. (2) respectively when the numbers of tag matching between two annotaters are as shown in Table 1.

$$d = \frac{\sum_{i=1}^{n} a_{ii}}{a_{00}} \tag{1}$$

$$\kappa = \frac{a_{00}\sum_{i=1}^{n} a_{ii} - \sum_{i=1}^{n} a_{i0}a_{0i}}{(a_{00})^2 - \sum_{i=1}^{n} a_{i0}a_{0i}} \tag{2}$$

The precisions, the recalls, and the F-measures are calculated as equ. (3), equ. (4), and equ. (5) when we have the set of tags as Figure 1.

$$p = \frac{n(x)}{n(c)} \tag{3}$$

$$r = \frac{n(x)}{n(a)} \tag{4}$$

$$f = \frac{2pr}{p+r} \tag{5}$$

4 Experiment

We used 136 texts extracted from BCCWJ, which are available as ClassA[5]. BCCWJ consists of six genres, "Q & A sites" (OC), "white papers" (OW), "blogs" (OY), "books" (PB), "magazines" (PM), and "newswires" (PN). Table 2 shows the summary of the numbers of documents and tags of each genre.

Sixteen non-experts assigned the nine types of NE tag of IREX to the plain texts after reading the definitions [6]. Every annotator annotated 34 texts, which is 17 texts via **KNP+M** and **Manual**, respectively, which makes two sets of corpus for each method. Eight annotators began with **KNP+M**, and the rest began with **Manual** to address the bias of the proficiency. Annotation time is recorded for each text. We calculated the averaged annotation time for one set of corpus, i.e., 136 texts, for each method. Therefore, the documents matched in size when the annotation times were compared. We used the newest corpus of BCCWJ by 2016/2/11 (Iwakura et al., 2016) [7] as the gold standard. We used KNP Ver. 4.11 and JUMAN Ver. 7.0 for windows [8].

The performances were evaluated based on the rules defined for IREX. In other words, the annotations were deemed correct if and only if both the tag and its extent were correct except for the cases of the optional tags. When the optional tag was assigned to some words in the gold standard, the annotations were deemed correct if (1) the words were not annotated by any tags or (2) a word or some words in that extent were annotated by any tags including the optional tag.

As we have two annotators for one file of each method, we evaluated the two performances based on golden standard, which are the averaged performances over the two annotators and the performances deeming the annotations correct when either of them is correct. We investigate the latter performances since we usually integrate the results of two annotators when we generate corpora.

In addition, we used the corpora which are annotated via **Manual** or **KNP+M** as the training data for supervised learning of NER to test the quality of the annotations for the machine learning. The training mode of KNP was used for the experiments. Therefore, the features for training are the same as the original KNP, which are the morpheme itself, character type, POS tag, category if it exists, cache features, syntactic features, and caseframe features (Sasano and Kurohashi, 2008). We used KNP Ver. 4.16 and JUMAN Ver. 7.01 for Linux for training-mode. We used the five-fold cross validation. Since two persons annotated each file for each method, we used two annotations for the training data of each method. Every test set of each validation includes the texts from as many genres as possible.

[5] http://plata.ar.media.kyoto-u.ac.jp/mori/research/NLR/JDC/ClassA-1.list

[6] KNP does not extract optional tags.

[7] https://sites.google.com/site/projectnextnlpne/en

[8] http://nlp.ist.i.kyoto-u.ac.jp/EN/index.php?JUMAN

Method	Observed	Kappa
KNP+M	**0.79**	**0.75**
Manual	0.57	0.50
Both	0.64	0.58

Table 3: Micro-averaged observed agreement and Kappa coefficient of each method (All)

5 Result

Tables 3 and 4 show the micro and macro-averaged observed agreement (Observed) and Kappa coefficients (Kappa) of each method of all the genres. Tables 5 and 6 summarize those of each genre. **KNP+M** and **Manual** in the tables are the agreement values between the two annotators of each method, respectively. **Both** in the tables are averaged values of every combination pairs in the four annotators of the both two methods. Table 7 shows the averaged annotation time for one text according to each method.

Tables 8 and 9 show the averaged precisions (P), recalls (R), and F-measures (F) of each method of all the genres. They are average over the two annotators. Tables 10 and 11 summarize those of each genre. The fully automatic annotation, which is the results of original KNP without revising are also shown in these tables as **KNP**. **Avg.** in the tables indicates the average of **KNP+M** and **Manual**. The higher observed agreements, Kappa coefficients, precisions, recalls, and F-measures among the two methods are written in bold.

Next, we investigated the performances deeming the annotations correct when either of the two annotators is correct. Tables 12 and 13 show the precisions (P), the recalls (R), and the F-measures (F) of each method of all the genres. Tables 14 and 15 summarize those of each genre. The fully

Genre	Doc	Artifact	Date	Location	Money	Organization	Percent	Person	Time	Optional	All
OC	74	44	18	65	9	18	0	6	0	8	168
OW	8	86	143	147	9	136	33	15	0	26	595
OY	34	23	61	59	7	64	10	79	3	17	323
PB	5	32	49	100	0	19	5	174	9	20	408
PM	2	9	24	36	5	18	1	216	3	1	313
PN	13	24	166	192	60	123	37	78	22	20	722
ALL	136	218	461	599	90	378	86	568	37	92	2,529

Table 2: Summary of number of documents and tags

Method	Observed	Kappa
KNP+M	**0.66**	**0.48**
Manual	0.52	0.29
Both	0.52	0.31

Table 4: Macro-averaged observed agreement and Kappa coefficient of each method (All)

Genre	Method	Observed	Kappa
OC	KNP+M	**0.62**	**0.54**
OC	Manual	0.47	0.34
OC	Both	0.52	0.41
OW	KNP+M	**0.78**	**0.73**
OW	Manual	0.41	0.28
OW	Both	0.55	0.46
OY	KNP+M	**0.69**	**0.63**
OY	Manual	0.58	0.50
OY	Both	0.57	0.49
PB	KNP+M	**0.76**	**0.68**
PB	Manual	0.67	0.56
PB	Both	0.71	0.61
PM	KNP+M	**0.87**	**0.84**
PM	Manual	0.61	0.55
PM	Both	0.69	0.64
PN	KNP+M	**0.86**	**0.75**
PN	Manual	0.81	0.65
PN	Both	0.80	0.65

Table 5: Micro-averaged observed agreement and Kappa coefficient of each method

Genre	Method	Observed	Kappa
OC	KNP+M	**0.58**	**0.27**
OC	Manual	0.50	0.15
OC	Both	0.47	0.14
OW	KNP+M	**0.80**	**0.73**
OW	Manual	0.45	0.36
OW	Both	0.59	0.50
OY	KNP+M	**0.63**	**0.47**
OY	Manual	0.50	0.29
OY	Both	0.47	0.30
PB	KNP+M	**0.63**	**0.54**
PB	Manual	0.60	0.43
PB	Both	0.62	0.48
PM	KNP+M	**0.87**	**0.83**
PM	Manual	0.62	0.55
PM	Both	0.69	0.63
PN	KNP+M	**0.88**	**0.74**
PN	Manual	0.74	0.56
PN	Both	0.77	0.59

Table 6: Macro-averaged observed agreement and Kappa coefficient of each method

Method	Averaged time
KNP+M	0:03:19
Manual	0:05:23

Table 7: Tagging time for each method

automatic annotation, which is the results of KNP without revising are also shown in these tables as **KNP** here again.

In addition, we examined the performances of the system trained with the corpora annotated via **KNP+M** and **Manual**. Tables 16 and 17 show the precisions (P), the recalls (R), and the F-measures (F) of each method of all the genres. Tables 18 and 19 summarize those of each genre. The results of original KNP are also shown in these tables as **KNP** here again.

The differences between **KNP** and **KNP+Manual**, **KNP** and **Manual**, and **Manual** and **KNP+Manual** of the precisions and the recalls in Tables 8 and 16 and those of the precisions in Table 14 are statistically significant according to chi-square test. However, the differences between **KNP** and **KNP+Manual** and **KNP** and **Manual** are statistically significant but that between **Manual** and **KNP+Manual** is not significant according to chi-square test when we compared the recalls of Table 12. In addition, the asterisk in the tables of micro-averaged accuracies for each genre, i.e., Tables 10, 14, and 18, means the difference between presicions or recalls of **Manual** and **KNP+Manual** is statistically significant according to a chi-square test. The level of significance in the test was 0.05. When macro-averaged accuracies were compared, the differences were not significant due to the decrease of the samples of the test.

Method	P	R	F
KNP	77.64%	68.09%	72.55%
KNP+M	**84.03%**	**81.41%**	**82.70%**
Manual	75.22%	72.74%	73.96%
Avg.	79.63%	77.07%	78.33%

Table 8: Micro-averaged precision, recall, and F-measure of each method (All)

Method	P	R	F
KNP	47.43%	39.81%	43.29%
KNP+M	**55.30%**	**54.72%**	**55.01%**
Manual	52.54%	51.06%	51.77%
Avg.	53.92%	52.87%	53.39%

Table 9: Macro-averaged precision, recall, and F-measure of each method (All)

6 Discussion

6.1 Agreements and Time

First, Tables 3 and 4 show that the observed agreements and Kappa coefficients of **KNP+M** are higher than those of **Manual** in both micro and macro averages. This is similar in every genre according to Tables 5 and 6. We think this is because that the tags assigned by KNP still remain after the annotators revised the results of KNP. The agreement values of **Both** are usually higher than or similar to those of **Manual** but the macro-averaged Kappa coefficient of **Both** (0.14) is lower than that of **Manual** (0.15) more than one point (0.01) in OC, which indicates the results of annotators greatly vary. These results indicate that there can be some NEs which require more rules to extract in OC because the definition we used was developed for only the newswires. In addition, Table 3 shows that Kappa coefficients indicate good agreement for **KNP+M** and moderate agreement for **Manual** when they are micro-averaged, and Table 4 shows that they indicate moderate agreement for **KNP+M** and poor agreement for **Manual** when they are macro-averaged. Since micro average is an average over NEs, and macro average is that over texts, it means that the agreement values of some texts which include a few NEs were low.

In addition, Table 7 shows that the annotation time for one text of **KNP+M** is approximately two minutes shorter on average than that of **Manual**. These results indicate that **KNP+M** is faster and shows better agreement than **Manual**. The difference in time was significant according to F test. The level of significance is 0.01.

Genre	Method	P	R	F
OC	KNP	72.38%	47.50%	57.36%
OC	KNP+M	***77.74%**	75.31%	**76.51%**
OC	Manual	66.93%	**80.06%**	72.91%
OC	Avg.	71.76%	77.69%	74.61%
OW	KNP	78.87%	78.60%	78.73%
OW	KNP+M	***81.68%**	***84.62%**	**83.12%**
OW	Manual	64.62%	67.22%	65.90%
OW	Avg.	73.11%	75.90%	74.48%
OY	KNP	73.42%	56.86%	64.09%
OY	KNP+M	***85.47%**	***75.00%**	**79.90%**
OY	Manual	79.81%	68.13%	73.51%
OY	Avg.	82.67%	71.56%	76.71%
PB	KNP	75.00%	59.54%	66.38%
PB	KNP+M	**78.54%**	**73.58%**	**75.98%**
PB	Manual	77.85%	72.84%	75.27%
PB	Avg.	78.20%	73.21%	75.62%
PM	KNP	60.61%	57.69%	59.11%
PM	KNP+M	88.51%	**86.38%**	**87.43%**
PM	Manual	**89.68%**	84.94%	87.24%
PM	Avg.	89.08%	85.66%	87.34%
PN	KNP	88.44%	78.49%	83.17%
PN	KNP+M	***87.87%**	***85.11%**	**86.47%**
PN	Manual	77.46%	72.12%	74.70%
PN	Avg.	82.77%	78.61%	80.64%

Table 10: Micro-averaged precision, recall, and F-measure of each method

6.2 Performances Averaged over Annotators

Next, we evaluate the performances of the methods based on the gold standard. First, we evaluate the average over the two annotators.

We can see the precisions, the recalls, and the F-measures of **KNP+M** are higher than those of **Manual** in both micro and macro averages, according to Tables 8 and 9. This is similar in every genre in micro average according to Table 10, except the recall of OC and the precision of PM. When we see these two exceptions, we can see that those of **KNP** are considerably lower than those of other genres. The topic of OC was far from newswires, and a name of person was misrecognized as name of location many times in PM. This fact indicates that the performances of **KNP+M** directly depend on those of **KNP**.

Table 11 shows that the macro-averaged precisions, recalls, and F-measurs of **KNP+M** are better than those of **Manual** in OW, OY, and PN but those of **Manual** are better in OC, PB, and PM, except the recall of PM. We think this is because **KNP** are better than **Manual** in the precisions, the recalls, and the F-measures in OW and PN and the precisions in OY. OW and PN are similar to the training data set of KNP, i.e., newswires, which makes the performances in them better (Ichihara et al., 2015). These results indicate that **KNP+M**

Genre	Method	P	R	F
OC	KNP	30.74%	25.55%	27.91%
OC	KNP+M	38.83%	40.75%	39.77%
OC	Manual	**41.80%**	**43.84%**	**42.79%**
OC	Avg.	40.31%	42.29%	41.28%
OW	KNP	76.84%	80.45%	78.60%
OW	KNP+M	**82.98%**	**85.47%**	**84.21%**
OW	Manual	69.91%	72.65%	71.25%
OW	Avg.	76.45%	79.06%	77.73%
OY	KNP	57.99%	44.37%	50.27%
OY	KNP+M	**68.33%**	**62.94%**	**65.53%**
OY	Manual	55.79%	49.32%	52.36%
OY	Avg.	62.06%	56.13%	58.95%
PB	KNP	66.04%	45.84%	54.12%
PB	KNP+M	71.02%	64.63%	67.67%
PB	Manual	**81.37%**	**67.48%**	**73.77%**
PB	Avg.	76.19%	66.05%	70.76%
PM	KNP	60.31%	66.37%	63.19%
PM	KNP+M	82.34%	**87.00%**	84.61%
PM	Manual	**85.64%**	83.94%	**84.78%**
PM	Avg.	83.99%	85.47%	84.73%
PN	KNP	87.51%	77.70%	82.31%
PN	KNP+M	**87.76%**	**85.06%**	**86.39%**
PN	Manual	78.37%	71.60%	74.83%
PN	Avg.	83.06%	78.33%	80.63%

Table 11: Macro-averaged precision, recall, and F-measure of each method

Method	P	R	F
KNP	77.64%	68.09%	72.55%
KNP+M	**91.34%**	**88.92%**	**90.11%**
Manual	86.76%	88.28%	87.53%

Table 12: Micro-averaged precision, recall, and F-measure of each method (All) deeming the annotations correct when either of two annotators is correct

is better than **Manual** to annotate corpora by non-experts, in particular, the texts in some genres similar to the training data of KNP. However, sometimes **Manual** should be used for some texts, whose genres are far from newswires.

6.3 Sum-Set Performances of Two annotators

Next, we investigate the performances deeming the annotations correct when either of the two annotators is correct. Tables 12 and 13 show that the precision, the recall, and F-measure of **KNP+M** are also better than those of **Manual** even if we deemed the annotations correct when either of the two annotators was correct. However, the difference greatly decreased comparing with Tables 8 and 9, i.e., the performances averaged over the annotators. In particular, the difference between **KNP+M** (62.92%) and **Manual** (62.09%) was less than one point when the macro-averaged F-measures were compared. We think

Method	P	R	F
KNP	47.43%	39.81%	43.29%
KNP+M	**63.48%**	**62.37%**	**62.92%**
Manual	61.96%	62.22%	62.09%

Table 13: Macro-averaged precision, recall, and F-measure of each method (All) deeming the annotations correct when either of two annotators is correct

Genre	Method	P	R	F
OC	KNP	72.38%	47.50%	57.36%
OC	KNP+Manual	**86.79%**	86.25%	86.52%
OC	Manual	85.63%	**90.51%**	**88.00%**
OW	KNP	78.87%	78.60%	78.73%
OW	KNP+Manual	***91.20%**	**91.20%**	**91.20%**
OW	Manual	75.71%	89.07%	81.85%
OY	KNP	73.42%	56.86%	64.09%
OY	KNP+Manual	**93.62%**	**87.13%**	**90.26%**
OY	Manual	92.91%	85.90%	89.27%
PB	KNP	75.00%	59.54%	66.38%
PB	KNP+Manual	87.05%	81.87%	84.38%
PB	Manual	**89.86%**	**86.32%**	**88.05%**
PM	KNP	60.61%	57.69%	59.11%
PM	KNP+Manual	92.65%	**93.55%**	93.10%
PM	Manual	***97.26%**	92.81%	**94.98%**
PN	KNP	88.44%	78.49%	83.17%
PN	KNP+Manual	***93.29%**	**90.33%**	**91.79%**
PN	Manual	89.19%	87.25%	88.21%

Table 14: Micro-averaged precision, recall, and F-measure of each method deeming the annotations correct when either of two annotators is correct

this is because the manual annotations vary and one of the two annotators usually annotates the NEs correctly. As Tables 8 and 9 showed, the non-expert annotators often make mistakes because the definitions of NEs for IREX include so many rules and therefore, the annotators sometimes overlooked some rules when they annotated the texts. However, the experimental results revealed that the performances of the fully manual annotations were almost comparable to those of the semi-automatically annotations when we have two annotators. Moreover, Tables 14 and 15 indicate that the F-measures of **Manual** are better than those of **KNP+M** in OC, PB, and PM. These results are like those in Table 11 but not like those in Table 10, which means that the better method varies depending on the genres even if the performances were micro-averaged when we deemed the results correct when either of two annotator was correct.

Furthermore, we compared Table 8 with Table 12 and Table 9 with Table 13 to compare the performances of annotations by one annotator and

Genre	Method	P	R	F
OC	KNP	30.74%	25.55%	27.91%
OC	KNP+M	46.30%	47.35%	46.82%
OC	Manual	**49.16%**	**50.88%**	**50.01%**
OW	KNP	76.84%	80.45%	78.60%
OW	KNP+M	**91.09%**	90.96%	**91.02%**
OW	Manual	82.55%	**91.39%**	86.74%
OY	KNP	57.99%	44.37%	50.27%
OY	KNP+M	**78.69%**	**73.63%**	**76.07%**
OY	Manual	67.84%	65.47%	66.63%
PB	KNP	66.04%	45.84%	54.12%
PB	KNP+M	83.51%	77.94%	80.63%
PB	Manual	**93.98%**	**85.91%**	**89.76%**
PM	KNP	60.31%	66.37%	63.19%
PM	KNP+M	85.74%	93.17%	89.30%
PM	Manual	**97.58%**	**93.45%**	**95.47%**
PN	KNP	87.51%	77.70%	82.31%
PN	KNP+M	**93.36%**	**90.09%**	**91.70%**
PN	Manual	88.94%	86.39%	87.64%

Table 15: Macro-averaged precision, recall, and F-measure of each method deeming the annotations correct when either of two annotators is correct

Method	P	R	F
KNP	77.64%	68.09%	72.55%
KNP+M	**74.14%**	**38.11%**	**50.34%**
Manual	67.21%	28.52%	40.05%

Table 16: Micro-averaged precision, recall, and F-measure of each method (All) when the annotated data were used for training

those by two annotators. The results in Tables 8 and 9 could be considered as the annotations by one annotator because they are averages over annotators. These four tables show that the results of annotations by two annotators are always better than those by one annotator. In particular, the performances by two annotators of **Manual** are always better than those by one annotator of **KNP+M**. Since the better methods varies depending on the genres in both micro and macro averages when the performances of annotations by two annotators are compared, these results indicate that we should use not only **KNP+M** but also **Manual** in real situation.

6.4 Annotated Corpora as Training Data

Finally, we evaluate the performances of machine learning when we used the annotated corpora via **KNP+M** and **Manual** as the training data. Tables 16 and 17 show that the precision, the recall, and F-measure of **KNP+M** are better than those of **Manual** when we used the annotated corpora as the training data for KNP. However, Tables 18 and 19 show that the micro-averaged precisions

Method	P	R	F
KNP	47.43%	39.81%	43.29%
KNP+M	**40.41%**	**23.55%**	**29.76%**
Manual	31.44%	16.16%	21.34%

Table 17: Macro-averaged precision, recall, and F-measure of each method (All) when the annotated data were used for training

Genre	Method	P	R	F
OC	KNP	72.38%	47.50%	57.36%
OC	KNP+M	**88.46%**	**28.75%**	**43.40%**
OC	Manual	84.21%	20.00%	32.32%
OW	KNP	78.87%	78.60%	78.73%
OW	KNP+M	***74.45%**	***53.16%**	**62.03%**
OW	Manual	54.69%	35.85%	43.31%
OY	KNP	73.42%	56.86%	64.09%
OY	KNP+M	**83.62%**	***31.70%**	**45.97%**
OY	Manual	80.00%	18.30%	29.79%
PB	KNP	75.00%	59.54%	66.38%
PB	KNP+M	70.41%	**30.67%**	**42.73%**
PB	Manual	**73.29%**	27.58%	40.07%
PM	KNP	60.61%	57.69%	59.11%
PM	KNP+M	**55.05%**	**19.23%**	**28.50%**
PM	Manual	51.76%	14.10%	22.17%
PN	KNP	88.44%	78.49%	83.17%
PN	KNP+M	76.00%	***43.30%**	**55.17%**
PN	Manual	**78.26%**	35.90%	49.22%%

Table 18: Micro-averaged precision, recall, and F-measure of each method when the annotated data were used for training

in PB and PN, the macro-averaged precisions in PB and PN, and the macro-averaged F-measure in PB were not the case. The exception of the macro-averaged F-measure shows that sometimes the annotation of **Manual** is better training data than **KNP+M**.

Tables 16 and 17 show the difference in the precisions between the original KNP and other methods are not so large comparing with those of the recalls. In particular, **KNP+M** and **Manual** were better than the original KNP when the micro-averaged precisions in OC and OY were compared according to Table 18. The performances of **KNP+M** and **Manual** were low because the amount of the training data was so small comparing with the original KNP. However, these results show that the precisions will be better than original KNP even if we use a small training data in some genres.

7 Conclusion

We compared the semi-automatic and fully manual annotations to investigate the annotation qualities by non-experts. The methods we investigated

Genre	Method	P	R	F
OC	KNP	30.74%	25.55%	27.91%
OC	KNP+M	**24.32%**	**15.88%**	**19.22%**
OC	Manual	17.34%	12.24%	14.35%
OW	KNP	76.84%	80.45%	78.60%
OW	KNP+M	**71.59%**	**56.71%**	**63.29%**
OW	Manual	62.55%	42.52%	50.63%
OY	KNP	57.99%	44.37%	50.27%
OY	KNP+M	**52.32%**	**24.40%**	**33.28%**
OY	Manual	30.82%	9.184%	14.15%
PB	KNP	66.04%	45.84%	54.12%
PB	KNP+M	51.46%	**23.63%**	32.39%
PB	Manual	**64.93%**	21.65%	**32.47%**
PM	KNP	60.31%	66.37%	63.19%
PM	KNP+M	**54.56%**	**29.20%**	**38.04%**
PM	Manual	53.43%	24.63%	33.72%
PN	KNP	87.51%	77.70%	82.31%
PN	KNP+M	75.21%	**43.71%**	**55.28%**
PN	Manual	**77.88%**	37.01%	50.17%

Table 19: Macro-averaged precision, recall, and F-measure of each method when the annotated data were used for training

were **KNP+M**, which was revising the results of the existing NE recognizer, and **Manual**, which was annotating NEs only by hand. We investigated Japanese NER task. We evaluated the annotation time, the observed agreement, Kappa coefficients, and the precisions, the recalls, and the F-measures based on the gold standard. As two annotators annotated each text for each method, we evaluated the precisions, the recalls, and the F-measures averaged over annotators and those deeming the results correct when either of them was correct. The experiments revealed that **KNP+M** was faster and showed better agreements and higher performances than **Manual** on average but sometimes **Manual** should have been used for some texts whose genres were far from newswires. Finally the experiments using the annotated corpora via **KNP+M** or **Manual** indicated that the F-measures sometimes could be better for some texts when we used **Manual** than when we used **KNP+M**.

Acknowledgments

This work was supported by JSPS KAKENHI Grant Number 15K16046 and contribution from Fujitsu Laboratories Ltd.

References

Bea Alex, Claire Grover, Rongzhou Shen, and Mijail Kabadjov. 2010. Agile corpus annotation in practice: An overview of manual and automatic annotation of cvs. In *Proceedings of Fourth Linguistic Annotation Workshop, ACL 2010*, pages 29–37.

Taiichi Hashimoto, Takashi Inui, and Koji Murakami. 2008. Constructing extended named entity annotated corpora (in japanese). *IPSJ SIG Technical Reports (NLP)*, 2008-NL-188:113–120.

Ai Hirata and Mamoru Komachi. 2015. Analysis of named entity recognition for texts of various genres (in japanese). *NLP2015 Error Analysis Workshop.* https://docs.google.com/viewer?a=v&pid=sites&srcid=ZGVmYXVsdGRvbWFpbnxwcm9qZWN0bmV4dG5scHxneDo1ZGYxOTg3YWE1MDIzOTRi.

Masaaki Ichihara, Kanako Komiya, Tomoya Iwakura, and Maiko Yamazaki. 2015. Error analysis of named entity recognition in bccwj. *NLP2015 Error Analysis Workshop.* https://docs.google.com/viewer?a=v&pid=sites&srcid=ZGVmYXVsdGRvbWFpbnxwcm9qZWN0bmV4dG5scHxneDoxZTY1MWY4YTBjNmNjNzIx.

Tomoya Iwakura, Ryuichi Tachibana, and Kanako Komiya. 2016. Constructing a japanese basic named entity corpus of various genres. *Proceedings of NEWS 2016.*

Tomoya Iwakura. 2015. Error analysis of named entity extraction (in japanese). *NLP2015 Error Analysis Workshop.* https://docs.google.com/viewer?a=v&pid=sites&srcid=ZGVmYXVsdGRvbWFpbnxwcm9qZWN0bmV4dG5scHxneDo1ZTg0ZmJmYmRjNThmN2I1.

Kikuo Maekawa. 2008. Balanced corpus of contemporary written japanese. In *Proceedings of the 6th Workshop on Asian Language Resources (ALR)*, pages 101–102.

Mitchell P. Marcus, Mary Ann Marcinkiewicz, and Beatrice Santorini. 1993. Building a large annotated corpus of english: the penn treebank. *Computational Linguistics - Special issue on using large corpora: II*, 19:313–330.

Tetsuro Sasada, Shinsuke Mori, Tatsuya Kawahara, and Yoko Yamakata. 2015. Named entity recognizer trainable from partially annotated data. In *Proceedings of the PACLING 2015*, pages 10–17.

Ryohei Sasano and Sadao Kurohashi. 2008. Japanese named entity recognition using structural natural language processing. In *Proceedings of IJCNLP 2008*, pages 607–612.

Rion Snow, Brendan O'Conner, Daniel Jurafsky, and Andrew Y. Ng. 2008. Cheap and fast – but is it good? evaluation non-expert annotation for natural lanugage tasks. In *Proceedings of the 2008 Conference on Emprical Methods in Natural Language Processing (EMNLP)*, pages 254–263.

Takenobu Tokunaga, Jin Nishikara, Tomoya Iwakura, and Nobuhiro Yugami. 2015. Analysis of eye tracking data of annotators for named entity recognition task (in japanese). *IPSJ SIG Technical Reports (NLP)*, 2015-NL-223:1 – 8.

Lonneke van der Plas, Tanja Samardžić, and Paola Merlo. 2010. Cross-lingual validity of propbank in the manual annotation of french. In *Proceedings of Fourth Linguistic Annotation Workshop, ACL 2010*, pages 113–117.

Different Flavors of GUM: Evaluating Genre and Sentence Type Effects on Multilayer Corpus Annotation Quality

Amir Zeldes
Department of Linguistics
Georgetown University
amir.zeldes@georgetown.edu

Dan Simonson
Department of Linguistics
Georgetown University
des62@georgetown.edu

Abstract

Genre and domain are well known covariates of both manual and automatic annotation quality. Comparatively less is known about the effect of sentence types, such as imperatives, questions or fragments, and how they interact with text type effects. Using mixed effects models, we evaluate the relative influence of genre and sentence types on automatic and manual annotation quality for three related tasks in English data: POS tagging, dependency parsing and coreference resolution. For the latter task, we also develop a new metric for the evaluation of individual regions of coreference annotation. Our results show that while there are substantial differences between manual and automatic annotation in each task, sentence type is generally more important than genre in predicting errors within our data.

1 Introduction

With the availability of increasingly diverse language resources and the viability of processing almost unrestricted Web data, domain adaptation and coverage of novel domains have become a major concern in NLP and corpus creation (see e.g. Daumé 2007, Finkel & Manning 2009, McClosky et al. 2010, Søgaard 2013). However, accuracy for both state of the art automatic tools and manual annotation of new tasks is typically reported on standard sources, typically newswire text, which often leads to overestimation of expected accuracy in both manual and automatic annotation. Manning (2011) points out that although we expect 97% accuracy from POS taggers on newswire, such a rate indicates an error every other sentence even within the training domain, and more in other domains or epochs. A major cause of problems in adaptation is the presence of unknown words from outside the training domain, which may be more influential than other aspects of the actual genre itself (cf. Plank 2011).

It has also been suggested that at least part of the source for these problems lies in less frequent kinds of utterances within and across domains, i.e. that domain adaptation may be folding in sentence type effects. For example, in an evaluation of the English Web Treebank, explicitly intended to expand the text types covered by reference Treebank data, Silveira et al. (2014:2898) remark that "[t]he most striking difference between the two types of data [Web and newswire] has to do with imperatives, which occur two orders of magnitude more often in the EWT." Specifically Silveira et al. found over 445 times more imperatives in EWT than in the Wall Street Journal corpus (Marcus et al. 1993). Despite this stark difference, there is remarkably little literature on sentence type as a factor in annotation quality or NLP tool performance. While sentence type is known to be important in computational models of language acquisition (see Frank et al. 2013), it has not been suggested that human annotators are affected by it. In the development of automatic annotation tools, explicit partitioning of sentence types for differential treatment is also rare (for an exception see Zhang et al. 2008 on machine translation).

Indeed, it is not clear whether sentence type is actually pertinent to annotation quality, especially for human annotators, who are generally able to understand most sentences without difficulty. The question we will be asking in this paper is

Proceedings of LAW X – The 10th Linguistic Annotation Workshop, pages 68–78,
Berlin, Germany, August 11, 2016.

therefore whether sentence types are a better predictor of annotation quality than text type or genre, which is often postulated to be central without consideration of alternative explanations.[1]

2 Data

For our evaluation we will use the GUM corpus (Zeldes 2016)[2], a class-sourced, richly annotated multilayer corpus containing freely available texts from four different types: news articles from Wikinews, Wikimedia interviews, travel guides from Wikivoyage and how-to guides from wikiHow (abbreviated 'whow'). Each of these sources corresponds more or less to a different communicative intent, which lends itself to different types of sentences: news articles are narrative, telling about events, often in indicative past tense; travel guides are informational, giving modals of possibility and general truths about places; how-to guides are instructional, containing many imperatives and lists of ingredients; and interviews are conversational, often containing question and answer pairs or sequences. Interviews in particular could be expected to differ from the other types, due to differences between spoken and written language. The corpus contains 54 documents, totaling just over 44,000 tokens, as outlined in Table 1.

text type	source	texts	tokens
Interviews	Wikinews	14	12,661
News	Wikinews	15	9,402
Travel guides	Wikivoyage	11	9,240
How-tos (instructional)	wikiHow	14	12,776
Total		**54**	**44,079**

Table 1: Composition of the GUM corpus.

Document structure is annotated using TEI XML labels, and each text is annotated with POS tags and lemmas, dependency and constituent syntax, entities (using a subset of categories from OntoNotes, Hovy et al. 2006), information status (the scheme in Dipper et al. 2007), coreference, Rhetorical Structure Theory (Mann & Thompson 1988), and crucially, sentence type (see below). In this paper we will be concerned with:

1. POS tags – annotated manually using the extended Penn tag set used by the TreeTagger[3] (Schmid 1994)
2. Manually corrected Stanford Typed Dependencies (de Marneffe & Manning 2013)
3. Coreference annotation, including pronominal anaphora, lexical coreference and appositions (but not bridging, which is also annotated in the corpus).

Finally, the sentence type annotation layer supplies a kind of rough speech act or sentence mood, using an extended form of the SPAAC annotation scheme (Leech et al. 2003). The sentence types distinguished are given in Table 2.

tag	type	example
q	polar yes/no question	*Did she see it?*
wh	WH question	*What did you see?*
decl	declarative (indicative)	*He was there.*
imp	imperative	*Do it!*
sub	subjunctive (incl. modals)	*I could go*
inf	infinitival	*How to Dance*
ger	gerund-headed clause	*Finding Nemo*
intj	interjection	*Hello!*
frag	fragment	*The End.*
other	other predication or combination	*Nice, that!'* Or: *'I've had it, go!'* (decl+imp)

Table 2: Sentence type annotation in GUM.

Given genre metadata and sentence type annotations in the corpus, we would like to know which is a better predictor of errors on each layer.[4]

Our analyses of each data type will be addressed in separate experiments, similar in general configuration but adapted to the needs of the data type: POS tags in Section 4, dependencies in Section 5, and coreference in Section 6.

[1] An anonymous reviewer has pointed out that many other covariates of genre could be subjected to a similar treatment, in the vein of Biber's multidimensional analysis (see Biber 2009 for an overview), such as tense and other grammatical features. We agree completely: we are only beginning to understand the components of genre variation and how it interacts with annotation quality.

[2] The data is freely available under a CC license from `http://corpling.uis.georgetown.edu/gum` . We would like to thank the annotators, a current list of which is found at the same Web site.

[3] The tag set used by TreeTagger distinguishes forms of *be* (VB, 3rd person present VBZ,..) from *have* (VH, VHZ, ...) and other verbs (VV, VVZ, ...), as well as several punctuation tags and a special tag for *that* as a complementizer (IN/that). GUM also contains a second POS layer using the CLAWS5 tags (Garside & Smith 1997), which will not be evaluated here.

[4] An anonymous reviewer has asked about the decision to include the *sub* type as distinct from *decl*: this type was already in the existing annotation of GUM and was not added for this study. However modality is expressed syntactically e.g. via auxiliaries, ultimately influencing sentence structure, and semantic influence on humans should not be ruled out either.

3 Experimental setup

For each of the three tasks, POS tagging, dependency annotation, and coreference resolution, we first split the corpus into each of the four text types and collate responses from manual, automatic and gold annotation in GUM. Ordinarily, the manual annotation data released for a corpus is the same as the gold data – for this study we obtained uncorrected, single annotator versions of the data to approach annotation quality effects in an initial manually produced analysis.

Since GUM is a 'class-sourced' corpus, the unadjudicated annotations always represent work from relatively inexperienced student annotators, which was subsequently corrected by an experienced instructor. These corrections will be considered the 'gold' data for our evaluation.[5]

Once we have annotation graphs and labels from all three sources, we can easily compare manual and automatic annotation with the gold standard in each subcorpus. However comparisons across sentence types can be less straightforward: while POS tags can be evaluated in the different sentence types in isolation, coreference annotation cannot be easily evaluated while ignoring certain parts of the text. We therefore develop some extended metrics for the evaluation in Section 6. For all data sets, we keep track of the documents (and by proxy annotators) that contain each annotation as a random effect, and we will consider some competing independent variables, such as sentence length, as alternative explanations for annotation quality.

4 Part of speech tagging

4.1 Method

For the evaluation, we compare data from the annotators, who received only brief training, to three popular taggers: TreeTagger (TT, Schmid 1994), the Stanford Tagger (Toutanova et al. 2003) and Spacy (`https://spacy.io/`). Double corrected gold data was available for only 38,022 tokens, which are evaluated below. Since GUM was annotated using the TreeTagger's extended tag set, the most comparable evaluation will be between TT and human annotators. However, it is fairly straightforward to collapse the extended tag set into the more compact 36 tags used by the other taggers (*VVZ* and *VHZ* become *VBZ*, etc.), so that results for those taggers can be evaluated as well (though with somewhat less potential for errors, especially for the tag *IN/that*).

While our primary interest lies in gauging the relative influence of genre and sentence type, we would also like to consider some alternative explanations. Using mixed effects models from R's lme4 package, we will take individual document effects into account as a random effect. Mixed effects models (see Baayen 2008: 263-327 for an overview) allow us to assign some of the variance we see in the data to random effects, such as ostensibly unpredictable interpersonal variation between annotators, or the difficulty of particular documents: these factors are assumed to have a mean influence of 0 (since they are random), while positing individual intercepts for higher/lower baselines observable in our dependent variable (the error rate). Additionally, we also suspect that sentence length is a possible predictor of errors: for example, longer sentences may be more grammatically complex; or it could turn out that very short sentences (for example headings) lead to part of speech ambiguities. We therefore model length as a further fixed effect, which could be an alternative explanation for differences in error rates.

Although our null hypothesis must be an equal distribution of errors, we do not expect strong effects for text or sentence type in manual annotation, since tagging decisions are relatively local: trained annotators should be able to discern parts of speech even in heterogeneous sentences. Automatic taggers, by contrast, rely on the Markov assumption and learn tag distributions from chains of tokens, meaning that a greater influence of input type effects can be expected, especially in text types more dissimilar to newswire, on which the taggers are trained.

4.2 Results

Tables 3 and 4 give raw breakdowns of error frequencies across text and sentence types (asterisks designate significant predictors of error proportion in a simple linear model, for the annotation strategy in the respective row). The figures for TT are the most comparable to the manual fig-

[5] We have no doubt that the gold data also contains some errors, and that class-sourced data may be more erroneous than data obtained in other settings. But our premise is that manual annotation difficulties depending on genre and sentence types should still emerge in the comparison, especially since we will allow for document-by-document random effects.

	decl	frag	ger	imp	inf	other	q	sub	wh
Manual	93.87	94.70	**90.28***	93.14	93.20	95.34	**96.59++**	94.13	93.32
TT	**95.33+++**	90.46	**93.52+**	93.16	**79.59*****	90.60	93.34	94.63	92.30
Stanford	**95.21+++**	88.57	88.89	91.24	**78.91*****	90.50	**93.00+**	94.98	**93.09++**
Spacy	**94.43+++**	**87.81*****	**87.04*****	91.91	**82.99*****	89.94	94.37	94.38	94.11
Tokens	27,440	1,321	219	4,313	147	1,074	586	2,011	883

Table 4: Tagging accuracy by sentence type for manual and automatic annotation. Significance only indicated for deviations of more than 2% below the mean (with *) or above (with +).

ures, since the other two taggers are evaluated against the unextended tagset.[6]

Table 3 shows that genre effect sizes are modest for tagging. Manual annotation from scratch performs similarly to all of the taggers, and is only better for the how-to guides, which are the most accurate for humans, but worst for POS taggers. TT loses about 1% accuracy on this genre, while the other taggers lose about 2% accuracy; in other categories all three taggers are largely neck-and-neck, with Spacy surprisingly somewhat behind on news compared to other taggers.

	interview	news	voyage	whow
Manual	93.55	93.52	94.06	94.30*
TT	94.73	95.57*	95.21	93.44*
Stanford	94.50	95.78*	94.80	92.54***
Spacy	94.03	94.71	94.15	92.44***

Table 3: Tagging performance by genre, with significance in a simple linear model (*p<0.05;**p<0.001;***p<0.0001)

While a simple a linear model significantly correlates text type with performance at the 5% threshold for all annotation sources, only the slight differences in *whow* and *news* are significant predictors. Moreover, even before we consider a full multifactorial model, if we add document identity as a random effect in a mixed effects model with only genre as a fixed effect, the genre effect largely disappears, with the exception of the low *whow* performance by Spacy and the Stanford tagger. This suggests that most of what we are seeing is due to specific documents being more difficult for the taggers. In other words, humans and taggers do almost exactly as well across these text types.

Sentence type, by contrast, shows some stronger effect sizes, shown in Table 4. Since there are many sentence types, all rows are significant and very many values are significant at a 5% threshold; to improve readability significance is only indicated for deviations of 2% accuracy from the mean or more. Despite their significance, some of these are however based on very little data and should be interpreted with caution.

Gerunds, which are usually headings as in (1), are significantly worse for manual annotation, and infinitives as in (2) are worst for automatic tagging, but these are based on only 219 and 147 tokens respectively, so that results should be taken with a grain of salt despite their significance.

(1) *Hiring*/VVG *employees*/NNS

(2) *How*/WRB *to*/TO *Grow*/VV *Basil*/NN

Though the data is limited, the fact that these are mostly headings means it is possible that capitalization is causing problems in mistagging common nouns as proper nouns, which manual annotation is less susceptible to. Another possibility is that the shorter, more condensed sentence length makes these harder on account of missing function word cues (articles signaling nouns, etc.), meaning that length is a possible confound for the sentence type effect.

The remaining discrepancies are more certain, with about 87-90% accuracy in automatic tagging for *frag* and around 90% for the *other* type, based on much more data (1,321 and 1,074 tokens). For *frag*, we can suspect the reason is verbs: fragments lack a VP, which, assuming the verb can be recognized, would have a positive effect on tagging the surrounding arguments as nouns and their modifiers. For all three taggers, declaratives perform best by a wide margin, and as the gaps marked in bold show, other types are very substantially worse.

While these results are based only on sentence and text type separately, we can also check whether the sentence and text type effects are significant overall in a model that takes both into consideration, as well as the possible sentence length confound. Table 5 gives t-test values for the fixed effects in four mixed effects models including document identity as a random effect, and fixed predictors for text and sentence type,

[6] For all taggers we used the default English models supplied by their Web pages. The Stanford tagger model (*english-bidirectional-distsim*) did not distinguish tags for opening and closing quotation marks, which slightly boosts its accuracy.

as well as length. Each column gives values for a different tagger or manual annotation.[7]

	Manual	TT	Stanford	Spacy
length	-0.38	-1.10	1.46	0.78
news	0.26	0.81	1.29	0.87
voyage	-0.05	0.00	-0.58	-0.52
whow	0.50	-1.30	-1.74	-1.84
frag	0.86	**-6.60*****	**-8.23*****	**-8.41*****
ger	-1.28	-1.60	**-4.22*****	**-4.52*****
imp	**-2.26***	**-2.60****	**-5.01*****	**-2.65****
inf	-0.61	**-8.00*****	**-7.90*****	**-5.24*****
other	0.55	**-5.80*****	**-4.90*****	**-5.17*****
q	1.29	**-2.10***	**-2.08***	-0.08
sub	-0.06	0.31	1.13	0.94
wh	0.55	-3.9	**-2.28***	-0.30

Table 5: t values for mixed effects models with document, genre, sentence and length effects (significant values bold).

The effects disappear almost entirely for manual annotation, suggesting document or annotator specific factors. The significant result for *imp* is related to the positive coefficient of *whow*, which is collinear with the presence of *imp* (r^2=-0.285).[8]

Results for the taggers remain highly significant and entirely restricted to sentence types: the model consistently chooses sentence type over genre, despite the presence of the length predictor, which is somewhat correlated with imperatives (0.16) and fragments (0.20). The overall picture emerging from these results is that sentence type is more influential than genre, and that effects in manual annotation are modest. For taggers, *decl* is much better than any other type.

5 Dependency parsing

5.1 Method

Of the three tasks examined in this paper, we expect the most marked input effects for syntactic parsing. Parsing is not only well known to be affected by genre and domain (Lease & Charniak 2005, Khan et al. 2013), as well as sentence length (Ravi et al. 2008), but it is also directly related to sentence type, since the unit of annotation is the sentence, and local problems in a parse can disrupt accuracy throughout each clause.

Unlike POS tagging, dependency annotations in GUM represent manually corrected output from the Stanford Parser (see Chen & Manning 2014; V3.5 was used). While the entire corpus was corrected by student annotators, only 4,872 tokens were corrected a second time by an experienced instructor. Although this is a small dataset, we choose to use it rather than the whole corpus both because it is more reliable, and because this allows us to evaluate human errors in the initial correction. Our results for manual annotation therefore apply to the task of parser correction, and not to annotation from scratch.

Here too, we consider text and sentence type, but also sentence length, as well as individual document effects. Our null hypothesis is an equal distribution of errors among all partitions. We suspect a stronger effect for sentence length, since long distance dependencies are likelier in long sentences and may be more difficult for humans and automatic parsing, by opening up more opportunities for actual and apparent ambiguities. Sentence type may also have a strong effect, especially for types underrepresented in parser training data (i.e. the Penn Treebank, Marcus et al. 1993). This is expected for imperatives and non-canonical clauses, whereas the *decl* and *sub* types are expected to perform best.

5.2 Results

Table 6 gives accuracy by genre and sentence type for dependency label and attachment. The types *intj* and *ger* have been dropped, since they were represented by fewer than 10 tokens in the doubly corrected data. Token counts in each partition are included for the remaining categories.

As expected, humans improved on the parser in all cases. Genre is only significant for *voyage*, and only in parser label assignment. More pronounced negative effects can be seen for *frag* and *other*, which carry over from parser to manual correction. Smaller effects for the question types can be observed, but are based on few tokens.

Although the results confirm the expected good performance on *decl* and lower importance of genre, imperatives emerge as unproblematic and only *frag* and *other* stand out. At the same time, it is possible there are alternative explana-

[7] Note that *decl* and *interview* represent the intercept for sentence and text type, meaning figures for other types represent deviations from these values.

[8] An anonymous reviewer has asked about other genre/type correlations in our data: beyond *imp+whow*, the more distant second is *wh* questions in the *interview* subcorpus: although the coefficient for *wh* is not significantly collinear in the model, these two category combinations together are responsible for almost 50% of the chi squared residuals for sentence type versus genre (*imp+whow*: 41.1%, *wh+interview*: 8.2%). Since *imp* forms 32.8% of the *whow* data but only 11.3% of all data, there is some potential for conflation between results for *imp* in *whow* and *whow* as a whole, whereas for interviews, *wh* is only 6.8% of the data – a very significant proportional deviation from the average of 2.3%, but still modest in absolute terms.

tions for the data, such as sentence length or individual document difficulty.

	manual		parser		
	attach	**label**	**attach**	**label**	**tok**
interv.	88.1	89.2	80.2	83.2	1405
news	89.9	90.5	80.9	82.5	1222
whow	87.0	87.5	80.7	82.1	1371
voyage	88.4	90.4	82.0	**87.1+**	1058
decl	93.6	94.8	87.0	90.3	3588
frag	**89.3*****	**89.0*****	**76.0*****	**72.1*****	337
sub	85.7	89.3	82.1	89.3	28
q	**100+**	100	86.3	87.7	73
imp	93.6	95.3	86.4	88.4	361
other	**87.3*****	**88.0*****	**70.6*****	**76.6*****	299
inf	100	93.1	96.6	89.7	29
wh	**88.0***	90.4	80.7	84.3	83

Table 6: Parser and corrector accuracies.

The four mixed-effects models summarized in Table 7 show that while sentence type survives, genre is no longer significant. Moreover, sentence length was disruptive only for humans (in contrast to Ravi et al.'s data, though that study did not include sentence type as a predictor).

	manual		automatic	
	label	**attach**	**label**	**attach**
length	-1.62	**-3.02****	1.70	-1.42
news	1.08	-0.13	-0.36	-0.34
voyage	0.93	-0.43	1.31	0.03
whow	-0.16	-0.76	0.25	-0.06
frag	**-4.48*****	**-5.15*****	**-7.09*****	**-5.34*****
imp	0.23	-0.17	-0.15	-0.24
inf	-0.19	0.90	0.27	1.03
other	**-3.85****	**-2.31***	**-5.71*****	**-4.84*****
q	1.29	0.28	-0.55	-1.59
sub	-1.01	-1.63	0.14	-0.69
wh	-1.29	**-2.23***	-1.06	**-2.07***

Table 7: t values from mixed effects models for parsing accuracy using sentence type, genre and length, with document random effects.

The most striking sentence type predictor is *wh*, though it is based on little data. As length has been factored in, these are cases where length is not a sufficient predictor of the observed error rate. Upon closer inspection, *wh* sentences are shorter overall – about 10 tokens on average – while declaratives are 21 tokens on average but similarly difficult. Both types are dense in the syntactic content that can lead to errors while easy to catch categories, such as trivial modifiers, are more rare - see the dearth of easy modifier functions despite complex syntax in examples (3–5).

(3) *What analysis did you perform on the specimens and what equipment was used?*

(4) *What are the startup costs involved?*

(5) *Why run for president?*

The type *frag* was a strong predictor of error. Many instances of *frag* in the data were more complex than a simple NP, such as captions for image credit (6), dates (7), NPs with foreign word heads (8) or potentially ambiguous NPs (9), among many other short bits of language with little else available to contextualize them.

(6) *Image: Mathias Krumbholz.*

(7) *Tuesday, September 1, 2015*

(8) *Beauveria bassiana on a cicada in Bolivia.*

(9) *Clothing supply closet*

Imperatives were not a strong predictor of error; this is surprising given Silvera et al. (2014)'s characterization of imperatives being an essential difference between newswire and non-newswire text. While lacking an overt subject, imperatives were largely syntactically conventional. Omitting the subject relation did not create difficulties for the parser or annotators.

6 Coreference resolution

6.1 Method

Domain adaptation in coreference resolution has been discussed often, both in the context of multiple text types within standard reference corpora (e.g. conversation, newswire and Web subcorpora in datasets such as the ACE corpus, see Yang et al. 2012) or novel domains that are not included in most reference corpora, such as Biomedical NLP (Apostolova et al. 2012, Zhao & Ng 2014). Such studies suggest a genre or text type effect for coreference; sentence type effects, by contrast, have not yet been studied.

Pradhan et al. (2014) give a detailed overview and reference implementation of evaluation metrics for coreference resolution, including the MUC, B^3 and CEAF scores, which are averaged to produce the standard CoNLL score. The metrics focus on correct links between postulated entities, correct mention recognition, and correct entity recognition across mentions (see Pradhan et al. for details and references). Using the metrics on subcorpora of genres is unproblematic: scores can be reported for each subcorpus. However for sentence types, we encounter problems: the metrics were designed for the evaluation of entire running documents and cannot be applied directly to parts of documents, since we will not be running systems or manually annotating only a subset of each document (e.g. interrogative sentences) without looking at other sentences.

More recently Martschat et al. (2015) introduced error analysis for mention pair types in the CORT system, which keeps track of each pair of mentions corresponding to a correct or incorrect linking decision in a mention-chain model.[9] For example, it is possible to diagnose precision or recall errors involving a pronominal anaphor with a common noun-headed antecedent, by counting correct and incorrect links of this type, in much the same way used by the MUC metric.

Building on Martschat et al.'s insights, we extend the MUC metric to features of single mentions involved in correct or incorrect links. We call this metric 'p-link', which stands for 'partitioned link score'. The basic idea is that a coreference failure (or success) has two equally responsible mentions in a consecutive mention-chain model. Each of the two mentions involved shares credit or blame for the classification decision. If a link partition is worth 1 precision or recall point, then involvement in a correct decision earns 0.5 points for the category that includes the mention at each end of the link.

Figure 1 illustrates this using the example from Pradhan et al. (2014), which has been extended with shading representing categories.

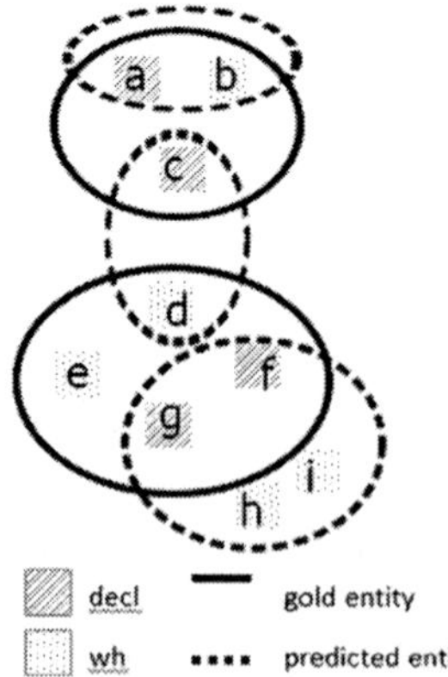

Figure 1: Gold (solid) and predicted (dashed) entities, with mentions in two categories distinguished by shading.

The solid oval represent two gold entities, with mentions {a,b,c} and {d,e,f,g}. Dashed ovals give three predicted entities, with mentions {a,b}, {c,d} and {g,f,h,i}. Note that mention e is not in any predicted entity, and h+i are not in the gold data. Pradhan et al.'s implementation of the MUC metric tallies the partitions with respect to gold and predicted mentions, such that a predicted link a+b is a correct positive (since a+b are in the same gold entity), c+d is a false positive, and the absence of predicted b+c is a false negative.

The p-link score builds on this by counting 0.5 points of correct positive, correct negative, etc. for each mention, such that points accrue for the respective category of that mention. The metric is a direct extension of Pradhan et al.'s definitions for recall (R) and precision (P):

$$p\text{-}link_{R,\pi} = \frac{\sum_{i=1}^{N_k}(|K_i^\pi| - p(K_i^\pi))}{\sum_{i=1}^{N_k}(|K_i^\pi| - 1)}$$

$$p\text{-}link_{P,\pi} = \frac{\sum_{i=1}^{N_r}(|R_i^\pi| - p'(R_i^\pi))}{\sum_{i=1}^{N_r}(|R_i^\pi| - 1)}$$

where K_i is the ith entity in the key (gold) data (and Ri is correspondingly the ith response entity); $|K_i^\pi|$ is the weighted partition magnitude within entity i, i.e. the number of instances of a mention from partition type π being either the source or target of a coreference link, multiplied by the weight 0.5 (since source and target may be of different types, and each is worth 'half a link'); and $p(K_i^\pi)$ is the set of elements of type π obtained by intersecting the key entities with the response entities, with each mention again being worth 0.5 points for its respective type π.[10]

Thus for the example in Figure 1, declaratives get 0.5 points for their correct involvement in a+b, but none for the missing link with c, and 1 point for their involvement in the correct g+f (since both are *decl*). The total possible links for declaratives in Figure 1 are worth 2 points (0.5 for a+b, 0.5 for b+c and 1 for g+f), so that *decl* scores a recall of 1.5/2 or 0.75 in this example. Indeed, only 1 of 4 *decl* link endpoints is missed in this example. We have implemented the p-link metric as an extension to Pradhan et al.'s original code, and our code is freely available.[11]

To test whether genre or sentence type has more influence on p-link, we evaluate manual and automatic coreferencer output, using a con-

[9] This approach assumes a 'mention-pair' model, in which each anaphor is linked to its antecedent in a chain. By contrast, 'mention-cluster' or 'entity-mention' models (see Rahman & Ng 2011) focus on entities as clustered groups of mentions referring to the same entity.

[10] Although we assign anaphors and antecedents equal weights of 0.5, other weights are conceivable.

[11] Code available at: `https://github.com/amir-zeldes/reference-coreference-scorers.`

figurable rule-based coreferencer called xrenner (Zeldes & Zhang 2016).[12] The tool can be set up to produce GUM's annotation scheme. The same data subset as for POS tagging was doubly corrected, and is used below.

6.2 Results

Table 8 gives p-link precision and recall for manual (double corrected) and automatic coreference resolution in the genre vs. sentence type partitions. The results show that differences between genres are comparatively small: although humans fare best on news and travel guides and worst on interviews, their performance is rather comparable, with a range of only .06 F1 points.

	manual			**automatic**		
	R	**P**	**F1**	**R**	**P**	**F1**
interview	0.67	0.86	0.75	0.59	0.60	0.60
news	0.74	0.90	0.81	0.53	0.56	0.54
voyage	0.77	0.83	0.80	0.51	0.49	0.50
whow	0.71	0.86	0.77	0.60	0.58	0.59
decl	0.72	0.86	0.78	0.56	0.57	0.56
frag	0.75	0.88	0.81	0.45	0.37	0.40
ger	0.68	0.86	0.76	0.59	0.59	0.59
imp	0.66	0.87	0.75	0.61	0.59	0.60
inf	0.65	0.80	0.72	0.46	0.63	0.53
other	0.79	0.91	0.84	0.54	0.58	0.56
q	0.67	0.86	0.76	0.62	0.65	0.63
sub	0.69	0.88	0.77	0.61	0.56	0.58
wh	0.71	0.91	0.80	0.66	0.75	0.70

Table 8: Partitioned precision and recall p-link scores.

Recall is universally lower than precision, suggesting that many cases of lexical coreference ('different names for the same thing') are left out by annotators with only minimal training (as we will see below, pronouns were overwhelmingly resolved correctly). The automatic coreferencer, by contrast, has the easiest time with interviews and how-to guides, due to two simple facts: the long chains of 'I' and 'you' boost scores in interviews, and the how-to guides tend to refer to the main subject of the guide repeatedly by name, making a lexical matching strategy work well. The range of F1 scores is within .1 points, larger but still modest.

Sentence types, by contrast, show much greater variance, with F1 scores ranging 0.72-0.84 for manual annotation and 0.40-0.70 for the coreferencer. Figure 2 plots the ranges of values.

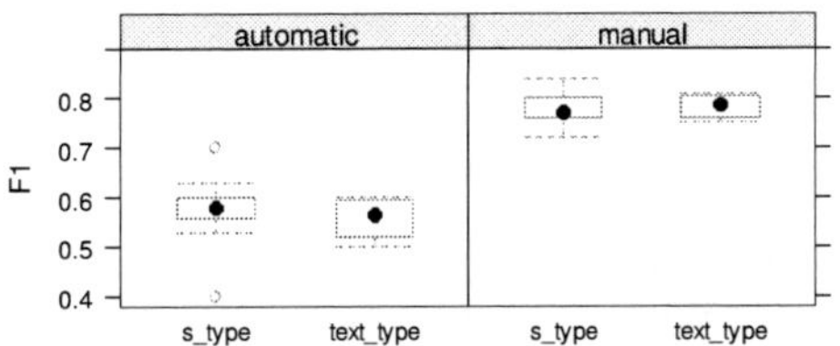

Figure 2: Box plots for p-link F-scores by partition using manual and automatic annotations.

It is clear that sentence types are more spread out, but for automatic annotation this is also due to two outliers: wh-questions as in (10), which do well, possibly due to a simpler information structure and fewer 'confusing' adjuncts, and fragments, which do badly for the coreferencer, possibly because of coreference via synonyms (see e.g. 12 below).

(10) *then circumstances allowed [her] to attend the exhibit. Why did [she] so badly want to attend?*

It is however possible that sentence types are more spread out because they form more categories, and some of the smaller ones may distort the skew of F1 scores. We would therefore like to know whether a model given both types of partitions would find either or both significant in predicting errors. Again we control for length (*imp* and *frag* are also short), but also for pronominality, since some sentence types may include more pronouns, for which recall is higher for both human and machine. Table 9 gives t values and significance for 4 mixed effects models predicting precision and recall errors, allowing for different error-rate intercepts for each document.

	manual		**automatic**	
	recall	**precision**	**recall**	**precision**
length	**-2.16***	-0.28	**-6.55*****	**-4.53*****
news	1.61	1.73	1.11	0.58
voyage	-1.29	1.90	-0.82	-1.08
whow	-0.79	1.50	0.17	0.11
frag	**2.02+**	1.46	**-5.69*****	**-3.95*****
ger	0.53	-1.45	-0.56	0.28
imp	**2.25+**	-1.13	**2.27+**	**3.00++**
inf	-0.98	-0.54	-0.37	-0.39
other	1.42	**2.88++**	-0.82	-0.51
q	-1.45	-0.38	-0.12	-1.57
sub	-0.82	-1.39	-0.15	-0.58
wh	1.72	1.52	**3.71++**	**2.69++**
pron	**11.96+++**	**14.56+++**	**17.71+++**	**21.38+++**

Table 9: t-values for mixed effects models of precision and recall for manual and automatic annotation.

All models predict highly significant positive scores for pronominality (i.e. pronouns are easi-

[12] The tool is open source and freely available at: http://corpling.uis.georgetown.edu/xrenner.

er). Sentence length is negatively correlated with manual precision and automatic recall (longer is harder), though there is no effect on manual precision. This can be explained by long sentences making human annotators miss mentions, but not resolve them incorrectly; the coreferencer, by contrast, prefers close antecedents, meaning long sentences offer more close competitors.

In terms of the partitions, none of the text type effects are significant, but several of the sentence types survive: fragments are still hard for the coreferencer, above and beyond prediction based on pronominality, sentence length and genre, but not for humans. Imperatives, by contrast, are significantly easier for everyone. These typically refer to at-issue, non-subject, lexical NPs, since imperatives have no overt subject. The imperatives in the data, typically instructions in how-to and travel guides are often adjacent to lexical remention of the same entities, making them easy to resolve via lexical identity (11). Fragments, by contrast, and especially very short ones that the model expects to be easy, sometimes corefer via synonyms, perhaps to deliberately avoid remention after headlines, as in (12). This makes them easy for humans, but difficult for the machine.

(11) *Read below for more of* [*the interview*] *in full.* [*Interview*] …

(12) [*Superstars*]
Each collection donated by the Andy Warhol Photographic Legacy Program holds Polaroids of [*well-known celebrities*]

Finally, the coreferencer is more likely than usual to get wh-referents right, beyond the positive effects of pronominality and short length. This suggests that wh-questions too have comparatively simple mention structure and tend to mention lexical NPs that are likely to recur verbatim or with identical heads, rather than more roundabout references (e.g. 13).

(13) - *What is [Heaven Sent Gaming]?*
- *[Heaven Sent Gaming] is basically me and Isabel*

7 Conclusion

The results from our data set indicate that, across the board, sentence type variation is a better predictor of annotation quality than genre. Although it is obvious that there are more sentence types than genres in our study, this result is not obvious: many patterns of style and vocabulary are specific to genres such as travel guides or interviews, and sentence types are cross-classified across all text types. There are more imperatives in how-to and travel guides, and more questions in interviews, but these types are attested in all genres, and the multifactorial models consistently choose sentence type with no remaining added effect for genre. Additionally, even a coarse binary factor such as pronominality can survive in a multifactorial model that finds sentence type significant, but not genre.

It should be noted that the genres surveyed here are not very distant: We are certain that adding Computer Mediated Communication (e.g. Twitter data) as a further text type would radically alter our results. However, given the scope of differences in annotation quality across sentence types, we would also expect to see strong effects of sentence type within and across more disparate genres, such as CMC data of various kinds.

A practical implication of this study is that it may be worth redoubling annotation quality control on sentence types known to be problematic for a certain task. As we have seen, these can vary between manual and automatic annotation, the automatic tool used, and the task itself. It is also clear that, as noted by Silveira et al. (2014), we are in great need of more diverse annotated datasets, and especially ones containing underrepresented sentence types, such as imperatives, questions and non-canonical sentences.

Acknowledgments

We would like to thank Shuo Zhang for helping to process the coreference data, the participants of the course LING-367 Computational Corpus Linguistics for contributing their annotations, and three anonymous reviewers for valuable comments on earlier versions of this paper. For a current list of contributors to GUM, see `http://corpling.uis.georgetown.edu/gum`.

References

Emilia Apostolova, Noriko Tomuro, Pattanasak Mongkolwat and Dina Demner-Fushman. 2012. Domain Adaptation of Coreference Resolution for Radiology Reports. In *Proceedings of the 2012 Workshop on Biomedical Natural Language Processing (BioNLP 2012)*. Montreal, 118–121.

R. Harald. Baayen. 2008. *Analyzing Linguistic Data. A Practical Introduction to Statistics using R*. Cambridge: Cambridge University Press.

Douglas Biber. 2009. Multi-Dimensional Approaches. In Anke Lüdeling & Merja Kytö (eds.), *Corpus*

Linguistics. An International Handbook. Vol. 2. Berlin: Mouton de Gruyter, 822–855.

Danqi Chen and Christopher D. Manning. 2014. A Fast and Accurate Dependency Parser using Neural Networks. In *Proceedings of the 2014 Conference on Empirical Methods in Natural Language Processing (EMNLP 2014).* Doha, Qatar, 740–750.

Hal Daumé III. 2007. Frustratingly Easy Domain Adaptation. In *Proceedings of ACL 2007.* Prague, Czech Republic, 256–263.

Stefanie Dipper, Michael Götze and Stavros Skopeteas (eds.). 2007. Information Structure in Cross-Linguistic Corpora: Annotation Guidelines for Phonology, Morphology, Syntax, Semantics, and Information Structure. *Interdisciplinary Studies on Information Structure* 7.

Jenny Rose Finkel and Christopher D. Manning. 2009. Hierarchical Bayesian Domain Adaptation. In *Proceedings of NAACL-HLT 2009.* Boulder, CO, 602–610.

Stella Frank, Sharon Goldwater and Frank Keller. 2013. Adding Sentence Types to a Model of Syntactic Category Acquisition. *Topics in Cognitive Science* 5(3):495–521.

Roger Garside and Nicholas Smith. 1997. A Hybrid Grammatical Tagger: CLAWS4. In Roger Garside, Geoffrey Leech and Tony McEnery (eds.), *Corpus Annotation: Linguistic Information from Computer Text Corpora.* London: Longman, 102–121.

Eduard Hovy, Mitchell Marcus, Martha Palmer, Lance Ramshaw and Ralph Weischedel. 2006. OntoNotes: The 90% Solution. In *Proceedings of the Human Language Technology Conference of the NAACL, Companion Volume: Short Papers.* New York: ACL, 57–60.

Mohammad Khan, Markus Dickinson and Sandra Kübler. 2013. Towards Domain Adaptation for Parsing Web Data. In *Proceedings of Recent Advances in Natural Language Processing (RANLP 2013).* Hissar, Bulgaria, 357–364.

Matthew Lease and Eugene Charniak. 2005. Parsing Biomedical Literature. In Robert Dale, Kam-Fai Wong, Jian Su and Oi Yee Kwong (eds.), *Proceedings of IJCNLP 2005.* Berlin: Springer, 58–69.

Geoffrey Leech, Tony McEnery and Martin Weisser. 2003. *SPAAC Speech-Act Annotation Scheme.* University of Lancaster, Technical Report.

William C. Mann and Sandra A. Thompson. 1988. Rhetorical Structure Theory: Toward a Functional Theory of Text Organization. *Text* 8(3):243–281.

Christopher D. Manning. 2011. Part-of-Speech Tagging from 97% to 100%: Is It Time for Some Linguistics? In Alexander Gelbukh (ed.), *Computational Linguistics and Intelligent Text Processing, 12th International Conference (Proceedings of CICLing 2011).* Tokyo, 171–189.

Mitchell P. Marcus, Beatrice Santorini and Mary Ann Marcinkiewicz. 1993. Building a Large Annotated Corpus of English: The Penn Treebank. *Special Issue on Using Large Corpora, Computational Linguistics* 19(2):313–330.

Marie-Catherine de Marneffe and Christopher D. Manning. 2013. *Stanford Typed Dependencies Manual.* Stanford University, Technical Report.

Sebastian Martschat, Thierry Göckel and Michael Strube. 2015. Analyzing and Visualizing Coreference Resolution Errors. In *Proceedings of NAACL-HLT 2015.* Denver, CO, 6–10.

David McClosky, Eugene Charniak and Mark Johnson. 2010. Automatic Domain Adaptation for Parsing. In *Proceedings of NAACL 2010.* Los Angeles, CA, 28–36.

Barbara Plank. 2011. *Domain Adaptation for Parsing.* PhD Thesis, University of Groningen.

Sameer Pradhan, Xiaoqiang Luo, Marta Recasens, Eduard Hovy, Vincent Ng and Michael Strube. 2014. Scoring Coreference Partitions of Predicted Mentions: A Reference Implementation. In *Proceedings of the 52nd Annual Meeting of the ACL.* Baltimore, MD, 30–35.

Altaf Rahman and Vincent Ng. 2011. Narrowing the Modeling Gap: A Cluster-Ranking Approach to Coreference Resolution. *Journal of Artificial Intelligence Research* 40(1):469–521.

Sujith Ravi, Kevin Knight and Radu Soricut. 2008. Automatic Prediction of Parser Accuracy. In *Proceedings of the 2008 Conference on Empirical Methods in Natural Language Processing (EMNLP 2008).* Honolulu, 887–896.

Helmut Schmid. 1994. Probabilistic Part-of-Speech Tagging Using Decision Trees. In *Proceedings of the Conference on New Methods in Language Processing.* Manchester, UK, 44–49.

Natalia Silveira, Timothy Dozat, Marie-Catherine de Marneffe, Samuel R. Bowman, Miriam Connor, John Bauery and Christopher D. Manning. 2014. A Gold Standard Dependency Corpus for English. In *Proceedings of the Ninth International Conference on Language Resources and Evaluation (LREC-2014).* Reykjavik, Iceland, 2897–2904.

Anders Søgaard. 2013. *Semi-Supervised Learning and Domain Adaptation in Natural Language Processing.* (Synthesis Lectures on Human Language Technologies.) San Rafael: Morgan & Claypool.

Kristina Toutanova, Dan Klein, Christopher D. Manning and Yoram Singer. 2003. Feature-Rich Part-of-Speech Tagging with a Cyclic Dependency Network. In *Proceedings of the 2003 Conference of the North American Chapter of the Association for Computational Linguistics on Human Language Technology (NAACL-HLT 2003).* Stroudsburg, PA: ACL, 252–259.

Jian Bo Yang, Qi Mao, Qiao Liang Xiang, and Ivor W. Tsang, Kian Ming A. Chai and Hai Leong Chieu. 2012. Domain Adaptation for Coreference Resolution: An Adaptive Ensemble Approach. In *Proceedings of the 2012 Joint Conference on Empirical Methods in Natural Language Processing and Computational Natural Language Learning (EMNLP 2012)*. Jeju Island, Korea, 744–753.

Amir Zeldes. 2016. The GUM Corpus: Creating Multilayer Resources in the Classroom. *Language Resources and Evaluation*.

Amir Zeldes and Shuo Zhang. 2016. When Annotation Schemes Change Rules Help: A Configurable Approach to Coreference Resolution beyond OntoNotes. In: *Proceedings of the NAACL-HLT 2016 Workshop on Coreference Resolution Beyond OntoNotes (CORBON)*. San Diego, CA, 92-101.

Jiajun Zhang, Chengqing Zong and Shoushan Li. 2008. Sentence Type Based Reordering Model for Statistical Machine Translation. In *Proceedings of the 22nd International Conference on Computational Linguistics (Coling 2008)*. Manchester, 1089–1096.

Shanheng Zhao and Hwee Tou Ng. 2014. Domain Adaptation with Active Learning for Coreference Resolution. In *Proceedings of the 5th International Workshop on Health Text Mining and Information Analysis, EACL 2014*. Gothenburg, 21–29.

Addressing Annotation Complexity: The Case of Annotating Ideological Perspective in Egyptian Social Media

Heba Elfardy
Department of Computer Science
Columbia University
New York, NY
heba@cs.columbia.edu

Mona Diab
Department of Computer Science
The George Washington University
Washington, DC
mtdiab@gwu.edu

Abstract

Automatically detecting the stance of people toward political and ideological topics –namely their "Ideological Perspective"– from social media is a rapidly growing research area with a wide range of applications. Research in such a field faces several challenges among which is the lack of annotated corpora and associated guidelines for collecting annotations. The problem is even more pronounced in situations where there is no clear taxonomy for the common community perspectives and ideologies. The challenges are exacerbated when the communities where we need to gather these annotations are in a state of turmoil causing *subjectivity* and *intimidation* to be factors in the annotation process. Accordingly, we present the process for creating a robust and succinct set of guidelines for annotating "Egyptian Ideological Perspectives". We collect social media data discussing Egyptian politics and develop an iterative feedback annotation framework refining the annotation task and associated guidelines attempting to circumvent both weaknesses. Our efforts lead to a significant increase in inter-annotator agreement measures from 75.7% to 92% overall agreement.

1 Introduction

With the rise of social media there has been a plethora of documented political and ideological discussions. These discussions typically represent polarizing topics and in doing so convey the participants' belief systems expressing their perspective (or stance) on contentious issues –namely their "Ideological Perspective". Identifying the perspective of users in such media is a challenging research problem that has a wide variety of applications from recommendation systems and targeted advertising to planning political campaigns, political polling and predicting possible future events. As a matter of fact, social media played a major role in the Arab Spring (2010– present). In Egypt, for example, activists and political leaders resorted to social media as an alternative to the censored and mostly biased state and privately owned media. Most of these activists used social media to make announcements, campaign for elections, spread awareness of important causes and conduct polls in order to predict election outcomes. After Egypt's Jan. 25th Revolution, alliances kept forming (and later breaking) between Islamist movements, Revolutionists, public figures from Mubarak's regime (the Old guard) and the Army. The formation and break-up of such alliances often triggered apparent perspective-shifts in the public sphere. These shifts in perspective can be best explained by Converse's concept of centrality in belief systems. Converse (2006) defines a belief system as the configuration of idea elements and attitudes that are bound together by some constraint. This constraint helps us in knowing that a person holds a specific attitude given knowledge that he/she holds another one (Converse, 2006). For example, if we know that an American citizen supports ObamaCare, can we predict that he/she supports gun control? While there are Americans who support ObamaCare and oppose gun control, the vast majority of people either support or oppose both issues because the stance toward these two issues is always backed by one's ideology or belief system, namely being of a Democratic Party leaning. Converse states that within a belief system, idea elements vary in "centrality". These variations always govern what happens when the status of one of the idea elements in a belief system changes. For example, what will a self-proclaimed Republican do if the Republi-

Proceedings of LAW X – The 10th Linguistic Annotation Workshop, pages 79–88,
Berlin, Germany, August 11, 2016. ©2016 Association for Computational Linguistics

can Party decided to change its stance on universal healthcare and started to support it? The reaction of the person will depend on which is more central to the person's belief system – political party affiliation or stance on healthcare. Many Egyptians were faced with such choices post the Jan. 25th Revolution as the stance of political leaders toward major political entities such as the Military, the Police, Islamists, the Revolution, etc. kept changing. This change of stance among the leaders often triggered perspective shifts among the mass public toward the entities that are less central to their belief systems.

Collecting annotations of such perspectives is quite challenging in a dynamic political setting since many of the political stances are emergent and shifting. The problem is two fold: (1) pinning down what the perspectives are; and, (2) gathering annotations on such perspectives while circumventing the subjectivity of the annotators themselves. Due to the nature of the data, we need to use the help of annotators who understand the nature of the political landscape, hence they had to be Egyptians familiar with the recent events. But by being Egyptian, they are not themselves naturally divorced from the events, thereby having their own perspectives and biases. In this paper, we present our iterative approach to building effective guidelines for collecting annotations that aims at decoupling the annotation process from possible subjective assessment of the annotators. We build a list of major political events and sample a set of social media data that was posted within one week from the start of each of these events. We come up with a hypothesis on the most important elements governing the Ideological Perspective of most Egyptians and develop a set of guidelines and an annotation task to identify the perspective from which a given comment was written. Our hypothesis is that a person's perspective has two major underlying dimensions: (1) a person's stance on political reform versus stability; and, (2) a person's stance on the role Islam/religion should play in the public sphere, in politics. We run our first annotation experiment where we ask annotators to identify the stance of a given comment toward several political entities such as Jan. 25th Revolution, Mubarak's Regime, Military Rule, Islamists and Secularists. Based on the feedback and error analysis of this pilot annotation, we note some interesting observations most impactful of which is the annotators' having significant reservations in making a judgment on comments. Accordingly, taking this feedback into consideration, we refine the guidelines and the annotation task and have the same set of comments annotated based on the refined guidelines. Given the new set of guidelines, annotators are asked to identify the top priorities expressed in the comment such as stability, supporting (or opposing) Islamists, supporting Jan. 25th Revolution, etc. The new task and guidelines yield better inter-annotator agreement and annotators give a more positive feedback on the clarity of the task.

2 Related Work

From a social-science viewpoint, the notion of "Perspective" is related to the concept of "Framing". Framing involves making some topics –or some aspects of the discussed topics– more prominent in order to promote the views and interpretations of the writer (communicator). (Entman, 1993). At the most basic level, these decisions are expressed in lexical choice. For example, a person who opposes gun rights is more likely to use words that emphasize "death" while a supporter is more likely to use ones that promote "self defense". As the saying goes, *"One man's terrorist is another man's freedom fighter"*. Perspective is also expressed on the syntactic and semantic levels. Greene and Resnik (2009) showed that the syntactic structure can be a strong indicator of a specific perspective, or bias. For example, using the passive voice puts less emphasis on the doer than using an active one. This is particularly important when the verb is sentiment bearing. In such case, the passive voice is less likely to associate the sentiment with the doer. Sentiment in itself serves as another important cue for identifying a person's perspective since it expresses one's opinion on different topics. In fact, from a computational point of view, the work on perspective-detection is closely related to subjectivity and sentiment analysis. One's perspective normally influences his/her sentiment toward different topics or targets. Conversely identifying the sentiment of a person toward multiple targets can serve as a cue for identifying this person's perspective. For example, we expect a typical Jan. 25th Revolutionist to express positive sentiment toward social justice, freedom of speech and the Revolution's public figures and negative sentiment toward the ousted ex-president Mubarak of Egypt and his regime.

Event	Date Range
1. Jan. 25th Revolution	Jan. 25 - Jan. 31, 2011
2. Battle of the camel	Feb. 2 - Feb. 8, 2011
3. Mubarak Stepping Down	Feb. 11 - Feb. 17, 2011
4. Referendum on amendments to old constitution	Mar. 19 - Mar. 25, 2011
5. Mohamed Mahmoud Protests *(Clashes between Army and Revolutionists)*	Nov. 19 - Nov. 25, 2011
6. Announcement of presidential election results	Jun. 24 - Jun. 30, 2012
7. Presidential decree and associated protests	Nov. 22 - Nov. 28, 2012
8. Ousting of President Mohamed Morsi	Jun. 30 - Jul. 6, 2013
9. Army calls for mandate to crack down on terrorism	Jul. 24 - Jul. 30, 2013
10. Rabia (Pro-Muslim Brotherhood) camp dismantling	Aug. 14 - Aug. 20, 2013

Table 1: List of events and their associated dates for which the data was selected.

Most of the currently available datasets that are annotated for Ideological Perspective are in English (Lin et al., 2006; Somasundaran and Wiebe, 2010; Abu-Jbara et al., 2012; Yano et al., 2010; Elfardy et al., 2015; Hasan and NG, 2012; Hasan and Ng, 2013). The only Arabic Ideological Perspective datasets that we are aware of are those of Abu-Jbara et al. (2013), Siegel (2014) and Borge-Holthoefer et al. (2015). Abu-Jbara et al. (2013)'s dataset is self annotated, and the annotations are more abstract –only provide the binary stance of each post toward the debate question. Siegel (2014) study whether Egyptian twitter users who are exposed to a more diverse twitter network become more tolerant toward people having different political and ideological leanings. On the other hand, Borge-Holthoefer et al. (2015) collect Arabic tweets posted between June and September 2013. They manually annotate a subset of 1000 tweets as either supporting, opposing or being neutral toward the Military and use this subset to build a classifier that they then apply to all unlabeled tweets. The authors then track users who change their position toward the Military across the studied timeline. As opposed to our work, Borge-Holthoefer et al. (2015)'s work focuses on a much shorter time-frame during which most people were polarized between either supporting the Military or supporting the Muslim Brotherhood (Islamists) hence the authors do not aim to identify the stance of the author toward other political entities such as Jan. 25th Revolution, Mubarak's regime, etc.

To the best of our knowledge, the presented work is the first attempt at creating guidelines for collecting fine-grained multidimensional annotations of Egyptian Ideological Perspectives that try to uncover the different underlying elements of a person's belief system.

3 Data Collection

We select a set of public social media discussion fora pages of renowned Egyptian activists and politicians of different political leanings and curate posts and comments from these pages. The "*post*" refers to some piece of content shared on a page while the "*comment*" is a response to this original piece of content. We filter spam/repetitive comments that do not respond to the original post. Moreover, only comments with no Latin words and that have a length of at least ten words were preserved.

After the initial cleanup of the data, we use a list of major events such as Jan. 25th demonstrations, major protests, Presidential elections, etc. to select our final dataset. Table 1 shows the list of events and the dates covered by the selected data. We split the data into two groups based on whether it was curated from a page that supports (1) Reform [RFM] (Supporting Jan. 25th Revolution); or, (2) Old Guard Rule [OGR] (ex. Supporting the ousted Egyptian President Mubarak and his regime, or supporting the current Egyptian President –Sisi– who was the ex-minister of Defense). We then select a sample of 31 comments per event for each of the two groups. It is worth mentioning that for the first event –Jan. 25th Revolution– no comments were posted in the pro-OGR pages accordingly we only have 31 pro-RFM comments for this event. This results in a total of 310 RFM and 279 OGR comments.

4 Egyptian Ideological Perspectives

Prior to collecting the annotations, we come up with a high level taxonomy for the most common

- All questions target the *comment*. (The *post* is meant to give you context)
- Please pay attention to the *post* and *comment* dates.
- Use your knowledge of the political events in Egypt when responding to the questions.
  ex. If a *comment* supports Jan. 25th Revolution and you know that this implies that it opposes Mubarak's regime then choose "*Oppose*" as an answer to Q4.
- If the answer to Q1 or Q2 is "*No*", then choose "*NA*" as an answer to all other questions
- Difference between "*NA/Does not apply*" and "*Not Sure*":
  - "*NA*" should be used when the *comment* does not discuss the subject of the question
    ex. If a given *comment* does not discuss Mubarak's regime then you should choose "*NA*" as an answer to Q4.
    If, on the other hand, the *comment* discusses Mubarak's regime but you are not sure whether it opposes it or supports it then choose "*Not Sure*"
- Q7 targets Military Rule at any point in time (not a specific Army leader)
- If a *comment* supports Islamists this does not necessarily mean that it opposes Seculars and vice versa. (Unless the author expresses anti-secular views)
- If you have any feedback, please respond to Q8.

Figure 1: Synopsis of annotation guidelines for Pilot annotation task

political leanings in Egypt for this timeframe. We base our taxonomy on the works of "The Hariri Center at the Atlantic Council",[1] and "Carnegie Endowment for International Peace".[2] As mentioned earlier, after Jan. 25th Revolution, the formation and breakup of alliances between different political entities resulted in a dynamic set of political leanings hence created a need for a dynamic classification. For the context of this paper, we reduce the very rich perspective map of a person to two underlying dimensions: (1) stance toward democracy and political reform versus stability at the expense of loss of civil liberties; (2) stance toward the role played by Islam/religion in the public sphere or politics, namely Islamist vs. Secular. Accordingly, we assume that these two dimensions constitute a person's perspective. So for example, a person can oppose involving Islam in politics and support political reform. Another person can focus on stability even if it brings autocracy while either supporting or opposing Islamists. As mentioned earlier, the dimension that is less central to a person's belief system is more likely to change over time.

5 Annotation

Noting how challenging the annotation will be, we wanted to get a sense of how to circumvent annotator bias. Accordingly we devise an iterative feedback loop for the annotation process. We first have the sampled comments annotated by four trained Egyptian annotators. We ask the annotators to self identify what their own positions are with respect to the two dimensions of interest. All annotators indicate that they support Jan. 25th Revolution. Additionally, three annotators (annotators 1-3) indicate that they are neutral toward the role of Islam in politics while the fourth annotator indicates support toward the Army's leadership in ousting Islamists. An annotation lead managed the process of (1) training the annotators, (2) relaying their feedback about the clarity of the task to the authors. Based on the feedback and inter-annotator agreement (IAA) from this round, we refine the guidelines and annotation task before having the same data annotated by the same set of annotators.

5.1 First Annotation Experiment

For each task, we present annotators with a post and an associated comment. Except for one optional question that asks for feedback about the overall annotation task, all questions are formatted as multiple choice and require one answer to be provided. We do not reveal the leaning of the source page from which the comments were curated to the annotators so as not to bias their judgments. Annotators were asked to answer the following questions for each task:

- Q1: Does the given *comment* discuss Egyptian politics? (Yes/No)
- Q2: Is there enough context to determine the political leaning of the *comment*? (Yes/No)

[1] http://www.atlanticcouncil.org/blogs/egyptsource/egyptian-politics

[2] http://carnegieendowment.org/2015/01/22/2012-egyptian-parliamentary-elections/

Does the given *comment* Support/Oppose/Not Sure/Not Applicable:

- Q3: Jan. 25th Revolution?
- Q4: Mubarak's regime?
- Q5: Seculars?
- Q6: Islamists?
- Q7: Military Rule?

- Q8: Do you have any feedback or suggestions?

Questions 3-7 aim to identify the two previously discussed dimensions that define a person's perspective. Questions 3, 4 and 7 attempt to uncover the first dimension –the person's position on political reform and democracy while questions 5 and 6 aim to identify the second dimension –the person's view on the role of Islam/religion in the political sphere/government.

Since the task is quite subjective, we tried to cover most possible scenarios and to provide examples in our guidelines. Moreover we attempted to the best of our knowledge to avoid any bias in the way the questions were phrased. Figure 1 shows the guidelines for this first annotation experiment.

5.2 Error Analysis

We calculate the pairwise and overall IAA for all questions. Table 2 shows the results. The average pairwise IAA for all questions is quite high ranging from 84.1% to 88.4%. However, achieving a complete-row agreement (Row) by all annotators is quite challenging. The four annotators achieved a perfect row agreement –chose the same answers for all questions pertaining to a particular comment– on only 25.5% of the comments. We also note that Annotator 1 and 3 exhibit the most agreement.

In order to get better insights into the source of disagreement between annotators, we perform a manual error analysis by looking into the confusable comments and find that most of them fall under the following categories:

1. Comments that provide cues for both supporting and opposing the topic the question is addressing **ex.** (Event 2)

   لازم نصبر ونشوف اللى حيحصل مفيش حاجة بتتغير
   بين يوم وليلة براحة علشان اللى عملناه ميتقلبش ضدنا
   يا جماعة خافوا على البلد شوية عايزين نعمرها تانى

   Translation: *We have to be patient and wait and see what will happen. Nothing changes in a day and night. Take it easy so what we did does not backfire on us. Care about the country. We need to rebuild it.*

   While above comment opposes the continued demonstrations, this does not necessarily mean that it opposes Jan. 25th Revolution since the author just prioritizes stability over immediate political reform.

2. Ambiguous pronouns **ex.** (Event 9)

   وقيادتهم اللى دفعوا بهم للتجارة بدمهم اليسوا اول
   المسئولين؟ واول من يستطيعوا ان يوقفوا اهدار دمهم
   وعدم دفعهم للانتحار

   Translation: *And their leaders that pushed them in order to sell their blood, aren't they the responsible ones? They could have stopped their bloodshed if they didn't push them to commit suicide.*

   In this comment, although "their leaders" refers to leaders of the Muslim Brotherhood, it can be easily confused with the Army leaders.

3. Comments where the stance toward one entity is implied from the stance toward another entity **ex.** (Event 6)

   يا ما انا فرحانة فيكوا يا وفي شفيق العتيه يا عبيييييد
   يا حرامية

   Translation: *I am gloating over the loss of the idiot Shafik, you slaves and thieves*

   In the above comment, the author gloats over the defeat of Ahmed Shafik (a key figure of the OGR) in the 2012 presidential elections.. While the comment clearly supports Jan. 25th Revolution and opposes Mubarak's regime, it is not clear whether the author actually supports or is indifferent toward the Muslim Brotherhood's candidate.

4. Authors that report the opinions of other people by quoting them instead of stating their own opinions in comments they post. **ex.** (Event 7)

	Q1 Egy. Politics	Q2 Context	Q3 Jan. 25th	Q4 Mubarak	Q5 Seculars	Q6 Islamists	Q7 Military Rule	Avg	Row
Ann.1-2	95.6	81.8	80.3	76.1	96.8	80.6	79.5	84.4	44.3
Ann.1-3	96.8	87.6	81	83.4	97.8	86.1	86.1	88.4	55.5
Ann.1-4	97.1	86.1	81.2	81.5	97.5	83	78.8	86.4	48.6
Ann.2-3	95.8	82.3	77.2	72.8	97.3	82.7	80.3	84.1	42.3
Ann.2-4	96.4	83.5	87.3	79.8	98.8	82.7	78.8	86.8	47.5
Ann.3-4	98	84.9	80	81.2	97.3	84.9	81.3	86.8	49.4
All Ann.	93.5	71.1	66.9	64.3	95.9	72.2	65.9	75.7	25.5

Table 2: Inter-Annotator agreement for the pilot annotation experiment

	Pro-RFM Pages				Pro-OGR Pages			
	Yes		No		Yes		No	
Q1. Egy. Politics	97.6		2.4		97.8		2.2	
Q2. Context	84.4		15.6		81.5		18.5	
	Support	Oppose	Not Sure	NA	Support	Oppose	Not Sure	NA
Q3. Jan. 25th Revolution	42.9	2.6	0.3	54.2	3.9	32.2	0.8	63.1
Q4. Mubarak	1.9	43.5	1.5	53.1	30.1	7.7	1.5	60.7
Q5. Seculars	0.2	2.6	0.2	96.9	0	1.3	0.3	98.4
Q6. Islamists	27.7	11.2	1.7	59.4	9.9	33.9	0.8	55.5
Q8. Military Rule	1.2	11.3	0.6	86.9	22.6	5.8	0.4	71.1

Table 3: Answer Distribution (averaged over all annotators) to each question in the pilot annotation split according to the leaning of the source page from which data is curated.

وكالات انباء عالمية: عدد المتظاهرين المعارضين لمرسي في التحرير يفوق عدد مؤيديه عند الاتحادية.

Translation: *International News Agencies: "The number of anti-Morsi protestors in Tahrir exceeds the number of his supporters at the Heliopolis Palace"*

5. Sarcastic comments where the annotator judges the comment based on the literal and not the intended meaning;
6. Comments that oppose a certain group of Islamists (ex. Muslim Brotherhood) and oppose other ones (ex. Salafis). To handle these cases, the annotation task should provide a "Mixed Views" option to Q6 (a comment's stance on Islamists).

5.3 Qualitative Assessment

To perform a qualitative assessment of the annotations, we begin by calculating the distribution of the answers to all questions. We further split the comments according to whether the source pages they were collected from support OGR or RFM. One should note that even if a page supports democracy this does not necessarily mean that all people who comment on that page share the same views. However, we do expect a higher number of pro-RFM authors to comment on the pro-RFM pages and vice versa. Table 3 shows the distribution. By analyzing the responses, we find that the majority of the given comments (>97%) discuss Egyptian politics, which indicates that our filtration process works well in excluding spam and irrelevant comments. Moreover the majority of comments (>84%) provide enough context to determine their stance. Another observation is that annotators are very conservative in using "*Not Sure*" category. As expected, we find a much higher percentage of comments that support Mubarak's regime and Military Rule and oppose Jan. 25th Revolution among the ones collected from pro-OGR pages. On the contrary, the majority of comments from pro-RFM pages that express a stance toward the different political entities support Jan. 25th Revolution and oppose both Military Rule and Mubarak's Regime. While pro-RFM pages have a higher percentage of comments that support Islamists (27.7%) and pro-OGR pages have a higher percentage of anti-Islamists comments (33.9%), a considerable number of comments in each of these pages follow the opposite trend. 11.2% of comments in pro-RFM pages oppose Islamists and 9.9% of those in pro-OGR pages support them.

We analyze the answers per event and find that the distribution of the answers aligns with our knowledge of the political events in Egypt. For example, we expect and find a higher percentage of "*NA*" for Q4 (Mubarak's Regime) as we move away from the start of Jan. 25th Revolution and more polarization on the stance toward Islamists for events 8 through 10. Almost all comments pertaining to the first three events do not convey any stance toward Islamists. In the days right after the start of Jan. 25th Revolution most of the discussions addressed political reform versus stability and not the role of religion in politics. For events 7 through 10 more comments express a stance toward Islamists. For "Event 6" (announcing the results of presidential elections in which the Muslim Brotherhood's candidate was elected) the majority of comments sampled from pro-RFM pages support Islamists indicating acceptance of the election outcome while the pro-OGR pages express negative stance toward Islamists indicating disappointment in election outcomes, namely, disappointment that the OGR candidate –former Prime Minister– Ahmed Shafik lost.[3]

5.4 Pilot Annotation Weaknesses

Based on the feedback collected from the annotators and our manual error analysis, we notice the following problems with the way the task is formulated:

- The main point of confusion among annotators is deciding when they should infer the stance of the comment toward an entity based on the stance toward another entity. For example, if a person opposes the Army during Morsi's presidency term, does it imply that he/she supports Islamists;
- The task does not model the people who mainly care about stability regardless of political reform or the role of religion in politics;
- Even though the comments were collected from a specific set of events, we do not present the annotators with the event each comment was discussing and rather relied on the comment-date and the annotators' knowledge of the timeline of political events in Egypt;
- Q7 (A comment's stance on Military Rule) relied to a great extent on each annotator's interpretation of the Military Rule. A better way to phrase the question is to simply ask about the comment's stance toward the Military leaders and tap into our knowledge of the political timeline in Egypt in order to identify the periods where the Army/Military was actually in charge of governance;
- Most of the comments we looked at expressed the author's top priority whether it is political reform, stability, supporting the army, opposing the intervention of religion in political governance, etc. but our task gives equal weight to all political entities and do not ask annotators the top priority that they think drives the author's stance on various issues;
- Annotators were tempted to choose "*NA*" for many comments because they were trying to identify the reason behind a comment's stance. For example, a comment might support Islamists during Rabia camp dismantling because the author is against civil rights infringement but not necessarily because that person is pro-Islamists in general. We clarified to the annotators that we are only interested in the stance of the given comment at the time of the event of interest, namely in the specific context of the comment, regardless of the reason behind this stance or the person' stance at other points in time. Hence changing the question from a confusable potential "why" question to a "what" question. As mentioned earlier, this might also reflect the annotators' own concern over expressing their opinion about the comments with such a contentious event, erring on the side of caution;
- Some annotators chose "Yes" as an answer to Q2 (Is there enough context to judge the comment) when they were able to identify the sentiment of the comment but not the target of the sentiment. We clarified that if knowing the target is needed to identify the leaning of the comment then they should choose "No" as the answer to Q2;
- The guidelines do not address the cases where a comment shows mixed views on different Islamist groups/parties;
- Finally, the task does not address how the cases of reported opinions should be handled.

[3]In the interest of space, we do not show the distribution per event.

	Q1 Egy Polit.	Q2 Context	Q3 Reported Op.	Q4 Priority	Q5 Jan.25	Q6 Mubarak	Q7 Army	Q8 Islamists	Avg	Row
Ann. 1-2	99.3	95.1	95.1	89.5	92.9	92.9	95.4	94.9	94.4	82.7
Ann. 1-3	99.2	97.5	97.1	92.9	94.2	94.2	96.3	95.6	95.9	86.2
Ann. 1-4	99.2	94.6	94.1	88.6	91.7	91.9	94.6	94.4	93.6	80.8
Ann. 2-3	99.5	95.6	95.4	89.5	94.4	94.4	96.1	94.7	94.9	83.9
Ann. 2-4	99.5	97.1	96.6	92.0	95.9	95.8	97.1	95.6	96.2	86.9
Ann. 3-4	100.0	95.4	95.2	91.5	95.1	94.9	96.4	96.3	95.6	87.9
All-Ann.	99.0	93.2	92.9	85.2	90.5	90.5	93.5	92.4	92.1	76.9

Table 4: Inter-Annotator agreement for the refined annotation experiment

5.5 Refined Annotation Experiment

In order to mitigate the sources of confusion in the original guidelines, we come-up with event-based guidelines where we clarify for each event whether or not the annotators should draw correlations between different entities. This is needed in order to rely less on each annotator's political leaning and more on the presented set of rules. Additionally, we ask annotators to identify the priority expressed by the comment and change the questions and answer choices as follows:

- Q1: Does the given *comment* discuss Egyptian politics? (Yes/No)
- Q2: Is there enough context to identify the political leaning of the *comment*? (Yes/No)
- Q3: Does the *comment* report the opinion of another person/entity and not the opinion of the author of the comment? (Yes/No/None)
- Q4: Which of the following do you think is the top priority for the comment: (1) Supporting Jan. 25th Revolution; (2) Stability; (3) Supporting Mubarak's Regime; (4) Supporting the Military; (5) Supporting Islamists; (6) Opposing Islamists; (7) Cannot determine the priority; (8) None.
- Q5: What is the *comment*'s stance on Jan. 25th Revolution? (Support/Oppose/None)
- Q6: What is the *comment*'s stance on Mubarak and his regime? (Support/Oppose/None)
- Q7: What is the *comment*'s stance on the Military leaders during the period the *comment* was posted in? (Support/Oppose/None)
- Q8: What is the *comment*'s stance on Islamists? (Support/Oppose/Mixed/None)

We split the comments according to the event they discuss and present the annotators with 10 sub-tasks for each one of the 10 events. Additionally we clarify the following in the refined guidelines:

- When choosing "No" as an answer to Q1 or Q2, choose "None" for Q3-Q8;
- For Q4, choose "Can't determine the priority" when there is more than one priority in the *comment* and you cannot choose between them;
- For Q5-Q8, choose "None" if you cannot determine the leaning of the comment toward the entity in question;
- For all questions if the *comment* expresses an opinion toward Jan. 25th Revolution or Mubarak's regime but not both of them, in most cases you can assume that supporting Jan. 25th Revolution implies opposing Mubarak's regime and vice versa;
- If a *comment* reports a opinion of another person/entity without opposing it, indicate in Q3 that it is a reported opinion then assume for all other questions that the reported opinion expresses the opinion of the author of the *comment*.
- For event 6:
  - Opposing the OGR candidate Ahmed Shafik does not imply supporting the Islamist candidate Mohamed Morsi while supporting Ahmed Shafik implies opposing Mohamed Morsi.
  - Similarly, opposing Mohamed Morsi does not imply supporting Ahmed Shafik while supporting Mohamed Morsi implies opposing Ahmed Shafik.
- For events 9 and 10, if a *comment* expresses an opinion toward the Military or Islamists (not both of them), in most cases you can assume that supporting Islamists implies opposing the Military and vice versa.

	Pro-RFM Pages				Pro-OGR Pages			
	Yes		No		Yes		No	
Q1. Egy Politics	97.7		2.3		97.9		2.1	
Q2. Context	85.9		14.1		87.7		12.3	
	Yes	No	None		Yes	No	None	
Q3. Rep. Opinion	2.3	83.6	14.1		0.4	87.3	12.3	
	Support	Oppose	None		Support	Oppose	None	
Q5. Mubarak	46	3.6	50.4		12.2	44.2	43.6	
Q6. Army	3.6	45.9	50.5		44	12.4	43.6	
Q7. Islamists	23.1	9.7	67.3		25	5.2	69.8	
	Support	Oppose	Mixed	None	Support	Oppose	Mixed	None
Q8. Islamists	29.4	12.9	57.3	0.3	12	37.7	0	50.3

Table 5: Answer distribution (averaged over all annotators) to questions Q1-3 and Q5-Q8 in the refined annotation experiment.

	Pro-RFM	Pro-OGR
Jan. 25th Revolution	33.5	3.3
Support Mubarak	0.6	31.5
Support Stability	9.4	7.8
Support Army	1.1	6.8
Support Islamists	28.5	11.5
Oppose Islamists	11.7	26.5
Can't Tell	1	0.4
None	14.1	12.3

Table 6: Answer distribution (averaged over all annotators) to Q4 (Identify the priority of the comment)

It is worth mentioning that for Q4 except for opposing Islamists, we only address what a comment supports (not opposes). We did an exercise where we annotated 400 comments ourselves and found that for many comments the most central element to the belief systems of the authors is whether or not Islam/religion should be involved in politics. A person who supports RFM might temporarily support OGR if it guarantees ousting Islamists from the political scene and vice versa. Moreover for all other aspects (Jan. 25th Revolution, Mubarak, Army, etc.) one can infer what a person opposes based on what this person supports and the event that is being commented on.

5.6 Results of Refined Annotation

Table 4 shows the IAA for the second annotation experiment. As expected, Q4 has a lower IAA than all other questions. Overall the new task yields a much higher agreement. The complete row agreement (Row) jumps from 25.5% to 76.9% and the average question agreement jumps from 75.7% to 92% comparing the pilot annotations to the refined annotations. Tables 5 and 6 show the distribution to all answers in the second annotation experiment. While the distribution of answers to Q1 almost remained the same, the distribution of Q2 changed. We attribute this to our emphasis on what constitutes enough context in the modified guidelines.

6 Conclusion

In this work we explain our process for collecting and annotating a dataset of social media commentaries discussing Egyptian politics. We propose a taxonomy of major Egyptian Ideological Perspectives, develop annotation guidelines and conduct a pilot experiment to collect annotations that try to uncover the underlying dimensions of the perspective from which a given comment was written. We refine the annotation task and the guidelines based on feedback collected from the annotators. In the refined task, in addition to asking about the comment's position on different ideological aspects such as Jan. 25th Revolution, the Military, Islamists, etc. we ask them to identify the priority expressed by the comment. Additionally to address the challenge of when they should imply a comment's stance on one political entity (ex. the Military) based on its stance toward another entity (ex. Islamists), we develop a set of event-based rules for these associations. IAA between all four annotators for the refined task ranges from 99% to 85.2% for the different questions. We pay close attention to annotator bias. We design the second set of guidelines in such a way to circumvent the role of annotator subjectivity, decoupling the "why" from the "what" in annotation. We plan on further refinement of the proposed guidelines to alleviate the points of confusion among the annotators. Moreover we plan on collecting more annotations from other informal genres testing the robustness of our annotation framework.

Acknowledgments

We would like to acknowledge the feedback of three anonymous reviewers that helped us shape the final version of this paper. We would also like to thank our annotators. Finally this work was funded by a Google Faculty award to the second author.

References

Amjad Abu-Jbara, Mona Diab, Pradeep Dasigi, and Dragomir Radev. 2012. Subgroup detection in ideological discussions. In *Proceedings of the 50th Annual Meeting of the Association for Computational Linguistics*. Association for Computational Linguistics.

Amjad Abu-Jbara, Ben King, Mona T Diab, and Dragomir R Radev. 2013. Identifying opinion subgroups in arabic online discussions. In *ACL (2)*.

Javier Borge-Holthoefer, Walid Magdy, Kareem Darwish, and Ingmar Weber. 2015. Content and network dynamics behind egyptian political polarization on twitter. In *Proceedings of the 18th ACM Conference on Computer Supported Cooperative Work & Social Computing*, pages 700–711. ACM.

Philip E Converse. 2006. The nature of belief systems in mass publics (1964). *Critical Review*, 18(1-3).

Heba Elfardy, Mona Diab, and Chris Callison-Burch. 2015. Ideological perspective detection using semantic features. *Lexical and Computational Semantics (* SEM 2015)*.

Robert M Entman. 1993. Framing: Toward clarification of a fractured paradigm. volume 43. Wiley Online Library.

Stephan Greene and Philip Resnik. 2009. More than words: Syntactic packaging and implicit sentiment. In *Proceedings of human language technologies: The 2009 annual conference of the north american chapter of the association for computational linguistics*, pages 503–511. Association for Computational Linguistics.

Kazi Saidul Hasan and Vincent NG. 2012. Predicting stance in ideological debate with rich linguistic knowledge. In *Proceedings of the 24th International Conference on Computational Linguistics*.

Kazi Saidul Hasan and Vincent Ng. 2013. Extra-linguistic constraints on stance recognition in ideological debates. In *Proceedings of the 51st Annual Meeting of the Association for Computational Linguistics*. Association for Computational Linguistics.

Wei-Hao Lin, Theresa Wilson, Janyce Wiebe, and Alexander Hauptmann. 2006. Which side are you on?: identifying perspectives at the document and sentence levels. In *Proceedings of the Tenth Conference on Computational Natural Language Learning*. Association for Computational Linguistics.

Alexandra Siegel. 2014. Tweeting beyond tahrir: Ideological diversity and political tolerance in egyptian twitter networks.

Swapna Somasundaran and Janyce Wiebe. 2010. Recognizing stances in ideological online debates. In *Proceedings of the NAACL HLT 2010 Workshop on Computational Approaches to Analysis and Generation of Emotion in Text*. Association for Computational Linguistics.

Tae Yano, Philip Resnik, and Noah A Smith. 2010. Shedding (a thousand points of) light on biased language. In *Proceedings of the NAACL HLT 2010 Workshop on Creating Speech and Language Data with Amazon's Mechanical Turk*. Association for Computational Linguistics.

Evaluating Inter-Annotator Agreement on Historical Spelling Normalization

Marcel Bollmann **Stefanie Dipper** **Florian Petran**
Ruhr-Universität Bochum
Department of Linguistics
{bollmann,dipper,petran}@linguistics.rub.de

Abstract

This paper deals with means of evaluating inter-annotator agreement for a normalization task. This task differs from common annotation tasks in two important aspects: (i) the class of labels (the normalized wordforms) is open, and (ii) annotations can match to different degrees. We propose a new method to measure inter-annotator agreement for the normalization task. It integrates common chance-corrected agreement measures, such as Fleiss's κ or Krippendorff's α. The novelty of our proposed method lies in the way the annotated word forms are treated. First, they are evaluated character-wise; second, certain characters are mapped to more general categories.

1 Introduction

In recent years, and in particular in the context of digital humanities, historical language data has been gaining increasing significance. The focus is on providing easy access to the information contained in the data. To this end, historical texts are digitized and processed by OCR or even transcribed manually. Due to the absence of standards, historical data often exhibits large variance, especially with regard to spelling. Hence, further processing either has to rely on fuzzy-matching strategies, or on standardization of the data.

In the Anselm project (Dipper and Schultz-Balluff, 2013), we opted for the second way. We provide normalized wordforms for the full corpus that have been manually annotated according to guidelines specifically created for this task (Krasselt et al., 2015). These normalizations can be useful for search queries, further downstream applications such as POS tagging, or as training data for automatic normalization methods.

This paper deals with means of quantitative evaluation of these normalization guidelines. We would like to quantify the degree of consistency that can be achieved with annotations according to the guidelines, i.e., the inter-annotator agreement (IAA). While a range of measures has been proposed for measuring agreement (e.g., see the survey by Artstein and Poesio (2008)), our task differs from common annotation tasks, such as part-of-speech tagging or semantic role labeling, in two important aspects: (i) the class of labels (the normalized wordforms) is open, and label distribution is sparse; and (ii) annotations are biased to be similar to the surface form of the token they belong to, and can match to different degrees. For example, we would like to score almost identical annotations like *nähme – nehme* 'take' (for the historical form *neme*) higher than annotations that are rather dissimilar, like *drückte* 'pressed' – *trocknete* 'dried' (for *trvckente*).

We investigate why conventional IAA measures are not suitable to the normalization task, and propose a new method that integrates common chance-corrected agreement measures, such as Fleiss's κ (Fleiss, 1971) or Krippendorff's α (Krippendorff, 1980). The novelty of our proposed method lies in the way the annotated wordforms are treated. First, we reframe normalization as a character-based task; and second, we model the inherent properties of normalization by mapping certain characters to more general categories.

We first present the annotation guidelines (Sec. 2) and the dataset that our evaluation is based on (Sec. 3). Sec. 4 discusses the problems that arise from applying common agreement measures to the normalization task. Sec. 5 introduces our new method, followed by an evaluation in Sec. 6, comparing and assessing the results of different ways of measuring agreement.

Proceedings of LAW X – The 10th Linguistic Annotation Workshop, pages 89–98,
Berlin, Germany, August 11, 2016.

2 Annotation of Language Changes

Languages evolve over time. This probably becomes most apparent in sound changes, which modify the way words are pronounced. In the long run, such changes are also reflected in the spelling of these words, cf. the pairs of word forms in (1), which are etymologically related, the ancestor being from Early New High German (ENHG, 1350–1650), the descendant from Modern German (MG).[1]

(1) a. *friund* / Fr**e**und 'friend' [N4]
    b. ***ch**ind* / **K**ind 'child' [M1]

Of course, language evolution concerns all other linguistic levels as well, e.g. (2) shows changes in morpho-syntax (inflection).

(2) *vnser vrow**en*** (acc.sg.) / unser**e** Frau 'our lady' [M1]

Finally, words can change semantically or even get lost. In both cases, there is no direct, i.e. etymologically-related, equivalent in the modern language, see (3).

(3) a. *geitig* (geizig, lit. 'stingy') / gierig 'greedy' [M1]
    b. *vnze* / bis 'until' [St2]

Since ENHG is already quite close to MG, it was decided to standardize ENHG forms to MG forms in the context of the Anselm project.[2] The question was now whether all the changes described above should be submitted to the same standardization procedure. For instance, if a word still exists in MG but with a different meaning (as in (3a)), should the word be replaced by the modern equivalent? What should be done with inflectional endings that have changed? After all, most inflectional differences would not hinder people from using and understanding the data, in contrast to clear semantic changes.

On the other hand, if we compare the effort it takes to automatically generate the forms, it is, of course, easier to generate forms that stay close to the original forms. However, for further use and processing of the data, forms are to be preferred in general that are maximally similar to modern data.

Ex	ENHG	Norm	Mod	Type
(1a)	*friund*	freund		
(1b)	*chind*	kind		
(2)	*vnser*	unser	unsere	INFL
	vrowen	frauen	frau	INFL
(3a)	*geitig*	geizig	gierig	SEM
(3b)	*vnze*	unz	bis	EXT

Table 1: Normalization, modernization and modernization type of the examples (1)–(3) in the text.

ENHG	Norm	Mod	Type
da	da	als	SEM
er	er		
sein	sein	ihn	INFL
zum	zum		
dritten	dritten		
mal	mal		
verlaugnent	verleugnet	verleugnete	INFL
zuhant	zehant	sogleich	EXT
da	da		
kraet	kräht	krähte	INFL
der	der		
han	hahn		

Table 2: Normalization, modernization and modernization type of the sentence 'As he disowned him for the third time, the rooster crowed immediately' [Hk1].

2.1 Annotation guidelines

Rather than opting for one of the two forms, the guidelines designed in the Anselm project serve both camps by providing two levels of standardization, called *normalization* and *modernization*, see Krasselt et al. (2015). Normalization maps a given historical word form to a close modern (lower-cased) word form, considering sound and spelling changes. Modernization goes one step further and adjusts this form to an inflectionally or semantically appropriate modern equivalent, if necessary. In the annotation, modernized forms

[1] In the following examples, ENHG forms are given first, MG forms follow after the slash. The labels [N4], [M1] etc. refer to the text the example comes from, see Sec. 3.

[2] Another option has been traditionally pursued by researchers working on texts from the earlier period of Middle High German (MHG, 1050–1350). They standardized MHG word forms to an artificially-created, "idealized" MHG form, which is supposed to abstract from dialectal variation while keeping the "common" MHG characteristics.

Text	Tokens	Date	Dialect	Norm-Type			Mod-Type		
				ORIG	NORM	BOTH	INFL	SEM	EXT
HK1	8,718	16th cent.	Central Bavarian	42.5	41.5	83.6	6.3	8.1	2.1
M1	10,274	14th cent.	Central Bavarian	41.3	40.8	82.1	8.4	7.4	2.1
N4	8,625	15th cent.	Alemannic + Bavarian	31.4	49.9	81.2	9.8	6.6	2.4
ST2	8,873	14th cent.	Alemannic	32.9	53.1	86.0	4.4	6.8	2.8

Table 3: The texts of the four annotated fragments, with information about their provenance and frequencies (%) of normalization and modernization types.

are marked according to their type: INFL for inflectional modifications, SEM for semantically-determined replacements, and EXT for extinct ENHG word forms.[3]

Table 1 illustrates the two levels of standardization for the examples in (1)–(3), Table 2 shows the annotations for a short fragment of one text. If no morphological and/or semantic adjustment is necessary, the modernization and type levels are not filled.

3 Data

Our data comes from the Anselm corpus[4] (Dipper and Schultz-Balluff, 2013), a collection of texts from Early New High German (1350–1650). For the IAA evaluation, we selected fragments of 1000–1200 tokens of four manuscripts; see Table 3 for more information on these texts. All texts are written in dialects that are part of the language area called Upper German. Two of the texts are written in Central Bavarian but come from different centuries, 14th vs. 16th. The two other texts are from the neighboring region, Alemannic (with one of the texts also showing traits from Bavarian).

Table 3 also shows how many ENHG words are identical to MG words and do not need to be modified at all (column ORIG). The amount of "simple" normalizations, which only require sound and spelling adjustments, is shown in column NORM. The table also includes the frequencies of the different modernization types (columns INFL/SEM/EXT).

The four texts behave quite differently with regard to normalization and modernization. Judging from column ORIG, the two Alemannic texts, N4 and ST2, seem more archaic than the two Bavarian ones, because they have a lower ratio of word forms that already correspond to MG. However, ST2 has a very high ratio of words that can be normalized by adjusting the spelling only (column NORM). In fact, from a grammatical point of view, text ST2 is the most modern one (see column BOTH). The fact that ST2 shows the smallest proportion of INFL-type modernizations also points in this direction.

Of course, these figures do not tell us how difficult it is to normalize the individual texts. Common annotation errors are shown in (4) and (5); the examples first specify the original word form, followed by different normalizations as proposed by the annotators.

(4) Proper nouns

a. *iudas:* iudas, judas 'Judas'
b. *ysmahelite:* ismaeliter, ismaeliten, ismaheliten 'Ismaelis'

(5) Imperatives; subjunctive mood

a. *sag:* sag, sage 'tell'
b. *hoer/hoere:* hör, höre 'listen'
c. *neme:* nähme, nehme 'take'

There are also serious disagreements, resulting in semantically different words even on the normalization layer, as in (6) and (7). Very often, context information helps in disambiguating and, hence, avoiding such cases, so such disagreements are considerably less frequent than the cases above.

(6) Function words

a. *das:* das 'that' (pronoun), dass 'that' (conjunction)
b. *in:* in 'in' (preposition), ihn 'him' (pronoun)

[3]The guidelines define that extinct forms are standardized at the normalization level to forms that are compliant with reference lexicons, e.g. Lexer: `http://woerterbuchnetz.de/Lexer` or Deutsches Wörterbuch by Jacob and Wilhelm Grimm: `http://woerterbuchnetz.de/DWB`. In the Anselm corpus, Lexer was used as the reference lexicon.

[4]`https://www.linguistics.rub.de/comphist/projects/anselm/`

(7) Content words

a. *pin:* bin '(I) am', pein 'torment'
b. *dinen:* deinen 'your', dienen 'serve'
c. *holen:* hohlen 'hollow', höhle 'cave'

For the evaluation, passages in Latin and punctuation marks were removed from the texts, and all words were lower-cased. Five trained student annotators annotated these fragments. These annotations serve as the basis of the evaluation in Sec. 6.

4 Agreement Measures

The simplest way to measure agreement between annotators is "percentage agreement" ($agr_{\%}$), i.e., counting the number of items on which they agree and dividing the result by the total number of items. Percentage agreement has the drawback that it does not account for agreement *by chance.* A high chance agreement can occur, for example, when the annotation scheme only has a low number of distinct labels, or when certain labels occur much more often than others.

Therefore, most measures of agreement try to correct for chance. Two of the most widely-used agreement coefficients for nominal data are Scott's π (Scott, 1955) and Cohen's κ (Cohen, 1960), which both use the formula:

$$\pi, \kappa = \frac{A_o - A_e}{1 - A_e}$$

Here, A_o stands for observed agreement between two annotators, while A_e is the agreement expected by chance. Both coefficients estimate A_e from the distribution of the observed annotations in the evaluation data, the difference being that κ uses the *individual* distributions of each annotator, while π assumes an *identical* distribution for each.

Krippendorff's α (Krippendorff, 1980) is a similar, but more versatile coefficient. Like π, it assumes an identical distribution of labels, but is defined by the observed and expected *disagreement* between annotators:

$$\alpha = 1 - \frac{D_o}{D_e}$$

Despite this difference in definition, α and π are roughly equivalent (Artstein and Poesio, 2008, p. 567). The main advantage of α lies in the fact that it can use arbitrary *distance functions* to measure distance between labels. This allows for a more fine-grained treatment of disagreement than the binary "correct" or "wrong" distinction.

In the context of normalization, a possible distance function is *normalized Levenshtein distance (NLD),* which we define as follows:

$$NLD(a, b) = \frac{LD(a, b)}{\max(|a|, |b|)}$$

Here, $LD(a, b)$ is the Levenshtein distance between *a* and *b*, defined as the number of edits required to change *a* into *b* (Levenshtein, 1966), and $|x|$ is the character length of *x*. By using this function with Krippendorff's α, the disagreement between two annotations *a* and *b* effectively depends on their string similarity, with disagreements being considered less severe the more similar the two strings are.

It is possible to generalize π and κ to more than two annotators. Fleiss's κ (Fleiss, 1971) is a generalization of π, which we will call π^* here to avoid confusion. Krippendorff's α already accounts for multiple annotators.

4.1 Challenges for the Normalization Task

Normalization can be seen as a labelling task with nominal categories, where tokens are the annotation units, and normalized wordforms are the labels. This would allow us to use the aforementioned coefficients for calculating agreement. However, we believe that a naive application of these measures is not useful, and can even be misleading, for this task.

First, the set of all possible labels in the normalization task is the set of all morphologically well-formed words in the target language, of which only a small percentage will actually be seen in the annotated data. Estimating the label distribution from this data is therefore problematic, especially if the dataset is small. When calculating chance agreement, plausible alternative normalizations that do not occur in the training data will be given a probability of zero, which is not a realistic model.

Second, when the labels are words, most of the observed label types will usually be rare. Chance-corrected coefficients such as $\pi/\kappa/\alpha$ give more weight to rare labels than to common ones, which is usually desired (Artstein and Poesio, 2008). In the case of normalization, this seems unsound: we would expect the difficulty of agreeing on a normalization to depend mainly on the spelling characteristics and the closeness of the historical wordform to the modern target language, and not (or at least not exclusively) on its lexical frequency.

Third, using words as labels does not model the inherent property of normalization that most normalized wordforms will be similar, if not identical, to the historical token. When calculating chance agreement, all normalization candidates are considered equally, regardless of their similarity to the historical token. In other words, label probabilities are not conditioned on the items when calculating chance (dis)agreement for $\pi/\kappa/\alpha$. This is true for all annotation tasks, of course; however, for normalization, the large size of the label set exacerbates this problem.

A consequence of these factors is that a naive calculation of agreement will usually overestimate the annotators' performance. Particularly the second and third issue cause the expected chance agreement to be extremely low, while at the same time giving strong weight to almost any item where the annotators agree. The evaluation in Sec. 6 confirms these expectations.

```
g e w a i n -     g e w a i n - -
g e w e i n t     - - w e i n t e
```

Figure 1: Character alignments using the Needleman-Wunsch algorithm

Units	Full		Diff	
	A	B	A	B
g	g	∅	_	∅
e	e	∅	_	∅
w	w	w	_	_
a	e	e	e	e
i	i	i	_	_
n	nt	nte	_t	_te

Table 4: Character-based representation of the token *gewain* being normalized as *geweint* (A) or *weinte* (B), showing either the full normalization (Full) or only the changes (Diff).

5 Normalization as a Character-Based Annotation Task

Motivated by the problems discussed in Sec. 4.1, we explore the option of reframing the normalization task in the following way:

1. consider characters as the units for annotation instead of words; and
2. introduce an "identity" label for all normalizations where the character was not changed.

We will first describe how the mapping of annotations to characters is performed before discussing how this reframed task relates to the issues raised in Sec. 4.1.

5.1 Mapping Normalizations to Characters

Instead of considering words as our annotation units, we choose to view each character in the historical wordform as a unit of annotation. This raises the question of how to map word-level normalizations to individual characters, particularly if the historical and modernized wordforms are of different lengths.

Since normalizations derive from their original wordform by making adjustments to its spelling where necessary, and leaving other parts unchanged, this should be reflected in the character-based normalization by having identical characters line up if possible. We can achieve this by using the Needleman-Wunsch algorithm for sequence alignment (Needleman and Wunsch, 1970),[5] which favors aligning identical matches over any modifications or "gaps" in the sequences.

Figure 1 shows an example of the Needleman-Wunsch algorithm being used to align the historical wordform *gewain* to its potential normalizations *geweint* and *weinte* 'cried'. While this alignment has the desired property of lining up identical characters, we cannot use it directly because it introduces "gaps" in the historical wordform where characters are inserted—the annotation units should be fixed, though, regardless of the value of the normalization. We resolve this issue by merging insertions with the nearest non-insertion character to the left, with the (rare) exception of word-initial insertions, which are merged to the right. Table 4, column "Full" shows how our units and annotations look like after this process.

Finally, we introduce an identity label to represent matching characters. We do this before

[5]We use the Python implementation from the LingPy library (List and Forkel, 2016).

	Tokens	Word-based			Character-based		
		$agr_{\%}$	π^*	α_{NLD}	$agr_{\%}$	π^*	α_{NLD}
ALL	4558	0.9262	0.9254	0.9736	0.9698	0.9155	0.9184
MEDIUM	2858	0.8822	0.8804	0.9579	0.9551	0.9102	0.9138
STRICT	2673	0.9126	0.9112	0.9691	0.9653	0.9327	0.9355

Table 5: Inter-annotator agreement on normalization across five annotators; ALL = all tokens, MEDIUM = at least one annotator made a change to the original token, STRICT = all annotators made a change to the original token.

the merging step by replacing all identity alignments in the Needleman-Wunsch alignment with the identity label. The result can be seen in table 4, column "Diff". Note how this representation specifically highlights the *changes* made to the original token.

5.2 Advantages of the Character-Based Representation

Using character-based representations with identity labels does not completely solve the problems described in Sec. 4.1, but alleviates them significantly.

Instead of words, our label set now contains all possible character n-grams. While this is still a potentially unbounded set, the vast majority of labels are single characters only. This means that the effective size of our label set has been greatly reduced, allowing for a better estimation of the label distribution and reducing the "rare label" problem.

Introducing the identity label models the assumption that leaving characters unchanged is the "default" action. Under this assumption, the identity label will now be the most common label by far, and all other labels (representing modifications) will be comparatively rare. Since the agreement coefficients give more weight to rare labels, this means that agreement on actual modifications is now considered to be much more important than agreement on characters that do not change, which is exactly what we want.

Note that simply using the character-based representation *without* identity labels will overestimate the annotators' performance even more, since it greatly increases the number of units where the annotators agree. On the other hand, using identity labels directly on a word level does nothing to alleviate the issue of a potentially infinite label set.

6 Evaluation

We first compare agreement scores of the naive word-based evaluation with those obtained using the character-based representation of the task. For both scenarios, we calculate average percentage agreement ($agr_{\%}$) and Krippendorff's α using the NLD distance function defined in Sec. 4. We find that values for π and κ, either naively averaged over all annotator pairs or using the generalization of π^*, almost always differ only after the fifth or sixth decimal place; we therefore restrict ourselves to reporting π^*.

We evaluate separately on all tokens (ALL), tokens where at least one annotator made a modification to the historical token (MEDIUM), and tokens where *all* five annotators made a modification (STRICT).

Table 5 shows the agreement scores for this evaluation. The average word-based agreement over all tokens is 92.62%, and π^* values for the word-based task are always similar to the percentage agreement. Values for α_{NLD} are naturally higher, since it also considers partial agreement within the normalizations. For the character-based task, percentage agreement is always much higher, but π^* values are now noticeably lower compared to the percentage values. This is a consequence of the character-based reframing of the task being much more sensitive to agreement on the actual modifications (cf. Sec. 5.2).

Comparing the different evaluation sets, percentage agreement on the STRICT set is noticeably higher than on the MEDIUM set. This is particularly remarkable since the MEDIUM set only has 185 tokens more. Therefore, cases where annotators disagree whether a change to the historical wordform is even needed appear to be particularly problematic. On the other hand, if all annotators agree that a change needs to be made, they seem to reliably produce similar normalizations.

	Tokens	Word-based			Character-based		
		$agr_{\%}$	π^*	α_{NLD}	$agr_{\%}$	π^*	α_{NLD}
HK1	1157	0.9255	0.9247	0.9741	0.9701	*0.8957*	*0.9017*
M1	999	0.9252	0.9244	*0.9701*	0.9696	**0.9287**	**0.9322**
N4	1195	**0.9316**	**0.9306**	**0.9757**	**0.9712**	0.9239	0.9265
ST2	1207	*0.9221*	*0.9213*	0.9738	*0.9683*	0.9174	0.9186

Table 6: Inter-annotator agreement on normalization, separately for each text; highest score for each measure shown in **bold**, lowest score shown in *italics*.

This is supported even further by the fact that the STRICT set has the highest π^*/α_{NLD} scores in the character-based evaluation.

It is also interesting to compare the agreement by chance (A_e) between the two approaches. For π^*, the naive word-based evaluation has an expected agreement of $A_e^{\pi^*} = 0.0103$, which is not surprising considering that the pool of possible annotations is the set of all observed wordforms. For the character-based task, the majority of annotations are the identity label, which results in a high chance agreement of $A_e^{\pi^*} = 0.6312$. A better agreement between the annotators is therefore required to obtain a good π^* value.

For these reasons, we believe that the high agreement values of $\pi^* \geq 0.91$ on the character-based task provide stronger evidence for a good inter-annotator agreement on our dataset than the naive word-based evaluation does.

6.1 Per-Text Evaluation

Our evaluation dataset consists of passages from four different texts that exhibit different spelling characteristics (cf. Sec. 3). Since it is conceivable that this affects the difficulty of the normalization task, we also choose to evaluate on each text excerpt separately.

The results are shown in Table 6. Generally, there are only minor differences between the texts: for the word-based evaluation, N4 consistently shows the highest agreement, while ST2 usually has the lowest values (except for α_{NLD}, where M1 ranks worse). The same is true for $agr_{\%}$ on the character-based task. However, the agreement coefficients for the character-based task show very different trends: here, M1 gets the highest scores, while the values for HK1 are lowest by a noticeably margin.

This evaluation shows that our character-based evaluation is also useful for providing a different perspective on the annotated data than word-based agreement.

	Tokens	$agr_{\%}$	π^*
ALL	4558	0.8857	0.8171
MEDIUM	1230	0.5907	0.4681
STRICT	329	0.8839	0.8081

Table 7: Inter-annotator agreement on type of modernization; ALL = all tokens, MEDIUM = at least one annotator chose a modernization category (INFL/SEM/EXT), STRICT = all annotators chose a modernization category.

6.2 Type of Modernization

So far, the evaluation has focused on normalization alone. However, as described in Sec. 2, the annotation guidelines also include an additional modernization layer, which accounts for changes to the historical wordforms that go beyond spelling modifications.

Whenever annotators assign a modernization, they also need to select which type of adjustment they have performed. This allows us to evaluate agreement on the "type of modernization" they have chosen; we extend the three modernization types from our guidelines with two types for cases where no modernization has been performed, leaving us with these five categories: ORIG = no change from the original token; NORM = normalization, but no modernization; INFL = inflectional adjustment; SEM = semantic adjustment in the modernization; EXT = adjustment due to extinct wordform.

Table 7 shows that we achieve a reasonable agreement of $\pi^* = 0.8171$ on the assignment of these categories. However, restricting the eval-

	ORIG	NORM	INFL	SEM	EXT
ORIG	1452	11	20	36	1
NORM	–	2125	68	60	29
INFL	–	–	233	11	4
SEM	–	–	–	154	15
EXT	–	–	–	–	71

Table 8: Confusion matrix of annotator judgments between modernization types, averaged across all annotator pairs

	Tokens	$agr_{\%}$	π^*	α_{NLD}
ORIG	1357	1.0000	–	–
NORM	1930	0.9932	0.9870	0.9878
INFL	148	0.9715	0.9559	0.9606
SEM	63	0.8650	0.8453	0.8535
EXT	37	0.7694	0.7188	0.7227

Table 9: Inter-annotator agreement on modernization, using character-based evaluation, separately for tokens where all annotators agree on the type of modernization.

uation to tokens where at least one annotator chose one of the actual modernization categories (INFL/SEM/EXT; row MEDIUM in Table 7) results in a very low score of 0.4681. A further restriction to tokens where *all* annotators chose one of these categories results in a much better score again, however, this was only the case for 329 tokens. These results show that our annotators disagree strongly on when to actually assign a modernized wordform at all; in the few cases where they all agree that a modernization has to be assigned, the agreement on the type of modernization is reasonably good.

To further illustrate this point, Table 8 shows a confusion matrix on modernization types. For each of INFL/SEM/EXT, the second most often selected category by another annotator was NORM, i.e., a normalization where no additional modernization was performed. However, disagreement within these categories of INFL/SEM/EXT occurs only rarely, confirming the interpretation of the values in Table 7. Also, confusion with the ORIG category is also comparatively rare, showing that wordforms which do not need to be changed are much less problematic.

6.3 Character-Based Evaluation of Modernization

Due to the nature of the modernization layer, a character-based evaluation of the wordforms is problematic, since modernized forms usually do not need to bear any resemblance to the historical token. An exception are modernized forms that have been assigned due to inflectional changes (INFL), which we would assume to be similar to the respective historical and normalized forms.

To test this assumption, we evaluate character-based agreement on the modernization layer for tokens where all annotators agree on a modernization type (Table 9). For ORIG and NORM, we assume the modernized wordform to be identical to the normalization. The results confirm our expectations: π^* on INFL is 0.9559, while it drops considerably for SEM and EXT; however, the significance of these results might be limited due to the low sample size for these cases.

Another notable result is the extremely high agreement ($\pi^* = 0.9870$) for tokens where all annotators agree on type NORM. This tells us that most of the disagreements from the normalization evaluation (cf. Table 5) stem from cases where at least one annotator decided that a modernization was necessary; these tokens therefore appear to be more difficult to agree on not only on the modernization layer, but already on the normalization layer.

While it is plausible that extinct wordforms, as well as words with different meaning or inflection than in modern language, are inherently more difficult to annotate, the intention of the guidelines was to move this difficulty to the modernization layer, while having unambiguous rules for the annotation of the normalization layer. These results show that while we achieve a good reliability overall, the guidelines were not able to remove this difficulty completely for these cases.

7 Discussion

In this paper, we presented and evaluated a method to measure inter-annotator agreement on normalization of historical data. We argue that our character-based evaluation approach is more appropriate for this task from a theoretical perspective, and showed that it behaves differently than a naive word-based measure.

We have found that the scores resulting from our method correspond well to our intuitive judgments. As a direction for future research, it would be useful to conduct a systematic evaluation of this notion. For that purpose, human annotators would rate normalizations for agreement, and the level of correspondence would be revealed by how well the metrics can reproduce the rankings of the human annotators. However, the rating of normalizations is not in itself a trivial task. It would also have to be based on entire texts rather than isolated pairs of normalizations, since expected agreement cannot be calculated for isolated pairs and, hence, a comparison with our scores would not easily be possible. For these reasons, we did not conduct such a study for this paper.

Our proposed method is certainly not the only way to accomodate the specific properties of the normalization task. Instead of viewing the task on a character level, normalizations could also be seen as sets of edit operations on a word. This can easily be derived from the Needleman-Wunsch alignment that we already use (cf. Fig. 1): instead of the normalization *geweint*, we could define the annotation of the token *gewain* to be a set of edit operations $\{4\colon a \rightarrow e, 6\colon n \rightarrow nt\}$, and use a set-based agreement measure on it—see, e.g., Passonneau (2004) for a set-based measure applied to coreference annotation. However, this approach is also not free of problems: in the annotated set, the position of edit operations is important, but for purposes of calculating chance agreement, positional information should not be included. While we believe this difficulty can probably be resolved, we did not explore this option further.

We are aware of only one approach that reports agreement figures on the task of normalizing historical data, Scheible et al. (2011), who deal with data from Early Modern German (1650–1800) and report word-based percentage agreement of 96.9%. As we have argued, word-based evaluation alone cannot adequately assess performance of the annotators because partial agreement is not considered, and also this measure does not try to correct for chance.

Normalization is also sometimes performed on other types of data, such as dialectal or social media texts. Our method of evaluating IAA can be generalized to these datasets as long as it is possible to frame them as a character-based annotation task, i.e., the annotation values should be derived from (and typically be similar to) the surface forms of their respective tokens. The same considerations apply when transferring this approach to other open-class annotations, e.g. lemmatization.

Acknowledgments

We would like to thank Julia Krasselt and all of our student annotators for their help in creating the evaluation dataset. The research reported here was supported by Deutsche Forschungsgemeinschaft (DFG), Grant DI 1558/4.

References

Ron Artstein and Massimo Poesio. 2008. Inter-coder agreement for computational linguistics. *Computational Linguistics*, 34(4):555–596.

Jacob Cohen. 1960. A coefficient of agreement for nominal scales. *Educational and Psychological Measurement*, 20(1):37–46.

Stefanie Dipper and Simone Schultz-Balluff. 2013. The Anselm corpus: Methods and perspectives of a parallel aligned corpus. In *Proceedings of the NODALIDA Workshop on Computational Historical Linguistics*, Oslo, Norway.

Joseph L. Fleiss. 1971. Measuring nominal scale agreement among many raters. *Psychological Bulletin*, 76(5):378–382.

Julia Krasselt, Marcel Bollmann, Stefanie Dipper, and Florian Petran. 2015. Guidelines for normalizing historical German texts. *Bochumer Linguistische Arbeitsberichte*, 15.

Klaus Krippendorff. 1980. *Content Analysis: An Introduction to Its Methodology*. SAGE, Beverly Hills, CA.

Vladimir I. Levenshtein. 1966. Binary codes capable of correcting deletions, insertions, and reversals. *Soviet Physics Doklady*, 10(8):707–710.

Johann-Mattis List and Robert Forkel. 2016. LingPy. A Python library for historical linguistics. Version 2.4. `http://lingpy.org`. With collaborations by Steven Moran, Peter Bouda, Johannes Dellert, Taraka Rama, Frank Nagel, and Simon Greenhill: Max Planck Institute for the Science of Human History.

Saul B. Needleman and Christian D. Wunsch. 1970. A gene method applicable to the search for similarities in the amino acid sequence of two proteins. *Journal of Molecular Biology*, 48:443–453.

Rebecca J. Passonneau. 2004. Computing reliability for coreference annotation. In *Proceedings of the 4th International Conference on Language Resources and Evaluation (LREC)*, volume 4, pages 1503–1506, Lisbon, Portugal.

Silke Scheible, Richard J. Whitt, Martin Durrell, and Paul Bennett. 2011. A gold standard corpus of Early Modern German. In *Proceedings of the ACL-HLT 2011 Linguistic Annotation Workshop (LAW V)*, pages 124–128, Portland, Oregon, USA.

William A. Scott. 1955. Reliability of content analysis: The case of nominal scale coding. *Public Opinion Quarterly*, 19(3):321–325.

A Corpus of Preposition Supersenses

Nathan Schneider
University of Edinburgh / Georgetown University
nschneid@inf.ed.ac.uk

Jena D. Hwang
IHMC
jhwang@ihmc.us

Vivek Srikumar
University of Utah
svivek@cs.utah.edu

Meredith Green **Abhijit Suresh** **Kathryn Conger** **Tim O'Gorman** **Martha Palmer**
University of Colorado at Boulder
{laura.green,abhijit.suresh,kathryn.conger,timothy.ogorman,martha.palmer}@colorado.edu

Abstract

We present the first corpus annotated with **preposition supersenses**, unlexicalized categories for semantic functions that can be marked by English prepositions (Schneider et al., 2015). The preposition supersenses are organized hierarchically and designed to facilitate comprehensive manual annotation. Our dataset is publicly released on the web.[1]

1 Introduction

English prepositions exhibit stunning frequency and wicked polysemy. In the 450M-word COCA corpus (Davies, 2010), 11 prepositions are more frequent than the most frequent noun.[2] In the corpus presented in this paper, prepositions account for 8.5% of tokens (the top 11 prepositions comprise >6% of all tokens). Far from being vacuous grammatical formalities, prepositions serve as essential linkers of meaning, and the few extremely frequent ones are exploited for many different functions (figure 1). For all their importance, however, prepositions have received relatively little attention in computational semantics, and the community has not yet arrived at a comprehensive and reliable scheme for annotating the semantics of prepositions in context (§2). We believe that such annotation of preposition functions is needed if preposition sense disambiguation systems are to be useful for downstream tasks—e.g., translation[3] or semantic parsing (cf. Dahlmeier et al., 2009; Srikumar and Roth, 2011).

This paper describes a new corpus, fully annotated with **preposition supersenses** (hierarchically

(1) I have been going **to**/DESTINATION the Wildwood_,_NJ **for**/DURATION over 30 years **for**/PURPOSE summer~vacations

(2) It is close **to**/LOCATION bus_lines **for**/DESTINATION Opera_Plaza

(3) I was looking~**to**/`i bring a customer **to**/DESTINATION their lot **to**/PURPOSE buy a car

Figure 1: Preposition supersenses illustrating the polysemy of **to** and **for**. Both can mark a DESTINATION or PURPOSE, while there are other functions that do not overlap. The syntactic complement use of infinitival **to** is tagged as `i. The **over** token in (1) receives the label APPROXIMATOR. See §3.1 for details.

organized unlexicalized classes primarily reflecting thematic roles; Schneider et al., 2015). Whereas fine-grained sense annotation for individual prepositions is difficult and limited by the coverage and quality of a lexicon, preposition supersense annotation offers a practical alternative (§2). We comprehensively annotate English preposition tokens in a corpus of web reviews (§3). It is the first English corpus with semantic annotations of prepositions that are both *comprehensive* (describing all preposition types and tokens) and *double-annotated* (to attenuate subjectivity in the annotation scheme and measure inter-annotator agreement). The corpus gives us an empirical distribution of preposition supersenses, and the annotation process has helped us improve upon the supersense hierarchy. Additionally, we examine the correspondences between our annotations and role labels from PropBank (§4). For some labels, clean correspondences between the two independent annotations speak to the validity of our hierarchy and annotation, but this analysis also reveals mismatches deserving of further examination. The corpus is publicly released (footnote 1).

2 Background and Motivation

Theoretical linguists have puzzled over questions such as how individual prepositions can acquire such a broad range of meanings and to what extent those meanings are systematically related (e.g.,

[1] STREUSLE 3.0, available at http://www.cs.cmu.edu/~ark/LexSem/

[2] http://www.wordfrequency.info/free.asp?s=y

[3] This work focuses on English, but adposition and case systems vary considerably across languages, challenging second language learners and machine translation systems (Chodorow et al., 2007; Shilon et al., 2012; Hashemi and Hwa, 2014).

Proceedings of LAW X – The 10th Linguistic Annotation Workshop, pages 99–109,
Berlin, Germany, August 11, 2016.

Brugman, 1981; Lakoff, 1987; Tyler and Evans, 2003; O'Dowd, 1998; Saint-Dizier and Ide, 2006; Lindstromberg, 2010). Prepositional polysemy has also been recognized as a challenge for AI (Herskovits, 1986) and natural language processing, motivating semantic disambiguation systems (O'Hara and Wiebe, 2003; Ye and Baldwin, 2007; Hovy et al., 2010; Srikumar and Roth, 2013b). Training and evaluating these requires semantically annotated corpus data. Below, we comment briefly on existing resources and why (in our view) a new resource is needed to "road-test" an alternative, hopefully more scalable, semantic representation for prepositions.

2.1 Existing Preposition Corpora

Beginning with the seminal resources from The Preposition Project (TPP; Litkowski and Hargraves, 2005), the computational study of preposition semantics has been fundamentally grounded in corpus-based lexicography centered around individual preposition types. Most previous datasets of English preposition semantics at the token level (Litkowski and Hargraves, 2005, 2007; Dahlmeier et al., 2009; Tratz and Hovy, 2009; Srikumar and Roth, 2013a) only cover high-frequency prepositions (the 34 represented in the SemEval-2007 shared task based on TPP, or a subset thereof).[4]

We sought a scheme that would facilitate *comprehensive* semantic annotation of all preposition tokens in a corpus, covering the full range of usages possible for all English preposition types. The recent TPP PDEP corpus (Litkowski, 2014, 2015) comes closer to this goal, as it consists of randomly sampled tokens for over 300 types. However, since sentences were sampled separately for each preposition, there is only one annotated preposition token per sentence. By contrast, we will fully annotate documents for all preposition tokens. No inter-annotator agreement figures have been reported for the PDEP data to indicate its quality, or the overall difficulty of token annotation with TPP senses across a broad range of prepositions.

2.2 Supersenses

From the literature on other kinds of supersenses, there is reason to believe that token annotation with **preposition supersenses** (Schneider et al., 2015) will be more scalable and useful than senses. The term **supersense** has been applied to lexical semantic classes that label a large number of word types (i.e., they are unlexicalized). The best-known supersense scheme draws on two inventories—one for nouns and one for verbs—which originated as a high-level partitioning of senses in WordNet (Miller et al., 1990). A scheme for adjectives has been proposed as well (Tsvetkov et al., 2014).

One argument advanced in favor of supersenses is that they provide a coarse level of generalization for essential contextual distinctions—such as artifact vs. person for *chair*, or temporal vs. locative **in**—without being so fine-grained that systems cannot learn them (Ciaramita and Altun, 2006). A similar argument applies for *human* learning as pertains to rapid, cost-effective, and open-vocabulary annotation of corpora: an inventory of dozens of categories (with mnemonic names) can be learned and applied to unlimited vocabulary without having to refer to dictionary definitions (Schneider et al., 2012). Like with WordNet for nouns and verbs, the same argument holds for prepositions: TPP-style sense annotation requires familiarity with a different set of (often highly nuanced) distinctions for each preposition type. For example, **in** has 15 different TPP senses, among them **in 10(7a)** 'indicating the key in which a piece of music is written: *Mozart's Piano Concerto in E flat*'.

Supersenses have been exploited for a variety of tasks (e.g., Agirre et al., 2008; Tsvetkov et al., 2013, 2015), and full-sentence noun and verb taggers have been built for several languages (Segond et al., 1997; Johannsen et al., 2014; Picca et al., 2008; Martínez Alonso et al., 2015; Schneider et al., 2013, 2016). They are typically implemented as sequence taggers. In the present work, we extend a corpus that has already been hand-annotated with noun and verb supersenses, thus raising the possibility of systems that can learn all three kinds of supersenses jointly (cf. Srikumar and Roth, 2011).

Though they go by other names, the TPP "classes" (Litkowski, 2015),[5] the "clusters" of Tratz and Hovy (2011), and the "relations" of Srikumar and Roth (2013a) similarly label coarse-grained semantic functions of English prepositions; notably, they group senses from a lexicon rather than directly annotating tokens, and restrict each sense

[4] A further limitation of the SemEval-2007 dataset is the way in which it was sampled: illustrative tokens from a corpus were manually selected by a lexicographer. As Litkowski (2014) showed, a disambiguation system trained on this dataset will therefore be biased and perform poorly on an ecologically valid sample of tokens.

[5] `http://www.clres.com/db/classes/ClassAnalysis.php`

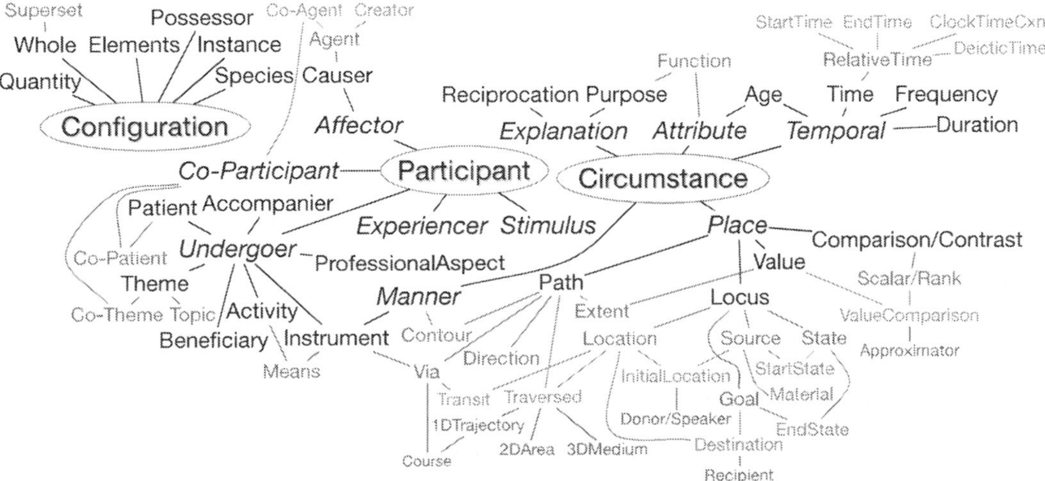

Figure 2: Supersense hierarchy used in this work (adapted from Schneider et al., 2015). Circled nodes are roots (the most abstract categories); subcategories are shown above and below. Each node's color and formatting reflect its depth.

to (at most) 1 grouping. Schneider et al. (2015) used the Srikumar and Roth (2013a) "relation" categories as a starting point in creating the preposition supersense inventory, but removed the assumption that each TPP sense could only belong to 1 category. Müller et al.'s (2012) semantic class inventory targets German prepositions.

2.3 PrepWiki

Schneider et al.'s (2015) preposition supersense scheme is described in detail in a lexical resource, PrepWiki,[6] which records associations between supersenses and preposition types. Hereafter, we adopt the term **usage** for a pairing of a preposition type and a supersense label (e.g., **at**/Time). Usages are organized in PrepWiki via (lexicalized) **senses** from the TPP lexicon. The mapping is many-to-many, as senses and supersenses capture different generalizations. (TPP senses, being lexicalized, are more numerous and generally finer-grained, but in some cases lump together functions that receive different supersenses, as in the sense **for 2(2)** 'affecting, with regard to, or in respect of'.) Thus, for a given preposition, a sense may be mapped to multiple usages, and vice versa.

2.4 The Supersense Hierarchy

Unlike the noun, verb, and adjective supersense schemes mentioned in §2.2, the preposition supersense inventory is hierarchical (as are Litkowski's (2015) and Müller et al.'s (2012) inventories). The hierarchy, depicted in figure 2, encodes inheritance: characteristics of higher-level categories are asserted to apply to their descendants. Multiple inheritance is used for cases of overlap: e.g., Destination inherits from both Location (because a destination is a point in physical space) and Goal (it is the endpoint of a concrete or abstract path).

The structure of the hierarchy was modeled after VerbNet's hierarchy of thematic roles (Bonial et al., 2011; Hwang, 2014). But there are many additional categories: some are refinements of the VerbNet roles (e.g., subclasses of Time), while others have no VerbNet counterpart because they do not pertain to core roles of verbs. The Configuration subhierarchy, used for **of** and other prepositions when they relate two nominals, is a good example.

The hierarchical structure will be useful for comparing against other annotation schemes which operate at different levels of granularity, as we do in §4 below. We expect that it will also help supervised classifiers to learn better generalizations when faced with sparse training data.

3 Corpus Annotation

3.1 Annotating Preposition Supersenses

Source data. We fully annotated the Reviews section of the English Web Treebank (Bies et al., 2012), chosen because it had previously been annotated for multiword expressions, noun and verb supersenses (Schneider et al., 2014; Schneider and Smith, 2015), and PropBank predicate-argument structures (§4). The corpus comprises 55,579 tokens organized into 3,812 sentences and 723 documents with gold tokenization and PTB-style POS

[6] `http://tiny.cc/prepwiki`

tags.

Identifying preposition tokens. TPP, and therefore PrepWiki, contains senses for canonical prepositions, i.e., those used transitively in the [$_{PP}$ P NP] construction. Taking inspiration from Pullum and Huddleston (2002), PrepWiki further assigns supersenses to spatiotemporal particle uses of **out**, **up**, **away**, **together**, etc., and subordinating uses of **as**, **after**, **in**, **with**, etc. (including infinitival **to** and infinitival-subject **for**, as in *It took over 1.5 hours **for** our food **to** come out*).[7]

Non-supersense labels. These are used where the preposition serves a special syntactic function not captured by the supersense inventory. The most frequent is `i, which applies only to infinitival **to** tokens that are not PURPOSE or FUNCTION adjuncts.[8] The label `d applies to discourse expressions like ***On** the other hand*; the unqualified backtick (`) applies to miscellaneous cases such as infinitival-subject **for** and both prepositions in the **as**-**as** comparative construction (***as** wet **as** water*; ***as** much cake **as** you want*).[9]

Multiword expressions. Figure 3 shows how prepositions can interact with multiword expressions (MWEs). An MWE may function holistically as a preposition: PrepWiki treats these as multiword prepositions. An idiomatic phrase may be headed by a preposition, in which case we assign it a preposition supersense or tag it as a discourse expression (`d: see the previous paragraph). Finally, a preposition may be embedded within an MWE (but not its head): we do not use a preposition supersense in this case, though the MWE as a whole may already be tagged with a verb supersense.

Heuristics. The annotation tool uses heuristics to detect candidate preposition tokens in each sentence given its POS tagging and MWE annotation. A *single-word expression* is included if: (a) it is tagged as a verb particle (RP) or infinitival **to** (TO), or, (b) it is tagged as a transitive preposition or subordinator (IN) or adverb (RB), and it is listed in PrepWiki (or the spelling variants list). A strong *MWE* instance is included if: (a) the MWE begins with a word that matches the single-word criteria (idiomatic PP), or, (b) the MWE is listed in PrepWiki (multiword preposition).

(4) [**Because_of**/EXPLANATION] the ants I dropped them **to**/ENDSTATE a 3_star .

(5) I was told **to**/`i take my coffee [**to**_go/MANNER] if I wanted **to**/`i finish it .

(6) **With**/ATTRIBUTE higher **than**/SCALAR/RANK average prices [**to**_boot/`d] !

(7) I worked~**with**/PROFESSIONALASPECT Sam_Mones who [took_ great _care_**of**] me .

Figure 3: Prepositions involved in multiword expressions. (4) Multiword preposition **because of** (others include **in front of**, **due to**, **apart from**, and **other than**). (5) PP idiom: the preposition supersense applies to the MWE as a whole. (6) Discourse PP idiom: instead of a supersense, expressions serving a discourse function are tagged as `d. (7) Preposition within a multiword expression: the expression is headed by a verb, so it receives a verb supersense (not shown) rather than a preposition supersense.

Annotation task. Annotators proceeded sentence by sentence, working in a custom web interface (figure 4). For each token matched by the above heuristics, annotators filled in a text box with the contextually appropriate label. A dropdown menu showed the list of preposition supersenses and non-supersense labels, starting with labels known to be associated with the preposition being annotated. Hovering over a menu item would show example sentences to illustrate the usage in question, as well as a brief definition of the supersense. This preposition-specific rendering of the dropdown menu—supported by data from PrepWiki—was crucial to reducing the overhead of annotation (and annotator training) by focusing the annotator's attention on the relevant categories/usages. New examples were added to PrepWiki as annotators spotted coverage gaps. The tool also showed the multiword expression annotation of the sentence, which could be modified if necessary to fit PrepWiki's conventions for multiword prepositions.

3.2 Quality Control

Annotators. Annotators were selected from undergraduate and graduate linguistics students at the University of Colorado at Boulder. All annotators had prior experience with semantic role labeling. Every sentence was independently annotated by two annotators, and disagreements were subse-

[7]PrepWiki does not include subordinators/ complementizers that cannot take NP complements: *that*, *because*, *while*, *if*, etc.

[8]Because the word **to** is ambiguous between infinitival and prepositional usages, and because infinitivals, like PPs, can serve as PURPOSE or FUNCTION modifiers, we allow infinitival **to** to be so marked. E.g., *a shoulder **to** cry on* would qualify as FUNCTION. By contrast, *I want/love/try **to** eat cookies* and ***To** love is **to** suffer* would qualify as `i. See figure 1 for examples from the corpus.

[9]Annotators used additional non-supersense labels to mark tokens that were incorrectly flagged as prepositions by our heuristics: e.g., *price was way <u>to</u> high* was marked as an adverb. We ignore these tokens for purposes of this paper.

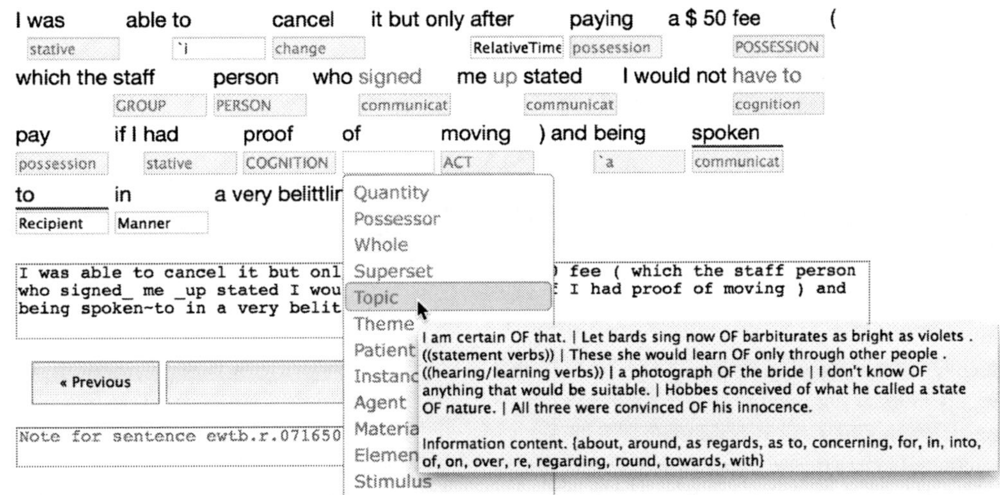

Figure 4: Supersense annotation interface, developed in-house. The main thing to note is that preposition, noun, and verb supersenses are stored in text boxes below the sentence. A dropdown menu displays the full list of preposition supersenses, starting with those with PrepWiki mappings to the preposition in question. Hovering the mouse over a menu item displays a tooltip with PrepWiki examples of the usage (if applicable) and a general definition of the supersense.

quently adjudicated by a third, "expert" annotator. There were two expert annotators, both authors of this paper.

Training. 200 sentences were set aside for training annotators. Annotators were first shown how to use the preposition annotation tool and instructed on the supersense distinctions for this task. Annotators then completed a training set of 100 sentences. An adjudicator evaluated the annotator's annotations, providing feedback and assigning another 50–100 training instances if necessary.

Inter-annotator agreement (IAA) measures are useful in quantifying annotation "reliability", i.e., indicating how trustworthy and reproducible the process is (given guidelines, training, tools, etc.). Specifically, IAA scores can be used as a diagnostic for the reliability of (i) individual annotators (to identify those who need additional training/guidance); (ii) the annotation scheme and guidelines (to identify problematic phenomena requiring further documentation or changes to the scheme); (iii) the final dataset (as an indicator of what could reasonably be expected of an automatic system).

Individual annotators. The main annotation was divided into 34 batches of 100 sentences. Each batch took on the order of an hour for an annotator to complete. We monitored original annotators' IAA throughout the annotation process as a diagnostic for when to intervene in giving further guidance. Original IAA for most of these batches fell between 60% and 78%, depending on factors such as the identities of the annotators and when the annotation took place (annotator experience and PrepWiki documentation improved over time).[10] These rates show that it was not an easy annotation task, though many of the disagreements were over slight distinctions in the hierarchy (such as PURPOSE vs. FUNCTION).

Guidelines. Though Schneider et al. (2015) conducted pilot annotation in constructing the supersense inventory, our annotators found a few details of the scheme to be confusing. Informed by their difficulties and disagreements, we therefore made several minor improvements to the preposition supersense categories and hierarchy structure. For example, the supersense categories for partitive constructions proved persistently problematic, so we adjusted their boundaries and names. We also improved the high-level organization of the original hierarchy, clarified some supersense descriptions, and removed the miscellaneous OTHER supersense.

Revisions. The changes to categories/guidelines noted in the previous paragraph required a small-scale post hoc revision to the annotations by the expert annotators. Some additional post hoc revisions were performed to improve consistency, e.g., some anomalous multiword expression annotations

[10] The agreement rate among tokens where both annotators assigned a preposition supersense was between 82% and 87% for 4 batches; 72% and 78% for 11 batches; 60% and 70% for 17 batches; and below 60% for 2 batches. This measure did not award credit for agreement on non-supersense labels and ignored some cases of disagreement on the MWE analysis.

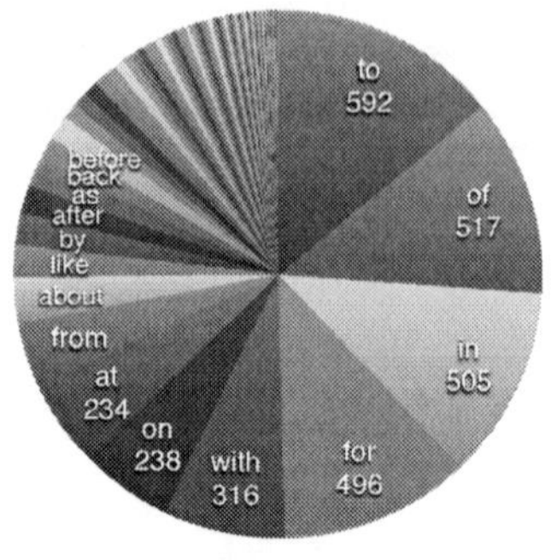

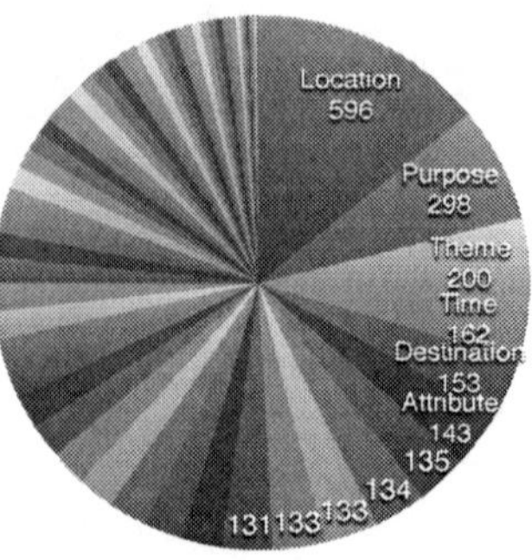

Figure 5: Distributions of preposition types and supersenses for the 4,250 supersense-tagged preposition tokens in the corpus. Observe that just 9 prepositions account for 75% of tokens, whereas the head of the supersense distribution is much smaller.

involving prepositions were fixed.[11]

Expert IAA. We also measured IAA on a sample independently annotated from scratch by both experts.[12] Applying this procedure to 203 sentences annotated late in the process (using the measure described in footnote 10) gives an agreement rate of 276/313 = 88%.[13] Because every sentence in the rest of the corpus was adjudicated by one of these two experts, the expert IAA is a rough estimate of the dataset's adjudication reliability—i.e., the expected proportion of tokens that would have been labeled the same way if adjudicated by the other expert. While it is difficult to put an exact quality figure on a dataset that was developed over a period of time and with the involvement of many individuals, the fact that the expert-to-expert agreement approaches 90% despite the large number of labels suggests that the data can serve as a reliable resource for training and benchmarking disambiguation systems.

3.3 Resulting Corpus

4,250 tokens in the corpus have preposition supersenses. 114 prepositions and 63 supersenses are attested.[14] Their distributions appear in figure 5. Over 75% of tokens belong to the top 10 preposition types, while the supersense distribution is closer to uniform. 1,170 tokens are labeled as LOCATION, PATH, or a subtype thereof: these can roughly be described as spatial. 528 come from the TEMPORAL subtree of the hierarchy, and 452 from the CONFIGURATION subtree. Thus, fully half the tokens (2,100) mark non-spatiotemporal participants and circumstances.

Of the 4,250 tokens, 582 are MWEs (multiword prepositions and/or PP idioms). A further 588 preposition tokens (not included in the 4,250) have non-supersense labels: 484 `i, 83 `d, and 21 `.

3.4 Splits

To facilitate future experimentation on a standard benchmark, we partitioned our data into training and test sets. We randomly sampled 447 *sentences* (4,073 total tokens and 950 (19.6%) preposition instances) for a held-out test set, leaving 3,888 preposition instances for training.[15] The sampling was stratified by preposition supersense to encourage a reasonable balance for the rare labels; e.g., supersenses that occur twice are split so that one instance is assigned to the training set and one to the test set.[16] 61 preposition supersenses are attested in the training data, while 14 are unattested.

4 Inter-annotation Evaluation with PropBank

The REVIEWS corpus that we annotated with preposition supersenses had been independently

[11]In particular, many of the borderline prepositional verbs were revised according to the guidelines outlined at `https://github.com/nschneid/nanni/wiki/Prepositional-Verb-Annotation-Guidelines`.

[12]These sentences were then jointly adjudicated by the experts to arrive at a final version.

[13]For completeness, Cohen's $\kappa = .878$. It is almost as high as raw agreement because the expected agreement rate is very low, but keep in mind that κ's model of chance agreement does not take into account preposition types or the fact that, for a given type, a relatively small subset of labels were suggested to the annotator. On the 4 most frequent prepositions in the sample, *per-preposition* κ is .84 for **for**, 1.0 for **to**, .59 for **of**, and .73 for **in**.

[14]For the purpose of counting prepositions by type, we split up supersense-tagged PP idioms such as those shown in (5) and (6) by taking the longest prefix of words that has a PrepWiki entry to be the preposition.

[15]These figures include tokens with non-supersense labels (§3.1); the supersense-labeled prepositions amount to 3,397 training and 853 test instances.

[16]The sampling algorithm considered supersenses in increasing order of frequency: for each supersense ℓ having n_ℓ instances, enough sentences were assigned to the test set to fill a minimum quota of $\lceil .195 n_\ell \rceil$ tokens for that supersense (and remaining unassigned sentences containing that supersense were placed in the training set). Relative to the training set, the test set is skewed slightly in favor of rarer supersenses. A small number of annotation errors were corrected after determining the splits. Entire sentences were sampled to facilitate future studies involving joint prediction over the full sentence.

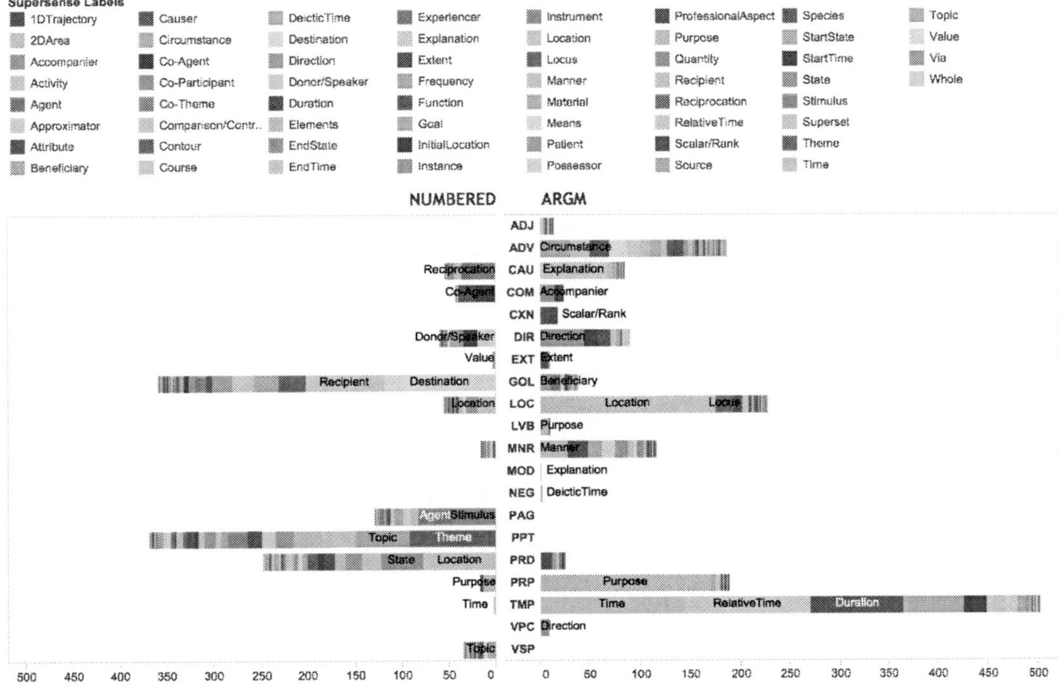

Figure 6: PropBank function tags on PP arguments and counts of their observed token correspondences with preposition supersenses. For each function tag, counts are split into numbered (core) arguments, left, and `ArgM` (modifier/non-core) arguments, right.

annotated with PropBank (Palmer et al., 2005; Bonial et al., 2014) predicate-argument structures. As a majority of preposition usages mark a semantic role, this affords us the opportunity to empirically compare the two annotation schemes as applied to the dataset—assessing not just inter-*annotator* agreement, but also inter-*annotation* agreement. (Our annotators did not have access to the PropBank annotations.) Others have conducted similar token-level analyses to compare different semantic representations (e.g., Fellbaum and Baker, 2013).

The supersense inventory is finer-grained than the PropBank function tags, ruling out a one-to-one correspondence. However, if the two sets of categories are both linguistically valid and correctly applied, then we expect that a label from either scheme will be predictive of the other scheme's label(s). Thus, we investigate the kinds and causes of divergence to see whether they reveal theoretical or practical problems with either scheme.

4.1 Function Tags in PropBank

In comparing our supersense annotation to the PropBank annotation of prepositional phrases, we focus on the mapping of the supersenses to PropBank's **function tags** marking location (`LOC`), extent (`EXT`), cause (`CAU`), temporal (`TMP`), and manner (`MNR`), among others.

Originally associated with modifier (`ArgM`) labels, function tags were recently added to all PropBank numbered arguments in an effort to address the performance problems in SRL systems caused by the higher-numbered arguments (Bonial et al., 2016).[17] In addition to the 13 existing function tags, three tags were introduced specifically for numbered roles: Proto-Agent (`PAG`), Proto-Patient (`PPT`), and Verb-Specific (`VSP`). These three tags are used, respectively, for `Arg0`, `Arg1`, and other arguments that simply do not have an appropriate function tag because they are unique to the lemma in question. Each of the numbered arguments has thus been annotated with a function tag. Unlike modifiers, where the function tag is annotated at the token level, function tags on the numbered arguments were assigned at the type level (in verbs' frameset definitions) by selecting the function tag most applicable to existing annotations.

Example (8) shows a sentence annotated for the predicate *going*; function tags appear in each argu-

[17] While automatic SRL performance is quite good for the detection of `Arg0` and `Arg1`, the performance on identification of higher-numbered arguments, 2–6, is relatively poor due to the variety of semantic roles they are associated with, depending on which relation is being considered.

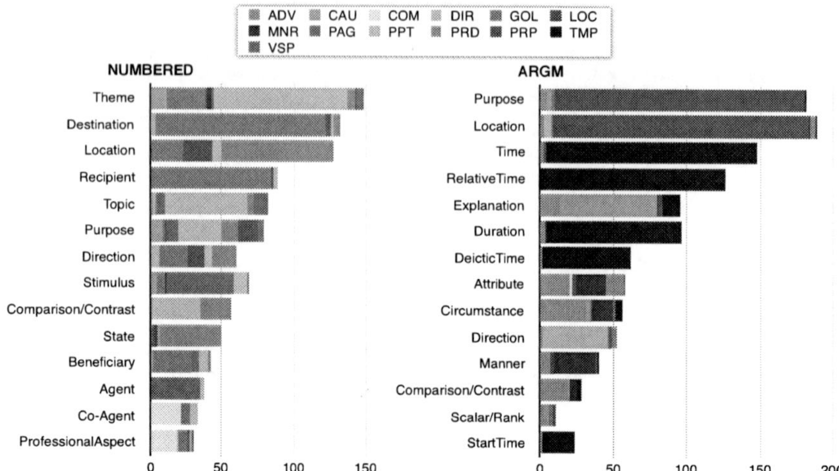

Figure 7: Distribution of PropBank function tags for the most frequent mapped supersenses. Counts are split into numbered (core) arguments, left, and `ArgM` (modifier/non-core) arguments, right.
Function tags mapped to fewer than 20 supersense-tagged prepositions overall are not displayed. (This accounts for why the bars are not strictly decreasing in width.) Numbered arguments tagged with `VPC` are mapped to DIRECTION in 8 instances. `ArgM-LVB` is mapped to PURPOSE in 8 instances, while `ArgM-CXN` is the dominant function tag mapped to SCALAR/RANK (18 instances).

ment name, following a hyphen:

(8) **I**$_{\text{Arg1-PPT}}$ have been **going**$_{\text{rel}}$ **[to the Wildwood, NJ]**$_{\text{Arg4-GOL}}$ **[for over 30 years]**$_{\text{ArgM-TMP}}$ **[for summer vacations]**$_{\text{ArgM-PRP}}$.

Of interest to this study are the three labels assigned to the prepositional phrases—`Arg4-GOL`, `ArgM-TMP`, and `ArgM-PRP`—and their corresponding supersense labels in (1). If the supersense annotation is valid, we should see a consistent correspondence between these PropBank function tags and semantically equivalent supersenses DESTINATION, DURATION, and PURPOSE, respectively, or their semantic relatives in the hierarchy.

Of the 4,250 supersense-annotated preposition tokens in the REVIEWS corpus (see §3.1), we were able to map 2,973 to arguments in the PropBank annotation—1,435 numbered arguments and 1,538 `ArgM` arguments.[18] Most of the remaining prepositions belong to non-predicative NPs and multiword expressions, which PropBank does not annotate.

4.2 Supersense and PropBank function tag correspondence

Figures 6 and 7 show the distribution of correspondences between the PropBank function tags and the supersense labels. Figure 6 visualizes all the mapped tokens, organized by function tag; figure 7 visualizes the function tag distributions for the most frequent supersenses that could be mapped.

Modifiers. We find that the supersense hierarchy captures some of the same generalizations as PropBank's coarser-grained distinctions. Most notably, the PropBank `ArgM` labels (visualized in the right-hand sides of figures 6 and 7) correspond relatively cleanly to the supersense labels: PropBank's `TMP` maps exclusively to the TEMPORAL branch of the hierarchy; and `PRP`, `CAU`, and to a slightly lesser extent `LOC`, map cleanly to their supersense counterparts PURPOSE, EXPLANATION, and LOCUS (and its subcategory LOCATION). The supersenses ATTRIBUTE, CIRCUMSTANCE, MANNER and the function tags `ADV`, `MNR`, `PRD`, and `GOL` stand out as warranting further scrutiny as applied to `ArgM`s.

Numbered arguments. The situation for numbered arguments is considerably messier. Note, for example, that in the left portion of figure 7, only a few of the supersenses map consistently to a single function tag: DESTINATION and RECIPIENT to `GOL`, STATE to `PRD`, and AGENT to `PAG`. The mappings for THEME, LOCATION, PURPOSE, and DIRECTION are extremely inconsistent. In part this is because PropBank captures predicate-centric, sometimes orthogonal distinctions: e.g., the copula is tagged as **be.01**, and its complement is always `PRD`—whether the PP describes a location (*It is in the box*), state (*We are in danger*), time (*That was 4 years ago*), etc. Other verbs, like *stay* and *find*, similarly have an argument tagged

[18] To perform the mapping, we first converted the gold PropBank annotations into a dependency representation using ClearNLP (`https://github.com/clir/clearnlp`; Choi and Palmer, 2012) and then heuristically postprocessed the output for special cases such as infinitival **to** marked as PURPOSE.

as PRD because that argument's function is to elaborate some other argument. Of course, *that* they elaborate some other argument is different from *how* (with respect to location, state, time, or other function conveyed by the preposition).

Because Arg0 and Arg1 had been consistently assigned to the verb's proto-agent (PAG) and proto-patient (PPT), respectively, we expected PAG to correspond cleanly to the AFFECTOR subhierarchy, and PPT to the UNDERGOER subhierarchy. We find that to a large extent, Arg0 does correspond to the AFFECTOR subhierarchy, which includes AGENT and CAUSER. However, Arg0 also maps to other supersenses such as STIMULUS (an entity that prompts sensory input), TOPIC (an UNDERGOER), and PURPOSE (a CIRCUMSTANCE). The source of the difference is partly due to a systematic disagreement on the status of a semantic label. Consider the following two PropBank frames:

amuse.01	**see.01**
Arg0-PAG: causer of mirth	Arg0-PAG: viewer
Arg1-PPT: mirthful entity	Arg1-PPT: thing viewed
Arg2-MNR: instrument	Arg2-PRD: attribute of Arg1
"Mary was amused **by** John"	"Mary was seen **by** John"

The preposition **by** for verbs *amuse* and *see* would carry the supersense labels of STIMULUS (entity triggering amusement) and EXPERIENCER (entity experiencing the sight), respectively. But PropBank's choice is verb-specific, assigning PAG based on which argument displays volitional involvement in the event or is causing an event or a state change in another participant (Bonial et al., 2012). Experiencer and Stimulus are known to compete over Dowty's Proto-Agent status, so this type of mismatch is not surprising (Dowty, 1991).

Arg1 is similarly muddled. Setting aside the expected mappings to THEME and TOPIC—both of which are undergoers—Arg1 overlaps with STIMULUS (for the same reasons as cited above) and, also, to a wide range of semantics including PURPOSE, ATTRIBUTE, and COMPARISON/CONTRAST.

Post hoc analysis. Well after the original annotation and adjudication, we undertook a post hoc review of the supersense-annotated tokens that were also PropBank-annotated to determine how much noise was present in the correspondences. We created a sample of 224 such tokens, stratified to cover a variety of correspondences (most supersenses were allotted 4 samples each, and for each supersense, function tags were diversified to the extent possible). Each token in the sample was reviewed independently by 4 annotators (all authors of this paper). Two annotators passed judgment on the gold supersense annotations; there were just 6 tokens for which they both said the supersense was clearly incorrect. The other two annotators (who have PropBank expertise) checked the gold PropBank annotations, agreeing that 5 of the tokens were clearly incorrect.

This analysis tells us that obvious errors with both types of annotation are indeed present in the corpus (11 tokens in the sample), adding some noise to the supersense–function tag correspondences. However, the outright errors are probably dwarfed by difficult/borderline cases for which the annotations are not entirely consistent throughout the corpus. For example, ***on time*** (i.e., 'not late') is variously annotated as STATE, MANNER, and TIME. Inconsistency detection methods (e.g., Hollenstein et al., 2016) may help identify these—though it remains to be seen whether methods developed for nouns and verbs would succeed on function words so polysemous as prepositions.

Summary. The (mostly) clean correspondences of the supersenses to the independently annotated PropBank *modifier* labels speak to the linguistic validity of our supersense hierarchy. On the other hand, the confusion evident for the supersense labels corresponding to PropBank's *numbered* arguments suggests further analysis and refinement is necessary for both annotation schemes. Some of these issues—especially correspondences between labels with unrelated semantics that occur in no more than a few tokens—are due to erroneous supersense or PropBank annotations. However, other categorizations are pervasively inconsistent between the two schemes, warranting a closer examination.

5 Conclusion

We have introduced a new lexical semantics corpus that disambiguates prepositions with hierarchical supersenses. Because it is comprehensively annotated over full documents (English web reviews), it offers insights into the semantic distribution of prepositions within that genre. Moreover, the same corpus has independently been annotated with PropBank predicate-argument structures, which facilitates analysis of correspondences and further refinement of both schemes and datasets. We expect that comprehensively annotated preposition supersense data will facilitate the development of automatic preposition disambiguation systems.

Acknowledgments

We thank our annotators—Evan Coles-Harris, Audrey Farber, Nicole Gordiyenko, Megan Hutto, Celeste Smitz, and Tim Watervoort—as well as Ken Litkowski, Michael Ellsworth, Orin Hargraves, and Susan Brown for helpful discussions. This research was supported in part by a Google research grant for Q/A PropBank Annotation.

References

Eneko Agirre, Timothy Baldwin, and David Martinez. 2008. Improving parsing and PP attachment performance with sense information. In *Proc. of ACL-HLT*, pages 317–325. Columbus, Ohio, USA.

Ann Bies, Justin Mott, Colin Warner, and Seth Kulick. 2012. English Web Treebank. Technical Report LDC2012T13, Linguistic Data Consortium, Philadelphia, PA. URL `http://www.ldc.upenn.edu/Catalog/catalogEntry.jsp?catalogId=LDC2012T13`.

Claire Bonial, Julia Bonn, Kathryn Conger, Jena D. Hwang, and Martha Palmer. 2014. PropBank: semantics of new predicate types. In Nicoletta Calzolari, Khalid Choukri, Thierry Declerck, Hrafn Loftsson, Bente Maegaard, Joseph Mariani, Asuncion Moreno, Jan Odijk, and Stelios Piperidis, editors, *Proc. of LREC*, pages 3013–3019. Reykjavík, Iceland.

Claire Bonial, Kathryn Conger, Jena D. Hwang, Aous Mansouri, Yahya Aseri, Julia Bonn, Timothy O'Gorman, and Martha Palmer. 2016. Current directions in English and Arabic PropBank. In Nancy Ide and James Pustejovsky, editors, *Handbook of Linguistic Annotation*. Springer, New York.

Claire Bonial, William Corvey, Martha Palmer, Volha V. Petukhova, and Harry Bunt. 2011. A hierarchical unification of LIRICS and VerbNet semantic roles. In *Fifth IEEE International Conference on Semantic Computing*, pages 483–489. Palo Alto, CA, USA.

Claire Bonial, Jena D. Hwang, Julia Bonn, Kathryn Conger, Olga Babko-Malaya, and Martha Palmer. 2012. English propbank annotation guidelines. *Center for Computational Language and Education Research Institute of Cognitive Science University of Colorado at Boulder*.

Claudia Brugman. 1981. *The story of 'over': polysemy, semantics and the structure of the lexicon*. MA thesis, University of California, Berkeley, Berkeley, CA. Published New York: Garland, 1981.

Martin Chodorow, Joel R. Tetreault, and Na-Rae Han. 2007. Detection of grammatical errors involving prepositions. In *Proc. of the Fourth ACL-SIGSEM Workshop on Prepositions*, pages 25–30. Prague, Czech Republic.

Jinho D. Choi and Martha Palmer. 2012. Guidelines for the CLEAR style constituent to dependency conversion. Technical Report 01-12, Institute of Cognitive Science, University of Colorado at Boulder, Boulder, Colorado, USA. URL `http://www.mathcs.emory.edu/~choi/doc/clear-dependency-2012.pdf`.

Massimiliano Ciaramita and Yasemin Altun. 2006. Broad-coverage sense disambiguation and information extraction with a supersense sequence tagger. In *Proc. of EMNLP*, pages 594–602. Sydney, Australia.

Daniel Dahlmeier, Hwee Tou Ng, and Tanja Schultz. 2009. Joint learning of preposition senses and semantic roles of prepositional phrases. In *Proc. of EMNLP*, pages 450–458. Suntec, Singapore.

Mark Davies. 2010. The Corpus of Contemporary American English as the first reliable monitor corpus of English. *Literary and Linguistic Computing*, 25(4):447–464.

David Dowty. 1991. Thematic proto-roles and argument selection. *Language*, pages 547–619.

Christiane Fellbaum and Collin F. Baker. 2013. Comparing and harmonizing different verb classifications in light of a semantic annotation task. *Linguistics*, 51(4):707–728.

Homa B. Hashemi and Rebecca Hwa. 2014. A comparison of MT errors and ESL errors. In Nicoletta Calzolari, Khalid Choukri, Thierry Declerck, Hrafn Loftsson, Bente Maegaard, Joseph Mariani, Asuncion Moreno, Jan Odijk, and Stelios Piperidis, editors, *Proc. of LREC*, pages 2696–2700. Reykjavík, Iceland.

Annette Herskovits. 1986. *Language and spatial cognition: an interdisciplinary study of the prepositions in English*. Studies in Natural Language Processing. Cambridge University Press, Cambridge, UK.

Nora Hollenstein, Nathan Schneider, and Bonnie Webber. 2016. Inconsistency detection in semantic annotation. In Nicoletta Calzolari, Khalid Choukri, Thierry Declerck, Marko Grobelnik, Bente Maegaard, Joseph Mariani, Asuncion Moreno, Jan Odijk, and Stelios Piperidis, editors, *Proc. of LREC*, pages 3986–3990. Portorož, Slovenia.

Dirk Hovy, Stephen Tratz, and Eduard Hovy. 2010. What's in a preposition? Dimensions of sense disambiguation for an interesting word class. In *Coling 2010: Posters*, pages 454–462. Beijing, China.

Jena D. Hwang. 2014. *Identification and representation of caused motion constructions*. Ph.D. dissertation, University of Colorado, Boulder, Colorado.

Anders Johannsen, Dirk Hovy, Héctor Martínez Alonso, Barbara Plank, and Anders Søgaard. 2014. More or less supervised supersense tagging of Twitter. In *Proc. of *SEM*, pages 1–11. Dublin, Ireland.

George Lakoff. 1987. *Women, fire, and dangerous things: what categories reveal about the mind*. University of Chicago Press, Chicago.

Seth Lindstromberg. 2010. *English Prepositions Explained*. John Benjamins, Amsterdam, revised edition.

Ken Litkowski. 2014. Pattern Dictionary of English Prepositions. In *Proc. of ACL*, pages 1274–1283. Baltimore, Maryland, USA.

Ken Litkowski. 2015. Notes on barbecued opakapaka: ontology in preposition patterns. Technical Report 15-01, CL Research, Damascus, MD. URL `http://www.clres.com/online-papers/PDEPOntology.pdf`.

Ken Litkowski and Orin Hargraves. 2005. The Preposition Project. In *Proc. of the Second ACL-SIGSEM Workshop on the Linguistic Dimensions of Prepositions and their Use in Computational Linguistics Formalisms and Applications*, pages 171–179. Colchester, Essex, UK.

Ken Litkowski and Orin Hargraves. 2007. SemEval-2007 Task 06: Word-Sense Disambiguation of Prepositions. In *Proc. of SemEval*, pages 24–29. Prague, Czech Republic.

Héctor Martínez Alonso, Anders Johannsen, Sussi Olsen, Sanni Nimb, Nicolai Hartvig Sørensen, Anna Braasch, Anders Søgaard, and Bolette Sandford Pedersen. 2015. Supersense tagging for Danish. In Beáta Megyesi, editor, *Proc. of NODALIDA*, pages 21–29. Vilnius, Lithuania.

George A. Miller, Richard Beckwith, Christiane Fellbaum, Derek Gross, and Katherine Miller. 1990. Five Papers on WordNet. Technical Report 43, Princeton University, Princeton, NJ.

Antje Müller, Claudia Roch, Tobias Stadtfeld, and Tibor Kiss. 2012. The annotation of preposition senses in German. In Britta Stolterfoht and Sam Featherston, editors, *Empirical Approaches to Linguistic Theory: Studies in Meaning and Structure*, Studies in Generative Grammar, pages 63–82.

Walter de Gruyter, Berlin.

Elizabeth M. O'Dowd. 1998. *Prepositions and particles in English: a discourse-functional account*. Oxford University Press, New York.

Tom O'Hara and Janyce Wiebe. 2003. Preposition semantic classification via Treebank and FrameNet. In Walter Daelemans and Miles Osborne, editors, *Proc. of CoNLL*, pages 79–86. Edmonton, Canada.

Martha Palmer, Daniel Gildea, and Paul Kingsbury. 2005. The Proposition Bank: an annotated corpus of semantic roles. *Computational Linguistics*, 31(1):71–106.

Davide Picca, Alfio Massimiliano Gliozzo, and Massimiliano Ciaramita. 2008. Supersense Tagger for Italian. In Nicoletta Calzolari, Khalid Choukri, Bente Maegaard, Joseph Mariani, Jan Odjik, Stelios Piperidis, and Daniel Tapias, editors, *Proc. of LREC*, pages 2386–2390. Marrakech, Morocco.

Geoffrey K. Pullum and Rodney Huddleston. 2002. Prepositions and preposition phrases. In Rodney Huddleston and Geoffrey K. Pullum, editors, *The Cambridge Grammar of the English Language*, pages 579–611. Cambridge University Press, Cambridge, UK.

Patrick Saint-Dizier and Nancy Ide, editors. 2006. *Syntax and Semantics of Prepositions*, volume 29 of *Text, Speech and Language Technology*. Springer, Dordrecht, The Netherlands.

Nathan Schneider, Dirk Hovy, Anders Johannsen, and Marine Carpuat. 2016. SemEval-2016 Task 10: Detecting Minimal Semantic Units and their Meanings (DiMSUM). In *Proc. of SemEval*. San Diego, California, USA.

Nathan Schneider, Behrang Mohit, Chris Dyer, Kemal Oflazer, and Noah A. Smith. 2013. Supersense tagging for Arabic: the MT-in-the-middle attack. In *Proc. of NAACL-HLT*, pages 661–667. Atlanta, Georgia, USA.

Nathan Schneider, Behrang Mohit, Kemal Oflazer, and Noah A. Smith. 2012. Coarse lexical semantic annotation with supersenses: an Arabic case study. In *Proc. of ACL*, pages 253–258. Jeju Island, Korea.

Nathan Schneider, Spencer Onuffer, Nora Kazour, Emily Danchik, Michael T. Mordowanec, Henrietta Conrad, and Noah A. Smith. 2014. Comprehensive annotation of multiword expressions in a social web corpus. In Nicoletta Calzolari, Khalid Choukri, Thierry Declerck, Hrafn Loftsson, Bente Maegaard, Joseph Mariani, Asuncion Moreno, Jan Odijk, and Stelios Piperidis, editors, *Proc. of LREC*, pages 455–461. Reykjavík, Iceland.

Nathan Schneider and Noah A. Smith. 2015. A corpus and model integrating multiword expressions and supersenses. In *Proc. of NAACL-HLT*, pages 1537–1547. Denver, Colorado.

Nathan Schneider, Vivek Srikumar, Jena D. Hwang, and Martha Palmer. 2015. A hierarchy with, of, and for preposition supersenses. In *Proc. of The 9th Linguistic Annotation Workshop*, pages 112–123. Denver, Colorado, USA.

Frédérique Segond, Anne Schiller, Gregory Grefenstette, and Jean-Pierre Chanod. 1997. An experiment in semantic tagging using hidden Markov model tagging. In Piek Vossen, Geert Adriaens, Nicoletta Calzolari, Antonio Sanfilippo, and Yorick Wilks, editors, *Automatic Information Extraction and Building of Lexical Semantic Resources for NLP Applications: ACL/EACL-97 Workshop Proceedings*, pages 78–81. Madrid, Spain.

Reshef Shilon, Hanna Fadida, and Shuly Wintner. 2012. Incorporating linguistic knowledge in statistical machine translation: translating prepositions. In *Proc. of the Workshop on Innovative Hybrid Approaches to the Processing of Textual Data*, pages 106–114. Avignon, France.

Vivek Srikumar and Dan Roth. 2011. A joint model for extended semantic role labeling. In *Proc. of EMNLP*, pages 129–139. Edinburgh, Scotland, UK.

Vivek Srikumar and Dan Roth. 2013a. An inventory of preposition relations. Technical Report arXiv:1305.5785. URL `http://arxiv.org/abs/1305.5785`.

Vivek Srikumar and Dan Roth. 2013b. Modeling semantic relations expressed by prepositions. *Transactions of the Association for Computational Linguistics*, 1:231–242.

Stephen Tratz and Dirk Hovy. 2009. Disambiguation of preposition sense using linguistically motivated features. In *Proc. of NAACL-HLT Student Research Workshop and Doctoral Consortium*, pages 96–100. Boulder, Colorado.

Stephen Tratz and Eduard Hovy. 2011. A fast, accurate, non-projective, semantically-enriched parser. In *Proc. of EMNLP*, pages 1257–1268. Edinburgh, Scotland, UK.

Yulia Tsvetkov, Manaal Faruqui, Wang Ling, Guillaume Lample, and Chris Dyer. 2015. Evaluation of word vector representations by subspace alignment. In *Proc. of EMNLP*. Lisbon, Portugal.

Yulia Tsvetkov, Elena Mukomel, and Anatole Gershman. 2013. Cross-lingual metaphor detection using common semantic features. In *Proc. of the First Workshop on Metaphor in NLP*, pages 45–51. Atlanta, Georgia, USA.

Yulia Tsvetkov, Nathan Schneider, Dirk Hovy, Archna Bhatia, Manaal Faruqui, and Chris Dyer. 2014. Augmenting English adjective senses with supersenses. In Nicoletta Calzolari, Khalid Choukri, Thierry Declerck, Hrafn Loftsson, Bente Maegaard, Joseph Mariani, Asuncion Moreno, Jan Odijk, and Stelios Piperidis, editors, *Proc. of LREC*, pages 4359–4365. Reykjavík, Iceland.

Andrea Tyler and Vyvyan Evans. 2003. *The Semantics of English Prepositions: Spatial Scenes, Embodied Meaning and Cognition*. Cambridge University Press, Cambridge, UK.

Patrick Ye and Timothy Baldwin. 2007. MELB-YB: Preposition sense disambiguation using rich semantic features. In *Proc. of SemEval*, pages 241–244. Prague, Czech Republic.

Focus Annotation of Task-based Data: Establishing the Quality of Crowd Annotation

Kordula De Kuthy **Ramon Ziai** **Detmar Meurers**
Collaborative Research Center 833
University of Tübingen
{kdk,rziai,dm}@sfs.uni-tuebingen.de

Abstract

We explore the annotation of information structure in German and compare the quality of expert annotation with crowd-sourced annotation taking into account the cost of reaching crowd consensus.

Concretely, we discuss a crowd-sourcing effort annotating *focus* in a task-based corpus of German containing reading comprehension questions and answers. Against the backdrop of a gold standard reference resulting from adjudicated expert annotation, we evaluate a crowd sourcing experiment using majority voting to determine a baseline performance. To refine the crowd-sourcing setup, we introduce the Consensus Cost as a measure of agreement within the crowd. We investigate the usefulness of Consensus Cost as a measure of crowd annotation quality both intrinsically, in relation to the expert gold standard, and extrinsically, by integrating focus annotation information into a system performing Short Answer Assessment taking into account the Consensus Cost.

We find that low Consensus Cost in crowd sourcing indicates high quality, though high cost does not necessarily indicate low accuracy but increased variability. Overall, taking Consensus Cost into account improves both intrinsic and extrinsic evaluation measures.

1 Introduction

This paper addresses the question of how to explore and evaluate the annotation of information structural concepts to support the analysis of authentic data. While the formal pragmatic concepts in information structure, such as the *focus* of an utterance, are precisely defined in theoretical linguistics and potentially very useful in conceptual and practical terms, it has turned out to be difficult to reliably annotate such notions in corpus data (Ritz et al., 2008; Calhoun et al., 2010).

Theoretical linguists have discussed the notion of focus for decades (cf., e.g., Jackendoff 1972; Stechow 1981; Rooth 1992; Schwarzschild 1999; Büring 2007). Following the work of Rooth (1992), one of the widely used definitions of focus is that "Focus indicates the presence of alternatives that are relevant for the linguistic expressions" (cf. Krifka 2007). Which part of an utterance is in the focus thus depends on the context of the utterance, as illustrated by the question-answers pairs in examples (1) and (2).

(1) A: *What did John show Mary?*
B: *John showed Mary* $[\![$*the PICTures*$]\!]_F$.

(2) A: *Who did John show the pictures?*
B: *John showed* $[\![$*MARy*$]\!]_F$ *the pictures.*

Since focus is signalled by prosodic prominence in an intonation language like English, the answers also show different prominence patterns, as indicated by the pitch accents on *picture* in (1) and *Mary* in (2).

The linguistic discussions of focus phenomena generally are based on few example sentences, without an apparent exploration of substantial amounts of authentic data. Only few attempts at systematically identifying focus in authentic data have been made (Ritz et al., 2008; Calhoun et al., 2010). They generally ran into significant problems trying to reach good inter-annotator agreement, as they tried to identify focus in newspaper text or other data types where no explicit questions are available, making the task of determining the question under discussion, and thus reliably annotating focus, particularly difficult.

Proceedings of LAW X – The 10th Linguistic Annotation Workshop, pages 110–119,
Berlin, Germany, August 11, 2016.

More recently, Ziai and Meurers (2014) showed that reliable focus annotation is feasible, even for somewhat ill-formed learner language, if one has access to explicit questions and takes them into account in an incremental annotation scheme. They demonstrate the effectiveness of the approach by reporting both substantial inter-annotator agreement and a substantial extrinsic improvement resulting from integration of focus information into a Short Answer Assessment system.

However, manual focus annotation by experts is time consuming, both for annotator training and the annotation itself. Additionally, in computational linguistics it has been argued (Riezler, 2014) that annotation of theoretical linguistic notions by experts should be complemented by external grounding, either in the form of extrinsic evaluation, as reported above, or by using crowdsourcing: by formulating the annotation task in such a way that non-experts can understand it and carry it out, one ensures that the task does not depend on implicit knowledge shared only by a team of experts.

In this paper, we explore the use of crowdsourcing – which has been shown to work well for a number of linguistic tasks (see, e.g., Finin et al. 2010; Tetreault et al. 2010; Zaidan and Callison-Burch 2011) – for focus annotation. We investigate how systematically the untrained crowd can identify a meaning-based linguistic notion like focus in authentic data and which characteristics of the data and context lead to consistent annotation results.

Having established the general feasibility of non-expert focus annotation, we refine the crowdsourcing approach by taking into account the variability within the set of crowd judgements. The approach is based on the idea that sentences with little variation in the annotation provided by the crowd are more reliably annotated, i.e., are of a higher quality. We spell out a measure of crowd diversity, Consensus Cost, and investigate its usefulness both intrinsically, by relating it to the expert-based gold-standard, and extrinsically, by integrating cost-based focus annotation data in a Short Answer Assessment system.

2 Data

We base our work on the CREG corpus (Ott et al., 2012), a freely available task-based corpus consisting of answers to reading comprehension questions written by American learners of German at the university level. The overall corpus includes 164 reading texts, 1,517 reading comprehension questions, 2,057 target answers provided by the teachers, and 36,335 learner answers. Each answer was rated by two annotators with respect to whether it is a correct (appropriate) answer or not. The CREG-5K subset used for the present annotation study is an extended version of CREG-1032 (Meurers et al., 2011), selected using the same criteria after the overall, four year corpus collection effort was completed. The criteria include balancedness (equal number of correct and incorrect answers), a minimum answer length of four tokens, and a language course level at the intermediate level or above.

(3) provides an example of a question-answer pair from the CREG corpus.

(3) Q: *Welches Thema wurde am 4. November nicht diskutiert?*
which topic was on the 4th November not discussed
'Which topic was not discussed on Nov. 4th?'

A: *Die deutsche Einheit stand nicht auf der Agenda.*
the German unity stood not on the agenda
'The German unification was not on the agenda.'

2.1 Gold Standard Annotation

As a reference point for the evaluation of the focus annotation by crowd workers, we first obtained a gold-standard annotation using experts. We based this effort on the focus annotation scheme and annotation of the CREG-1032 data set provided in Ziai and Meurers (2014). We extended this by manually focus-annotating both target answers and student answers in the larger CREG-5K data set. The annotation was performed by two graduate research assistants in linguistics using the *brat*[1] rapid annotation tool directly at token level. An important characteristic of the annotation scheme is that it is applied incrementally: annotators first look at the surface question form, then determine the set of alternatives (Krifka, 2007, sec. 3), and finally mark instances of the alternative set in answers. The following three types of categories are distinguished:

- **Question Form** encodes the surface form of a question (e.g., `WhPhrase`, `Yes/No` or `Alternative`).

[1] `http://brat.nlplab.org`

- **Focus** marks the focused words or phrases in an answer.
- **Answer Type** expresses the semantic category of the focus in relation to the question form. Examples include `Time/Date`, `Location`, `Entity`, `Action`, and `Reason`.

Figure 1 shows a brat screen shot with an example including a `WhPhrase` Question Form and two answers, a target answer (TA) and a student answer (SA), containing a word selected as focus with Answer Type `Action`.

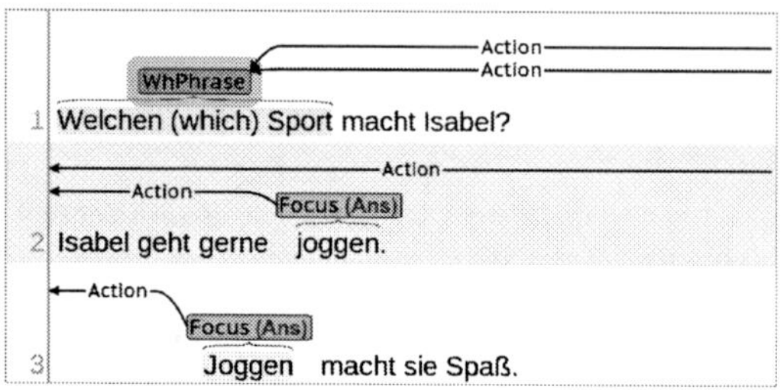

Q: '*Which sport* does Isabel do?'

TA: 'She likes to go ⟦jogging⟧$_F$.'

SA: '⟦Jogging⟧$_F$ is fun for her.'

Figure 1: Brat annotation example

In the following we will only evaluate the agreement results for the category *Focus* of our annotation scheme. Ziai and Meurers (2014) annotated 1,255 answers (1,032 student answers and 223 target answers of CREG-1032) and reported 88.1% percentage agreement for focus in all answers, with $\kappa = 0.75$, calculated over all answer tokens. We applied the approach to another 2,922 answers (2,155 student answers and 767 target answers) of CREG-5K using two annotators and obtained a percentage agreement for focus annotation calculated over all answer tokens of 86.3%, with $\kappa = .70$, demonstrating the robustness of the annotation approach when applied to new data. Altogether, 4,177 answers (3,187 student answers and 990 target answers) of the CREG-5K corpus are manually annotated with focus. The overall percentage agreement for focus is 86.6% with a κ of 0.71.

To obtain the gold standard focus annotation of the combined corpus, the two annotation versions were merged into one focus annotation by a third expert, who determined the annotation in case the two annotators disagreed.

3 Crowd Annotation

3.1 Setup of the crowd-sourcing experiment

To study non-expert focus annotation, we implemented a crowd-sourcing task using the crowd-sourcing platform CrowdFlower[2] to collect focus annotations from crowd workers. CrowdFlower makes it possible to require workers to come from German speaking countries, a feature that other platforms like Amazon Mechanical Turk do not provide as transparently, and it has a built-in quality control mechanism ensuring that workers throughout the entire job maintain a certain level of accuracy on interspersed test items.

As data for our crowd-sourcing experiment, we used 5,597 question-answer pairs from the CREG-5K corpus and 100 manually constructed test question-answer pairs. The task of the crowd workers was to mark those words in an answer sentence that "contain the information asked for in the question". Workers were shown five question-answer pairs at a time. One of those five was from our set of hand-crafted test question-answer pairs. The workers were paid two cents per annotated sentence.

Since CREG-5K consists of reading comprehension questions and answers provided by learners of German, there are cases where a student response does not answer a given question at all, for example, when the learner misunderstood the question. In the gold standard annotation described in section 2.1, the annotators had the option to mark such cases as "question ignored". Since we also wanted to provide the crowd workers with this option, we included a checkbox "Frage nicht beantwortet" ("*question not answered*"). When this option is selected, no word in the answer sentence can be marked as focus.

Figure 2 shows an example CrowdFlower task with the marked words in yellow. These marked words are the ones that we counted as focus. The English translation shown below was not part of the CrowdFlower task.

We collected 11 focus annotations per answer sentence and crowd workers had to maintain an accuracy of 60% on the test question-answer pairs. Altogether we collected 62,247 annotated sentences.

[2] `http://www.crowdflower.com/`

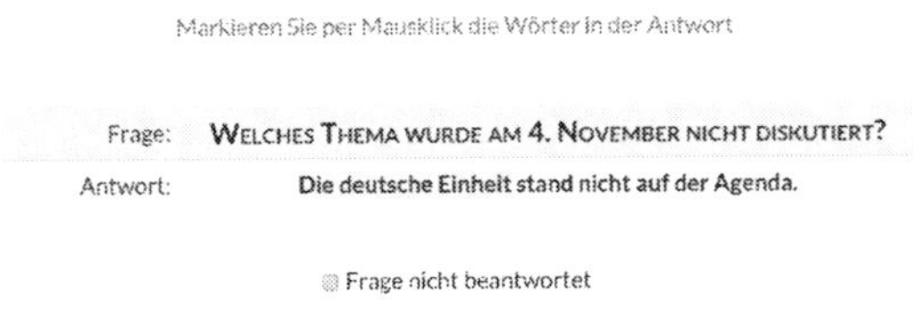

Markieren Sie per Mausklick die Wörter in der Antwort

Frage: WELCHES THEMA WURDE AM 4. NOVEMBER NICHT DISKUTIERT?

Antwort: Die deutsche Einheit stand nicht auf der Agenda.

Frage nicht beantwortet

Q: 'Which topic was not discussed on November 4th?'
A: '$[\![$The German unification$]\!]_F$ was not on the agenda.'

Figure 2: Example CrowdFlower annotation task

3.2 Evaluation

To evaluate the quality of our crowd focus annotation, we wanted to find out how the annotations produced by the crowd workers compare to the gold standard expert annotation described in section 2.1. We therefore chose to calculate all possibilities of combining one through eleven workers into one "virtual" annotator using majority voting on individual word judgments. Ties in voting are resolved by random assignment. The procedure is similar to the approach described by Snow et al. (2008). We did not employ any bias correction or other types of weighting schemes, as discussed, e.g., by Qing et al. (2014), but plan to do so in future research.

In measuring agreement between crowd workers and the expert gold-standard on the word level, for the following reasons we opted for percentage agreement instead of Kappa or other measures that include a notion of expected agreement: *i)* Kappa assumes the annotators to be the same across all instances and this is systematically violated by the crowd-sourcing setup, and *ii)* calculating Kappa on a per-answer basis is not sensible in cases where only one class occurs, as in all-focus and no-focus answers.

3.2.1 Overall agreement of crowd with gold

We performed the evaluation on the CREG-5K data subset for which we obtained both expert and crowd annotations. Figure 3 shows the observed per-token percentage agreement reached by the crowd workers compared to the gold standard annotation.

As reference, the dotted lines show the percentage agreement between the two expert annotators. We see that the quality improves from 74.9% for one worker to 79.8% for eleven workers[3]. Given

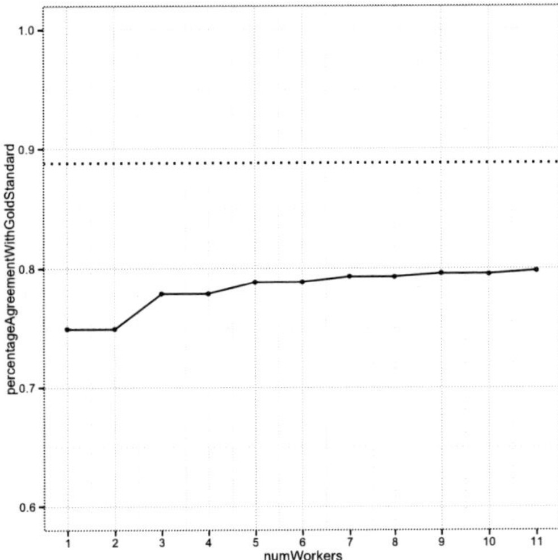

Figure 3: Agreement of crowd with gold standard

that this is below the agreement of 88.8% reached by the expert annotators for this data set, we next investigated which cases the crowd can handle, and which ones turn out to be difficult for the non-experts.

3.2.2 Evaluation for different question forms

To identify patterns that show which types of data can be annotated with focus most consistently by crowd workers compared to the experts, we particularly want to look at properties of our data that take characteristics of the context into account – which in our case is the question context in which an answer annotated with focus occurs. We therefore investigated the impact of different types of questions on annotation agreement.

We carried out the comparison for the specific question form subtypes distinguishing surface forms of *wh*-questions as annotated in CREG (Meurers et al., 2011). Figure 4 shows how the different question form subtypes impact the agreement between the crowd and the gold-standard focus annotation.

As reference, the dotted lines again show the percentage agreements between the two expert annotators for the different question forms. The question forms make the answers fall into three broad categories in terms of worker-gold agreement: the most concrete ones (*who*, *when* and *where*) in terms of surface realization in answers come out on top with percentage agreements at 91% (*where*), 87% (*who*), and 86% (*when*).

[3]Note that agreement does not improve when increasing from odd to even worker numbers, which is due to the fact that the probability of drawing a majority does not increase in these cases.

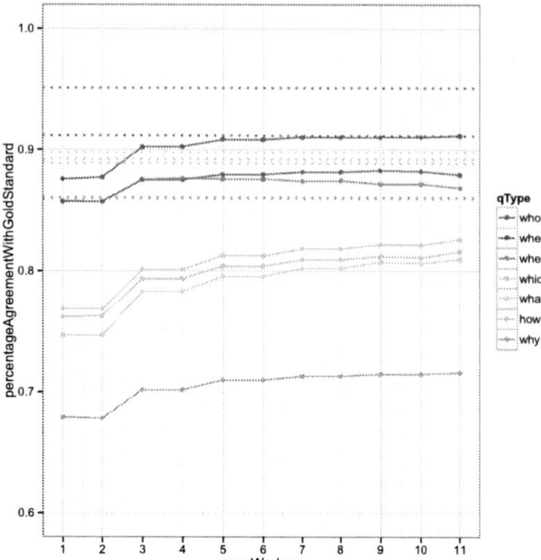

Figure 4: Agreement by question form

The second group (*which*, *what* and *how*) are at 80–82% percentage agreement, which is likely due to their more ambiguous answer realization possibilities, e.g., a *what*-question can ask for an activity ('What did Peter do?') or an object ('What does Peter wear?').

The third group consists only of *why*-questions at an agreement level of 71%. For such questions asking for reasons, the range of possible answer realizations arguably is the greatest given that reasons are typically expressed by whole clauses. However, for the gold expert-annotation, the more explicit guidelines seem to have paid off in this case, as *why*-questions come out at a much higher agreement level of 86%.

To test whether more explicit guidelines could also help the crowd annotators to be more systematic in their focus annotation, we conducted a small additional crowdsourcing annotation study with a smaller data set only containing answers to *why* and *what*-questions. While the general set up was the same as described in section 3.1, we provided the crowd workers with more examples illustrating focus in different kind of answers. The result was only a small improvement in agreement between crowd and gold standard annotation, with answers to *what*-questions 1% higher than before, and 2% higher for *why*-questions. Even more explicit guidelines thus do not seem to help the non-experts to handle answers occurring with *why*-questions when annotating focus.

Summing up the results so far, the crowd annotation study shows that i. the percentage agreement improves the more crowd workers are taken into account, and ii. majority voting on crowd worker judgments compared to the expert gold annotation can reach the expert level for specific cases (e.g., *where*-questions).

3.2.3 Qualitative discussion

To gain a better understanding of why the annotation agreement differs so widely with respect to question types for the crowd annotators, we take a closer look at the variation in the linguistic material that apparently impacts focus annotation. We discuss a typical example for a *who*-question (4) and a *why*-question (5) together with a sample of given answers from the CREG-5K data set as the two most extreme cases with respect to the observed annotation agreement.

In the case of the different answers to the *who*-question shown in (4), we can see that the variation both in meaning and form is very limited:

(4) Q: *Wer war an der Tür?*
who was at the door

A1: ⟦*Drei Soldaten*⟧$_F$ *waren an der Tür.*
three soldiers were at the door

A2: ⟦*Drei Männer in alten Uniformen*⟧$_F$ *waren an der Tür.*
three men in old uniforms were at the door

A3: ⟦*Die drei Männer*⟧$_F$ *waren an der Tür.*
the three men were at the door

A4: ⟦*Drei alte Uniformen*⟧$_F$ *waren an der Tür.*
three old uniforms were at the door

Syntactically, the focused part of the answers shown in ⟦. . . ⟧$_F$ is expressed as a nominal phrase. Contentwise, the same type of entity (a person) is expressed by semantically related words. The rest of the sentence shows no variation at all. The only inconsistency in annotation by the crowd occurred with NPs such as *Die drei Männer* in answer A3 in (4), where some of the crowd annotated the entire NP as the focus, while the rest of the crowd annotators only marked *drei Männer* as the focus, leaving out the definite article.

In the case of the various answers to the *why*-question shown in (5), multiple ways of answering the same questions can be observed, both syntactically and semantically.

(5) Q: *Warum ist das Haus der Kameliendame*
why is the house of the lady of the camellias
so interessant?
so interesting

A1: ⟦*Ein Klimacomputer regelt Temperatur,*
a air computer regulates temperature
Belüftung, Luftfeuchte und Beschattung.⟧$_F$
ventilation humidity and shading

A2: *Das Haus der Kamelie ist so interessant,*
the house of the camellia is so interesting
⟦*weil es 230 Jahre alt und 8,90 m hohe ist.*⟧$_F$
because it 230 years old and 8.90 m high is

A3: ⟦*In der warmen Jahreszeit wird das Haus*
in the warm season is the house
neben die Kamelie gerollt.⟧$_F$
next to the camellia rolled

A4: *Das Haus der Kamelie ist so interessant,*
the house of the camellia is so interesting
⟦*weil es ist ein fahrbares Haus.*⟧$_F$
because it is a mobile house

A5: *Der Kamelie ist interessant* ⟦*wegen des*
the camellia is interesting because of the
Computers.⟧$_F$
computer

Syntactically, the focused part of the answer is either expressed as the entire sentence as in A1 and A3 in (5), the subordinate clause starting with *weil* (because) as in A2 and A4 in (5), or as a PP introduced by *wegen* (because of) as in A5. Semantically, all four answers present a different propositional content. The relation between the question and potential answers thus is not particularly obvious or direct. Establishing the relation between question and answer – as needed to identify the focus of the answer – thus requires more effort by the annotator. This leads to less consistent results in the annotation for the crowd. For example, parts of the crowd annotators did not interpret the sentence A3 in (5) as an answer to the *why*-question in (5) at all and consequently did not mark any words in that sentence as focus, while the rest of the crowd annotators marked the entire clause as the focus.

For the expert annotators, the more explicit guidelines including a conceptual discussion of the key notions and explicit tests with minimal pairs, results in less pronounced differences in annotation quality for the different question types.

4 Predicting when the crowd is reliable

Apart from taking the question type into account, is it possible to predict when crowd focus annotation is particularly reliable based on characteristics of the crowd judgements?

Previous research on this issue has looked primarily at individual crowd worker characteristics, such as worker trustfulness (cf., e.g., Hantke et al. (2016). Hsueh et al. (2009) calculate sentiment ambiguity by considering the strength and the polarity of the sentiment's ratings. We here go into a similar direction for focus annotation, investigating the idea to take into account the diversity of the crowd performance, i.e., how diverse the focus annotations obtained from crowd workers for individual sentences are. Our hypothesis here is that sentences where the crowd agrees more on the annotation are annotated more reliably.

4.1 Calculating the cost of crowd consensus

We propose to measure the diversity of the focus annotation provided by the crowd workers in terms of the *Consensus Cost* in annotating a sentence of length n. The Consensus Cost (CC) is defined to be the sum of the minority annotation (i.e., focus or background) for all tokens in a sentence divided by the total number of tokens and the largest possible minority annotation for a token (in our case 5, since 6 would be a majority with 11 workers).

$$CC = \frac{\sum_{w=0}^{n} changeNeededForConsensus(w)}{largestPossibleMinority \times n}$$

The formula measures how many annotation changes would be needed to reach total consensus in annotating a given token. Sentences where the crowd workers mostly agreed on an annotation have a low consensus cost, because for every token only few annotation changes are needed to reach total agreement. Sentences where a larger number of workers diverge from the majority annotation have a higher consensus cost, since more changes would be needed in order to reach complete consensus on that annotation.

Figure 5 exemplifies the calculation of the Consensus Cost for the actual eleven crowd annotations from the crowdsourcing experiment for the short example answer *Die/the drei/three Männer/men war/was an/at der/the Tür/door* from our CREG data.

For the first word *die*, only two of the 11 crowd workers marked the word as Focus, so the cost to reach total agreement (in this case that the token is (b)ackground, i.e., not focus) is 2. The next two words (*drei/three*) and *(Männer/men)* were marked as focus by 10 of the 11 of workers and thus each have a cost of one. The rest of the words in the sentence were unanimously not marked as focus by the crowd workers and thus have a cost

	Die	drei	Männer	war	an	der	Tür
1	**F**	F	F	b	b	b	b
2	**F**	F	F	b	b	b	b
3	b	F	F	b	b	b	b
4	b	F	F	b	b	b	b
5	b	F	F	b	b	b	b
6	b	F	F	b	b	b	b
7	b	F	F	b	b	b	b
8	b	F	F	b	b	b	b
9	b	F	F	b	b	b	b
10	b	F	F	b	b	b	b
11	b	**b**	**b**	b	b	b	b
Cost	2	1	1	0	0	0	0

$$\text{ConsensusCost} = \frac{4}{5 \times 7} = 0.11$$

Figure 5: Calculating the Consensus Cost

of 0. The resulting Consensus Cost for the focus annotation for this sentence according to our formula is 0.11.

Since not all crowd workers perform equally well, it would in principle make sense to incorporate their individual reliability. As a first step towards this idea, we are excluding all workers from annotation who fail to reach a particular accuracy threshold (0.66) on the test questions.

We can now investigate whether the Consensus Cost, i.e., the amount of agreement within the crowd, can serve as an indicator of the quality of the annotations provided by the crowd.

4.2 Consensus Cost and Annotation Quality

In order to determine whether Consensus Cost can function as a proxy for annotation quality, let us compare it to the agreement of the crowd workers with the gold standard expert annotation we discussed in section 3.2.

To explore the relation between Consensus Cost and quality of the annotation of an answer, we divided the possible values (0.0 to 1.0) of Consensus Cost into four ranges, using 0.25, 0.5 and 0.75 as boundaries. Figure 6 shows the boxplots for each of the four groups of answers by Consensus Cost, with the percentage agreement with the gold standard shown on the y-axis. The width of the box plots indicates the number of instances represented, whereas the height represents the distribution of agreement values.

For answers annotated with low Consensus Cost (< 0.5), the quality of annotation is generally high, with agreement with the gold standard between 0.7 and 1.0. The majority of data points fall into this interval. Interestingly, answers annotated

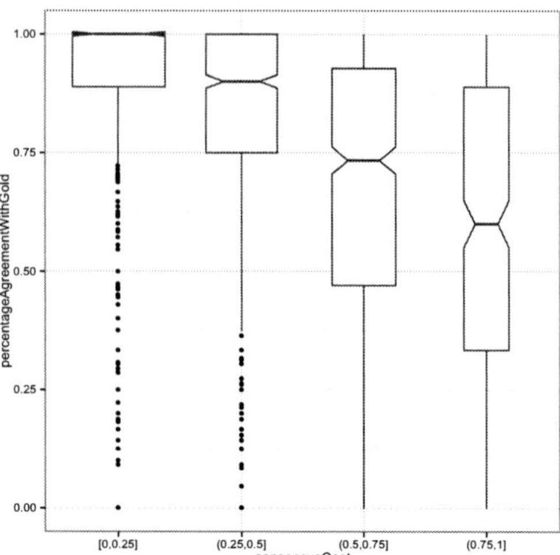

Figure 6: Consensus Cost and Annotation Quality

with higher Consensus Cost values, in the intervals (0.5,0.75] and (0.75,1], show a more heterogeneous picture. While their median agreement is much lower, they also show a more varied distribution, including some high quality annotations.

In sum, we can conclude that there is a clear association between Consensus Cost and annotation quality. A low Consensus Cost can serve as a proxy for high annotation quality. The relationship is not a simple linear one, though, so that some annotations with high Consensus Cost may also be of high quality.

4.3 Consensus Costs by Question Type

When we evaluated the quality of the crowd focus annotation in relation to the gold-standard expert annotation in section 3.2, we found that the crowd annotations fall into three groups with respect to question types: Answers to the *who*, *when* and *where* questions showed a high percentage agreement with the expert annotation, answers to *which*, *what* and *how* questions had a much lower percentage agreement and answers to *why* questions were the most difficult ones for the crowd and had the lowest agreement numbers. The data by question type thus makes an interesting test case for Consensus Cost as a proxy for annotation quality. If sentences with a low consensus cost provide annotation of higher quality, we should be able to find a similar division of the annotation in terms of question types as as in comparison with the expert annotation.

Figure 7 shows the consensus cost of our crowd annotation plotted according to question types.

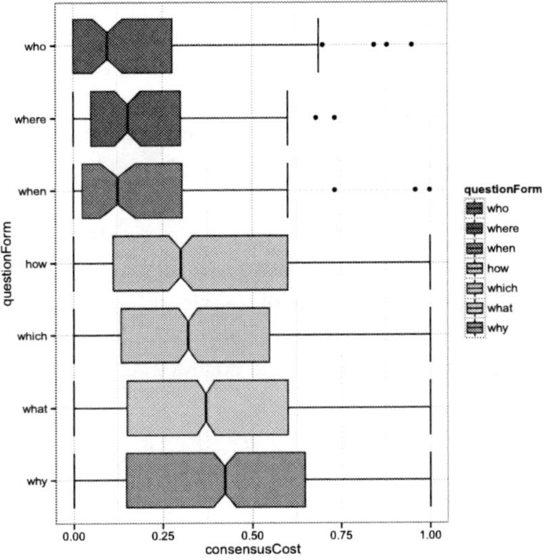

Figure 7: Consensus Cost per Question Type

The figure shows clear differences by question type: The annotations of answers to *who*, *when*, and *where* questions have the lowest consensus costs, while answers to *why* questions have highest cost. And in addition, focus annotations of answers to *why* and *how* are most varied.

Consensus cost by question type thus patterns parallel to the quality of the crowd annotation compared to the expert annotation. The analysis by question type thus confirms the overall analysis in the previous subsection establishing a low Consensus Cost in crowd annotation as a proxy for high quality annotation.

4.4 Extrinsic evaluation

To externally establish the relevance and quality of the crowd focus annotation, we extrinsically evaluated the expert gold standard annotation in an independent task, Short Answer Assessment, specifically the automatic assessment of answers to reading comprehension questions. For this purpose, we employed the CoMiC system (Meurers et al., 2011), which assesses student answers by analyzing the quantity and quality of alignment links it finds between the student and the target answer.

Our goal here is twofold: on the one hand, we want to find out whether the previously introduced Consensus Cost measure is helpful in determining the quality of focus annotation as measured by its impact on Short Answer Assessment. On the other hand, it is interesting to determine whether the state of the art in automatic answer assessment can be advanced by integrating non-expert annotation of focus (as a step towards automatic focus annotation developed using the crowd-annotated data).

To cleanly separate the data used for testing the Answer Assessment system CoMiC from the data used for training CoMiC, we randomly sampled approximately 20% of the CREG-5K data set and set it aside as the final test set. The remaining 80% was used as training set.

In exploring the impact of different Consensus Costs, we used the same four cutoffs as before: 0.25, 0.5, 0.75 and the maximum value 1.0. For each cutoff, we picked the answers with crowd focus annotations satisfying the cutoff constraint in training and test set, and ran CoMiC on the resulting data excerpt, aligning only words in student and target answer that are focused. For the rest of the data, which did not meet the Consensus Cost criterion or for which no focus annotation was available, we used the standard version of CoMiC that only aligns words not previously mentioned in the question. We then calculated a weighted average (by number of test instances) of both system accuracies in order to arrive at an overall system result for the respective Consensus Cost value. The results are displayed in Table 1.

Cost	Focus		Given		Avg
≤	train/test	%	train/test	%	%
base	–		4136/1001	81.5	81.5
0.25	1009/252	88.1	3127/749	80.4	82.3
0.5	2019/489	84.5	2117/512	80.7	82.5
0.75	3087/747	84.5	1049/254	79.5	**83.2**
1.0	3638/882	82.7	498/119	76.5	81.9

Table 1: Results on the "unseen answers" test set

The 'train/test' column shows the number of training and test instances each system was run on, and the '%' column shows the classification accuracy achieved. The 'base' row gives the baseline resulting from using CoMiC as-is, without any focus information.

Looking at the results for the focus partition of the data, one can see that accuracy drops when taking into account focus annotation with higher Consensus Cost, even though thereby in principle more training data is becoming available.

For the 'Given' column, when data with higher Consensus Cost is used for the 'Focus' version of the system and thereby less data is available for training the 'Given' system, accuracy of the latter decreases.

Overall, a Consensus Cost cutoff of 0.75 gives the optimal trade-off between both system variants, yielding 83.2% classification accuracy.

Test with answers to unseen questions In a second experiment, we also compiled a question-based train/test split, meaning that for approximately 20% of randomly picked questions in CREG-5K, all answers were held out as the test set. This is a much harder benchmark since the system in the test has to classify answers to previously unseen questions, providing some indication of the system's ability to learn something general rather than about specific question-answer pairs. The remainder of the testing procedure was the same as described above, yielding the results detailed in Table 2.

Cost	Focus		Given		Avg
≤	train/test	%	train/test	%	%
base	–		4016/1121	78.8	78.8
0.25	970/291	81.4	3046/830	78.2	79.0
0.5	1938/570	80.4	2078/551	78.2	79.3
0.75	2973/861	81.6	1043/260	76.9	**80.6**
1.0	3515/1005	79.6	501/116	78.4	79.5

Table 2: Results on the "unseen questions" test set

The accuracies are generally lower due to the harder test scenario. Moreover, the clear trends observed above with regard to training and test size do not seem to apply as clearly here, likely again owing to the 'unseen questions' scenario. Given the many different types of potential questions and the relatively small number of different questions the system sees during training, it is more important for which questions the system has seen answers, than how many. However, despite the differences to the previous experiment, the optimal result is again achieved with a Consensus Cost of 0.75, supporting the conclusion that Consensus Cost supports a systematic characterization of annotation quality.

5 Conclusion

We described a crowd-sourcing experiment for the annotation of focus, establishing its success both intrinsically by comparing it to a gold-standard expert annotation, and extrinsically by using the resulting annotations successfully in an independent CL task, Short Answer Assessment.

In order to distinguish between high and low quality crowd annotations, we define the measure of Consensus Cost, which essentially is the number of minority votes for each markable. We show that low values of Consensus Cost indicate high annotation quality and that training data selection based on Consensus Cost is beneficial in the Short Answer Assessment task.

In the future, we plan to extend our assessment of annotation quality beyond simple Consensus Cost cut-offs to a supervised machine-learning approach that can also take other characteristics of the authentic data (e.g., the question type) into account. The relationship between Consensus Cost and annotation quality is not simply linear and the additional information could help determine which of the more variable-quality data with high Consensus Cost is of high quality.

References

Daniel Büring. 2007. Intonation, semantics and information structure. In Gillian Ramchand and Charles Reiss, editors, *The Oxford Handbook of Linguistic Interfaces*, Oxford University Press.

Sasha Calhoun, Jean Carletta, Jason Brenier, Neil Mayo, Dan Jurafsky, Mark Steedman, and David Beaver. 2010. The NXT-format switchboard corpus: A rich resource for investigating the syntax, semantics, pragmatics and prosody of dialogue. *Language Resources and Evaluation* 44:387–419.

Tim Finin, Will Murnane, Anand Karandikar, Nicholas Keller, Justin Martineau, and Mark Dredze. 2010. Annotating named entities in twitter data with crowdsourcing. In *Proceedings of the NAACL HLT 2010 Workshop on Creating Speech and Language Data with Amazon's Mechanical Turk*. Association for Computational Linguistics, Stroudsburg, PA, USA, CSLDAMT '10, pages 80–88.

Simone Hantke, Erik Marchi, and Björn Schuller. 2016. Introducing the weighted trustability evaluator for crowdsourcing exemplified by speaker likability classification. In Nicoletta Calzolari (Conference Chair), Khalid Choukri, Thierry Declerck, Sara Goggi, Marko Grobelnik, Bente Maegaard, Joseph Mariani, Helene

Mazo, Asuncion Moreno, Jan Odijk, and Stelios Piperidis, editors, *Proceedings of the Tenth International Conference on Language Resources and Evaluation (LREC 2016)*. European Language Resources Association (ELRA), Paris, France.

Pei-Yun Hsueh, Prem Melville, and Vikas Sindhwani. 2009. Data quality from crowdsourcing: A study of annotation selection criteria. In *Proceedings of the NAACL HLT 2009 Workshop on Active Learning for Natural Language Processing*. Association for Computational Linguistics, Stroudsburg, PA, USA, HLT '09, pages 27–35.

Ray Jackendoff. 1972. *Semantic Interpretation in Generative Grammar*. MIT Press, Cambridge, MA.

Manfred Krifka. 2007. Basic notions of information structure. In Caroline Fery, Gisbert Fanselow, and Manfred Krifka, editors, *The notions of information structure*, Universitätsverlag Potsdam, Potsdam, volume 6 of *Interdisciplinary Studies on Information Structure (ISIS)*, pages 13–55.

Detmar Meurers, Ramon Ziai, Niels Ott, and Janina Kopp. 2011. Evaluating answers to reading comprehension questions in context: Results for German and the role of information structure. In *Proceedings of the TextInfer 2011 Workshop on Textual Entailment*. ACL, Edinburgh, pages 1–9.

Niels Ott, Ramon Ziai, and Detmar Meurers. 2012. Creation and analysis of a reading comprehension exercise corpus: Towards evaluating meaning in context. In Thomas Schmidt and Kai Wörner, editors, *Multilingual Corpora and Multilingual Corpus Analysis*, Benjamins, Amsterdam, Hamburg Studies in Multilingualism (HSM), pages 47–69.

Ciyang Qing, Ulle Endriss, Raquel Fernandez, and Justin Kruger. 2014. Empirical analysis of aggregation methods for collective annotation. In *Proceedings of COLING 2014, the 25th International Conference on Computational Linguistics: Technical Papers*. Dublin City University and Association for Computational Linguistics, Dublin, Ireland, pages 1533–1542.

Stefan Riezler. 2014. On the problem of theoretical terms in empirical computational linguistics. *Computational Linguistics* 40(1):235–245.

Julia Ritz, Stefanie Dipper, and Michael Götze. 2008. Annotation of information structure: An evaluation across different types of texts. In *Proceedings of the 6th International Conference on Language Resources and Evaluation*. Marrakech, Morocco, pages 2137–2142.

Mats Rooth. 1992. A theory of focus interpretation. *Natural Language Semantics* 1(1):75–116.

Roger Schwarzschild. 1999. GIVENness, AvoidF and other constraints on the placement of accent. *Natural Language Semantics* 7(2):141–177.

Rion Snow, Brendan O'Connor, Daniel Jurafsky, and Andrew Y. Ng. 2008. Cheap and fast—but is it good?: Evaluating non-expert annotations for natural language tasks. In *Proceedings of the Conference on Empirical Methods in Natural Language Processing*. Association for Computational Linguistics, Stroudsburg, PA, USA, EMNLP '08, pages 254–263.

Arnim von Stechow. 1981. Topic, focus, and local relevance. In Wolfgang Klein and W. Levelt, editors, *Crossing the Boundaries in Linguistics*, Reidel, Dordrecht, pages 95–130.

Joel Tetreault, Elena Filatova, and Martin Chodorow. 2010. Rethinking grammatical error annotation and evaluation with the amazon mechanical turk. In *NAACL-HLT: 2010 Proceedings of the 5th Workshop on Building Educational Applications (BEA-5)*. Association for Computational Linguistics.

Omar F. Zaidan and Chris Callison-Burch. 2011. Crowdsourcing translation: Professional quality from non-professionals. In *Proceedings of the 49th Annual Meeting of the Association for Computational Linguistics: Human Language Technologies - Volume 1*. Association for Computational Linguistics, Stroudsburg, PA, USA, HLT '11, pages 1220–1229.

Ramon Ziai and Detmar Meurers. 2014. Focus annotation in reading comprehension data. In *Proceedings of the 8th Linguistic Annotation Workshop (LAW VIII, 2014)*. COLING, Association for Computational Linguistics, Dublin, Ireland, pages 159–168.

Part of Speech Annotation of a Turkish-German Code-Switching Corpus

Özlem Çetinoğlu
IMS
University of Stuttgart
Germany
ozlem@ims.uni-stuttgart.de

Çağrı Çöltekin
Department of Linguistics
University of Tübingen
Germany
ccoltekin@sfs.uni-tuebingen.de

Abstract

In this paper we describe our efforts on POS annotation of a code-switching corpus created from Turkish-German tweets. We use Universal Dependencies (UD) POS tags as our tag set. While the German parts of the corpus employ UD specifications, for the Turkish parts we propose annotation guidelines that adopt UD's language-general rules when it is applicable and adapt its principles to Turkish-specific phenomena when it is not. The resulting corpus has POS annotation of 1029 tweets, which is aligned with existing language identification annotation.

1 Introduction

Multilingual speakers cover a higher percentage of the world population than monolingual speakers (Tucker, 1999). Acting multilingual, that is, mixing languages is commonly observed among these multilingual speakers (Auer and Wei, 2007). The definition, types, and use of language mixing have long been studied by researchers, especially from a sociolinguistic perspective (Gumperz, 1964; Sankoff, 1968; Lipski, 1978). Some linguists make distinctions in the terminology according to the level of the language mixing, e.g. use *code-mixing* for sentence-internal alternations, some others use either *code-mixing* or *code-switching* for all types of mixing (Poplack, 1980; Myers-Scotton, 1997). In this paper we use code-switching (CS) as an umbrella term.

Unlike linguistic studies, computational research on code-switching has recently accelerated, although the first theoretical framework to parse code-switched sentences has been proposed by Joshi back in the 80s (Joshi, 1982). Several studies has emerged on word-level language identification (Nguyen and Doğruöz, 2013; Das and Gambäck, 2014; cf. Solorio et al., 2014), predicting code-switching points (Solorio and Liu, 2008a; Elfardy et al., 2013), and POS tagging (Solorio and Liu, 2008b; Vyas et al., 2014; Jamatia et al., 2015).

Computational approaches often need annotated data. The number of CS corpora annotated with language identification information has also increased proportional to the interest in the field (Nguyen and Doğruöz, 2013; Barman et al., 2014; Das and Gambäck, 2014; Maharjan et al., 2015).

Part of speech (POS) annotation of CS data, on the other hand, is not very common yet. To our knowledge, there are only three code-switching corpora with POS annotation:[1] one on Spanish-English (Solorio and Liu, 2008b) and two on Hindi-English (Vyas et al., 2014; Jamatia et al., 2015). These are valuable resources as part of speech tags can provide more insight on the nature of code-switching and pave the way for syntactic annotation.

Here in this work, we present a fourth CS corpus annotated with POS information. The corpus contains 1029 Turkish-German tweets, already annotated with language information (Çetinoğlu, 2016). We add the POS tag layer following Universal Dependencies (UD) (Nivre et al., 2016). German is one of the languages UD already covers. Turkish on the other hand is under development. Therefore, our work also contributes to the discussions on POS tagging and segmentation of Turkish in the UD framework.

The rest of the paper is as follows: We discuss previous annotation efforts in CS and POS annotation in social media in Section 2. The data is described in Section 3 and annotation decisions are explained in Section 4. Processing steps are given

[1]There are some POS-annotated corpora that contain CS instances although the intention of collection is different. For instance the KiezDeutsch corpus (Rehbein et al., 2014) has a small number of utterances with Turkish-German CS. Old German Reference Corpus (Dipper et al., 2004) has examples of mixing Old High German and Latin.

Proceedings of LAW X – The 10th Linguistic Annotation Workshop, pages 120–130,
Berlin, Germany, August 11, 2016.

in Section 5. We analyse the data and processing in Section 6 and conclude in Section 7.

2 Related Work

Corpora created for studying code-switching computationally mostly focus on data annotated with language information. Nguyen and Doğruöz (2013) collect Turkish-Dutch posts from an online discussion forum and annotate words as Turkish or Dutch. A small amount of English words are also annotated as Dutch. Punctuation, numbers, emoticons, links, chat language, meta forum tags, proper names are ignored during annotation. Barman et al. (2014) create a CS corpus of Bengali-Hindi-English from Facebook comments. They define English, Bengali, Hindi, Mixed tags, and annotate named entities, acronyms, and universal expressions such as symbols, numbers, emoticons as separate tags. The Shared Task on Language Identification in Code-Switched Data also uses social media, namely Twitter, as their main source in collecting code-switching data. They present corpora in pairs Spanish-English, Nepali-English, Mandarin-English, and Modern Standard Arabic-Egyptian Arabic (Maharjan et al., 2015).

POS tagged data sets are fewer as compared to ones annotated with language information. Solorio and Liu (2008b) are the first to annotate POS tags on code-switched data. They recorded conversations between bilingual speakers of Spanish and English. Then they transcribed this data and manually annotated with POS tags. They used a fine-grained tagset which is a combination of English and Spanish TreeTagger (Schmid, 1994) tags (a version of Penn Treebank tag set for English and 75 tags for Spanish). Out of the 922 sentences they collected, 576 are monolingual English. There are 239 switches throughout the conversations, 129 of them are intra-sentential.

Following studies on annotating code-switching data with POS tags come years later. Vyas et al. (2014) chose Facebook celebrity pages and BBC Hindi as their media and collected user posts mixed in English and Hindi. Their annotation is in multiple layers. First the posts were splitted into fragments so that they would have a unique matrix language English or Hindi. Each word in a matrix is identified as English, Hindi, or Other. The POS layer employs 12 Universal POS tags (Petrov et al., 2011) and three additional tags for named entities (people, location, organisation). They have a corpus of 381 posts which corresponds to 4135 words. 17.2% of these posts contains intersentential or intrasentential code-switching.

Jamatia et al. (2015) utilised both Facebook and Twitter in compiling their English-Hindi data. They divided posts and tweets into utterances and automatically tokenised them. Manual POS annotation uses a fine-grained tag set which could be mapped to a coarse-grained one. The fine-grained set combines tags developed for Indian languages with Twitter-specific tags from Gimpel et al. (2011). The coarse-grained version retains the Twitter-specific tags and maps the rest to Universal POS tags. The resulting corpus consists of 2583 utterances, with 68.2% being monolingual.

Efforts on POS annotation of social media started with using the Penn TreeBank tag set (Marcus et al., 1993) for English (Foster et al., 2011; Petrov and McDonald, 2012). Ritter et al. (2011) extended PTB tagset with Twitter-specific tags for retweets, usernames, hashtags, and URLs. Gimpel et al. (2011) designed a completely new set tailored to Twitter. For German, Neunerdt et al. (2013) use the standard STTS POS tag set (Schiller et al., 1995) to annotate web comments. Rehbein (2013) adopts the same tag set and introduces new tags for usernames, URLs, hashtags, and emoticons for POS tagging German tweets. Similarly for Turkish, Pamay et al. (2015) use the standard POS tag set of Oflazer (1994) and add tags for abbreviations, emoticons, mentions, hashtags, and URLs to cover the non-canonical content of a web treebank.

3 Data

We use the data that Çetinoğlu (2016) has collected on code-switching Turkish-German tweets. It consists of 1029 tweets, each having at least one code-switching point. Tweets are automatically collected and manually filtered. Before adding language identification annotation tokenisation and normalisation is applied based on Turkish and German orthography rules.

The tag set is based on the 2014 Shared Task on Language Identification in Code-Switched Data (Solorio et al., 2014; Maharjan et al., 2015): TR (Turkish), DE (German), LANG3 (third language), MIXED (intra-word CS), NE (named entity), AMBIG (words belong to both languages and cannot be disambiguated with the given context), OTHER (punctuation, numbers, URLs, emoticons, symbols, any other token that do not belong to previous classes). The Shared Task labels the tokens that belong to a third language as OTHER, Çetinoğlu (2016) introduces the LANG3 tag for them. Additionally, named entities are tagged both as NE as in the Shared Task, and with their language label TR, DE, or LANG3. MIXED tokens are also marked with the code-switching boundary, represented with the symbol '§'.

There are 16992 tokens in total, that corresponds to 16.51 tokens per tweet. Half of the tokens are Turkish, it is followed by OTHER and German, both being around 20%. In 790 tweets, there are more tokens labelled as TR than DE. Details of the data collection, correction, and annotation processes are explained in Çetinoğlu (2016).

4 Annotation Guidelines

The annotation process follows the Universal Dependencies (Nivre et al., 2016) conventions as much as possible.[2] We only use the POS tag labels from the UD inventory, and follow the general principles of UD as well as the available language-specific documentation for each language in the corpus. Although we do not explicity annotate in the syntactic level, we have to take into account UD syntax representation, especially for segmenting Turkish words.

Besides the recent popularity of the UD-based annotations, the major advantage of UD in our work is that the UD guidelines are intended to be as language-general as possible. For a multilingual corpus, such as ours, the importance of uniform annotations within the corpus cannot be overstated. The downsides, on the other hand, are potential confusion due to already established annotation conventions (such as STTS (Schiller et al., 1995) for German), and the fact that UD is an ongoing project, and parts of the formalism is still in development.

In this section we describe the annotation guidelines we follow briefly, focusing more on the aspects that differ from UD or the common conventions used in relevant monolingual corpora.

4.1 Segmentation

Following Universal Dependencies guidelines, we mark POS tags on *syntactic* words,[3] which results in segmenting some of the surface tokens in both German and Turkish. For German, the only case that require segmentation is the contraction of prepositions and definite articles. For example, the word *zur* 'to the' is tokenised into its parts as *zu* and *der*. The segmentation of Turkish syntactic words is more involved, and at present, the UD guidelines for Turkish tokenization are still a moving target. We describe the approach we employed for segmentation of Turkish below.

Turkish is a morphologically complex language. In addition to a large set of inflectional morphemes that can attach to verbal or nominal stems, some productive (derivational) morphemes may change the POS tag of an already inflected word. In Turkish NLP literature, this phenomenon is addressed with sub-word units that are often called *inflectional groups* (IGs) (Oflazer, 1999), which correspond to one or more morphemes grouped by derivational boundaries. In this work, we also follow the same convention, however, similar to Çöltekin (2016), we follow a more conservative approach to segmentation in comparison to most earlier work. Instead of segmenting a word into IGs after each derivation, we segment only before the morphemes that introduce a new syntactic word, such that parts of the word may carry conflicting morphological features, or participate in separate syntactic relations. In other words, we segment words to avoid potential ambiguous or conflicting morphosyntactic annotations.

An example of this is presented in (1) below,[4] which also coincides with an instance of word-internal code switching. As introduced earlier, the symbol '§' indicates the code switching boundary within a word. We mark inflectional group boundaries with the symbol '•' in the examples.

(1) sabah
morning.NOUN.Sg
Internetseite§-de•ki-ler-i
website.NOUN.Sg-Loc•ki.NOUN-Pl.Acc
ausdrucken ed-eceğ-im
print.VERB.Inf do.VERB-Fut-1Sg
'I will print the ones from the website in the morning'

The singular German noun *Internetseite* 'website' is inflected with the Turkish locative case marker *de*. This is the code-switching point. The

[2]More specifically we follow UD version 1.2.

[3]Segmentation is not in the morpheme level, yet words are not necessarily phonological or orthographic. http://universaldependencies.org/u/overview/tokenization.html

[4]Notation of examples and gloss descriptions are given in Appendix A.

rest of the word takes Turkish inflectional and derivational suffixes. The part *Internetseitede* 'on the website' functions as an adjective when it gets the derivational suffix *-ki* (e.g. *Internetseitedeki foto* 'the photo on the website'). With a zero derivation, the derived adjectival behaves as a noun, thus can bear a plural suffix and a case marker. In it is final form, the word *Internetseitedekileri* 'the ones on the website' refers to a set of objects (e.g., documents or pictures) on a website. Without segmentation, we cannot represent the fact that there is only one website but multiple items within the website. Similarly, the direct object of the predicate is the items on the website, not the website (which could have been a direct object of another predicate). As a result, annotations that allow correct interpretations of words like *Internetseitedekileri* above require further segmentation.

Besides the relativiser *-ki* discussed above, we mark the following suffixes which may introduce similar ambiguous or conflicting morphosyntactic annotations.[5]

- *-lH* deriving nouns and adjectives from a noun (N) with the meaning of 'with N' (*dondurmalı* '(the one) with ice cream', deriving adjectives and nouns from location names with the meaning 'from N' (*Berlinli* '(the person) from Berlin'
- *-sHz* deriving nouns and adjectives from a noun with the meaning of 'without N' (*eğitimsiz* '(the person) **without** education')
- *-lHk* deriving nouns and adjectives from a noun with the meaning of 'fit/suitable for N' (*senlik* **'fit for** you')
- *-CH* deriving nouns and adjectives from a noun with the meaning of 'preferring N' (*biracı* '(the one) who prefers beer'), as well as mostly lexicalized use of deriving nouns referring to occupations (*fizikçi* 'physic**ist**')
- *-lAş* deriving verbs from nouns with the meaning of 'become N' (*özgürleşmek* 'to **become** free')
- Copular suffixes (*sizdendi* '(he/she) **was** one of you')

[5]Capital letters in suffixes denote allomorphs. A = {a,e}, H = {ı,i,u,ü}, C = {c, ç}.

Similar to *-ki*, the first four suffixes form either adjectives or nouns from nouns. In their adjectival use, segmentation is not strictly necessary as the adjectives in Turkish do not inflect. We segmented productive uses of these suffixes regardless of whether they derive nouns or adjectives for the sake of easier and more accurate annotation.

The last two examples in the above list form predicates form nouns and adjectives. When these suffixes are attached to simple nouns or adjectives, one may avoid segmentation. However, the copular suffixes may also attach to subordinate verbs, in which case, the same word carries two predicates with potentially conflicting sets of inflections and syntactic relations outside the word. For example, if we do not segment the copular part of *gördüğüyüz* in (2) below, we cannot identify the facts that the verb *gör* 'see' is inflected for past tense, while the copula is in present tense. Furthermore, the subject of the copula is *o* 'he/she', while the subject of the verb *gör* is *biz* 'we'.

(2) Biz o-nun
We.PRON he/she.PRON-Gen
rüya-sı-nda
dream.NOUN-P3S-Loc
gör-düğü•yüz
see.VERB-Past-3Sg•VERB-Cop-1Pl
'We are the ones that he/she saw in his/her dream'

We segment words before productive uses of all of the suffixes listed in this section. However, we do not segment words if they are lexicalised. For example the suffix *-siz* 'without' is segmented in ***arabasız** gidemeyiz* 'we cannot go (there) **without a car**', but not in ***evsizler** için yardım* 'help for the **homeless**'.

To decide if a word is lexicalised, we test if the parts of the segmented version can have syntactic dependencies. For instance, *futbolcu* 'footballer' is lexicalised although it is derived from *futbol* 'football' with the agentive suffix *-CH*. In the expression *Amerikan futbolcu*, *Amerikan* 'American' modifies the footballer. An expression where American modifies football requires a third word: *Amerikan futbolu oyuncusu* 'American football player'. In contrast, unless we introduce a new IG with the suffix *-CH*, *eski kitap•çı* have ambiguous interpretations 'old [book shop]' and '[old book] shop/seller'. In other words, parts of the word referring to the 'book' and the 'book shop' can participate in separate syntactic relations.

Another difference from the use of IGs in earlier Turkish NLP literature is that we do not admit 'zero derivations'. All tokens correspond to non-empty surface strings. This results in an inconsistency in the representation of copular suffixes, since a nominal/adjectival predicate in present tense with the third person singular subject does not have a corresponding surface suffix. As a result, the predicate in *Ben hasta-yım* 'I am sick' is segmented, while the predicate *o hasta* 'he is sick' is not segmented. This case poses no problem for our POS annotation purposes, although it would lead inconsistencies in syntactic representation.

4.2 POS Tagging

For both languages, we follow the Universal Dependencies POS tag scheme as closely as possible. UD defines a coarse set of 17 tags listed in Table 1. As in segmentation, the German POS tagging scheme is better defined and more standardised. Despite some existing work, Turkish POS tagging standards for UD is under development.[6] As a result, we focus more on some aspects of Turkish POS tagging in our work. Detailed POS tagging guidelines are included in the distribution of the corpus.

Special word and symbol sequences, such as mentions, hashtags and URLs, are also tagged using the UD POS tag set. We tag mentions (always coded as `@username`) as `PROPN`. The hashtags are tagged as usual when they are a single word with a clear POS tag. For example, `#Berlin` is tagged as `PROPN`, and `#happy` is tagged as `ADJ`. If the hashtag is a multi-word string that cannot be treated as a single word, e.g., `#GiveVoiceToCizre`, it is tagged as `X`. We keep multi-word hashtags intact as we prefer to retain their hashtag property.

Unintelligible alphanumeric sequences and words from other languages whose POS tag could not be determined by the annotators are also tagged as `X`. URLs, emoticons and non-alphanumeric tokens are tagged as `SYM` as per UD specification. We also use the tag `SYM` for the Twitter tags `RE`, `RT` and, the new line representation `<NL>`.

[6]The UD version 1.3, which is released while the present paper was under review, contains a Turkish treebank. However, the treebank is still in development state, and the documentation is mainly based on Çöltekin (2015), which is not (yet) fully complient with the UD.

Tag	explanation
`ADJ`	adjective
`ADP`	adposition
`ADV`	adverb
`AUX`	auxiliary verb
`CONJ`	coordinating conjunction
`DET`	determiner
`INTJ`	interjection
`NOUN`	noun
`NUM`	numeral
`PART`	particle
`PRON`	pronoun
`PROPN`	proper noun
`PUNCT`	punctuation
`SCONJ`	subordinating conjunction
`SYM`	symbol
`VERB`	verb
`X`	other

Table 1: Universal dependencies tag set.

All forms of verbs, including verbs that are derived into other categories by subordinating suffixes are tagged as `VERB`. This is in line with the UD guidelines, but unlike most Turkish NLP work where subordinate word structures are typically segmented into multiple IGs, and the last IG (the head) is marked as `NOUN`, `ADJ` or `ADV` depending on whether the verbal form is a *verbal noun*, *participle*, or *converb* respectively.

Auxiliary verbs are tagged as `AUX`, and copulars as `VERB` for both Turkish and German. Similar to German verb *sein* 'to be', the Turkish copula *ol* 'to be/become' can act both as an auxiliary (`AUX`) or as a copula (`VERB`). Examples (3) and (4) show its verb and auxiliary uses respectively from the corpus we annotated.

(3) **Frau** **Geiger**§'i
Ms.NOUN.Sg Geiger.PROPN.Sg.Acc
gör-dü-m çok mutlu
see.VERB-Past-1Sg very.ADV happy.ADJ
ol-du-m
become.VERB-Past-1Sg
'I saw Ms Geiger I became very happy.'

(4) Osmanlı
Ottoman.PROPN.Sg
hayal-i
daydream.NOUN.Sg-P3S
kur-an-lar duvar-a
fancy.VERB.Part-3Pl wall.NOUN.Sg-Dat

tosla-mış ol-acak
bump.VERB-Evid-Past be.AUX-Fut.3Sg
'The ones who daydream of Ottomans will have bumped the wall.'

Substantivised adjectives are marked as ADJ. In Turkish it is common to use an adjective as noun with the meaning of 'the object or person with the property described by the adjective'. We mark adjectives as ADJ regardless of their use. This contrasts with most Turkish NLP work to date, since these words are typically analyzed as two separate IGs one of which is introduced by a zero-derivation. In both languages, we also use the tag ADJ for adjectives that are used as predicates.

Multi-word named entities are annotated as normal linguistic units. That is, the words that form a multi-word named entity are not marked as PROPN but as the POS tags they would normally be assigned to. For example in (5) the German word *Aufbruch* and the Turkish word *Derneği* are marked as NOUN even though they are part of a multi-word named entity. The original annotations (Çetinoğlu, 2016) mark the named entities and language IDs as shown in the third row of (5).

(5) **Aufbruch**
Emergence.NOUN.Sg
NE.DE
Neukölln Derneğ-i
Neukölln.PROPN.Sg Society.NOUN-P3S
NE.DE NE.TR
'Emerging Neukölln Society'

Non-root inflectional groups in Turkish that are split off from the root part during the segmentation step are assigned POS tags that reflect their function. For example, the IG introduced by the suffix *-siz* in ***eğitim****-siz insan* 'uneducated person' is tagged as ADJ, while in ***eğitim****-sizler çoğunlukta* 'uneducated (people) are in majority' it is tagged as NOUN.

Particles of German separable verbs are, following the UD principle, tagged as ADP. This is in contrast with the most common tagging scheme, STTS, used in German NLP so far.

5 Processing

The team for segmentation and POS tagging consists of four annotators and two researchers. All annotators are Turkish-German bilingual undergraduate students. Three of them study computational linguistics, and one studies linguistics.

5.1 Segmentation

Before the task, the annotators were not familiar with the idea of segmenting Turkish words into sublexical units. Thus, the training included the concept of inflectional groups and the current take on segmentation through recent work (Nivre et al., 2016; Çöltekin, 2016). For the actual task, they have given segmentation guidelines. They are also told to oversegment rather than undersegment in case of doubt. Each tweet is segmented by two annotators, and then merged and corrected if necessary, by the researchers. Lexicalised derivations were the source of main conflicts or sometimes non-conflicting oversegmentation. This is expectable, as lexicalisation decisions are rather a continuum. The German side of the segmentation was straightforward and on few cases; annotators easily accomplished this part.

5.2 Restoring Language Identification

When the German and Turkish segmentation has altered, language identification assigned to each token should be altered too. We restored language information in a semi-automatic way. There are three possible scenarios of segmentation. First, when a token identified as German is segmented, all segments are German. Second, similarly, a segmented Turkish token has Turkish segments.

The third scenario is more complex. How the segments of a MIXED token are labelled depends on segmentation boundaries. In our corpus the mixed words to segment are all examples of German-Turkish code-switching (with a single English-Turkish code-switching example). If the segmentation boundary is after the code-switching boundary as in the earlier ***Internetseite****§de-kileri* 'the ones on the website' (1), repeated as (6) below as it is coded in the corpus, the first segment remains MIXED and the second segment is tagged as Turkish. If the segmentation boundary is also the code-switching boundary, then each part is annotated using the corresponding language tags, as in ***kreativ****§miş* 'she/he was creative' demonstrated in (7) below. The fact that these are examples of word-internal code-switching can still be recovered based on the symbols we use for marking code-switching boundaries (§) and non-root IGs (-).

(6) `Internetseite§de` `MIXED` `NOUN`
`-kileri` `TR` `NOUN`

(7) `kreativ§` `DE` `ADJ`
`-miş` `TR` `VERB`

We treated all scenarios automatically, and double-checked the third scenario manually.

5.3 POS Tagging

We started annotator training with existing guidelines and treebank demos from Universal Dependencies.[7] We employed two different training sets for POS tagging. As the first set, we gave annotators 20 tweets separate from the data set and ask them to annotate 10 of them to have double annotation for each. We used these annotations to discuss confusing points. As the second set we gave each annotator up to 15 phrases that are potentially hard to annotate, and ask them to label and add a source, e.g. one of the UD links, to make sure they are aware of multiple sources. Some of these phrases are later used as examples in annotation guidelines.

All tweets are annotated twice. Each annotator is assigned half of the corpus, and each half is annotated by two annotators. The inter-annotator agreement is calculated separately for each half, and then the researchers went through those tweets to resolve conflicts, correct mistakes, and ensure consistency.

6 Analysis

Our annotations are based on the twitter corpus of Çetinoğlu (2016). Originally, the corpus contains 1029 tweets, and 16922 tokens (See Section 3 for more details). After word segmentation, the number of tokens increase to 17274. All tokens are annotated with a POS tag from the Universal Dependencies POS tag inventory, as explained in Section 5. In this section, we provide statistics about the resulting corpora and present some preliminary analyses.

Majority of the segmented tokens are Turkish. In total, 226 Turkish words were segmented. Except three tokens that were tokenised as three IGs, all multi-IG words consist of two IGs. The resulting ratio of IGs per surface word is 1.02 (cf. 1.20 in METU-Sabancı Treebank (Oflazer et al., 2003)). Besides completely Turkish words, 18 mixed words are segmented into two tokens. 17 of these words are German stems with Turkish suffixes, and one is an English word with a Turkish suffix. On the German side, 31 contracted preposition+article combinations were segmented.

The overall inter annotator agreements (IAA) as measured by Cohen's kappa (Cohen, 1960) between two teams are 78.78 and 77.77 for the first and the second team respectively. The IAA per language differ. For Turkish, the agreement scores are lower, averaging 70.39 for both teams. The low score is partially due to the difficulty of the task in Turkish, which is also accented by the fact that our annotators have not received formal education in Turkish, but in German. However, the overall low score also has to do with the fact that non-linguistic tokens (e.g., punctuation, special Twitter symbols) are not included in this calculation. The common disagreements (that are resolved during correction phase) that stand out are, `AUX–VERB`, `ADJ–ADV`, `DET–PRON`, `NOUN–PRON`, `NOUN–PROPN`, `INTJ–NOUN` and between `VERB` and `ADJ`, `ADV` and `NOUN` (in subordinate structures). The IAA for German is higher, averaging at 74.24. The confusion in German POS tagging is almost exclusively between `AUX–VERB`, `ADJ–ADV`, `NOUN–PROPN`, and `DET–PRON`. The agreement is the lowest for language ID LANG3 (57.92), and highest for OTHER (86.33, non-linguistic tokens, and tokens whose language ID could not be determined).

The confusion between `DET–PRON` is common in both languages, since they share the same frequent word forms. The `ADJ–ADV` confusion seems to stem from the same reason. Again, `AUX–VERB` confusion is due to copular and auxiliary use of the same frequent tokens. Most `NOUN–PROPN` disagreements happen since, following UD, we tag parts of named entities as their respective POS tags, not as `PROPN` (for an example, see (5) in Section 4). Annotators tend to go against this guideline, and often tag parts of named entities as `PROPN`. Similarly, the guidelines require that parts of multi-word interjections should be tagged as their base POS tags. For example, the tokens in *Allaha şükür* 'Thank God' should be tagged `PROPN` and `NOUN`, while annotators may sometimes decide for `INTJ` for both.

Table 2 presents the distribution of POS tags

[7] http://universaldependencies.org/u/pos/index.html
http://universaldependencies.org/de/pos/index.html
http://bionlp-www.utu.fi/dep_search/

for each label used during language identification. Our total number of tokens per language is slightly different from Çetinoğlu (2016) due to segmentation. Majority of the tokens are Turkish. German follows Turkish after the label OTHER which includes all punctuation, symbols, numbers, URLs and Twitter-specific tokens.

One of the interesting observations in Table 2 is the high proportion of Turkish verbs (25% of all Turkish tokens) in comparison German verbs (15%). The reason for high rate of verbs are partially due to the fact that we mark all verbal forms, including all verbs derived into verbal nouns, participles, or converbs as VERB. However, this is true for both languages. The difference between the ratio of verbs in two languages has to do with the fact that most of the sentence are Turkish sentences. As a result, the predicates of main (and subordinate) clauses tend to be in Turkish, where German words are included in the (host) Turkish sentence. This is in line with the finding reported in Çetinoğlu (2016) that most tweets in this corpus have a majority of Turkish words. The ratio of nominals (NOUN, PRON and PROPN) are similar, having a distribution of 41% for German, and 40% for Turkish. POS tags with grammatical functions, such as ADP, AUX, DET and PART, are proportionally higher for German in comparison to Turkish. This is expected, since many of these grammatical functions are carried out as morphological processes in Turkish.

An interesting aspect of this corpus is rather high rate of MIXED tokens. Table 2 also shows that majority of the MIXED class involve PROPN and NOUNs, which is expected. In cases of mixed nouns or proper nouns, the mixed words are almost exclusively, DE or LANG3 (mostly English) words affixed by Turkish suffixes, e.g., (8) below. The mixed tokens that include verbs are predominantly German words with Turkish copular suffixes (9) or suffixes that derive verbs from nominals, as in *-len* suffix in (10). In some cases, German infinitives or participles are suffixed with Turkish nominal inflections (11). One last interesting case in (12) demonstrates that Turkish derivational suffixes that are normally attached to nouns or adjectives to form verbs may be attached to German (or, as in the example, English) verbs. In example (12), the suffix *-lu*[8] is attached to an English verb in a way to allow further verbal inflections.

(8) Bak şu benim
Look.VERB.Imp that.DET my.PRON
Lieblingsschwester§-im-a
favourite sister.NOUN.Sg-P1S-Dat
'Look at that favourite sister of mine'

(9) çok
very.ADV
kreativ§•miş
creative.ADJ•Cop.VERB.Evid.Past.3Sg
'he/she was very creative'

(10) **Kopie**§-len-ip
copy-Become.VERB-Sub
yapış-tır-ıl-mış
paste.VERB-Caus-Pass-Evid.Past.3Sg
'it was copied and (then) pasted'

(11) şu **kopieren**§-i
that.DET copy.VERB.Inf-Acc
icat ed-en
invention.NOUN.Sg do.VERB-Sub
'(the person) who invented (that) copying'

(12) Ben aslında
I.PRON in fact.ADV
FB§•lu-lar-ı
FB.PROPN.Sg•From.NOUN-Pl-Acc
follow§•lu-yor-du-m
follow.VERB•Derv-Prog-Past-1Sg
nur
only.ADV
'In fact, I was only following the ones of/from FB'

Turkish to German word-internal switches seem to predominantly involve introducing German nominals in Turkish host sentences. In 53% of the Turkish to German switches, the German word is NOUN, PROPN or PRON, in contrast to expected 41% in the complete corpus. The switches from German to Turkish does not have a clear pattern. For example, the ratio of Turkish nominals in German to Turkish switches amount to 40%, exactly as expected from the general corpus distribution.

7 Conclusion

In this work we present the POS annotation of a code-switching corpus created from Turkish-German tweets. The corpus has already been tokenised, normalised, and annotated with word-level language identification information.

[8]The original surface form of this suffix is -lA (-le/-la), it undergoes vowel harmony due to following suffix *-yor*.

Language	ADJ	ADP	ADV	AUX	CONJ	DET	INTJ	NOUN	NUM	PART	PRON	PROPN	PUNCT	SCONJ	SYM	VERB	X	TOTAL
TR	767	289	1026	112	205	367	293	2563	52	41	691	428	3	40	1	2289	7	9174
DE	365	219	458	112	82	203	108	867	8	47	531	195	1	25	0	581	3	3805
LANG3	14	8	4	1	0	2	10	45	5	1	5	83	0	0	0	9	11	198
MIXED	10	0	1	0	1	0	0	97	0	0	1	73	0	0	0	6	1	190
AMBIG	4	0	1	0	0	0	7	18	0	0	0	11	0	0	0	1	0	42
OTHER	0	0	0	0	0	0	176	8	160	0	0	780	1820	0	820	0	101	3865
TOTAL	1160	516	1490	225	288	572	594	3598	225	89	1228	1570	1824	65	821	2886	123	17274

Table 2: Distribution of POS tag labels for each language identification label.

For POS annotation, we follow Universal Dependencies tokenisation and POS tagging policies as closely as possible. This requires revisiting tokenisation and aligning the language identification information with the new tokenisation as the first step.

Universal Dependencies is an evolving project. In its current version, German has a rather standardised tokenisation and less open questions regarding to POS and syntactic annotation as compared to Turkish. UD provides online documentation for German, the one for Turkish is work in progress. While we took the UD specifications as is for German, we developed our own annotation guidelines for Turkish, by adopting UD rules where applicable and by proposing our solutions to unresolved cases.

The resulting corpus contains 1029 tweets (17274 tokens) annotated with 7 different language IDs and 17 different POS tags. An obvious extension is to add morphological features as the next layer. This way we can better describe the distinctions among the words in the same category. For instance, it would be possible to distinguish Turkish verbal nouns, participles, and converbs that all have the `VERB` tag. We leave this finer-grained annotation as future work.

Another direction we want to pursue is experiments with automatic language identification and POS tagging. For other researcher who would like to conduct similar experiments, the corpus and the annotation guidelines are made available at `http://www.ims.uni-stuttgart.de/institut/mitarbeiter/ozlem/LAW2016.html`.[9]

Acknowledgments

We thank Sevde Ceylan, Hasret el Sanhoury, Esra Soydoğan, and Cansu Turgut for the annotation processes. This work was funded by the Deutsche Forschungsgemeinschaft (DFG) via SFB 732, project D2.

[9] We follow the restrictions of Twitter's Terms of Service and distribute the tweet IDs instead of actual tweets. The scripts that combine downloaded tweets with annotations are also provided.

References

Peter Auer and Li Wei. 2007. *Handbook of multilingualism and multilingual communication*, volume 5. Walter de Gruyter.

Utsab Barman, Amitava Das, Joachim Wagner, and Jennifer Foster. 2014. Code mixing: A challenge for language identification in the language of social media. In *Proceedings of the First Workshop on Computational Approaches to Code Switching*, pages 13–23, Doha, Qatar, October. Association for Computational Linguistics.

Özlem Çetinoğlu. 2016. A Turkish-German code-switching corpus. In *The 10th International Conference on Language Resources and Evaluation (LREC-16)*, Portorož, Slovenia.

Çağrı Çöltekin. 2015. A grammar-book treebank of Turkish. In Markus Dickinson, Erhard Hinrichs, Agnieszka Patejuk, and Adam Przepiórkowski, editors, *Proceedings of the 14th workshop on Treebanks and Linguistic Theories (TLT 14)*, pages 35–49.

Çağrı Çöltekin. 2016. (When) do we need inflectional groups? In *The First International Conference on Turkic Computational Linguistics*, page (to appear).

Jacob Cohen. 1960. A coefficient of agreement for nominal scales. *Educational and Psychological Measurement*, 20:37–46.

Amitava Das and Björn Gambäck. 2014. Identifying languages at the word level in code-mixed indian social media text. In *Proceedings of the 11th International Conference on Natural Language Processing, Goa, India*, pages 169–178.

Stefanie Dipper, Lukas Faulstich, Ulf Leser, and Anke Lüdeling. 2004. Challenges in modelling a richly annotated diachronic corpus of German. In *Workshop on XML-based richly annotated corpora, Lisbon, Portugal*, pages 21–29.

Heba Elfardy, Mohamed Al-Badrashiny, and Mona Diab. 2013. Code switch point detection in Arabic. In *Natural Language Processing and Information Systems*, pages 412–416. Springer.

Jennifer Foster, Özlem Çetinoğlu, Joachim Wagner, Joseph Le Roux, Joakim Nivre, Deirdre Hogan, and Josef van Genabith. 2011. From news to comment: Resources and benchmarks for parsing the language of web 2.0. In *Proceedings of 5th International Joint Conference on Natural Language Processing*, pages 893–901, Chiang Mai, Thailand, November. Asian Federation of Natural Language Processing.

Kevin Gimpel, Nathan Schneider, Brendan O'Connor, Dipanjan Das, Daniel Mills, Jacob Eisenstein, Michael Heilman, Dani Yogatama, Jeffrey Flanigan, and Noah A Smith. 2011. Part-of-speech tagging for twitter: Annotation, features, and experiments. In *Proceedings of the 49th Annual Meeting of the Association for Computational Linguistics: Human Language Technologies: short papers-Volume 2*, pages 42–47. Association for Computational Linguistics.

John J. Gumperz. 1964. Linguistic and social interaction in two communities. *American Anthropologist*, 66(6):137–153.

Anupam Jamatia, Björn Gambäck, and Amitava Das. 2015. Part-of-speech tagging for code-mixed english-hindi twitter and facebook chat messages. In *Proceedings of the International Conference Recent Advances in Natural Language Processing*, pages 239–248, Hissar, Bulgaria, September. INCOMA Ltd. Shoumen, BULGARIA.

Aravind K Joshi. 1982. Processing of sentences with intra-sentential code-switching. In *Proceedings of the 9th conference on Computational linguistics-Volume 1*, pages 145–150. Academia Praha.

John Lipski. 1978. Code-switching and the problem of bilingual competence. *Aspects of bilingualism*, 250:264.

Suraj Maharjan, Elizabeth Blair, Steven Bethard, and Thamar Solorio. 2015. Developing language-tagged corpora for code-switching tweets. In *Proceedings of The 9th Linguistic Annotation Workshop*, pages 72–84, Denver, Colorado, USA, June. Association for Computational Linguistics.

Mitchell P Marcus, Mary Ann Marcinkiewicz, and Beatrice Santorini. 1993. Building a large annotated corpus of english: The penn treebank. *Computational linguistics*, 19(2):313–330.

Carol Myers-Scotton. 1997. *Duelling languages: Grammatical structure in codeswitching*. Oxford University Press.

Melanie Neunerdt, Bianka Trevisan, Michael Reyer, and Rudolf Mathar. 2013. Part-of-speech tagging for social media texts. In *Language Processing and Knowledge in the Web*, pages 139–150. Springer.

Dong Nguyen and A. Seza Doğruöz. 2013. Word level language identification in online multilingual communication. In *Proceedings of the 2013 Conference on Empirical Methods in Natural Language Processing*, pages 857–862, Seattle, Washington, USA, October. Association for Computational Linguistics.

Joakim Nivre, Marie-Catherine de Marneffe, Filip Ginter, Yoav Goldberg, Jan Hajič, Christopher Manning, Ryan McDonald, Slav Petrov, Sampo Pyysalo, Natalia Silveira, Reut Tsarfaty, and Daniel Zeman. 2016. Universal dependencies v1: A multilingual treebank collection. In *Proceedings of the Tenth International Conference on Language Resources and Evaluation (LREC'16)*, page (accepted).

Kemal Oflazer, Bilge Say, Dilek Zeynep Hakkani-Tür, and Gökhan Tür. 2003. Building a Turkish treebank. In Anne Abeille, editor, *Building and Exploiting Syntactically-annotated Corpora*. Kluwer Academic Publishers, Dordrecht.

Kemal Oflazer. 1994. Two-level description of Turkish morphology. *Literary and Linguistic Computing*, 9(2):137–148.

Kemal Oflazer. 1999. Dependency parsing with an extended finite state approach. In *Proceedings of the 37th annual meeting of the Association for Computational Linguistics on Computational Linguistics*, pages 254–260. Association for Computational Linguistics.

Tuğba Pamay, Umut Sulubacak, Dilara Torunoğlu-Selamet, and Gülşen Eryiğit. 2015. The annotation process of the itu web treebank. In *Proceedings of The 9th Linguistic Annotation Workshop*, pages 95–101, Denver, Colorado, USA, June. Association for Computational Linguistics.

Slav Petrov and Ryan McDonald. 2012. Overview of the 2012 shared task on parsing the web. In *Notes of the First Workshop on Syntactic Analysis of Non-Canonical Language (SANCL)*, volume 59.

Slav Petrov, Dipanjan Das, and Ryan McDonald. 2011. A universal part-of-speech tagset. *arXiv preprint arXiv:1104.2086*.

Shana Poplack. 1980. Sometimes I'll start a sentence in Spanish y termino en Espanol: toward a typology of code-switching. *Linguistics*, 18(7-8):581–618.

Ines Rehbein, Sören Schalowski, and Heike Wiese. 2014. The KiezDeutsch korpus (KiDKo) release 1.0. In *The 9th International Conference on Language Resources and Evaluation (LREC-14)*, Reykjavik, Iceland.

Ines Rehbein. 2013. Fine-grained pos tagging of German tweets. In *Language Processing and Knowledge in the Web*, pages 162–175. Springer.

Alan Ritter, Sam Clark, Oren Etzioni, et al. 2011. Named entity recognition in tweets: an experimental study. In *Proceedings of the Conference on Empirical Methods in Natural Language Processing*, pages 1524–1534. Association for Computational Linguistics.

Gillian Sankoff. 1968. *Social aspects of multilingualism in New Guinea.* Montreal, McGill U.

Anne Schiller, Simone Teufel, and Christine Thielen. 1995. Guidelines für das tagging deutscher textcorpora mit stts. *Manuscript, Universities of Stuttgart and Tübingen*, 66.

Helmut Schmid. 1994. Probabilistic part-of-speech tagging using decision trees. In *Proceedings of the international conference on new methods in language processing*, volume 12, pages 44–49. Citeseer.

Thamar Solorio and Yang Liu. 2008a. Learning to predict code-switching points. In *Proceedings of the Conference on Empirical Methods in Natural Language Processing*, EMNLP '08, pages 973–981, Stroudsburg, PA, USA. Association for Computational Linguistics.

Thamar Solorio and Yang Liu. 2008b. Part-of-Speech tagging for English-Spanish code-switched text. In *Proceedings of the 2008 Conference on Empirical Methods in Natural Language Processing*, pages 1051–1060, Honolulu, Hawaii, October. Association for Computational Linguistics.

Thamar Solorio, Elizabeth Blair, Suraj Maharjan, Steven Bethard, Mona Diab, Mahmoud Ghoneim, Abdelati Hawwari, Fahad AlGhamdi, Julia Hirschberg, Alison Chang, and Pascale Fung. 2014. Overview for the first shared task on language identification in code-switched data. In *Proceedings of the First Workshop on Computational Approaches to Code Switching*, pages 62–72, Doha, Qatar, October. Association for Computational Linguistics.

G Richard Tucker. 1999. A global perspective on bilingualism and bilingual education. *Georgetown University Round Table on Languages and Linguistics*, pages 332–340.

Yogarshi Vyas, Spandana Gella, Jatin Sharma, Kalika Bali, and Monojit Choudhury. 2014. Pos tagging of english-hindi code-mixed social media content. In *Proceedings of the 2014 Conference on Empirical Methods in Natural Language Processing (EMNLP)*, pages 974–979, Doha, Qatar, October. Association for Computational Linguistics.

Appendix A. Notation of Examples

German words are represented in bold and English words in italics in the examples. The POS tags in glosses correspond to the UD tags used in annotation. Gloss descriptions are given in Table 3.

Gloss	Explanation
Acc	Accusative case
Loc	Locative case
Dat	Dative case
Gen	Genitive case
Sg	Singular
Pl	Plural
1Sg	1st person singular
1Pl	1st person plural
3Pl	3rd person plural
P1S	1st person possessive
P3S	3rd person possessive
Past	Past tense
Fut	Future tense
Prog	Progressive tense
Caus	Causative
Pass	Passive
Imp	Imperative
Part	Participle
Inf	Infinitive
Evid	Evidentiality
Cop	Copular
Become	Derivational suffix with semantics 'become'
From	Derivational suffix with semantics 'of/from'
Sub	Subordinating derivational suffix
Derv	Derivational

Table 3: Gloss descriptions

Dependency Annotation Choices:
Assessing Theoretical and Practical Issues of Universal Dependencies

Kim Gerdes
Sorbonne Nouvelle
ILPGA, LPP (CNRS)
kim@gerdes.fr

Sylvain Kahane
Université Paris Ouest Nanterre
Modyco (CNRS)
sylvain@kahane.fr

Abstract

This article attempts to place dependency annotation options on a solid theoretical and applied footing. By verifying the validity of some basic choices of the current dependency reference framework, Universal Dependencies (UD), in a perspective of general annotation principles, we show how some choices can lead to inconsistencies and discontinuities, partly due to UD's alternation between syntax and semantics. For some constructions, we propose better suited alternative structures with a clear-cut distinction of syntax and semantics. We propose a classification of conception-oriented, annotator-oriented, and finally, treebank end-user-oriented considerations to be used in the creation of new annotation schemes.

1 Introduction

Every project of corpus annotation is about making choices. Astonishingly little research is actually going into this founding act of every treebank.

1.1 Justifications of treebank annotation

In the literature, the discussions of the considerations taken into account in treebank and annotation scheme constructions are rather scarce. Treebank guidelines commonly make do with the *'what choices'* rather than the *'why those choices'*. Justifications are given in theoretical works only, if the treebank is based on a framework. For the Prague Dependency Treebank (Böhmová et al. 2003) for example, choices are based on theoretical works of the Prague team (Sgall et al. 1986) and if adaptations have been done for the annotation proper they are stated neither on the PDT website nor in the guidelines. For the French Treebank (Abeillé et al. 2003), the annotation choices are guided by the desire to be "*compatible with various syntactic frameworks*" and "*as theory neutral as possible*" (FTB home page) notwithstanding that we do not know how this is even possible. However, this does not explain under which considerations particular choices have been done. For Universal Dependencies (de Marneffe et al. 2014, Nivre 2015), "*The goal of the typed dependency relations is a set of broadly observed "universal dependencies" that work across languages. Such dependencies seek to maximize parallelism by allowing the same grammatical relation to be annotated the same way across languages, while making enough crucial distinctions such that different things can be differentiated.*" (UD home page) This general manifest is used to justify some choices: "*Preferring content words as heads maximizes parallelism between languages because content words vary less than function words between languages.*" But this is of course insufficient to justify numerous other choices that have been done (some of which we will discuss here).

If annotation guidelines of treebanks do not answer our question, studies dedicated to the analysis and comparison of treebanks do not help much more. Kakkonen (2005) is a good example of the kinds of questions investigated in such papers, which he resumes by "*What types of annotation schemes and formats are applied?*" or "*What kinds of annotation methods and tools are used for creating the treebanks?*". For instance, Ivanova et al. (2012) compare 7 dependency treebanks and identify "*a large variation across formats*". They note that "*divergent representations are in part owed to relatively superficial design decisions, as well as in part to more contentful differences in underlying linguistic assumptions*", but do not investigate further what kinds of considerations have led

Proceedings of LAW X – The 10th Linguistic Annotation Workshop, pages 131–140,
Berlin, Germany, August 11, 2016.

to such divergences. They are more interested in "*contrastive studies*" and present an "*automatic conversion procedure*".

Corpus linguistics and annotation handbooks that we are aware of are also mainly presenting different annotation schemes. Kübler & Zinsmeister (2015) describe how "*the different tagsets impose different restrictions on which phenomena can be looked up in corpora*", but the same is not done for structural annotation choices and *a fortiori* no guideline for choosing the most appropriate annotation scheme is put forward.

1.2 Delimitations of our study

We are here interested in syntactic and semantic dependency annotations. By *dependency annotation* we mean an annotation based on a tokenization of the text in basic units (morphemes, words, multi-word expressions, ...) and a labeled directed graph of relations between the tokens.

Deciding to use a dependency annotation is a choice in itself and, as every annotation choice, must be supported by different considerations which we propose to organize in three main groups:

1. **Theory-oriented considerations**: Adequacy of dependency has been proven for syntactic as well as semantic representations (Kern 1883, Tesni'ere 1959, Mel'čuk 1988, Hudson 2006). For instance, predicate-argument structures can be encoded by a dependency graph between lexical units, including idioms (Mel'čuk 1988, Kahane 2003, Copestake 2005, Banarescu et al. 2013).

2. **End-User-oriented considerations**: Dependency treebanks allow training of efficient parsers (Nivre et al. 2007, Bohnet 2010) and developing text generation systems (Bohnet et al. 2010) or translation system (Čmejrek et al. 2004). Specialized query systems exist but are still rather complex and difficult to use for the common linguist (Krause & Zeldes 2015). Dependency can also be used for grammar learning and language learning.[1] The usability of the resulting treebanks for the training of statistical parsers is also an important usage consideration (Schwartz et al. 2012).

3. **Annotator-oriented considerations**: Dependency structures are a light-weight annotation in terms of graph complexity (compared for example to phrase structure trees) and various ergonomic annotations tools have been developed (Gerdes 2013). Moreover, the annotators' evaluation is straightforward on dependency structures (labeled and unlabeled attachment scores, see Nilsson et al. 2007).

In this paper, we will explore the various choices that must be made when developing a dependency-based annotation, compare choices made by different frameworks (especially UD), evaluate on which considerations their annotation choices are based, and explore whether better choices could have been done with similar or other considerations.

The next sections will study some phenomena where basic annotation choices are traditionally made: Tokenization in section 2 exemplifies the choice of minimal units. Grammatical functions in section 3 exemplify labeling choices. In section 4, coordinations, prepositions, and light verbs exemplify structural choices. Section 5 presents an overview of the different considerations that can influence annotations choices. This last section can be read before the others and we will refer to it all along the paper.

2 Tokenization

Determining the units that constitute the base of the dependency structure, the tokens, is a central choice of the annotation scheme. In a syntactic treebank, basic units are words or lexemes, while in a semantic treebank, basic units are lexical units, including idioms which are multi-word expressions (MWEs).

2.1 Syntactic tokenization

Two options are possible: the tokenization can be based on theoretical considerations of *wordness* (*adequacy*)[2] (in which case each token has to be validated and possibly disambiguated before the dependency annotation can even start) or on purely

[1] Kahane & Osborne (2015) point out the pedagogical orientation of the Reeds & Kellogg (1877) diagrams as well as Tesnière's work whose basic goal was advances in language learning. See also Gerdes (2013), Zeldes (2016) who uses dependency annotation of a corpus for teaching syntax.

[2] These keywords refer to different considerations in annotation choices. They will be summarized in section 5.

formal spelling-based criteria like space and punctuation of the text (or the transcription for spoken corpora) (*simplicity*). The non-congruence between these considerations is an important problem for any kind of annotation scheme and calls for special annotation devices. The rules of what signs constitute word segmenters are language dependent. For example hyphens and apostrophes: The apostrophe is rather seen as part of the preceding word in French (*l' ami* 'the friend') and of the following word in English (*I 'm*). But as always, exceptions exist: Fr. *aujourd'hui* 'today', En. *isn't*. In any case, we recommend a purely formal tokenisation based on orthography and a few formal rules (*formalization*). A too fine-grained tokenisation can be handled by a special dependency relation.[3]

2.2 Multi-word expressions

Suppose now that we develop a semantic treebank. If we want the token to be our basic semantic unit (*adequacy*) (choice A), we need a lexicon of MWEs, which is a very large resource (the number of MWEs is greater that the number of lexemes) the outlines of which are fuzzy and controversial. This is why we recommend a tokenization at the syntactic level with an encoding of MWEs by means of an additional annotation at the dependency level. This choice gives way to several options.

The seemingly most simple annotation is the one advocated by UD: Tokens which are part of a MWE are connected with a special dependency (called *mwe*[4]) and each token of the MWE as well as the MWE's external relations depend on one fixed (the first) token (*formalization*) (choice B) (Fig. 1).

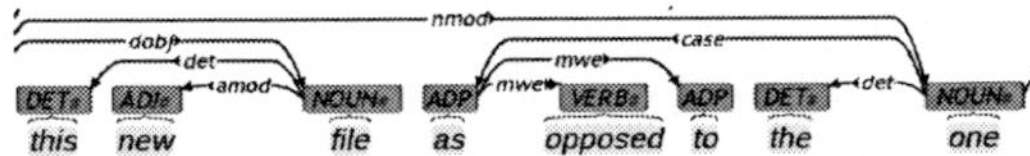

Figure 1: 'as opposed to' as an example of a MWE, extract from UD 1.2 English

[3]If, inversely, the spelling based units are too large, like in German N-N constructions that are written without spaces, the decomposition into semantic units requires a specific encoding mechanism. A tokenization into lexemes will need access to a lexicon, which can be costly (*concision*) and every change in the lexicon or error of tokenization implies a drastic change of the dependency structure.

[4]Additionally, UD distinguishes *compound, goeswith, name, foreign* for various cases of semantic units beyond the token.

Another solution is to systematically preserve the internal syntactic structure of MWEs (*level coverage*) (choice C), the majority of which have a regular syntactic pattern (Fig. 2).

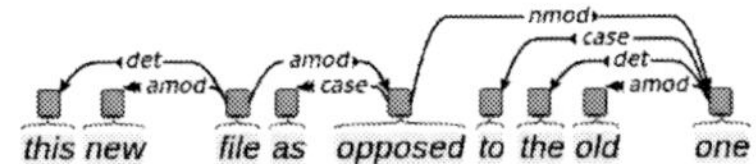

Figure 2: compositional UD-style analysis of 'as opposed to' preserving regular syntactic labels

Most syntacticians would agree that *as opposed to* is rather idiomatic and *as a great alternative to* isn't. The continuum between the two structures does not have a clear and consensual break-off point: *as opposed to, as relating to, as referred to, as commonly referred to, as a great alternative to,* etc.

UD's MWE analysis therefore gives rise to a *catastrophe*, in a strictly matematical sense of Thom's catastrophe theory (Saunders 1980), i.e. a brutal structural change in a continuum: The UD annotators have to give drastically different structures the moment they detect idiomaticity, which necessarily leads to low inter-annotator agreement, whereas the systematically compositional annotations would all look similar (*independence*) (Fig. 3).

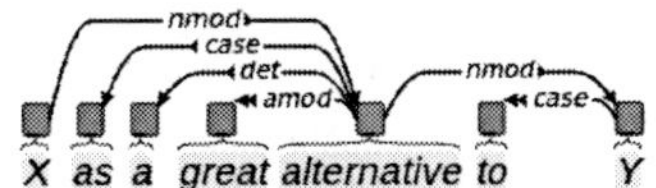

Figure 3: compositional UD-style analysis of 'as a great alternative to'

An annotation of MWEs is compatible with the compositional structure of choice C. Two solutions are possible to add the MWE information. Choice C1: replacing the regular syntactic label with the *mwe* label (*simplicity*); or choice C2: preserving the regular syntactic label and combining it with the *mwe* label (*separability*) (Fig. 4).

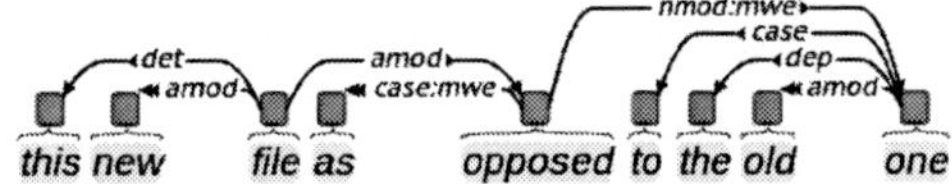

Figure 4: complex function names of choice C2

As most of the MWEs are either lexically or structurally non-ambiguous, obtaining C2 is not more complicated than B for the annotator (*naturalness*). Moreover, both choices C1 and C2 are structurally more informative than choice B: They can trivially and automatically be transformed into choice B, whereas the inverse automatic transformation is impossible without strong resources (*transformability*). Choice C2 is the richer solution: It is possible to project C2 onto C1.

C2's additional *mwe* tag relies again on access to a MWE lexicon but the likely inter-annotator disagreement caused by the identification of MWEs exclusively consists in this additional label, no other parts of the structure are concerned (*quality*). This additional *mwe* tag can partly be added automatically, using a MWE lexicon indicating which MWE are non ambiguous. Most grammatical MWE (such as complex prepositions) can be unambiguously detected, as soon as the syntactic structure of the text is given (*minimality*).

Another advantage of the syntactically valid internal annotation of MWEs is that the transparency of the internal structure gives rise to combinatorial properties of the semantic unit for example in coordination. Consider the following example: *oneself as opposed to other selves and to everything that is "not-self." (fakebuddhaquotes.com)* Here the preposition *to* as part of the complex preposition is coordinated with a simple *to*, thus revealing that a more adequate analysis is to consider that *as opposed* is the MWE proper and *to* its subcategorization marker (see Fig. 4). This also causes the parser to have more similar training examples and fewer ambiguities to resolve (*precision*).

From the end user's point of view, too, the advantage of, for example, encoding the MWE *as opposed (to)* compositionally are obvious: The user of the treebank has to know only the treebank's analysis of noun and prepositional phrases to query the treebank (*readability*).

3 Labeling Choices

The labels of syntactic dependencies traditionally encode grammatical functions, i.e. the role the dependent plays vis-à-vis its governor and in the construction. The label can also encode categorical information (i.e. information concerning the token and not only its role). This is what UD does when they distinguish *nsubj* and *csubj*, i.e. nominal vs. clausal subjects or *nmod* and *amod*, i.e. nominal vs. adjectival modifiers. This goes against the minimality of the label set (*concision, separability*).

UD also makes the distinction between *nsubj* and *nsubjpass* (as well as *csubj* and *csubjpass*), which is a combination of syntactic and semantic information: An *nsubjpass* is a syntactic subject that does not correspond to the first actant of the verb (cf. Mel'čuk 1988, partially following Tesnière 1959[2015]: ch. 51). Maybe it would have been better to clearly separate syntax and semantics since *nsubjpass* can designate a second or third actant (*A book* ←nsubjpass– *was given to Craig* vs. *Craig* ←nsubjpass– *was given a book*). This could be done by indicating the semantic actance number, which subsumes UD's analysis and the distinction between *nsubj* and *nsubjpass*: *it* ←subj:0– *is raining* (non actancial subject), *Ann* ←subj:1– *gives Craig a book, A book* ←subj:2– *was given to Craig*, *Craig* ←subj:3– *was given a book* (*separability, transformability, level coverage*).

Redistribution between second and third actants also exists in some languages (antipassive, including dative-shift in English for some linguists (Bresnan 1981)), which cannot be encoded cleanly without introducing similar distinctions for *dobj* (Mel'čuk 1993). UD uses the label *nmod* for a dative object when it is indirect (*give a book to Craig*: *give* –nmod→ *Craig* –case→ *to*) and *iobj* when it is shifted (and direct!) (*give Craig a book*: *give* –iob→ *Craig*), which is quite counterintuitive (*intuitiveness*). Again a clear separation between syntax and semantic would be better: *Ann gives Craig a book*: *gives* –dobj:3→ *Craig*; *give* –dobj:2→ *book* vs. *Ann give a book to Craig*: *give* –nmod:3→ *Craig* –case→ *to* (*separability, adequacy, level coverage*).

4 Structural Choices

Orthogonally to tokens and function labels, the structure itself is matter of central choices. The basic constraint that most annotation schemes put up is the tree structure, i.e. each token has exactly one governor (including the root that can be governed by an anchor). There are many practical reasons for this choice ranging across the whole spectrum of considerations that we propose: Theoretical as well as practical, in particular as the annotation tasks get considerably harder when annotating graph structures (*simplicity, minimality*).

4.1 Position of the preposition

UD favors links between content words. For this

reason, prepositions that mark the relation between the content words are dependents of the word they mark: *Ann talked to Craig: talk –* nmod→ *Craig* –case→ *to*. Consequently, every preposition is treated as a leaf of the tree, which is problematic because some prepositions are content words: *Ann talked during the play*: *talked* - nmod→ *play* -case→ *during* (*adequacy*). At first sight UD's solution seems to give the advantage of *uniformity*, but languages use compositional expressions (such as *in the (exact) middle of*, *on the (very) left of* ...), which occupy the same syntactic position as prepositions while not being treated in the same way (Fig. 5). Experiments on training of different parsers (Schwartz et al. 2012) also show that prepositions as heads give higher accuracy than when they are nominal dependents (*learnability*).

Because of the high degree of compositionality and modifiability of expressions like *in the middle of*, UD chooses to encode these complex "prepositions" compositionally and not as MWEs (see 2.2) and consequently not as prepositions. Indeed, *middle* is treated as a content word, depends on the verb, and governs a complement (Fig. 5). In other words, the catastrophe that UD avoids in treating all prepositions uniformly is just relegated to the border between simple prepositions (such as *during*) and compositional prepositional expressions (such as *in the middle of*).

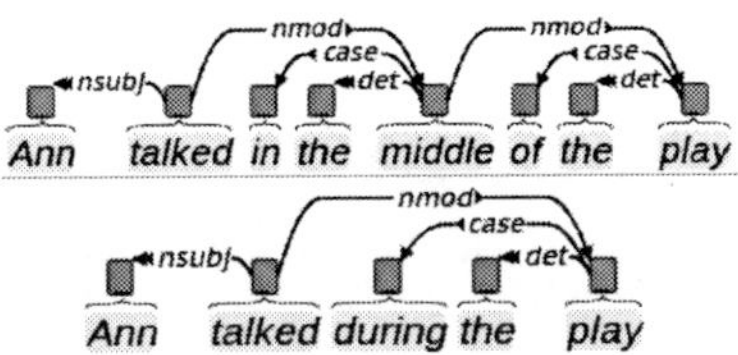

Figure 5: analyses of both a simple and a complex semantically full preposition in UD 1.2 English

Even *universality* cannot be ensured because parallel expressions can be expressed differently in other languages. For example, the English structure of *in the middle of* will not be easily comparable to its German adverbial counterpart *mitten* and both constructions receive quite different structures (Fig. 6).

To avoid a catastrophe, it is better to preserve the syntactic structure and to have the preposition as the head of its complement (we might call this function *pobj*, for *object of the proposition*) (Fig. 7). This solution is equivalent to UD's solution (each one can automatically be transformed into the other), but our solution avoids a catastrophe (*uniformity*).

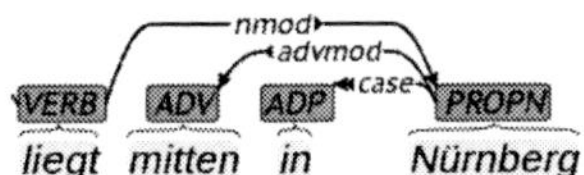

lies midway in Nuremberg

Figure 6: German adverbial construction translating the English "in the middle of", extract from UD 1.2

An additional label on the dependency (and/or on the preposition node) can indicate that the preposition is empty and only serves as a subcategorization marker (Fig. 8). This solution is now richer than UD's solution since it distinguishes content and phrasal verb prepositions (*transformability, level coverage, separability*).

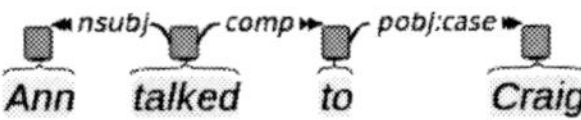

Figure 7: Proposed analysis of a phrasal verb

Even for the comparison of languages and paraphrases it will be better (*universality*): For instance, *X cause Y* and *Y because X* will be much more parallel with our analysis, the synonymous content words *cause* and *because* being linked to their two actants in both constructions.[5]

4.2 Coordination

Structural analyses that go beyond the tree structure are frequently encountered for constructions involving coordination. Paradigmatic relations between words are orthogonal to government-dependent links (Tesnière 1959, Blanche-Benveniste 1990, Gerdes & Kahane 2009) and are difficult to encode in simple tree structures. Moreover, paradigmatic relations are involved in complex deletion rules that some syntactic frameworks analyze with empty nodes, something that dependency theory traditionally attempts to avoid.

A simple coordination such as *we have apples and bananas* already gives rise to various links that could be encoded in the annotation scheme: *have → apples, have → bananas, apples → and, apples → bananas, and → bananas.* The direction

[5]As already stated by Mel'čuk (1988), paraphrasing is a particular case of translation (i.e. intra-language translation) and an analysis cannot be universal (and translation-invariant) without being paraphrasing-invariant.

of some links is also open for debate, in particular *apples* → *bananas* and *and* → *bananas*.

From a theoretical standpoint we would like to obtain the complete graph (Gerdes & Kahane 2015), but practical considerations of annotation and query opens the question whether the structure can be simplified to a tree without loosing important information (*minimality, readability*).

Mel'čukian surface syntax handles the coordinative conjunction as a head of the second conjunct which gives an asymmetrical analysis *apples* → *and* → *bananas* (Mel'čuk 1988). UD proposes both a complete graph and a reduced tree structure. For the reduced tree structure, UD selects the paradigmatic relation *apples* → *bananas* consistent with UD's basic concept of relegating function words to lower positions in the tree (although a word like *and* is far from being semantically empty) (*adequacy*). This choice also allows for a consistent analysis of the frequent cases where the coordinating conjunction is absent (*uniformity*).

It remains to choose where to attach the coordinating conjunction, on the head of the first or of the second conjunct? Here UD selects the first conjunct, without further justification. Where to attach the conjunction may not be relevant from a semantic point of view, but syntactically, *and bananas* clearly is a phrase (that can be separated prosodically and also added by a second speaker in a dialogue) whereas *apples and* does not have these properties. Here the *adequacy* and the *level coverage* considerations should make us prefer the opposite choice of UD.

Shared dependents, as in *we have rotten apples and bananas*, cannot be cleanly expressed with a simple tree structure (some frameworks attach the shared adjective on a different level, e.g. the coordinating conjunction; others like Mel'čuk have specialized function labels to indicate the scope) and UD offers to either not encode the scope of the adjective (*precision*) or to upgrade to a graph structure (*adequacy*) (Gerdes & Kahane 2015).

Contrarily to the Dutch CGN corpus that skips reparanda (Schuurman et al. 2003), UD proposes to encode them with a special *reparandum* link that goes from the "correct" *repair* part to the "incorrect" *reparandum* (*text coverage*), but in the opposite direction of the *conj* link that goes from left to right. This is again a semantic choice where the semantically peripheral elements are relegated to the lower parts of the tree. Gerdes & Kahane (2009) (following Blanche-Benveniste 1990), however, show that there is a continuum between elaboration and disfluency with frequent borderline cases like "*I saw a room, a bright room, a room with red lights...*", which makes them postulate the same dependency analysis for all those cases ranging from coordination to disfluency. Thus, in UD, we again have an annotational catastrophe: The direction of the central paradigmatic link between the conjuncts depends on whether the annotator considers the second conjunct to be a correction of the first (*independence*).

The UD guidelines also include the analysis of non-constituent coordination (NCC) as in *Marie went to Paris and Miriam to Prague* by means of a specific *remnant* link that connects the elements that play the same role in both conjuncts: *Marie* –remnant→ *Miriam* and *to Paris* –remnant→ *to Prague*. Again, to prioritize on these links in a manually corrected annotation setting is a reasonable choice from a *minimality* and *naturalness* point of view.

However, *Miriam to Prague* also forms a constituent according to autonomy criteria (prosody and stand-alone properties, see Gerdes & Kahane 2013). This constituent is disconnected in the UD analysis and it would be preferable, if we allowed ourselves a graph structure, to add a link between *Miriam* and *to Prague*. We claim that this link is more visible on the surface than UD's *remnant* links.

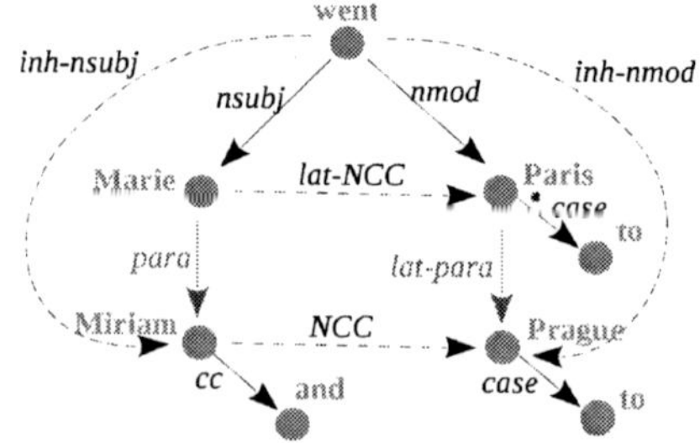

Figure 8: NCC structure in "Marie went to Paris and Miriam to Prague" *following Gerdes & Kahane (2015), prepositions analyzed in UD style*

Gerdes & Kahane (2015) show a complete schema of relations[6] that arise in an NCC from which one has to choose a possible tree structure, with

[6]The graph also includes the "inherited" links *Miriam* ←inh-nsubj– *went* and *went* –inh-nmod→ *to Prague*, which also undergo semantic and restrictional selection (see Tesnière 1959[2015]: ch. 143).

para and *lat-para* being UD's *remnant*, *NCC* and *lat-NCC* linking the constituents involved in the same unique coordination (Fig. 8). The idea is that, from a theoretical point of view, *para* and *NCC* are the primitive links, while *lat-para* and *lat-NCC* are "lateral" links, inherited from them and "symmetrizing" the structure. Nevertheless, it is a symmetric problem to automatically compute the NCC links (*NCC* and *lat-NCC*) from the paradigmatic links (*para* and *lat-para*) or the inverse: computing the paradigmatic links from the NCC links. However, only UD's choice of *remnant* links results in a tree structure and is thus preferable (*transformability, naturalness*).

Concerning coordination, we can sum up our observations by noting that in general the UD choices are well-founded in the proposed considerations with few exceptions, but these considerations are not made explicit.

4.3 Light verb constructions

A governed preposition (like *to* in *talk to Craig*) can be seen as reification of the semantic link between the verb and its actant. This tendency to reify semantic relation is not limited to government: copula or light verbs have the same role:

a red book vs. *the book is red*
Ann's slap on Craig
vs. *Ann gave Craig a slap*
vs. *Graig got a slap from Craig*

UD favors the semantic relations in all the cases of prepositions and copula, but not for light verbs. As explained in Nivre & Vincze (2015), the predicative noun is encoded as the *dobj* of the light verb in all UD treebanks, which is incoherent with the analysis of the copula (as a dependent of the predicative noun or adjective) (*uniformity*) and actants of the light verb construction are linked to the verb, which is incoherent with UD principles because the predicative noun is the content word (*adequacy*). Fig. 9b gives an analysis coherent with UD principles, to be compared with the present analysis of UD.

Of course, such an analysis is also problematic because the frontier between light verbs and content verbs is quite fuzzy (see for instance the very rich classification of support verbs in Mel'čuk (1998), cf. *feel fear* vs. *shake with fear*).

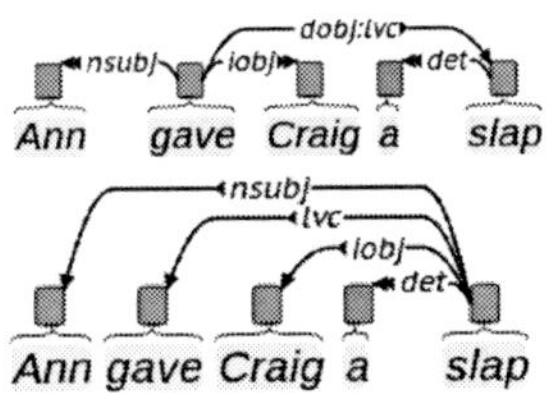

Figure 9:
a. UD analysis of a light verb construction
b. coherent analysis of a light verb construction

We then recommend maintaining the present annotation of LVC, which is similar to the syntax-based annotation of prepositions we have recommended. But to avoid a catastrophe, the same analysis should be used for the predicative construction: *book* ← nsubj- *is* -dobj:lvc→ *red*.

5 Overview of considerations about annotation choices

In this section, we propose to categorize the different types of considerations that we exemplified in the preceding sections. There are three stages in the development of a resource: conception, realization, and usage.

5.1 Conception-oriented consideration

The first decision concerns the kind of linguistic information we want to develop in our annotation. According to our theoretical goals, our annotation must respond to the following considerations:

A1. **Adequacy**: Our annotation must be as adequate as possible given our theoretical framework and the criteria validating a correct analysis.

A2. **Uniformity**: Similar constructions must be annotated in similar ways. Catastrophes must be avoided.

A3. **Level coverage**: Our annotation must be as informative as possible and must cover the maximum of linguistic levels. It can be costly to develop a too fine-grained annotation, but for a comparable cost, the more precise annotation must be chosen.

A4. **Text coverage**: Our annotation must cover the maximal range of relevant data. In terms of dependency annotation, it means that the graph must be as connected as possible. A text is cohesive and for instance many relations may not be limited to sentence boundaries.

5.2 Annotator-oriented considerations

The realization of a treebank supposes an annotation stage, but also some steps of validation of the annotation, as well as an easy maintenance and expansion of the treebank.

According to the need for efficiency in the annotation process, our annotation must respond to the following considerations:

B1. **Formalization**: Annotation criteria must be well formalized in order to avoid inter-annotator disagreement and to speed up annotators' decisions. A good formalization also means that part of the annotation process can be computer-assisted, by an automatic pre-annotation or by a tool pointing out inadequate annotations.

B2. **Simplicity**: The annotation process must be as simple as possible and complex or open decisions must be avoided. In particular, a tree structure can be preferred because each token has exactly one governor (except the root), which also enables an economic encoding (tabular, CoNLL) and a faster search.

B3. **Minimality**: The annotation can be enriched automatically (by deterministic and local rules) if it contains all information and all distinctions we want to make. It means that the annotation delivered by the annotators must be as minimal as possible to avoid useless work. Again, a tree structure can be preferred because, for a connected graph, a tree has the minimal number of links.

B4. **Concision**: Not only the annotation itself must be minimal but information needed to annotate must also be minimized. Tag sets as well as the guideline must be concise. Consultation of an external resource (for instance, a lexicon of multi-word expressions) must be avoided unless it is automatic and at no cost for the annotator.

B5. **Naturalness**: Annotators are humans and some decisions are easier than others for humans. Paradoxically, some high-level decisions, close to semantics for instance, can be easier than some low-level decisions, that would be much easier for a machine.

B6. **Separability**: The annotation can involve information of different levels. The choice between a unistratal annotation (combining different levels) and a multistratal annotation (separating everything that can be separated) must be made. As long as the size of the tag set remains reasonable, it could be more efficient to combine, but choosing between n tags and then m tags is quickly faster than choosing between nm tags.

B7. **Independence**: A change of annotation in a particular level must not drastically affect other levels of annotation.

B8. **Intuitiveness**: Annotation is labeling. Label terms must be intuitive. Terminology must be coherent with traditional uses.

5.3 End User-oriented considerations

An annotation project must be aware of the applications of the developed resource. Different goals can be considered:

- **Theory**: Annotating a corpus following a particular framework can be a means of proving the adequacy of the theory and evaluating its coverage.

- **NLP**: Many tools can be developed from a treebank, in particular using machine learning methods.

- **Pedagogy**: The annotation itself can be a good exercise to practice linguistics. And an annotated corpus can be a source of knowledge for learners (and other researchers).

According to our practical goal, our annotation must respond to the following considerations:

C1. **Quality**: The annotation must be reliable. In particular inter-annotator agreement must be as high as possible.

C2. **Precision**: The annotation must be fine-grained enough for the expected applications. But too much precision is unnecessary and removing a distinction (e.g. the categorical distinction between French *des* DET vs. *des* PREP+DEP) can speed up the annotation process and lower the error rate.

C3. **Learnability**: An annotation scheme is preferable if it gives higher accuracy when used for training a statistical parser. This point is strongly dependent on the state of the art of statistical parsing as well as on the size of the developed resource.

C4. **Readability**: The annotation must be easily interpretable by a user by a direct reading or via a query system.

C5. **Universality**: The annotation must not be too specific to a particular language or genre in order to allow extrapolation to other corpora (especially under-resourced languages) and comparisons. This concerns also spoken corpora and sign languages.

C6. **Transformability**: Annotation standards must be developed. But it is unproblematic to develop a new annotation if it can be transformed into other standards. It is essential to preserve inter-operability of resources and tools.

This list does not close the considerations taken into account. We have focused on scientific considerations, but in the end choices are political. For questions of visibility, availability of tools and guidelines, and perspective of richer collaborations, many teams choose to use the most visible annotation styles, which is a reasonable choice.

6 Conclusion

Every project of treebank development needs to make choices between different possible annotations. Conceptualizers of the treebank generally expose the general principles that underlie the main choices. These principles reduce the space of possible choices but as soon as we get into the details, several options remains possible, many particular choices are not argued for and it is not easy to know what considerations have at last been decisive.

In this article we concentrated on the UD annotation choices, refuting some and corroborating others based on our list of principles. This list as well as the corresponding example discussions might prove useful for future treebank development choices, in this or an extended format.

References

Abeillé, Anne, Lionel Clément, and François Toussenel. "Building a treebank for French." *Treebanks*. Springer Netherlands, 2003. 165-187.

Banarescu, L., Bonial, C., Cai, S., Georgescu, M., Griffitt, K., Hermjakob, U., Knight, K., Koehn, P., Palmer, M., and Schneider, N. "Abstract meaning representation for sembanking." *Proceedings of the 7th Linguistic Annotation Workshop and Interoperability with Discourse*. 2013.

Blanche-Benveniste, Claire, et al. *Le français parlé (études grammaticales)*. Sciences du langage, 1990.

Böhmová, Alena, Jan Hajič, Eva Hajičová, and Barbora Hladká. "The Prague dependency treebank." *Treebanks*. Springer Netherlands, 2003. 103-127.

Bohnet, Bernd. "Very high accuracy and fast dependency parsing is not a contradiction." *Proceedings of the 23rd International Conference on Computational Linguistics*. ACL, 2010.

Bohnet, Bernd, Leo Wanner, Simon Mille, and Alicia Burga, A. "Broad coverage multilingual deep sentence generation with a stochastic multi-level realizer." *Proceedings of the 23rd International Conference on Computational Linguistics*. ACL, 2010.

Bresnan, Joan. "An approach to Universal Grammar and the mental representation of language." *Cognition, 10(1)*. 1981. 39-52.

Copestake, Ann. "Slacker semantics: why superficiality, dependency and avoidance of commitment can be the right way to go." *Proceedings of the 12th Conference of the European Chapter of the Association for Computational Linguistics*. ACL, 2005.

Čmejrek, Martin, Jan Hajič, and Vladislav Kuboň. "Prague Czech-English dependency treebank: Syntactically annotated resources for machine translation." *Proceedings of the 10th Conference of the European Association for Machine Translation*. 2004.

Gerdes, Kim and Sylvain Kahane. "Defining dependencies (and constituents)." *Frontiers in Artificial Intelligence and Applications, Volume 258: Computational Dependency Theory*, 2013. 1-25.

Gerdes, Kim. "Collaborative Dependency Annotation." *Proceedings of the 2nd Confenrence on Dependency Linguistics,* 2013.

Gerdes, Kim and Sylvain Kahane. "Speaking In Piles: Paradigmatic Annotation Of French Spoken Corpus."*Proceedings of the 5th Corpus Linguistics Conference*, Liverpool. 2009.

Gerdes, Kim and Sylvain Kahane. "Non-constituent coordination and other coordinative constructions as dependency graphs." *Proceedings of the 3rd international conference on Dependency Linguistics*. 2015.

Hudson, Richard. *Language Networks: The New Word Grammar*. OUP Oxford, 2006.

Ivanova A., Oepen S., Øvrelid L., Flickinger D. "Who Did What to Whom? A Contrastive Study of Syntacto-Semantic Dependencies." *Proceedings of the 6th Linguistic Annotation Workshop (LAW VI)*, ACL, 2012.

Kahane, Sylvain. "The meaning-text theory." *Dependency and Valency.* An International Handbook of Contemporary Research 1. 2003. 546-570.

Kahane, Sylvain, and Timothy Osborne. "Translators" introduction." In Tesnière Lucien, *Elements of structural syntax*. 2015. xxix–lxxiv.

Kakkonen, Tuomo. "Dependency Treebanks: Methods." Annotation Schemes and Tools. *Proceedings of the 15th Nordic Conference of Computational Linguistics*. 2005.

Kern, Franz. *Zur Methodik des deutschen Unterrichts*, Nicolai, Berlin. 1883.

Krause, Thomas and Zeldes, Amir "ANNIS3: A New Architecture for Generic Corpus Query and Visualization." *Digital Scholarship in the Humanities, 31(1)*. 2015. 118-139.

Kübler, Sandra, & Zinsmeister, Heike. (2015). *Corpus Linguistics and Linguistically Annotated Corpora*. Bloomsbury Publishing.

De Marneffe, Marie-Catherine, et al. "Universal Stanford dependencies: A cross-linguistic typology." *Proceedings of 9th International Workshop on Language Resources and Evaluation*. 2014.

Mel'čuk, Igor. *Dependency syntax: Theory and Practice.* SUNY Press. 1988.

Mel'čuk, Igor. "The inflectional category of voice: towards a more rigorous definition." *Causatives and transitivity, 23*. 1993.

Mel'čuk, Igor. "Collocations and lexical functions." In A.P. Cowie (ed.) *Phraseology. Theory, Analysis, and Applications.* Clarendon Press, Oxford. 1998. 23-53.

Nilsson, Jens, Sebastian Riedel, and Deniz Yuret. "The CoNLL 2007 shared task on dependency parsing." *Proceedings of the CoNLL shared task session of EMNLP-CoNLL*, 2007.

Nivre, Joakim, et al. "MaltParser: A language-independent system for data-driven dependency parsing." *Natural Language Engineering, 13(2)*. 2007. 95-135.

Nivre, Joakim. "Towards a universal grammar for natural language processing." *Computational Linguistics and Intelligent Text Processing*. Springer International Publishing. 2015. 3-16.

Nivre, Joakim, and Veronika Vincze. 2015. "Light Verb Constructions in Universal Dependencies." Technical report, Parseme workshop.

Reed, A. and Kellogg B. *Higher Lessons in English: A Work on English Grammar and Composition*. Clark and Maynard, New-York. 1877.

Saunders, Peter T. *An introduction to catastrophe theory*. Cambridge University Press, 1980.

Schwartz, Roy, Omri Abend, and Ari Rappoport. "Learnability-Based Syntactic Annotation Design." *Proceedings of Coling*. 2012.

Schuurman, Ineke et al. "CGN, an annotated corpus of spoken Dutch." *Proceedings of 4th International Workshop on Language Resources and Evaluation*. 2003.

Sgall, Petr, Eva Hajicová, and Jarmila Panevová. *The meaning of the sentence in its semantic and pragmatic aspects*. Kluwer, Dordrecht. 1986.

Tesnière L. 1959. *Éléments de syntaxe structurale.* Paris: Klincksieck [transl. by Osborne T., Kahane S. *Elements of structural syntax.* Benjamins, 2015].

Zeldes, Amir. "The GUM corpus: creating multilayer resources in the classroom." *Language Resources and Evaluation.* 2016.1-32.

Conversion from Pāṇinian Kārakas to Universal Dependencies for Hindi Dependency Treebank

Juhi Tandon, Himani Chaudhary, Riyaz Ahmad Bhat and **Dipti Misra Sharma**
Kohli Center on Intelligent Systems (KCIS),
International Institute of Information Technology,Hyderabad (IIIT-H)
Gachibowli,Hyderabad 500 032, India
{juhi.tandon,himani,riyaz.bhat}@research.iiit.ac.in , dipti@iiit.ac.in

Abstract

Universal Dependencies (UD) are gaining much attention of late for systematic evaluation of cross-lingual techniques for cross-lingual dependency parsing. In this paper we present our work in line with UD. Our contribution to this is manifold. We extend UD to Indian languages through conversion of Pāṇinian Dependencies to UD for the Hindi Dependency Treebank (HDTB). We discuss the differences in annotation in both the schemes, present parsing experiments for both the formalisms and empirically evaluate their weaknesses and strengths for Hindi. We produce an automatically converted Hindi Treebank conforming to the international standard UD scheme, making it useful as a resource for multilingual language technology.

1 Introduction

Universal Dependencies is a project undertaken to develop an inventory of languages that have treebanks annotated in a consistent scheme (McDonald et al., 2013). The UD annotation has evolved by reconstruction of the Standford Dependencies (De Marneffe and Manning, 2008) and it uses a slightly extended version of Google universal tag set for part of speech (POS) (Petrov et al., 2011). This is done with the motivation to facilitate the efforts in building of cross-linguistic tools such as parsers, translation systems, search engines, etc.

The efforts in building similarly structured or annotated treebanks have invoked a lot intreset from researchers around the world. The first release of UD treebanks included six languages where English and Swedish were created by automatic conversion. Thereafter several other treebanks have been developed automatically such as Italian (Bosco et al., 2013), Russian (Lipenkova and Soucek, 2014), and Finnish (Pyysalo et al., 2015). Several treebanks have also been created using manual annotation procedures. For languages where a treebank is already available, automatic conversion process is more suitable than manual annotation which is expensive and time consuming. It should be noted here that while for some languages conversion between the original and the UD representations can be accurate, for others it may introduce too much noise.

There have been few attempts that have tried to convert the annotation scheme used for Indian languages to other schemes such as the annotation style of Prague Dependency Treebank (Zeman et al., 2012). Our work, instead, aims to convert HDTB annotation scheme to UD.

Keeping in line with the ongoing efforts in this direction, our work is a volunteer effort to harmonize the Hindi Dependency Treebank according to the UD formalism, making it a more available resource for multilingual parsing. In doing so, we have converted the dependency relations in Pāṇinian framework and the POS tag set followed by Hindi to the Universal Dependency scheme. This conversion had its challenges, as many language specific phenomena had to be addressed in the process. However, there was no requirement to develop a new, language specific UD-scheme, unlike some other treebanks, for instance Russian (Lipenkova and Soucek, 2014).

The rest of the paper is organized as follows: In Section 2, we describe the annotation scheme used for the Indian language treebanking and Universal Dependency treebanking. Section 3 talks about the granularity of the Pāṇinian scheme. In Section 4, we elaborate upon the differences in design between the two schemes, how existing dependency scheme and POS tags for Hindi map onto the universal taxonomy, the issues that were faced

Proceedings of LAW X – The 10th Linguistic Annotation Workshop, pages 141–150,
Berlin, Germany, August 11, 2016.

Count of	HDTB
Types	22,171
Tokens	434,856
Chunks	233,864
Sentences	20,783
Avg. Tokens/Sentence	20.92
Avg. Chunks/Sentence	11.25

Count of	Training	Testing
Tokens	3,47,744	87,112
Chunks	1,87,029	46,835
Sentences	16,629	4,154

Table 1: General Treebank Statistics and training-testing split for all the experiments reported in this work.

and how they have been resolved. The conversion process and program is discussed in Section 5. Section 6 discusses the parsing performance of the two schemes, assesses the learnability of the automatic parser for the UD scheme and its suitability for Hindi. Lastly, we conclude and discuss future work in Section 7.

2 The Two Schemes

2.1 Hindi Dependency Treebank and Computational Paninian Grammar

The Hindi Treebank contains text from news articles and heritage domain. It consists of 434,856 tokens in 20,783 sentences with an average of 20.92 words per sentence as can be seen in Table 2. It is multi-layered and multi-representational (Bhatt et al., 2009; Xia et al., 2009; Palmer et al., 2009; Bhat et al., 2014). It contains three layers of annotation namely **dependency structure (DS)** for annotation of modified-modifier relations, **PropBank-style annotation** for predicate-argument structure, and an independently motivated **phrase-structure annotation**. Each layer has its own framework, annotation scheme, and detailed annotation guidelines.

Dependency Structure–the first layer in these treebanks–involves dependency analysis based on the Pāṇinian Grammatical framework (Bharati et al., 1995; Begum et al., 2008). Pāṇini was an Indian grammarian who is credited with writing a comprehensive grammar of Sanskrit. The underlying theory of his grammar provides a framework for the syntactico-semantic analysis of a sentence. The grammar treats a sentence as a series of modified-modifier relations where one of the elements (usually a verb) is the primary modified. This brings it close to a dependency analysis model as propounded in Tesnière's Dependency Grammar (Tesnière, 1959).

The syntactico-semantic relations between lexical items provided by the Pāṇinian grammatical model can be split into two types[1]:

1. **Kāraka**: These are semantically related to a verb as the direct participants in the action denoted by a verb root. The grammatical model has six 'kārakas', namely **'kartā'** (the doer), **'karma'** (the locus of action's result), **'karaṇa'** (instrument), **'sampradāna'** (recipient), **'apādāna'** (source), and **'adhikaraṇa'** (location). These relations provide crucial information about the main action stated in a sentence.

2. **Non-kāraka**: These relations include reason, purpose, possession, adjectival or adverbial modifications etc.

Both the **Kāraka** and **Non-kāraka** relations in the scheme are represented in Figure 1; glosses of these relations are given in Table 2 . The purpose of choosing a hierarchical model for relation types is to have the possibility of underspecifying certain relations.

2.2 Universal Dependencies

As mentioned by (Nivre et al., 2016) and also discussed by (Johannsen et al., 2015), the driving principles of UD formalism are:

1. **Content over function:** Content words form the backbone of the syntactic representation. Giving priority to dependency relations between content words increases the probability of finding parallel structures across languages, since function words in one language often correspond to morphological inflection (or nothing at all) in other languages. Functional heads are instead represented as specifying features of content words, using dedicated relation labels.

[1]The complete set of dependency relation types can be found in (Bharati et al., 2009)

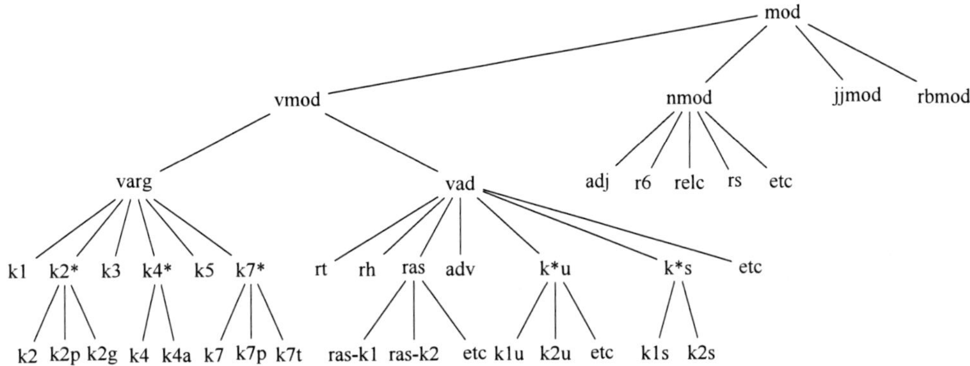

Figure 1: Inter-chunk dependency labels

Relation	Meaning
k1	Agent / Subject / Doer
k2*	Theme / Patient / Goal
k3	Instrument
k4*	Recipient / Experiencer
k5	Source
k7*	Spatio-temporal
rt	Purpose
rh	Cause
ras	Associative
k*u	Comparative
k*s	(Predicative) Noun / Adjective Complements
r6	Genitives
relc	Modification by Relative Clause
rs	Noun Complements (Appositive)
adv	Verb modifier
adj	Noun modifier

Table 2: Some major dependency relations depicted in Figure 1.

2. **Head-first:** In spans where it is not immediately clear which element is the head (the content-over-function rule does not apply straightforwardly), UD takes a head-first approach: the first element in the span becomes the head, and the rest of the span elements attach to it. This applies mostly to coordinations, multiword expressions, and proper names.

3. **Single root attachment:** There should be just one node with the root dependency relation in every tree, attached to the artificial root governor.

3 Granularity

Hindi is a morphologically rich, free word-order language. For such languages syntactic subject-object positions are not always able to elegantly explain the varied linguistic phenomena. As mentioned in the previous section, syntactico-semantic dependency relations and their labels defined in the CPG formalism are very fine grained to account for the rich grammatical functions. The number of distinct dependency labels are 82 as per the scheme (both interchunk and intrachunk). It has been observed that the more semantically oriented annotation schemes make labeled parsing more difficult than the schemes based on more surface-oriented grammatical functions. Further many applications do not require finer dependency labels and running a full parser with such a large set of labels can be too expensive. This further motivated us to convert the Hindi treebank to the UD scheme, with a relatively sparse taxonomy and observe the effects.

4 Differences in Design

While mapping the two annotation schemes we found that most of the tags entailed multiple correspondences, either one-to-many or many-to-one mappings between their tags. Below, some of the differences are discussed in detail.

4.1 Part of Speech Tags

The UD POS tag-set comprises 17 different tags only, whereas the POS tag set developed for Indian Languages (Bharati et al., 2006), has 32 tags.

One to many (HDTB to UD) The POS tag WQ used in the Hindi treebank for question words maps to DET, PRON and ADV in the UD.

Many to one (HDTB to UD) Similarly several tags on the Hindi treebank side RB, WQ etc. map with the UD POS tag ADV. Though we have a POS tag RB which directly maps with the grammatical category Adverb, our POS tagging scheme being more granular, we have various tags to annotate different kinds of adverbs. Tags such as WQ for question words ('kaha.N' कहाँ (where), 'kab' कब (when), 'kaise' कैसे (how)), NN (for words such as 'kal' कल (yesterday/tomorrow), 'Aj' आज (today)), NST, INTF, etc. are covered by UD under the umbrella tag ADV.

Hindi has compound conjunctions like 'aur to aur' और तो और (all the more) and 'jaisA ki' जैसा कि (like/as) etc. In HDTB these are tagged as follows:
और_CCC
तो_CCC
और_CC.
Multiword names are marked by POS tags NNPC and NNP. However in UD compounding is marked at the level of dependency relations by three tags: compound, mwe and name.

The Hindi tag set does not tag subordinate and coordinate conjunct differently. Our tags CC and CCC map with both, CONJ and SCONJ of UD for all simple and compound conjunctions.

There is not always a straight forward equivalence class mapping from HDTB to UD. The correct mapping of some tags requires the knowledge of lemma or the syntactic context. For example, the ambiguity in WQ and CC is resolved by using a word list corresponding to each Universal POS mapping and a few heuristics derived from the dependency tree structure.

In Indian Languages, there is a phenomenon called reduplication that involves the doubling of a lexical item to convey a grammatical function, such as plurality or intensification. The first word in such reduplicative construction is tagged by its respective lexical category and the second word is tagged as RDP to indicate that it is a case of reduplication, thus distinguishing it from a normal sequence (Bharati et al., 2006). UD does not have a corresponding tag for RDP which marks reduplication.

A mapping of all the 17 UD POS Tags to HDTB POS Tag set can be seen in the Table 3.

UD	HDTB
ADJ	JJ, JJC, QO
ADP	PSP, PSPC
ADV	RB, RBC, INTF, INTFC, NST, WQ, PRP, NN
AUX	VAUX, VAUXC
AUX	VAUXC
CONJ	CC, CCC
DET	DEM, QF, QFC, WQ
INTJ	INJ
NOUN	NN, NNC
NUM	QC, QCC
PART	RP, RPC, NEG
PART	NEG
PRON	PRP, PRPC, WQ
PROPN	NNP, NNPC
PUNCT	SYM
SCONJ	CC, CCC
VERB	VM, VMC
X	UNK

Table 3: Mappings of HDTB and Universal Dependencies POS tags.

4.2 Dependency Relations

In the above section, we found profound ambiguity in mapping the Hindi POS tags to their corresponding UD tags. In case of dependency relations, we also witnesses many cases of many-to-one and one-to-many mappings. For example dependency relations such as k3 (instrument of an action), k7t, k7p (location in time and space respectively), r6 (possession relation between two nouns), are all mapped to the label nmod (denoting nominal modifiers) in the UD scheme. Likewise, the Pāṇinian relation label k2 maps to xcomp, ccomp and dobj, based on 'Chunk[2] condition' described in section 5. The relation labels k1, k4a, pk1 (loosely corresponding to agent, experiencer, causer respectively) all map to the label nsubj of the UD scheme.

[2] A chunk (with boundaries marked), in HDTB, by definition, represents a group of adjacent words in a sentence, that are in dependency relation with each other, and where one of these words is their head (Chaudhry and Sharma, 2011)

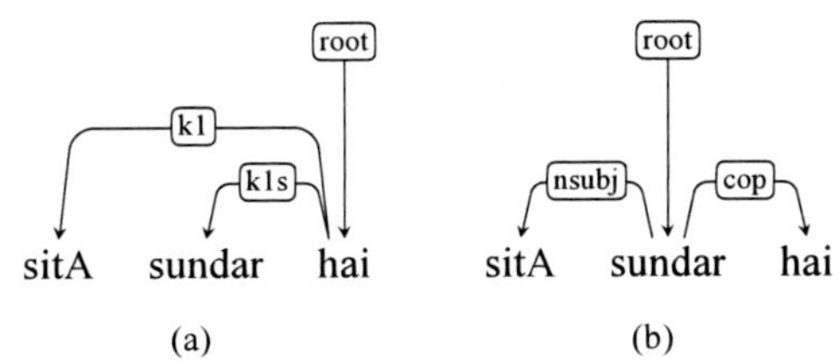

Figure 2: Dependency tree for a) HDTB and b) UD copula constructions.

4.3 Dependency Structure

In the Pāṇinian scheme there are about 82 kāraka and non kāraka relations. However, in UD there are only 40 dependency relations now, as opposed to 42 which were mentioned in (De Marneffe et al., 2014). The mapping between the two scheme can be seen in Table 4. One of the major challenges we came across during the conversion process was the conversion of elliptical constructions.

4.3.1 Copula

Currently in our scheme, a copular verb is considered as the head of a copula construction. During the conversion to UD, predicative nominal in the copula construction is marked as the head instead, while the 'be' verb becomes a cop dependent. For example in sentence (1) Sita is beautiful, 'sundar' सुंदर (beautiful) is treated as the head, while 'sItA' सीता (Sita) and the be verb 'hai' है (is) are its dependents of the type nsubject and cop, respectively.

(1) \`सीता सुंदर है.'
'sItA sundar hai.'

sItA *sundar* *hai*
sita beautiful is
'Sita is beautiful.'

For conversion to UD, these relations must be reversed, not just relabeled, which in turn may cause structural changes of other kinds. For example, a reanalysis must be done for dependents of the previous governor and decision be made whether they should attach to the new governor or remain as they were. Thus, for conversion to UD these relations are reversed though it leads to structural changes as can be seen in Figure 2.

4.3.2 Conjunctions

Another type of constructions we handle are those with conjunctions. In HDTB annotation scheme a conjunction, either coordinating or subordinating is the head of the clause and the other elements of the clause are its dependents. In the sentence such as in Example (2), 'aur' (and) is annotated the head with 'rAm' (Ram), 'mohan' (Mohan), 'sItA' (Sita), and 'mIrA' (Meera) as its dependents.

(2) \`राम, मोहन, सीता और मीरा आज आए थे.'
'rAm, mohan, sItA aur mIrA Aj Aye the.'

rAm, *mohAn,* *sItA* *aur* *mIrA* *Aj*
rAm mohAn sItA and mIrA today
Aye-the
came-PAST
'Ram, Mohan, Sita and Meera came today.'

Whereas in UD the first element of the coordinated construction is taken as the head. The conjunct and the other coordinated elements are annotated as its dependents. Given this sentence, in UD, 'rAm' is the head of the construction while 'mohan', 'sItA', 'mIrA' and 'aur' depend on it. Further, while 'mohan', 'sItA', 'mIrA' are annotated with the label conj, 'aur' is annotated with the label CC, since it is a coordinating conjunction, as can be seen in Figure 3. Also, UD annotates subordinating conjunction as mark, which is a dependent of the head of the subordinate clause. For the sake of conversion from HDTB to UD we distinguish between coordinating and subordinating conjunctions annotating them as conj and mark. For this we have enlisted them as two separate classes.

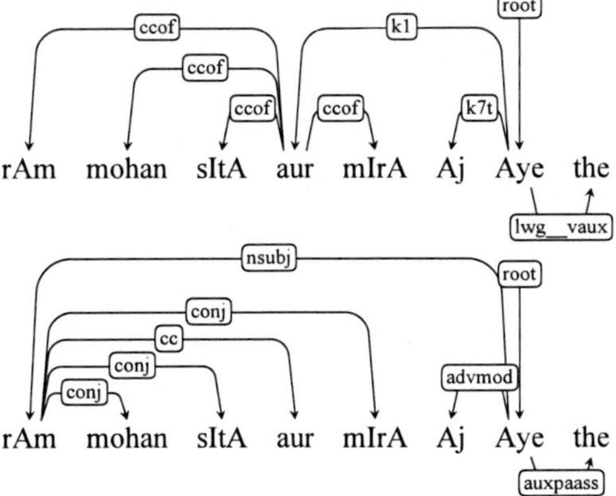

Figure 3: Dependency tree for a) HDTB and b) UD conjunctions constructions

4.3.3 Multiword names

As has been observed by (Johannsen et al., 2015), "In spans where it is not immediately clear which element is the head, UD takes a head-first approach: the first element in the span becomes the head, and the rest of the span elements attach to it. This applies mostly to coordinations, multiword expressions, and proper names." For example, in a name such as 'Atal Bihari Vajpayee', in UD, the first word in a compound name 'Atal', becomes the head and the rest its dependents. Whereas in HDTB, 'Vajpayee' is annotated the head and 'Atal' and 'Bihari' its dependents.

4.3.4 Ellipsis

Instances of ellipsis are abundant in the Hindi Treebank. While we are able to handle some in our current conversion, there are others we still need to work on. One such type which we have addressed is the 'yah-ki' यह-कि (this-that) complement constructions which follow the pattern: yah (*'यह)-its property-VP-ki कि clause'* (Mannem et al., 2009). In cases of ellipsis, a `NULL` node is introduced to facilitate annotation, since the entire 'ki' (that) clause is annotated as the child of 'yaha' (this) /`` `NULL' `` node here.

In Hindi, sentences such as in Example (3):

(3) \`गौरतलब है कि गोपाल को नासा आमंत्रित किया गया था.'
'gaurtalab hai ki gopAl ko nAsA Amantrit kiyA gayA thA.'

gaurtalab *hai* *ki* *gopAl-ko* *nAsA*
to-be-noted is that Gopal to-NASA
Amantrit-kiyA-gayA-thA.
invited-was

'Is to be noted that Gopal was invited to NASA.

'gaurtalab hai ki gopAl ko nAsA Amantrit kiyA gayA thA' (Is to be noted that Gopal was invited to NASA.) can come with the referent 'yah' यह (this) elided (a case of Pronoun drop) or explicitly manifested in the sentence. The 'ki' कि (that) clause and its referent are both modifiers (child) of the verb. However, in HDTB annotation the 'ki' clause is annotated a modifier of its referent which in turn is marked as the child of the verb. For the sake of consistency in cases where 'yah', the referent, does not manifest explicitly, a 'NULL' node is introduced in its stead. However, the UD scheme does not introduce `NULL` tokens to represent elided elements. Therefore to map all 'ki' complement constructions, with the UD scheme, we drop the 'NULL' node, and the 'ki' complement clause is annotated a dependent of the head of the removed `` `NULL' `` node (usually the verb) as illustrated in Figure 4.

Universal	Pāṇinian
acl	nmod__k1inv, nmod__k2inv, nmod__relc, rs, k2g, k2s, rbmod__relc
neg	nmod__neg
dislocated	fragof
iobj	k4
nmod	k2u, jk1, k1u, k3, k3u, k2p, k4u, k5, k7, k7a, k7p, k7pu, k7t, k7tu, k7u, r6, r6-k1, r6-k2, r6v, ras-k1, ras-k1u, ras-k2, ras-k4, ras-k4a, ras-k7, ras-k7p, ras-neg, ras-pof, ras-r6, ras-r6-k2, ras-rt, nmod__emph
punct	rsym
vocative	rad
advmod	rd, rsp, lwg__intf, vmod__adv, jjmod__intf, jjmod, adv, rbmod
dep	lwg__rp, lwg__unk, undef, enm
compound	pof__cn, pof__redup, lwg__rdp, lwg__vm, nmod__pofinv, pof, pof__inv
case	lwg__psp, lwg__nst, psp__cl
neg	lwg__neg
det	mod__wq
dobj	k2, k1s, mk1
amod	nmod__adj, nmod
parataxis	vmod
ccomp	k2
xcomp	k2
aux	lwg__vaux
auxpass	lwg__vaux
nsubj	k1, k4a, pk1
nsubjpass	k1
advcl	rh, rt, rtu, sent-adv, vmod

Table 4: Universal mapping of Pāṇinian Dependencies used in HDTB.

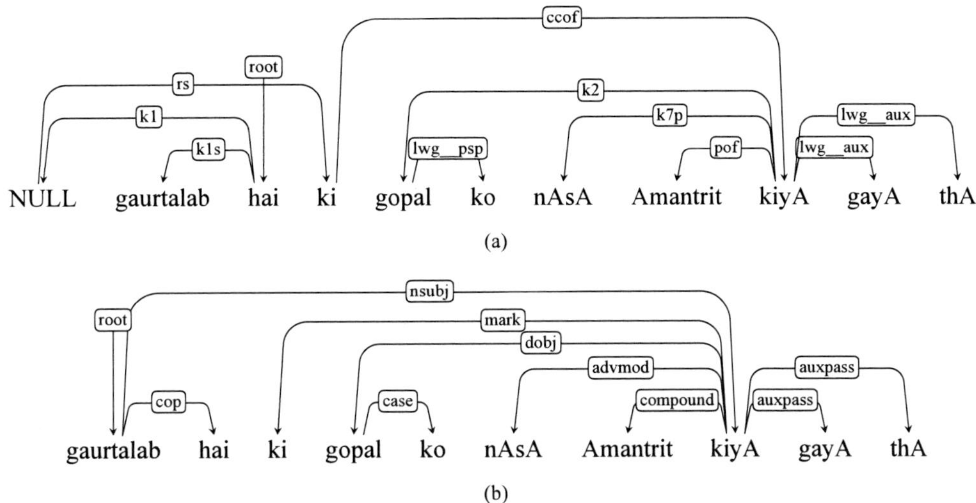

Figure 4: Dependency tree for a) HDTB and b) UD ellipsis constructions.

5 Conversion Process

During conversion it must be noted that we are moving from a very detailed and granular format to a format which is under-specified. The implementation of the conversion was based on the mapping between schemes described above. The conversion script executes as a pipeline of three components, each of which takes as input data in CONLL format and outputs data in the same format. During conversion, structure is handled before labels. The first module harmonizes the structural differences from HDTB to UD by handling ellipsis (and thereafter aligning nodes in the tree after NULL removal), copula constructions, mutliword names and conjunctions. It updates the nodes as modifier-modified relations have been changed. The second and third module converts POS and Dependency relations from HDTB to UD, respectively. The conversion is based on certain heuristics which involve conditions specified in terms of lexical, structural, morphological information and Part of Speech tags. Examples for the different types of conversion conditions are as follows:

- Lexical condition: The POS tag `WQ` of HDTB is converted to `ADV` of UD when expressed by word form or lemma 'kab' (कब), 'kahA.N' (कहाँ), 'kaisA' (कैसा), 'kyun' (क्यों). Else if the node has chunk type as child in its features, it is converted to `DET` of UD; otherwise to `PRON` of UD.
- Morphological condition: If the dependency relation is any of `k1`, `pk1`, `k4a` and the current node's parent has TAM (Tense, Aspect, Modality) feature as *'yA_jA'* (या_जा), the relation is converted to `nsubjpass`; if dependency relation is `lwg__vaux` and there is a presence of the TAM feature, it is converted to `auxpass`. In the absence of this morph feature `lwg__vaux` is converted to `aux`, while `k1`, `pk1`, `k4a` are converted to `nsubj`.
- Chunk condition: If the dependency relation is `k2` and the current node's chunk id is `VGF` (Finite Verb Chunk), the relation is converted to `ccomp`; else if chunk id is `VGNN` (Verb Chunk - Gerund) it is converted to `xcomp`; otherwise to `dobj`.
- POS condition: If the dependency relation is any of `nmod__adj` or `nmod` and the node's POS Tag is `DET` or `DEM` the relation is converted to `det`; if POS is `NUM` it is converted to `nummod`; else if POS is any of `NNP`, `NNPC`, `PRP`, `NN` or `NNC`, it is converted to `nmod`.

During conversion from HDTB to UD we lose 3852 sentences that cannot be restructured according to our current scheme, they are mostly cases of ellipsis (gapping).

6 Parsing Experiment

Our motive of conversion from HDTB to UD was not keeping the increase/decrease of parsing accu-

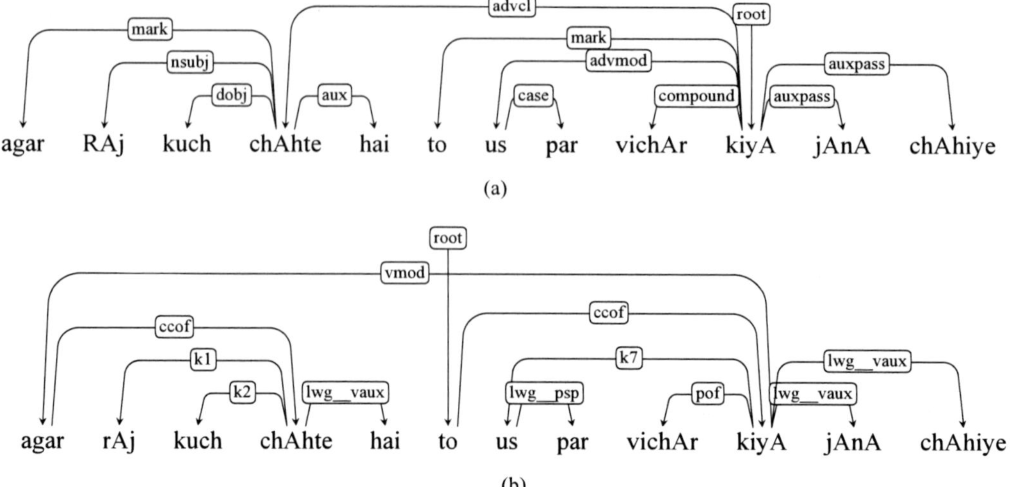

Figure 5: Dependency tree for paired connective 'agar-to' for a) UD and b) HDTB.

racy in consideration. The design choices taken, such as the head-first approach, as described in Section 2.2, led to changes in a lot of attachments like that of Copula and decreased the learnability of the parser for the syntactic structure of Hindi. We conduct parsing experiments to quantify these effects and also do a manual error analysis to point out the constructions which are not learnt efficiently by the parser.

For experiment purposes, we are using MALT [3] with parser settings from (Ambati et al., 2010). The metrics used for evaluation are Labeled and Unlabeled attachment score (LAS, UAS) and Label accuracy score (LS). The average accuracy of 10 fold cross validation is reported in Table 5.

We experience an accuracy drop of ~2% in UAS in conversion from HDTB to UD. This is not surprising as the two are now quite different treebanks. The drop in accuracy can be attributed to the numerous changes in attachment of edges while conversion. However the increase in accuracy of LS is intuitive because of the reduced number of classes of classification for dependency relations.

On doing a manual error analysis we observe the following patterns:

- The parser is not able to learn copula constructions properly, the 'be' verb is not recognised as 'cop' in most cases, it is made the root of the sentence or head of the phrase, instead. This is at odds with the general structure where verb is a root of a dependency tree as it is the primary modified. These structures also cannot be learnt efficiently based on lexicalism as the 'be' verb is also used as an auxillary in most cases.
- For control constructions which have more than one verb, the first non-finite verb is marked as the head instead of the finite verb.
- Sentences having paired connectives like 'agar-to' (अगर-तो), 'yadi-to' (यदि-तो) corresponding to 'if-then', do not have their governors and dependents correctly marked. This is because they are handled differently in both the schemes. In HDTB 'agar'and 'to' are clausal heads. The 'to'-clause is modified by the 'agar'-clause. Whereas in UD 'agar'and 'to' must be dependents of the main verb of their respective clauses as can be seen in Figure 5.

7 Conclusion and Future Work

In this paper we briefly described the process of conversion of Hindi Treebank to UD annotation scheme. It was an attempt to release the resource in a widely accepted international format so that it becomes more usable for a variety of multilingual NLP tasks. The conversion was a challenging task and there are constructions which are yet to be addressed to be fully compliant with the UD scheme

[3] MALT version 1.8.1 , http://www.maltparser.org/

	LAS	UAS	LS
Pāṇinian	90.97	95.206	92.908
UD	90.237	93.193	94.053

Table 5: Average accuracy of 10-fold cross validation using Pāṇinian and UD framework.

like that of ellipsis etc. As a part of future work, we propose to come up with better techniques to resolve empty nodes in the absence of predicational or verbal heads. Also a few attachment schemes must be reanalyzed and revised to handle long distance dependencies efficiently. We performed experiments using MALT parser on both the source treebank HDTB and the converted UD Hindi Treebank, to find that the performance is slightly deteriorated after conversion.

Acknowledgments

We would like to thank anonymous reviewers for their valuable comments that helped to improve the quality of this paper.
The work reported in this paper is supported by the NSF grant (Award Number: CNS 0751202; CFDA Number: 47.070)[4]

References

Bharat Ram Ambati, Samar Husain, Joakim Nivre, and Rajeev Sangal. 2010. On the role of morphosyntactic features in hindi dependency parsing. In *Proceedings of the NAACL HLT 2010 First Workshop on Statistical Parsing of Morphologically-Rich Languages*, pages 94–102. Association for Computational Linguistics.

Rafiya Begum, Samar Husain, Arun Dhwaj, Dipti Misra Sharma, Lakshmi Bai, and Rajeev Sangal. 2008. Dependency annotation scheme for indian languages. In *IJCNLP*, pages 721–726. Citeseer.

A. Bharati, V. Chaitanya, R. Sangal, and KV Ramakrishnamacharyulu. 1995. *Natural Language Processing: A Paninian Perspective*. Prentice-Hall of India.

Akshar Bharati, Rajeev Sangal, Dipti Misra Sharma, and Lakshmi Bai. 2006. Anncorra: Annotating corpora guidelines for pos and chunk annotation for indian languages. *LTRC-TR31*.

[4]Any opinions, findings, and conclusions or recommendations expressed in this material are those of the author(s) and do not necessarily reflect the views of the National Science Foundation.

Akshar Bharati, DM Sharma S Husain, L Bai, R Begam, and R Sangal. 2009. Anncorra: Treebanks for indian languages, guidelines for annotating hindi treebank (version–2.0).

Riyaz Ahmad Bhat, Rajesh Bhatt, Annahita Farudi, Prescott Klassen, Bhuvana Narasimhan, Martha Palmer, Owen Rambow, Dipti Misra Sharma, Ashwini Vaidya, Sri Ramagurumurthy Vishnu, et al. 2014. The hindi/urdu treebank project. In *Handbook of Linguistic Annotation*. Springer Press.

Rajesh Bhatt, Bhuvana Narasimhan, Martha Palmer, Owen Rambow, Dipti Misra Sharma, and Fei Xia. 2009. A multi-representational and multi-layered treebank for hindi/urdu. In *Proceedings of the Third Linguistic Annotation Workshop*, pages 186–189. Association for Computational Linguistics.

Cristina Bosco, Simonetta Montemagni, and Maria Simi. 2013. Converting italian treebanks: Towards an italian stanford dependency treebank. In *Proceedings of the 7th Linguistic Annotation Workshop and Interoperability with Discourse*, pages 61–69. Citeseer.

Himani Chaudhry and Dipti M Sharma. 2011. Annotation and issues in building an english dependency treebank.

Marie-Catherine De Marneffe and Christopher D Manning. 2008. The stanford typed dependencies representation. In *Coling 2008: Proceedings of the workshop on Cross-Framework and Cross-Domain Parser Evaluation*, pages 1–8. Association for Computational Linguistics.

Marie-Catherine De Marneffe, Timothy Dozat, Natalia Silveira, Katri Haverinen, Filip Ginter, Joakim Nivre, and Christopher D Manning. 2014. Universal stanford dependencies: A cross-linguistic typology. In *LREC*, volume 14, pages 4585–4592.

Anders Johannsen, Héctor Martínez Alonso, and Barbara Plank. 2015. Universal dependencies for danish. In *International Workshop on Treebanks and Linguistic Theories (TLT14)*, page 157.

Janna Lipenkova and Milan Soucek. 2014. Converting russian dependency treebank to stanford typed dependencies representation. In *EACL*, pages 143–147.

Prashanth Mannem, Himani Chaudhry, and Akshar Bharati. 2009. Insights into non-projectivity in hindi. In *Proceedings of the ACL-IJCNLP 2009 Student Research Workshop*, pages 10–17. Association for Computational Linguistics.

Ryan T McDonald, Joakim Nivre, Yvonne Quirmbach-Brundage, Yoav Goldberg, Dipanjan Das, Kuzman Ganchev, Keith B Hall, Slav Petrov, Hao Zhang, Oscar Täckström, et al. 2013. Universal dependency annotation for multilingual parsing. In *ACL (2)*, pages 92–97. Citeseer.

Joakim Nivre, Marie-Catherine de Marneffe, Filip Ginter, Yoav Goldberg, Jan Hajic, Christopher D Manning, Ryan McDonald, Slav Petrov, Sampo Pyysalo, Natalia Silveira, et al. 2016. Universal dependencies v1: A multilingual treebank collection. In *Proceedings of the 10th International Conference on Language Resources and Evaluation (LREC 2016)*.

Martha Palmer, Rajesh Bhatt, Bhuvana Narasimhan, Owen Rambow, Dipti Misra Sharma, and Fei Xia. 2009. Hindi syntax: Annotating dependency, lexical predicate-argument structure, and phrase structure. In *The 7th International Conference on Natural Language Processing*, pages 14–17.

Slav Petrov, Dipanjan Das, and Ryan McDonald. 2011. A universal part-of-speech tagset. *arXiv preprint arXiv:1104.2086*.

Sampo Pyysalo, Jenna Kanerva, Anna Missilä, Veronika Laippala, and Filip Ginter. 2015. Universal dependencies for finnish. In *Proceedings of NoDaLiDa*, pages 163–172.

Lucien Tesnière. 1959. *Eléments de syntaxe structurale*. Librairie C. Klincksieck.

Fei Xia, Owen Rambow, Rajesh Bhatt, Martha Palmer, and Dipti Misra Sharma. 2009. Towards a multi-representational treebank. In *The 7th International Workshop on Treebanks and Linguistic Theories. Groningen, Netherlands*, pages 159–170.

Daniel Zeman, David Marecek, Martin Popel, Loganathan Ramasamy, Jan Stepánek, Zdenek Zabokrtskỳ, and Jan Hajic. 2012. Hamledt: To parse or not to parse? In *LREC*, pages 2735–2741.

Phrase Generalization: a Corpus Study in Multi-Document Abstracts and Original News Alignments

Ariani Di-Felippo
Federal University of São Carlos
Language and Literature Dept.
Rod. Washington Luis, km 235 (SP-310)
São Carlos, SP 13565-905, Brazil
arianidf@gmail.com

Ani Nenkova
University of Pennsylvania
Computer and Information Science Dept.
3330 Walnut St.
Philadelphia, PA 19104, USA
nenkova@seas.upenn.edu

Abstract

Content can be expressed at different levels of specificity, varying the amount of detail presented to the reader. The need to transform specific content into more general form naturally arises in summarization, where people and machines need to convey the gist of a text within imposed space constraints. Completely removing sentences and phrases is one way to reduce the level of detail. The bulk of work on summarization content selection and compression deal with these tasks. In this paper, we present a corpus study on a more subtle and understudied phenomenon: noun phrase generalization. Based on multi-document news and abstract alignments at the phrase level, we arrive at a five category classification scheme and find that the most common category requires semantic interpretation and inference. The others rely on lexical substitution or deletion of details from the original expression. We provide a systematic analysis, elucidating the capabilities needed for automating the generation of more general or more specific references.

1 Introduction

Summarization involves a number of complex transformations to condense the gist of a text into a short summary (Nenkova and McKeown, 2011). One of these transformations is changing the amount of detail in the original news texts. Removing entire sentences is one of the fairly well-understood ways for changing the amount of detail. Which sentences to remove can be decided in a system's content selection module by a number of competitive approaches (Gillick and Favre, 2009; Lin and Bilmes, 2011; Kulesza and Taskar, 2011). Similarly, one can perform sentence compression, removing words or phrases from a sentence in the original text to form a summary sentence (Knight and Marcu, 2000; Riezler et al., 2003; Turner and Charniak, 2005; McDonald, 2006; Galley and McKeown, 2007; Cohn and Lapata, 2008) or perform sentence selection and compression jointly (Berg-Kirkpatrick et al., 2011).

In this paper, we focus our attention on a much finer level to study the changes of specificity on the phrase level. The existence of these changes have been documented in prior work (Jing and McKeown, 2000; Marsi and Krahmer, 2010). Jing and McKeown (2000) analyzed 30 single document articles and their summaries and characterized the transformations performed on the original text to form a summary. They did not give statistics about the relative frequency of each transformation operation but list "add descriptions or names for people and organizations" and "substitute phrases with more general or specific information" as two of the summarization operations. In a more recent study, Marsi and Krahmer (2010) analyzed the phrase alignment between original spoken news in a Dutch television news program and the subtitles for the same broadcast. They aligned the transcript and the subtitles and analyzed the transformations performed on the phrase level. The authors distinguished five mutually exclusive similarity relations in the corpus: `equals` (the aligned phrases are identical), `restastes` (the aligned phrases convey the same information but with different wording), `specifies` (the subtitle phrase is more specific than the transcript phrase), `generalizes` (the subtitle phrase is more general than the transcript phrase), and `intersects` (the aligned phrases share some informational content, but each also expresses some information not expressed in the other). The second most frequent

Proceedings of LAW X – The 10th Linguistic Annotation Workshop, pages 151–159,
Berlin, Germany, August 11, 2016. ©2016 Association for Computational Linguistics

class is `generalizes`[1]. In about 14% of the aligned phrases, the subtitle contained a more general phrase than the original. Only a small percentage of `specifies` pairs is present: in about 3% of the phrases the subtitles were more specific than the transcripts.

Here we present an analysis of generalization operations that occur in abstracts produced for clusters of topically related news articles in Brazilian Portuguese. In the vast majority of cases these require transformations at the phrase level. We observed five types of generalization: interpretation, detail removal, class, role, and whole. Named entity (NE) generalizations, in particular, belong to four categories: detail removal (removing some of the information contained in the original article, similar to compression on the phrase level), role (substituting a reference by name with a reference by the role the entity plays in the described events), class (substituting a reference with a superordinate concept, i.e. "swimmer – "athlete") , and whole (a reference to a member of a group or area is substituted by a reference to the whole, i.e. "Jamaica" – "the Caribbean". In each category, we identified a set of syntactic-semantic operations related to each type of named entities (person, organization, location and sports event). Such operations include substitutions and phrase reductions. Their automation would require the development of capabilities that are not available to current systems.

The remainder of this paper is structured as follows. In Section 2, we introduce our corpus, explaining the manual alignment between the human abstract and the multiple news text inputs, and the pre-processing of such alignments. In Section 3, we describe the analysis of the alignment pairs containing generalization and the categorization of each instance in according to the five-class typology of transformations. Then, in Section 4, our focus relies on the generalization of phrases containing named entities. Specifically, we describe the syntactic and semantic properties of such phrases considering both the different types of generalization and entities. In Section 5, we discuss what we learned and close with discussion of perspectives for automatic summarization.

[1] `Equals` is the most common relation between aligned phrases, accounting for 67% of the alignments

2 The Corpus

We used the CSTNews (Cardoso et al., 2011) corpus of multi-document abstracts and the associated news articles. The corpus comprises 50 clusters of news texts in Brazilian Portuguese from a range of categories: daily news (14), world (14), domestic politics (10), sports (10) , economy (1), and science (1). There are 140 documents in total in the corpus.

Each cluster contains two or three news articles on the same topic, with 42 sentences per cluster on average. There are six manual multi-document abstracts for each cluster. The abstract-writers were instructed to produce abstracts of length equal to 30% of the longest article in the cluster. The resulting abstracts were on average seven sentences (132 words) long. CSTNews has annotated versions of the source texts and summaries in different linguistic levels, e.g., intra- and inter-textual discourse relations, classification of temporal expressions, semantic annotation of nouns and verbs, and subtopic segmentation. The corpus also contains alignments between each human abstract and the source texts at the sentence level. Each sentence in the abstract is associated with all of the sentences in the original articles that support the information expressed in the abstract.

For our work, we use the existing manual annotations, pairing sentences from the abstract with their corresponding sentences in the original article (Camargo et al., 2013). The annotators identified 1,007 alignments, involving 334 summary sentences and 877 document sentences: 99.4% of the summary sentences were aligned to some document sentence and 42.43% of the document sentences were aligned to some some summary sentence.

In addition, for each pair of summary-original sentences, annotators included labels describing the sub-sentential relations between the sentences in the pair. Among other tags, the annotators labeled when a summary sentence contained parts that were more general or more specific than the semantically corresponding part in the document sentence. They however did not mark the exact spans of text involved in the generalization.

The alignment in (1) shows an example of a summary and document sentence that share information and in which one can observe changes in the specificity of reference. The summary sentence has more general content, referring to "many states" and "the operation" while the document sentence has a list of Brazilian states and the name of the police investigation (shown in bold).

(1) Summary: *Mais de 300 policiais de [**vários estados**] participaram d[**a operação**]* ("More than 300 officers from [many states] were part of the operation").
Document: *Ao menos 300 policiais de [**Amapá, Distrito Federal, Mato Grosso, Acre and Rondônia**] participaram da [**Operação Dominó**]* ("More than 300 officers from [Amazonas, Distrito Federal, Mato Grosso, Acre and Rondônia] were part of the [Operação Dominó"]).

Overall, 13% of summary-document pairs involved a generalization or a specification operation. There are 80 pairs tagged as containing generalization and 47 pairs tagged as containing specification (Camargo et al., 2013). The label describes the change that occurred to transform the document sentence into the summary sentence, i.e. generalization means some information is expressed in more general terms in the summary sentence than it was in the original document sentence.

2.1 Pre-Processing Steps

With the aim categorizing the type of every generalization case in the summary-documents alignments, we performed two manual pre-processing steps: (i) expansion and revision of the alignments with generalization, and (ii) delimitation of the generalization cases and indexing of the textual spans involved in each case.

Abstracts contained both generalizations and specifications of entities. Assuming that the underlying process involved in modifying the reference is the same in both cases, we augment our corpus of generalizations by "inverting" the 47 specification alignments to obtain 47 examples of generalization, as illustrated in (2). The pair is from a news article about the schedule of the Brazilian men's volleyball team. It was originally tagged as specification, since the summary sentence contains more detail than the original; it details that the team aim is to win "the gold medal". We swap the direction of the relation between the sentences and consider the resulting sentences as examples of generalization.

In this way, we obtained a set of 127 pairs of aligned sentences with differences in the specificity of reference. Next, each alignment was manually revised by the first author: 12 of them were excluded because the author did not find clear portions of the summary sentence that generalize information expressed in the original document. An example of sentence that was excluded is given in (3). The final set consists of a total of 115 aligned pairs.

(2) Summary: *O próximo objetivo da seleção é [**a medalha de ouro nos Jogos Pan-Americanos do Rio**]* ("The next goal of the team is [the gold medal in the Pan American Games in Rio]").
Document: *O próximo objetivo é [**os Jogos Pan-Americanos do Rio**]* ("The next goal is [the Pan American Games in Rio]").

(3) Summary: *A pressão argentina continuou no segundo tempo, mas o Brasil fechou a goleada com um gol marcado pela sua dupla de volantes* ("Argentina struggled to make any impact in the 2nd half, but Brazil sealed the victory with a goal made by one of its midfields").
Document: *Os argentinos, com um time repleto de craques favoritos ao título, e com campanha irrepreensível até o momento, pareciam não acreditar no que viam* ("Argentina, a team full of stars and favorite to win, could not believe what was happening").

Next, we carried out an annotation of each pair in order to answer two questions: (1) Which text spans in the respective sentences are involved in the generalization operation? (2) What is the linguistic-level characterization of the spans? The description captured the changes of content from specific to general. Clause generalization was restricted to cases where the summary noun phrase (NP) generalizes a proposition. In order to answer the questions, the spans were marked and labeled according to the corresponding generalization level (C for clause, and P for phrase). If the sentences had more than one case of generalization, they were also numbered according to the order of occurrence in the document, following the notation C/P_NUM. Examples of annotated phrases and clauses are given in (4) and (5), respectively. We extracted a total of 136 pairs of specific-general phrases from the 115 sentence alignments. There are more aligned phrases with difference in specificity than aligned sentences because some sentence pairs contained more than one case of phrase generalization case.

(4) Document: [O presidente dos EUA, George Bush]**P1**, pediu que o Exército turco busque [uma solução diplomática para a questão]**P2** ("[President of the US, George Bush], asked the Turkish Army to seek [a diplomatic solution to the issue]")
Summary: [Washington]**P1** e a Comissão Européia também pedem [uma solução diplomática]**P2** ("[Washington] and European Commission also ask for a [diplomatic solution]")

(5) Document: Na Jamaica, [muitos estocaram comida, água, lanternas e velas]**C** ("In Jamaica, many stock food, water, flashlights and candles")
Summary: [Muitos moradores e turistas estão se preparando para a passagem do furação. ("[Many locals and tourists prepare for the hurricane]")

3 Typology of Transformations

Further, we iteratively analyzed the types of the 136 cases of generalization to come up with categories that cover all examples in the corpus. We converged on a classification scheme with five categories: (i) **Interpretation**, i.e., generalization based on sophisticated inferences over the source text and additional information such as transforming "200 people were injured" to "the human toll was high"; (ii) **Detail removal**, i.e, generalization by omitting details of a specific textual segment; (iii) **Role**, i.e., replacement of person entities by their title or role; (iv) **Class**, i.e., substitution of a subordinate concept by a superordinate one, and (v) **Whole**, i.e., concepts representing parts are replaced by concepts that indicate the whole. The typology reveals that humans carry out a variety of inferences based on rich world and domain knowledge to produce generic information. Table 1 shows the distribution of the categories divided by clause and phrase levels.

Interpretation is the most frequent category in the corpus (45.6%) and the only one that occurs in both clause and phrase levels. However, 83.8% of the cases (52 out of 62) occur at the clause level and involve propositional generalizations. We show an example in (5). It involves

Category	Phrase	Clause	Total
Interpretation	10 (7.4)	52 (38.2)	62 (45.6)
Detail removal	32 (23.5)	0	32 (23.5)
Role	18 (13.2)	0	18 (13.2)
Class	13 (9.6)	0	13 (9.6)
Whole	11 (8.1)	0	11 (8.1)
Total	84 (61.8)	52 (38.2)	136 (100)%

Table 1: Number and percentage of the generalizations

Category	Noun	Named entity	Total
Interpretation	10 (11.9)	0	10 (11.9)
Detail removal	14 (16.7)	18 (21.4)	32 (38.1)
Role	2 (2.4)	16 (19)	18 (21.4)
Class	5 (6)	8 (9.5)	13 (15.5)
Whole	2 (2.4)	6 (10.7)	11 (13.1)
Total	33 (39.3)	51 (60.7)	84 (100)%

Table 2: Number and percentage of general NPs and NEs

an inference that "stocking food, water, flashlights and candles" is a preparedness activity against hurricane. Detail removal is the second most frequent, with 32 instances (23.5%), followed by Role, with 18 instances (13.2%). The distribution of cases in Class and Whole is quite similar, 13 (9.6%) and 11 (8.1%), respectively. Next, we turn our description to generalizations that occur at the phrase level[2], specifically to those involving named entities.

4 Named Entity Generalization

We first computed the number of cases that involve named entities or general NPs per category. Table 2 shows the results.

Looking briefly at the 33 common noun pairs, we found that Interpretation tends to be associated with numbers (25%). The substitution of "about 300 buildings" with "many buildings" illustrates this. Interpretation also results from different inferences, e.g., when a cause (e.g., 'the fog") is replaced by its effect (e.g., "the bad weather"). The Role case where "the 16 children and 14 adults" was replaced with "the 30 hostages" is the only one involving generation of a numeric expression. Detail removal occurs by deleting noun adjuncts (shown in italics) (e.g., "a *university* campus") or complements (e.g., "the inspection *of income tax declarations*").

Studying in detail the 51 generalizations involving NEs, we found four types of NEs: 26 persons (51%), 16 organizations (31.4%), 7 locations (13.7%), and 2 sports events (2%). We also identified sub-categories of generalization for three en-

[2]Appendix 1 (Table 4) provides examples of phrase generalizations.

Entity	Category	Sub-category	Document Phrase	Summary Phrase
Event (2)	Class (2)	–	Name (2)	Noun+Post-mod (2)
Location (7)	Whole (4)	Island-to-region (1) City-to-state (1) City-to-country (2)	Name (4)	Name (4)
	Detail removal (3)	–	Pre-mod+Name (1) Name (2)	Noun (3)
Organization (16)	Class (6)	–	Name (6)	Noun (6)
	Detail removal (6)	–	Name (4) Name+Post-mod (2)	Noun (4) Acronym (2)
	Whole (4)	Member-to-organization (4)	Name (2) Name (2)	Noun (2) Noun (1), name (1)
People (26)	Role (16)	–	Pre-mod+Full Name (6) First Name (4) Last name (3) Pre-mod+First name (1) Pre-mod+Last name (1) Acronym (1)	Noun (16)
	Detail removal (9)	–	Pre-mod+Full name (5)	Noun (3), First name (2)
			Full name (3)	First name (3)
			Pre-mod+Last name (1)	Noun (1)
	Whole (1)	Person-to-place (1)	Pre-mod+Full name (1)	Noun (1)

Table 3: Semantic and syntactic properties of named entity phrase generalization

tity types and some syntactic patterns in the transitions, related to the type of the phrase head and the occurrence of pre- and post-modifiers. The results are shown in Table 3. The numbers in parenthesis show how many times the given category and syntactic form have occurred in the pairs.

The sports event generalizations consist in substituting the multi-word expression (MWE) phrase "the American Cup" with two different general NPs: "the continental competition" and "the oldest soccer tournament". These are the only instances where the summary phrases include modification. Thus, both general mentions put the referent in a class and provide further details about it as well.

According to Table 3, there are three types of Whole generalizations for locations that solely involve names: (i) `island-to-region`, such as the replacement of "Haiti" and "Dominican Republic" with "the Caribbean"; (ii) `city-to-state`, such as "Maceió, which was substituted by "Alagoas", and (iii) `city-to-country`, such as the replacement of "Boston" with "United States". There is also one particular type of Detail removal by deleting names from phrases of the form premodifier + name (e.g., "the capital Kingston") to produce mentions whose head was the modifying noun of the specific phrase ("the capital"). Location names, specifically MWEs (e.g., "International Airport of São Paulo") that are made up of a place (possibly a MWE itself, such as "São Paulo") and additional information (e.g., "international"), are also replaced with common nouns ("the airport"). The replacement of such proper names with common nouns result from removal of all the details about the referent description.

Organization names are mostly generalized by means of common nouns that express class or whole. The substitution of "Brazil" with "the country" illustrates the Class category. The Whole generalization occurs through `member-to-organization` substitution, i.e., the replacement of "the Military Police Shock Troop" with "the police" illustrates this. The only case of name generalization is the substitution of "the Archdiocese of Los Angeles" with "the Catholic Church". There are also cases where names followed by acronyms in parenthesis, such as "National Institute of Social Security (INSS)", are reduced to the acronym only.

It can be seen that document mentions to people have different head types: full name, first name, last name, and acronym. With the exception of acronyms, the heads usually occur with two types of pre-modifiers (shown in italics): titles (e.g.,"*president* of the Senate, Renan Calheiros") and roles (e.g., "the *goalkeeper* Vieri"). In general, the document mentions are commonly replaced with common nouns only. The substitution of the first name "João Pedro" with "the senator" illustrates this. The summary writers also chose the modifying noun (shown in italics) from phrases of the form pre-modifier + name (e.g., "the *goalkeeper* Vieri") for generalization, deleting the last or fulll name (e.g., "the goalkeeper").

The reduction of full name by deleting surname (shown in italics) (e.g., "Renan *Calheiros*"), yielding phrases containing first name only (e.g., "Renan"), is another common type of operation. The case that belong to the Whole category is the only one involving two different types of named entity. In particular, "President of the United States, George Bush" was substituted by "Washington", in a `person-to-place` operation.

5 Discussion

This study provides an initial characterization for phrase generalizations that arise in summarization. It is evident that our results should be validated on a larger sample of summarization data. Nevertheless our findings can be seen as a good start for understanding the phenomenon. One of the practical outcomes from our work is the generalization typology which can be applied for the analysis of other data.

Interpretation is the most common category, resulting from inferences over propositions and covering a variety of operations. Its automatic treatment would be a major endeavor in natural language processing research because it is at the intersection of semantic interpretation and text generation.

Another challenge for summarization systems is how to deal with mentions of numbers, which form a special class of the interpretation transformation. We found that references to date, time, and general quantities accounted for 25% (8 out of 33 instances) of common noun phrase alignments in our corpus. Only in one case the numeric expression was transformed in an alternative numeric expression. All other phrases involving numbers were lexicalized alternatively. Then the task of a system would be to identify which references to numbers should be generalized and how to generate the generalization of numbers.

In our study, 61% of the generalizations involve operations over specific mentions to named entities. These have been studied computationally in the past, to predict the appropriate form of the name in references to people (Siddharthan et al., 2011) and to exploit the person name repetition in the summary to find the salience of entities (Dunietz and Gillick, 2014). Neither of these prior studies analyzed reference to named entities by common noun, which we provided in the analysis of our data, nor do they look at non-person references. In fact, substituting names with generic nouns was the most common operation in our data and it calls for the development of new capabilities, both to decide which entities should be mentioned generically and how to generate the reference itself.

Moreover, specific mentions to sports events, locations and organizations do not include modification in 88% (22 out of 25) of the pairs. Specific mentions to people have an accompanying description in around half the cases (57.6%). The occurrence of a pre-modifying word that identify the person's title or role provides more details about the referent. Thus, such mentions have a higher level of specificity than other with name only. Moreover, only few generic phrases contain a name, and, when it occurs, the names have particular types, e.g., first name in the case of people, and acronyms for organization.

On the operations concerning named entities, we provide some insights for substitution and reduction approaches to obtain general phrases.

Substitution is the most common operation (76.5%) (out of 51 cases), and its automatic process would require structured knowledge that includes at least three relationships: (i) **is-a** to express the rough notion of "a kind of", (ii) **part-whole** to express `island-to-region`, `city-to-state`, `city-to-country`, `member-to-organization`, and `person-to-place`, and (iii) **instance-role**, for entities of the person category. Since such knowledge is very particular to some domains, specially global and local sports, politics, and geography, we believe that it would possible to model it in handcrafted lexicons. It could also be derived automatically for some types of reference (McKinlay and Markert, 2011; Mitchell et al., 2015). In addition, modules to decide when substitution is necessary or appropriate would be needed.

Phrase reduction (i.e., deletion of words or phrases) occurs in 23.5% of the cases (out of 51). Although it is less frequent, detail removal include cases where specific phrases could be automatically converted into general in a more feasible way. This observation is based on the fact that summary phrases are made up of linguistic material that came from the document phrases. Thus, we can conceive phrase reduction as a similar task to sentence compression, where the operations are learned by analyzing pair of sentences, one from the source text, and other from human-written abstracts such that they both have the same content. Specifically, 4 reduction rules could be defined: (i) removing pre-modifier from phrase of the form modifier + location name, yielding a common noun mention; (ii) removing name from phrase of the form organization name + parenthetical acronym, generating an mention with acronym only; (iii) deleting name from phrase of the form title/role + person name, producing a common noun mention, and (iv) removing surname from person full name, generating a first name mention.

We may also contribute for generating references, since referring expressions in extracts can be problematic because the sentences compiled from different documents might contain too little, too much, or repeated information about the referent. Our results show that 76.5% of the 51 generalizations with named entities (e.g., "the coach Bernardinho") are made solely with a common noun phrase (without the inclusion of the entity's name) (e.g., "the coach"), and thus a task to be considered is the generation of common noun references to named entities. Such generation would allow the production of a more natural summary.

We are aware of full coreference resolution is a very difficult problem and there are no systems that can reliably perform it on free texts. But we believe that the availability of cross-document information can facilitate the resolution of common noun phrases. This assumption is built on the fact that most common nouns in summary phrases were contained in the input texts. For example, the head of the summary NP "the coach", which generalizes the name "Bernardinho", is contained in a different sentence of the same input, as part of the mention "the coach Bernardinho". This means that lexical overlap would indicate that these three NPs refer to the same entity. Common noun generation would increase the genericity level of summaries, and avoid the repetition of forms produced by some rewriting methods (Siddharthan et al., 2011).

6 Future work

Our research both provides a preliminary characterization of generalization in document-summary alignments and a discussion of some insights for Natural Language Processing. For future work, we plan to increase the sample of specific-generic pairs by aligning the five new abstracts recently added to each cluster of CSTNews in order to validate our results. We could repeat the manual alignment or use automatic methods (Agostini et al., 2014). To identify the categories, we intend to carry out a manual annotation with multiple judges.

Moreover, we have been performing a manual annotation of coreference chains that consist of all the mentions of an entity in abstracts with different lengths in two languages, Portuguese and English. Our goal is to explore human preferences in mention realization, and possible differences across languages. We also aim at exploring whether the abstract length has influence on the syntactic forms and sequences of mentions, and on the amount of information included in the mentions.

Acknowledgment: We thank the State of São Paulo Research Foundation (FAPESP) (#2015/01450-5) for the financial support.

References

Verônica Agostini, Roque E.L. Condori, and Thiago A. S. Pardo. 2014. Automatic alignment of news texts and their multi-document summaries: Comparison among methods. In *Proceedings of the 11st International Conference on Computational Processing of Portuguese*, pages 286–291, São Carlos, SP, Brazil.

Taylor Berg-Kirkpatrick, Dan Gillick, and Dan Klein. 2011. Jointly learning to extract and compress. In *Proceedings of the 49th ACL/HLT - Volume 1*, pages 481–490. Association for Computational Linguistics.

Renata T. Camargo, Verônica Agostini, Ariani Di-Felippo, and Thiago A. S. Pardo. 2013. Manual typification of source texts and multi-document summaries alignments. *Procedia Social and Behavioral Sciences*, 95:498–506.

Paula C. F. Cardoso, Erick G. Maziero, Maria Lucia R. Castro Jorge, Eloize M. R. Seno, Ariani Di-Felippo, Lucia Helena M. Rino, Maria das Graas V. Nunes, and Thiago Pardo. 2011. Cstnews - a discourse-annotated corpus for single and multi-document summarization of news texts in brazilian portuguese. In *Proceedings of the 3rd RST Brazilian Meeting*, pages 88–105, Cuiabá, MT, Brazil.

Trevor Cohn and Mirella Lapata. 2008. Sentence compression beyond word deletion. In *Proceedings of the 22nd International Conference on Computational Linguistics-Volume 1*, pages 137–144.

Jesse Dunietz and Dan Gillick. 2014. A new entity salience task with millions of training examples. In *Proceedings of the European Association for Computational Linguistics*, pages 2282–2287.

Michel Galley and Kathleen McKeown. 2007. Lexicalized markov grammars for sentence compression. In *HLT-NAACL*, pages 180–187.

Dan Gillick and Benoit Favre. 2009. A scalable global model for summarization. In *Proceedings of the Workshop on Integer Linear Programming for Natural Language Processing*, pages 10–18.

Hongyan Jing and Kathleen R. McKeown. 2000. The decomposition of human-written summary sentence. In *Proceedings of the 1st NAACL Conference*, pages 178–185, Stroudsburg, PA, USA. Association for Computational Linguistics.

Kevin Knight and Daniel Marcu. 2000. Statistics-based summarization - step one: Sentence compression. In *Proceedings of the Seventeenth National Conference on Artificial Intelligence and Twelfth Conference on on Innovative Applications of Artificial Intelligence*, pages 703–710, Austin, Texas, USA.

Alex Kulesza and Ben Taskar. 2011. Learning determinantal point processes. In *Proceedings of the Twenty-Seventh Conference Annual Conference on Uncertainty in Artificial Intelligence (UAI-11)*, pages 419–427.

Hui Lin and Jeff Bilmes. 2011. A class of submodular functions for document summarization. In *Proceedings of the 49th Annual Meeting of the Association for Computational Linguistics: Human Language Technologies - Volume 1*, HLT '11, pages 510–520.

Erwin Marsi and Emiel Krahmer. 2010. On the limits of sentence compression by deletion. In Erwin Marsi and M. Theune, editors, *Empirical Methods in Natural Language Generation*, pages 45–66. Springer-Verlag, Berlin, Heidelberg.

Ryan T McDonald. 2006. Discriminative sentence compression with soft syntactic evidence. In *EACL*.

Andrew McKinlay and Katja Markert. 2011. Modelling entity instantiations. In *Proceedings of the International Conference on Recent Advances in Natural Language Processing*, pages 268–274.

Tom M. Mitchell, William Cohen, Estevam Hruschka, Partha Talukdar, Justin Betteridge, Andrew Carlson, Bhavana Dalvi Mishra, Matthew Gardner, Bryan Kisiel, Jayant Krishnamurthy, Ni Lao, Kathryn Mazaitis, Thahir Mohamed, Ndapa Nakashole, Emmanouil Antonios Platanios, Alan Ritter, Mehdi Samadi, Burr Settles, Richard Wang, Derry Wijaya, Abhinav Gupta, Xinlei Chen, Abulhair Saparov, Malcolm Greaves, and Joel Welling. 2015. Never-ending learning. In *Proceedings of the European Association for Computational Linguistics*, pages 2302–2310.

Ani Nenkova and Kathleen McKeown. 2011. Automatic summarization. *Foundations and Trends in Information Retrieval*, 5(2-3):103–233.

Stefan Riezler, Tracy H King, Richard Crouch, and Annie Zaenen. 2003. Statistical sentence condensation using ambiguity packing and stochastic disambiguation methods for lexical-functional grammar. In *Proceedings of the NAACL/HLT'03*, pages 118–125.

Advaith Siddharthan, Ani Nenkova, and Kathleen McKeown. 2011. Information status distinctions and referring expressions: An empirical study of references to people in news summaries. *Computational Linguistics*, 37(4):811–842.

Jenine Turner and Eugene Charniak. 2005. Supervised and unsupervised learning for sentence compression. In *Proceedings of the 43rd Annual Meeting on Association for Computational Linguistics*, pages 290–297.

Types	Specific segment	Generic segment
Interpret.	cerca de 22 pessoas *("about 22 of the victims")*	a maioria das vítimas *("the most victims")*
	os primeiros 4 minutos de jogo *("the fourth minute of the match")*	the fourth minute of the match *("the begnning of the match")*
	casas e viadutos destruídos *("destroyed houses and viaducts")*	grandes danos materiais *("great damage")*
	dois terços das autuações de contribuintes *("two-thirds of the taxpayers' infractions")*	as irregularidades mais comuns *("the most common infractions")*
	(às) 11h40 *("at 11h40")*	(por) a manhã *("(in) the morning ")*
	cerca de 300 edifícios *("about 300 buildings")*	vários edifícios *("several buildings")*
	a polícia *("the police")*	o governo *("the government")*
	o nevoeiro *("the fog")*	o mau tempo *("the bad weather")*
	o ajuizamento de uma ação civil pública *("the filing of a public civil action")*	medidas necessárias *("necessary measures")*
Detail removal	um campus universitário *(an university campus)*	um campus *("a campus)*
	o goleiro Vieri *("the goalkeeper Vieri")*	o goleiro *("the goalkeeper")*
	as Ilhas Cayman *("the Cayman Islands")*	as ilhas *("the islands")*
	quase metade dos voos *("almost half of the flights")*	metade dos voos *("half of the flights")*
	a Operação Farrapos, da Polícia Federal *("the Federal Police's "Operation Farrapos"")*	a operação *("the operation")*
	Instituto Nacional do Seguro Social (INSS) *("National Institute of Social Security (INSS)")*	INSS *INSS*
	a pista principal do aeroporto *("the main runway")*	uma das pistas *("one of the runways")*
	a medalha de ouro nos Jogos Pan-Americanos *("the gold medal in the Pan-American Games")*	os Jogos Pan-Americanos *("the Pan American Games")*
	o Aeroporto Internacional de Guarulhos *("the International Airpot of Guarulhos")*	o Aeroporto de Guarulhos *("the Guarulhos Airport")*
	a capital Kingston *("the capital Kingston")*	a capital *("the capital")*
	falência de órgãos secundária à insuficiência cardíaca *("organs failure secondary to heart disease")*	insuficiência cardíaca *("heart failure")*
Role	Peterka (*Roberto Peterka)	um perito aposentado *("a retired expert")*
	o advogado das supostas vítimas, R. Boucher *("the lawyer of the alleged victims, Boucher")*	os advogados *("the lawyers")*
	as 16 crianças e 14 adultos *("the 14 children and 14 adults")*	as 30 vítimas *("the 30 hostages")*
	uma quadrilha de altos funcionários públicos *("a group of high-level public officials (accused of fraud)"*	pessoas suspeitas *("suspicious people")*
Class	os Estados Unidos *("the United States")*	o país *("the country")*
	o revólver *("the revolver/gun")*	as armas *("the weapons")*
	Abadia (*Juan Carlos Ramírez Abadía)	o colombiano *("the Colombian")*
	a queda (do avião) *("the crash")*	o acidente *("the accident")*
	a Schincariol *("the Schincariol")*	a empresa *("the company")*
Whole	Maceió (*capital of Alagoas)	Alagoas (*Brazilian state)
	a Arquidiocese de Los Angeles *("The Archdiocese of Los Angeles")*	a Igreja Católica *("The Catholic Church")*
	o Depart. de Investigações sobre Crime Organizado *("the State Department of Criminal Investigation")*	a polícia *("the police")*

Table 4: Examples of phrase-level generalization from the CSTNews corpus (Appendix 1)

Generating Disambiguating Paraphrases for Structurally Ambiguous Sentences

Manjuan Duan and **Ethan Hill** and **Michael White**
Department of Linguistics
The Ohio State University
Columbus, OH 43210, USA
{duan,mwhite}@ling.osu.edu, hill.1303@gmail.com

Abstract

We present a method that, for the first time in a broad coverage setting, uses natural language generation to automatically construct disambiguating paraphrases for structurally ambiguous sentences. By simply asking naive annotators to clarify which paraphrase is closer in meaning to the original sentence, the resulting paraphrases can potentially enable meaning judgments for parser training and domain adaptation to be crowd-sourced on a massive scale. To validate the method, we demonstrate that meaning judgments crowd-sourced in this way via Amazon Mechanical Turk have reasonably high accuracy—e.g. 80%, given a strong majority choice between two paraphrases—with accuracy increasing as the level of agreement among annotators increases. We also show that even with just the limited validation data gathered to date, the crowd-sourced judgments make it possible to retrain a parser to achieve significantly higher accuracy in a novel domain. We conclude with lessons learned for gathering such judgments on a much larger scale.

1 Introduction

While early dialogue systems such as SHRDLU (Winograd, 1973) were capable of asking questions to clarify the meaning of structurally ambiguous sentences, to our knowledge the task of generating questions to clarify structural ambiguities has not been investigated on a broad scale. Given the development in recent years of statistical parsers and realizers using a reversible grammar or a common set of dependencies, one might expect that in principle it should be possible today to generate paraphrases to help clarify the meaning of structurally ambiguous sentences simply by chaining the parser and realizer end-to-end. However, realization ranking models are typically trained to prefer corpus sentences over possible variants, and thus statistical realizers chained with statistical parsers are apt to just reproduce the input sentence, which is of no help for disambiguation. Moreover, while it is easy enough to require the realizer to output a distinct sentence, for most realizers there is no guarantee that the realization will in fact unambiguously express one or the other possible meaning.

In early work in natural language generation, Neumann and van Noord (1992) investigated algorithms for avoiding ambiguity in surface realization. More recently, Duan and White (2014) developed a method for using statistical parsers together with a realization ranking model to balance the competing concerns of fluency and ambiguity avoidance, given that sentences of even moderate length are rarely unambiguous according to a broad coverage grammar. In this paper, we present and validate a related method that aims to ensure that the difference in dependencies between two competing parses is unambiguously expressed in the realization corresponding to each parse (albeit at the expense of fluency), so that the realizations can serve as disambiguating paraphrases for the input sentence. To the extent that the method is successful, it then becomes possible to clarify the meaning of structurally ambiguous sentences simply by asking naive annotators which paraphrase is closer in meaning to the original sentence.

As is well known, the performance of most NLP tools such as statistical parsers has remained much higher for the domains and genres for which large-scale annotated training corpora are available. Domain adaptation techniques are not always successful (Dredze et al., 2007), and while

Proceedings of LAW X – The 10th Linguistic Annotation Workshop, pages 160–170,
Berlin, Germany, August 11, 2016.

self-training can yield substantial error reductions (McClosky and Charniak, 2008; Honnibal et al., 2009), large gaps in performance persist. Consequently, to achieve high performance, there remains a need to collect new annotated data in the target domain and genre. Moreover, experience with ImageNet (Deng et al., 2009; Russakovsky et al., 2015) in vision research suggests that breakthroughs in NLP performance might likewise be enabled by collecting annotated data across domains and genres on a massive scale.

As a first step towards that end, we present a validation experiment which demonstrates that our method enables meaning judgments to be crowd-sourced on Amazon's Mechanical Turk (AMT) with reasonably high accuracy, achieving 80% agreement with our own gold standard judgments when there is a strong majority choice between two paraphrases. Moreover, accuracy remains satisfactorily high for the subset of sentences where the top parse is incorrect. We also present a preliminary experiment which shows that even with just the limited validation data gathered to date, the "silver standard" crowd-sourced judgments make it possible to retrain a parser to achieve significantly higher accuracy in a novel domain.

In a previous study on obtaining crowd-sourced syntactic annotations, Jha et al. (2010) presented results indicating that with some training, annotators on AMT could accurately select prepositional phrase (PP) attachment sites, with accuracy also increasing with the level of agreement among annotators. Gerdes (2013) and Zeldes (2016) also found that it was possible to obtain fairly high quality class-sourced annotations where students only received a modest amount of training. Our work is quite different in that we aim to gather meaning judgments with no training whatsoever, simply by asking questions in natural language. Our work also differs from Jha et al.'s in that it is not limited to PP-attachment ambiguities. Since the Jha et al. study used a different corpus, our results are not directly comparable, though we note that our method also achieves satisfactory accuracy on PP-attachment cases. Finally, we note that our paper shows that the crowd-sourced data can enable parser improvements, while their study does not include parser retraining results.

The paper is structured as follows. In Section 2, we review the parsing and realization ranking models that serve as a starting point for the paper. In Section 3, we present our method for generating disambiguating paraphrases. In Section 4, we present our experiment validating the accuracy of naive annotator choices on AMT. In Section 5, we present an analysis of errors and a regression analysis investigating the factors affecting annotator decisions. In Section 6, we present our preliminary parser retraining experiment. In Section 7, after briefly comparing our results with Jha et al.'s, we discuss the implications of the analyses for future data collection and parser adaptation experiments. Finally, in Section 8, we conclude with a summary of the lessons learned.

2 Background

To generate disambiguating paraphrases, we use OpenCCG, an open source framework for parsing and realization with Combinatory Categorial Grammar (Steedman, 2000). It comes with a broad coverage English grammar extracted from a version of the CCGbank (Hockenmaier and Steedman, 2007) enhanced to include (inter alia) assignment of consistent semantic roles across diathesis alternations (Boxwell and White, 2008), using PropBank (Palmer et al., 2005). The parser can be used with a reimplemented version of Hockenmaier & Steedman's (2002) generative model or with the Berkeley parser (Petrov et al., 2006; Fowler and Penn, 2010); in this paper we use the Hockenmaier & Steedman model. The outputs of the parser—and the inputs to the realizer—are semantic dependency graphs, or logical forms, examples of which are given in the next section. In these graphs, nodes correspond to discourse referents labeled with lexical predicates and semantic attributes, and dependency relations between nodes encode argument structure.

The realizer uses a chart-based algorithm (White, 2006) together with a "hypertagger" for probabilistically assigning lexical categories to lexical predicates in the input (Espinosa et al., 2008). To select preferred outputs from the chart, we use an averaged perceptron realization ranking model (White and Rajkumar, 2009) that combines Clark & Curran's (Clark and Curran, 2007) normal-form syntactic model and various n-gram models including a large-scale 5-gram model based on the Gigaword corpus together with a feature for dependency length minimization (White and Rajkumar, 2012) and features for enhanced syntactic agreement (Rajkumar and White, 2010).

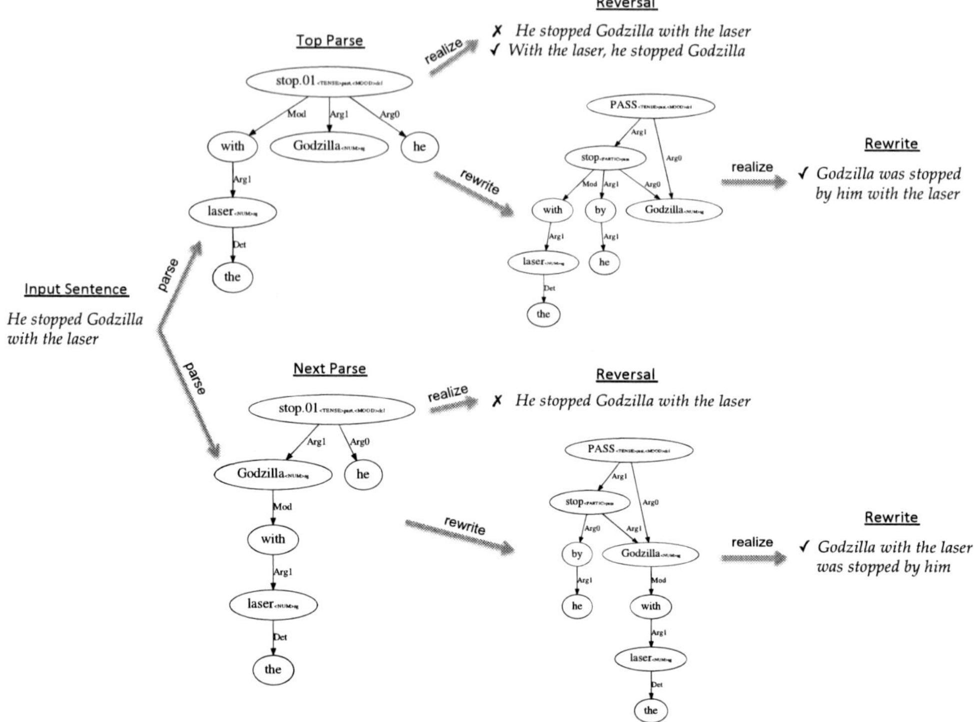

Figure 1: Overview of paraphrasing process (see text)

3 Generating Disambiguating Paraphrases

3.1 Parsing

At an overview level, the process for automatically generating disambiguating paraphrases is shown in Figure 1.[1] The first step is to obtain n-best parses of the input sentence (with $n = 25$ in our experiments).[2] Any structurally broken parses, such as those with two roots, are filtered out. Next, the remaining parses are examined successively to determine whether there is a parse that is *sufficiently distinct* from the top parse so that paraphrases generated from these two parses can be meaningfully distinguished. In order to locate a meaningful difference between two parses, the unlabeled and unordered dependencies extracted from the the top parse and a parse from the n-best parse list are compared. To be considered sufficiently distinct, the symmetric difference between the simplified dependencies must be non-empty, with neither set of dependencies a superset of the other, so that the difference between the parses represents a distinct attachment decision. For example, ambiguities involving only POS, named entity or word sense differences are not considered sufficiently distinct. If successful, this phase yields a *top* and *next* parse, whose distinct dependencies indicate the meaning difference for which the parser has the greatest uncertainty, given the relatively high probabilities assigned to both interpretations.

3.2 Reverse Realizations

Once the top and next parses have been selected, the next step is to realize the two distinct parses into their respective surface realizations, choosing the realizations which meet the criteria listed below for being disambiguating paraphrases of the original sentences. Paraphrases obtained in this process are called *reversals* in our study. Specifically, each parse is realized back into a n-best re-

[1] The input sentence *He stopped Godzilla with the laser* is one of the simplest in our test domain of Wikipedia articles on prehistoric reptiles, which contains occasional references to such creatures appearing in popular media.

[2] Although it is possible that some parses which represents meaningful structure differences might fall outside of the top 25 parses, we choose n to be 25 because the quality of parses generally goes down quickly when moving down the list.

alization list (with $n = 25$), which is traversed in order to find a qualifying paraphrase. The first criterion is that the realization needs to be different from the original sentence to be qualified as a paraphrase; in Figure 1, such non-helpful exact matches are crossed off. However, not just any realization that differs from the original sentence is necessarily disambiguating: it may just have a minor change in a part of the sentence unrelated to the ambiguity in question. Thus, we define the relevant *ambiguity span* for the sentence, and ensure that this span is altered in the realization.

Take a sentence from *Prehistoric Reptiles* corpus as an example.

(1) The two adult T-Rex and their baby are shown to have been returned safely.

Here the unlabeled dependency set of the top parse contains the dependency *returned* → *safely*, while a parse down in the n-best list has the dependency *shown* → *safely*. The three words *shown* < *returned* < *safely* form an ambiguity span in the original sentence for this ambiguity. When selecting the paraphrases from the n-best realizations, we choose the realization which has different relative distances for the words involved in the ambiguity span in the original sentence. For the dependency *returned* → *safely*, the realization *The two adult T-Rex and their baby are* ***shown*** *to have been* ***safely returned***, in which the relative distances between *shown*, *safely* and *returned* are changed, is selected. In the same way, for the other dependency *shown* → *safely*, the realization *The two adult T-Rex and their baby are* ***shown safely*** *to have been* ***returned*** is selected. The two realizations are then parsed to verify that the most likely interpretation does include the two dependencies from which they are generated. By doing so, we want to make sure that the realizations are structurally representative of the meaning for which it is chosen. If they pass the verification, these two realizations will be selected as the two paraphrases of the original sentence, each paraphrase representing a possible interpretation of the original sentence. These two paraphrases are called *two-sided* paraphrases of the original sentence.

In some cases, we fail to find two paraphrases of the original sentence, i.e. the algorithm fails to find a sentence in the n-best realizations of one of the distinct parses which is different from the original sentence, breaks up the ambiguity span and passes the verification. In these cases, we only generate one paraphrase for the original sentence, with the assumption that the other interpretation of the sentence is expressed by the original sentence. We call these cases *one-sided* paraphrases here.

3.3 Logical Form Rewrites

As noted above, there are some cases where it is impossible to generate a reversal that expresses one of the possible interpretations of the original sentence without repeating the original sentence. For example, the sentence *He stopped Godzilla with the laser* is ambiguous about whether the prepositional phrase *with the laser* is modifying *Godzilla* or the verb *stop*, as shown in Figure 1. It is impossible to have a reversal which expresses the interpretation where the prepositional phrase is modifying *Gozilla* and where the ambiguity span is altered, as the figure shows. In cases like these, we force structure changes in the dependency graphs, which, when realized, can demonstrate the parse's interpretation more adequately. The resulting realizations are referred to as *rewrites*.

Specifically, we experiment with three types of logical form rewriting: passive rewrites, cleft rewrites and coordination rewrites. Passive and cleft rewrites are designed for PP-attachment ambiguities, while coordination rewrites are for ambiguities in the scope of modifiers with coordinated phrases.[3]

For passive and cleft rewrites, we first detect the presence of a PP-attachment ambiguity by examining the POS tags of the dependents involved in the ambiguous dependencies. If we find the same prepositional phrase is attaching to different heads in distinct parses, we regard this as a PP-attachment ambiguity case. We then examine the main verb of the sentence to make sure the verb can be passivized or clefted. To force a passive rewrite, we create a passive node with the same tense as the original sentence and make the Arg1 of the main verb the Arg0 of the new node and attach the main verb to the passive node as a complement. The original Arg0 is replaced by a prepositional phrase *by Arg0* attached to the main verb, as illustrated in Figure 1.

For cleft rewrites (not shown in the figure), we create a *be* verb node, with the same tense as the original sentence, above the main verb of the clause containing the PP-attachment ambigu-

[3]These ambiguities are frequently found to be involved in the errors of most parsers; we leave experimenting with other kinds of rewrites for future work.

ity. We then create a *what* reference node taking the whole verb phrase as its complement and attach the *what* reference node to the verb *be* as a complement, yielding for example *Godzilla with the laser was what he stopped.*[4]

A coordination ambiguity refers to the cases where a modifier can be modifying the first conjunct or modifying the whole conjoined phrase, e.g. the modifier *East/West* in *He also was selected to play in [the] East/West Shrine game and Hula bowl.*[5] For the parse in which the modifier modifies the first conjunct only, we swap the order of the two conjuncts, so the conjunct with a modifier will occur after the conjunction, as in *He also was selected to play in [the] Hula bowl and [the] East/West Shrine game.* In the case where the modifier is modifying the whole conjoined phrase, we force verbosity in the logical form by moving the modifier to each conjunct and then swap the order of the two conjuncts, as in *He also was selected to play in [the] East/West Hula bowl and [the] East/West Shrine game.*

4 Validation Experiment

4.1 Data

We collected 6,335 sentences from *Prehistoric Reptiles* and 7,779 from *Big 10 Conference Football* from English Wikipedia. Only sentences with length of 5 to 20 words were selected to parse, assuming simple sentences would generalize better for parser adaptation. After parsing these sentences, for 2,458 sentences (38.8% of total sentences) from *Prehistoric Reptiles* and 2,605 sentences (33.5% of total sentences) on *Big 10 Conference Football*, we found meaningfully distinct parses in their n-best parse list. Of these 5,063 sentences, valid paraphrases are generated for 3605 sentences (71.2% of 5,063).

From these sentences, we randomly chose 515 sentences from each domain to be our test set, weighted to favor two-sided cases. In these 1030 sentences, 75% are two-sided cases and 25% are one-sided cases; 65% are reversals and 35% are rewrites (15% from cleft rewrites, 15% from coordination rewrites, and 10% from passive rewrites).

[4]The *what*-node is actually underspecified between *what* and *who(m)*, leaving the realizer to make the choice.

[5]This sentence, from our test domain of Big 10 Football, is mistakenly missing the determiner *the* in Wikipedia.

4.2 Annotation

For the 1030 sentences, we decided on the optimal ('gold') interpretation of the disputed dependencies represented by the two distinct parses. We annotated the correct parse by examining the dependency graphs. If the top parse was correct in the ambiguous dependency, the sentence was annotated as 'top'. A sentence was annotated as 'next' if the next best parse was correct in terms of the disputed dependencies. When neither of the two parses was more correct than the other one (e.g., when neither parse had the correct PP-attachment), the sentence was annotated as 'neither'; this label also covered some cases where there was no discernible semantic difference between the cases.

100 sentences were triple-annotated; for these sentences, inter-annotation agreement was **82.5%** for all three labels and **90.8%** excluding the 'neither' cases. The remaining sentences were single-annotated, with discussion of difficult cases. Of the 1030 sentences, 56.3% were annotated as top, 25.4% were 'next' and 18.3% were 'neither' cases. To calculate accuracy of Turker judgments below, we excluded the 'neither' cases; however, we included them for data collection since in a typical (non-validation) data collection scenario, the identity of the 'neither' cases would not be known.

4.3 Judgment Collection

For each of the 1030 sentences, we collected 5 judgments from the workers on Amazon Mechanical Turk. For each sentence, we provided a comprehension question to prevent random choosing; accuracy on comprehension questions was 93%, indicating that workers were paying attention to the task. For the sentences with two paraphrases, we asked the worker to choose which out of these two was closer to the original sentence in terms of meaning. For the one-sided cases, we simply asked them to decide whether that paraphrase had the same meaning as the original sentence.

We put 25 sentences into each survey and paid \$2 per survey. It took around 20 minutes on average to finish a survey. In total, we paid \$400 for 5000 judgments from AMT workers. While it took the authors days to come up with the gold annotations by examining the parses, the AMT judgments were collected in just a few hours.

	Maj	S. Maj	Unani
Coverage	99.3	69	36
Accuracy	68.1	76.4	82.6

Table 1: Coverage and Accuracy

	Maj	S. Maj	Unani
One-sided	59.1	65.2	70.6
Two-sided	71	79.9	87.2
Reversals	69.3	79.9	88.2
Rewrites	74.8	79.8	84.6
Cleft	79.7	82.1	83.3
Passive	68	71.4	66.6
Coordination	70	79.2	88

Table 2: Accuracy of AMT workers' judgments

4.4 Results

Table 1 shows the trade-off between the accuracy of the judgments collected from AMT and the coverage of the data. In Table 1, sentences which have more than 50% agreement from AMT workers are called 'Majority' cases (Maj); those with more than 75% agreement are 'Strong Majority' cases (S. Maj) and those with 90% or more agreement are 'Unanimity' cases (Unani).[6] As the table shows, the 'unanimity' sentences have the highest accuracy, however, at the expense of losing the coverage of 64% data.

Table 2 shows the accuracy of the AMT workers' judgments under different settings. The results shown in Table 2 are all significantly better than random choice (p = 0.5) at a level $\alpha = 0.05$ (binomial sign test). Table 2 shows that two-sided paraphrases have considerably higher accuracy than one-sided cases, which means two-sided paraphrases are better in highlighting the ambiguity in the original sentence.

Table 2 also shows the accuracy of reversals and rewrites for the two-sided paraphrases. It is good to see that reversals work better than rewrites in strong majority cases and unanimity cases, because reversals can be obtained without any changes to the logical forms and are able to capture various kinds of structural ambiguities detected by the automatic parser, not just those the rewrites have been designed to capture. 'Strong majority' two-sided cases appear to offer the best balance between coverage and accuracy.

[6]There are a few duplicated sentences in the validation dataset. For each of these sentences, we might have 10 or 15 Turker judgments. As such, we define 'Strong Majority' as agreement more than 75% and 'Unanimity' as agreement more than 90%.

	Maj	S. Maj	Unani
Total	**59.6**	**68**	**74.6**
One-sided	49.1	53.5	70.6
Two-sided	**63.2**	**73.9**	**87.2**
Reversal	55.3	**66.3**	**75.9**
Rewrite	**67.5**	**70.5**	**85.7**
Cleft	**81.8**	**86.6**	85.7
Passive	58.8	57.1	62.5
Coordination	63.2	**68.8**	**78.6**

Table 3: Accuracy of 'next' parses (accuracies significantly higher than chance in bold)

In order to judge whether the crowd-sourced judgments can be potentially beneficial for parser retraining, we need to examine the proportion of 'next' cases (i.e., those sentences one of whose non-top parses is more accurate than the top parse) that can be correctly annotated. Table 3 shows that majority, strong majority and unanimous annotations are all significantly better than chance overall in these cases ($p \leq 0.05$, exact binomial test). Some of the individual results in Table 3, however, fail to reach the significance level because of the small sample sizes. For example, the unanimous annotations for cleft are correct in 6 sentences out of 7 sentences; although the accuracy is as high as 85.7%, it still fails to be significant because of the small sample size. In general, two-sided paraphrases still work better than the one-sided ones and rewrites work better than reversals in terms of correctly annotating 'next' cases.

5 Error Analysis

5.1 Manual analysis

We did not directly evaluate paraphrase quality in this study, as we were primarily concerned with whether they sufficed to enable accurate crowd-sourced judgments. However, we did manually analyze 43 sentences where the unanimous AMT worker judgments do not agree with the expert annotations and found the following reasons: incompetent or broken realizations (29 out of 43); bad parses (11 out of 43); lack of context (3 out of 43).

Incompetents realizations refer to those paraphrases which fail to convey the distinct meanings in the parses in a distinguishable way. Sometimes a change of adverbial position in a sentence or punctuation deletion/insertion does not alter a human reader's interpretation of the sentence. For example, in (2) below, (2a) is the original sentence, which is ambiguous as to whether *with* attaches to the verb *crush*, which is realized as (2c), or to the noun *animal*, whose realization is the same as the original sentence. The correct interpretation is that *with* attaches to *animals*, so the expert annotation is (2b). Compared with the original sentence, (2c) has a comma inserted after *animals*. However, all 5 AMT workers think (2c) has the same meaning as the original sentence in spite of this change, as the punctuation difference is too subtle for reliable interpretation.

(2) a. The teeth were adapted to *crush* bivalves, gastropods and other *animals* **with** a shell or exoskeleton.

b. (animals→with): *Same as original sentence*

c. (crush→with): The teeth were adapted to crush bivalves, gastropods and other animals**,** with a shell or exoskeleton.

In some cases, the AMT workers fail to choose the correct parse because the realization of the correct parse is much less fluent than the other one. In (3) below, (3a) is the original sentence, and it is ambiguous as to whether the prepositional phrase *during the Triassic-Jurassic extinction event* modifies *gone* or *thought*. The correct interpretation is that the *during* prepositional phrase modify *gone*. However, the paraphrase of the correct parse, (3b), is not very fluent because the long prepositional phrase separates the verb and its complement, which causes the AMT workers to all choose (3c) as the best paraphrase. A disfluent paraphrase usually happens when the realizer needs to go far down the n-best realization list to find a realization which is different from the original sentence.

(3) a. They are *thought* to have *gone* extinct **during** the Triassic-Jurassic extinction event.

b. (gone→during): They are thought to have **gone during** the Triassic-Jurassic extinction event extinct.

c. (thought→during): They are **thought during** the Triassic-Jurassic extinction event to have gone extinct.

In other cases, although one parse is better than the other one for the disputed dependency, the rest of both parses is so broken that the realization cannot represent the meaning effectively. In those cases, the AMT workers usually could not give reliable annotations, because the realizations of the mangled parses make it hard for the AMT workers to see any reliable meaningful difference.

In some rare cases (3 out of 43), the AMT workers fail to choose the correct parse because they do not have the specific context to correctly understand the original sentence:

(4) a. Michigan's backup center, Gerald Ford, *expressed* a desire to *attend* the fair **while** in Chicago.

b. (attend→while): Michigan's backup center, Gerald Ford, expressed a desire to **attend while** in Chicago the fair.

c. (expressed→while): Michigan's backup center, Gerald Ford, **expressed while** in Chicago a desire to attend the fair.

The original sentence in (4a) is ambiguous as to whether the *while* adverbial phrase is modifying *attend* or *expressed*. After consulting the context of the Wikipedia article we know that when Gerald Ford made this speech, he was actually in Michigan and expressed this desire to visit the fair in Chicago. Accordingly, we annotated that *while* modifies *attend*. However, this information might not be available for the AMT workers. Also, perhaps because (4b) is a less fluent sentence where the *while* adverbial occurs between the verb *attend* and its object *the fair*, AMT workers all chose (4c) as the better paraphrase.

5.2 Regression analysis

We also conducted a regression analysis to determine the factors that affect AMT workers' choices. The predictors included in the analysis are ranks of the underlying parse of the paraphrase (parse), an arithmetic-mean approximation of BLEU between the paraphrase and the original sentence (bleu), and the fluency score of the paraphrase calculated by OpenCCG realizer, normalized globally across all the realizations in the data set (rlz.glb). For the two-sided paraphrases, all four predictors are calculated as the corresponding value of the paraphrase of the top parse minus the value of the paraphrase of the 'next' parse. The dependent variable in two-sided cases is 1 if the top parse is correct, 0 otherwise.

We fit four regression models respectively for the four combinations of majority (Maj) and strong majority (S. Maj) choices with one- and two-sided paraphrases. The regression analysis shows *bleu* has a significant effect on AMT workers' choice across all four settings. The positive coefficients of the predictor *bleu* indicates that AMT workers tend to choose the paraphrase that is similar to the original sentence in terms of its surface form. In some cases this likely means that the

	One-sided		Two-sided	
	Maj	S. Maj	Maj	S. Maj
parse	-0.03	-0.05	0.01	0.01
bleu	3.05*	4.38**	1.68*	3.07**
rlz.glb	0.01	0.01	0.07**	0.103***

Table 4: Coefficients of regression analysis of AMT workers' choice (significance codes are *: $p \leq 0.05$; **: $p \leq 0.01$; ***: $p \leq 0.001$)

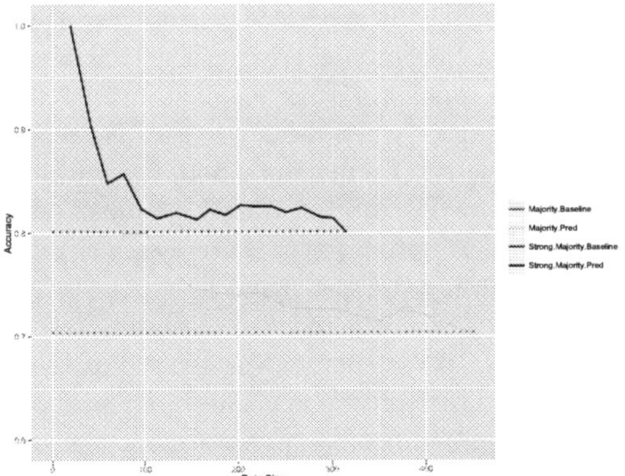

Figure 2: Accuracy and coverage trade-off plot for majority and strong majority choices

annotator is overly influenced by superficial similarity, which may partially explain the poor performance of one-sided paraphrases. We also observe a significant effect from the fluency score of the paraphrases in the two-sided case.

Inspired by the results above, we investigate the possibility of increasing the accuracy at the expense of coverage. We trained a logistic regression model on AMT workers' majority correct choices and plotted the accuracy of their choices in decreasing order of their likelihood of correctness, also plotting the accuracy of corresponding strong majority choices for comparison.

Figure 2 shows that in order to improve the accuracy of majority choices to 80%, we will lose around 80% data. However, the accuracy of strong majority choices, with 40% less coverage, is above 80%. Thus the results show that if we are willing to sacrifice some data coverage for higher quality annotation, strong majority choices are the better option. If data is quite plentiful (or nearly unlimited), only the most fluent items could be selected for annotation, in which case accuracy could potentially be pushed up past 90%.

	Dinosaur	Football
Train size	471	356
Eval size	291	226
Original acc.	0.701	0.668
Retrained acc.	**0.749**	**0.717**
Correction rate	0.243	0.32

Table 5: Parser retraining

6 Parser Retraining

As a preliminary experiment just using the validation data gathered to date, we retrained the OpenCCG parser with the majority judgments collected from AMT (along with the original CCGbank data). Results appear in Table 5. The training set of the dinosaur domain contains 471 parses and that of the football domain contains 356 parses, corresponding to the parses chosen by majority judgments of the AMT workers. We trained the OpenCCG parser on the two domains separately with ten-fold cross validation, and evaluated the parsing performance of the retrained parsers against our manually annotated gold dependencies (excluding 'neither' cases). Parses were considered correct if the parse matching the gold correct dependencies ranked higher than the parse matching the gold incorrect dependencies in the n-best list. For some sentences, we could not find a parse to match the annotated correct or wrong dependencies in the n-best list, especially the annotated wrong dependencies; we also excluded these sentences from the evaluation. In the end, we had 291 sentences in the dinosaur domain and 226 sentences in football for evaluation. *Original acc.* is the accuracy of the original OpenCCG parser evaluated on the gold annotated dependencies, while *Retrained acc.* is the accuracy of the retrained parsers and *Correction rate* is the proportion of original mistakenly parsed sentences that are correctly parsed by the retrained parsers.

MacNemar's chi-square test shows that the retrained parser achieves significantly higher accuracy in the dinosaur domain ($p = 0.02$). The same test on football data shows a trend but not a significant improvement ($p = 0.1$), most likely due to the smaller size of the training and evaluation sets for this domain. Meanwhile, the performance of the retrained parsers on the CCGbank development section does not differ significantly from the original parser ($p > 0.05$ for both).

7 Discussion

By directly asking AMT annotators to specify the attachment site for a PP, Jha et al. (2010) achieve 84% accuracy overall, rising to an impressive 95% in strong majority cases. However, their results are not directly comparable to our PP-disambiguation items since the texts are different and since they consider all PPs, rather than just the ones that the parser finds the most difficult. In addition, they allow annotators to indicate additional attachment sites if none of the automatically suggested ones are correct, yielding a considerably more complex annotation task than ours that requires explicit upfront instruction on the notion of PP-attachments; moreover, to extend their method to additional kinds of structural ambiguities, the instructions would be elaborated in each case.

The results and analysis indicate that the accuracy of our method could be improved simply by leaving aside the one-sided cases, where the AMT annotators may have been overly influenced by superficial similarity, as well as the passive rewrites, which performed much worse than the cleft rewrites on PP-attachment cases for reasons that are not clear. Realization fluency was also found to be a significant predictor of annotator choices in the two-sided cases, suggesting that accuracy could be further improved by taking this factor into account when selecting sentences if domain data is plentiful. Another alternative worth pursuing in future work would be to split sentences whose realizations are not sufficiently fluent, borrowing methods employed in syntactic simplification (Siddharthan, 2006; Siddharthan, 2011).

In future work we also plan to experiment with multiple parsers and additional collected data in order to measure the extent to which parsing performance on all attachments can be improved in new domains. Here we plan to use not only the OpenCCG reimplementation of the Hockenmaier & Steedman generative model, but also the Berkeley latent variable model and the Clark & Curran CCG parser, along with additional dependency parsers. To do so, we will take into account the "silver standard" nature of the annotations, namely that the parse corresponding to the selected disambiguating paraphrase may not be entirely correct, just closer than its competitor parse. In particular, using just the dependencies that differ between these two parses, we will select the highest-ranked parse that retains more of the correct (unlabeled, unordered) dependencies than any other in the n-best list. In this way, the dependencies yielded by each parser need not closely match the ones used to collect the data.

8 Conclusion

In this paper, we have shown that it is possible to obtain accurate crowd-sourced judgments of meaning by simply asking naive annotators to answer clarification questions, namely which of two automatically generated disambiguating paraphrases is closer to the original sentence in meaning. In a validation experiment, accuracy reached 80% or higher when there was a strong majority among the AMT annotators, both when using LF rewrites for PP-attachment and coordination ambiguities, as well as for direct reverse realizations, which cover a broader range of ambiguity types. Moreover, accuracy remains reasonably high for the subset of sentences where the top parse is incorrect, sufficiently so to enable a retrained parser to achieve significantly higher accuracy in a novel domain, even using just the limited validation data gathered to date. Data from the validation experiment is made available as a supplement to the paper.[7]

An analysis of errors revealed that one-sided cases (where only one disambiguating paraphrase could be generated) performed poorly, as did passive rewrites, and a regression analysis also revealed that realization fluency was a significant factor in predicting annotator decisions. In future work, we plan to take these lessons into account when collecting a much larger dataset in order to enable experiments on parser adaptation with multiple parsers, treating the crowd-sourced annotations as "silver standard" when retraining the parsers on in-domain sentences.

Acknowledgments

We thank James Curran, Eric Fosler-Lussier, the OSU Clippers Group and the anonymous reviewers for helpful comments and discussion. This work was supported in part by NSF grant 1319318.

[7] http://www.ling.osu.edu/~mwhite/data/law-x-2016-duan-hill-white-data.zip

References

[Boxwell and White2008] Stephen Boxwell and Michael White. 2008. Projecting Propbank roles onto the CCGbank. In *Proc. LREC-08*.

[Clark and Curran2007] Stephen Clark and James R. Curran. 2007. Wide-Coverage Efficient Statistical Parsing with CCG and Log-Linear Models. *Computational Linguistics*, 33(4):493–552.

[Deng et al.2009] J. Deng, W. Dong, R. Socher, L.-J. Li, K. Li, and L. Fei-Fei. 2009. ImageNet: A Large-Scale Hierarchical Image Database. In *CVPR09*.

[Dredze et al.2007] Mark Dredze, John Blitzer, Partha Pratim Talukdar, Kuzman Ganchev, João Graca, and Fernando Pereira. 2007. Frustratingly hard domain adaptation for dependency parsing. In *Proceedings of the CoNLL Shared Task Session of EMNLP-CoNLL 2007*, pages 1051–1055, Prague, Czech Republic, June. Association for Computational Linguistics.

[Duan and White2014] Manjuan Duan and Michael White. 2014. That's not what I meant! Using parsers to avoid structural ambiguities in generated text. In *Proceedings of the 52nd Annual Meeting of the Association for Computational Linguistics (Volume 1: Long Papers)*, pages 413–423, Baltimore, Maryland, June. Association for Computational Linguistics.

[Espinosa et al.2008] Dominic Espinosa, Michael White, and Dennis Mehay. 2008. Hypertagging: Supertagging for surface realization with CCG. In *Proceedings of ACL-08: HLT*, pages 183–191, Columbus, Ohio, June. Association for Computational Linguistics.

[Fowler and Penn2010] Timothy A. D. Fowler and Gerald Penn. 2010. Accurate context-free parsing with Combinatory Categorial Grammar. In *Proceedings of the 48th Annual Meeting of the Association for Computational Linguistics*, pages 335–344, Uppsala, Sweden, July. Association for Computational Linguistics.

[Gerdes2013] Kim Gerdes. 2013. Collaborative dependency annotation. In *Proceedings of the Second International Conference on Dependency Linguistics (DepLing 2013)*, pages 88–97, Prague, Czech Republic, August. Charles University in Prague, Matfyzpress.

[Hockenmaier and Steedman2002] Julia Hockenmaier and Mark Steedman. 2002. Generative models for statistical parsing with Combinatory Categorial Grammar. In *Proc. ACL-02*.

[Hockenmaier and Steedman2007] Julia Hockenmaier and Mark Steedman. 2007. CCGbank: A Corpus of CCG Derivations and Dependency Structures Extracted from the Penn Treebank. *Computational Linguistics*, 33(3):355–396.

[Honnibal et al.2009] Matthew Honnibal, Joel Nothman, and James R. Curran. 2009. Evaluating a statistical CCG parser on Wikipedia. In *Proceedings of the 2009 Workshop on The People's Web Meets NLP: Collaboratively Constructed Semantic Resources*, pages 38–41, Suntec, Singapore, August. Association for Computational Linguistics.

[Jha et al.2010] Mukund Jha, Jacob Andreas, Kapil Thadani, Sara Rosenthal, and Kathleen McKeown. 2010. Corpus creation for new genres: A crowd-sourced approach to PP attachment. In *Proceedings of the NAACL HLT 2010 Workshop on Creating Speech and Language Data with Amazon's Mechanical Turk*, pages 13–20, Los Angeles, June. Association for Computational Linguistics.

[McClosky and Charniak2008] David McClosky and Eugene Charniak. 2008. Self-training for biomedical parsing. In *Proceedings of ACL-08: HLT, Short Papers*, pages 101–104, Columbus, Ohio, June. Association for Computational Linguistics.

[Neumann and van Noord1992] Günter Neumann and Gertjan van Noord. 1992. Self-monitoring with reversible grammars. In *Proceedings of the 14th conference on Computational linguistics - Volume 2*, COLING '92, pages 700–706, Stroudsburg, PA, USA. Association for Computational Linguistics.

[Palmer et al.2005] Martha Palmer, Dan Gildea, and Paul Kingsbury. 2005. The Proposition Bank: A corpus annotated with semantic roles. *Computational Linguistics*, 31(1).

[Petrov et al.2006] Slav Petrov, Leon Barrett, Romain Thibaux, and Dan Klein. 2006. Learning accurate, compact, and interpretable tree annotation. In *Proceedings of COLING-ACL*.

[Rajkumar and White2010] Rajakrishnan Rajkumar and Michael White. 2010. Designing agreement features for realization ranking. In *Coling 2010: Posters*, pages 1032–1040, Beijing, China, August. Coling 2010 Organizing Committee.

[Russakovsky et al.2015] Olga Russakovsky, Jia Deng, Hao Su, Jonathan Krause, Sanjeev Satheesh, Sean Ma, Zhiheng Huang, Andrej Karpathy, Aditya Khosla, Michael Bernstein, Alexander C. Berg, and Li Fei-Fei. 2015. ImageNet Large Scale Visual Recognition Challenge. *International Journal of Computer Vision (IJCV)*, 115(3):211–252.

[Siddharthan2006] A. Siddharthan. 2006. Syntactic simplification and text cohesion. *Research on Language & Computation*, 4(1):77–109.

[Siddharthan2011] Advaith Siddharthan. 2011. Text simplification using typed dependencies: A comparision of the robustness of different generation strategies. In *Proceedings of the 13th European Workshop on Natural Language Generation*, pages 2–11, Nancy, France, September. Association for Computational Linguistics.

[Steedman2000] Mark Steedman. 2000. *The syntactic process*. MIT Press, Cambridge, MA, USA.

[White and Rajkumar2009] Michael White and Rajakrishnan Rajkumar. 2009. Perceptron reranking for CCG realization. In *Proceedings of the 2009 Conference on Empirical Methods in Natural Language Processing*, pages 410–419, Singapore, August. Association for Computational Linguistics.

[White and Rajkumar2012] Michael White and Rajakrishnan Rajkumar. 2012. Minimal dependency length in realization ranking. In *Proceedings of the 2012 Joint Conference on Empirical Methods in Natural Language Processing and Computational Natural Language Learning*, pages 244–255, Jeju Island, Korea, July. Association for Computational Linguistics.

[White2006] Michael White. 2006. Efficient Realization of Coordinate Structures in Combinatory Categorial Grammar. *Research on Language & Computation*, 4(1):39–75.

[Winograd1973] Terry Winograd. 1973. A procedural model of language understanding. In Roger Schank and Ken Colby, editors, *Computer Models of Thought and Language*, pages 152–186. W.H. Freeman. Reprinted in Grosz et al. (eds), Readings in Natural Language Processing. Los Altos CA: Morgan Kaufmann Publishers, 1986, pp.249-266.

[Zeldes2016] Amir Zeldes. 2016. The GUM corpus: Creating multilayer resources in the classroom. *Language Resources and Evaluation*, pages 1–32.

Applying Universal Dependency to the Arapaho Language

Irina Wagner[1], Andrew Cowell[1], Jena D. Hwang[2]
[1]University of Colorado Boulder, Department of Linguistics; [2]IHMC
{irina.wagner, james.cowell}@colorado.edu, jhwang@ihmc.us

Abstract

This paper discusses the use of Universal Dependency for annotations of a Native North American language Arapaho (Algonquian). While some relations of the universal dependency perfectly correspond with those in Arapaho, language specific annotations of verbal arguments elucidate problems of assuming certain syntactic categories across languages. By critiquing the influence of grammatical structures of major European and Asian languages in establishing the UD framework, this paper develops guidelines for annotating a polysynthetic agglutinating language and sets a path to developing a more comprehensive cross-linguistic approach to syntactic annotations of language data.

1 Introduction

The recent initiatives to create a cross-linguistic scheme of annotation rely on Universal Dependency (UD) as a system of describing the syntactic connection between words (Nivre, 2015; de Marneffe et al., 2014). While research shows this annotation type is effective not only for monolingual parsers but also cross-linguistically across multiple platforms, the universality of this approach is based on the assumptions of similar syntactic structures of major, often European, languages (McDonald et al., 2013). Without doubt, those are also the languages that receive predominant attention in the computational sphere, the languages whose technological presence requires a thorough analysis and annotation. However, if the goal of natural language processing is truly to develop a universal cross-linguistic strategy for annotating and analyzing linguistic data, it is important to attend to lesser described languages that may present strikingly different syntactic structures and dependencies.

Applying the UD rules while annotating the data from the Arapaho (Algonquian) language, several specific features were observed to fall outside of the charted labels. Since the language does not have a fixed word order and allows discontinuous constituency, dependencies on the previous word were avoided and re-analyzed. The most problematic dependency distinction in this language is the variation in relations between a verb and its arguments. This paper examines the correlation of the dependency relations in the UD scheme and their practical application for the Arapaho data. Using the UD framework, we create guidelines for annotating this data. In considerations of space, this paper primarily focuses on the argument structures defined by the UD and their correspondences to the Arapaho syntactic patterns. An additional discussion of non-verbal roots and topicality problematizes some of the common assumptions in discounting pragmatic features while analyzing syntactic dependencies.

In the following pages, we first provide a short note on the Arapaho language and the procedures of annotations (2); discuss issues of mapping the labels for subject, objects, and noun modifiers of the UD onto the Arapaho dependencies (3); define the mechanism of analysis of non-verbal roots (4); and suggest further ways of developing these annotation guidelines (5).

2 Arapaho data and annotations

Arapaho is an Algonquian poly-synthetic agglutinating language spoken by less than 200 people in the Wind River Indian Reservation in Wyoming. Because the language is in critical condition, there have been attempts at documenting and preserving it. A large transcribed and annotated spoken corpus has been created and parts of it are now available in the Endangered Languages Archive[1]. A

[1]http://elar.soas.ac.uk/deposit/0194

Proceedings of LAW X – The 10th Linguistic Annotation Workshop, pages 171–179,
Berlin, Germany, August 11, 2016.

total of around eighty thousand lines transcribed, translated, and grammatically analyzed is available for further processing. The current attempts at establishing the dependency scheme for this language initiate the new type of analysis of this data to allow machine processing.

2.1 Some features of the Arapaho language

The current paper largely relies on the previous description of the Arapaho grammar by Cowell and Moss (2008). There are several intriguing features of the grammar, but the ones most relevant to this study are its complex verbal morphology, split semantic and syntactic transitivity, and the system of obviation.

2.1.1 Verbal complexity

As is observed in many other poly-synthetic languages, Arapaho verbs are highly complex and mark multiple grammatical and semantic features. So, in example (1), a single verb demonstrates incorporation of not only the usual tense, aspect, mode, person, and number features, but also the manner of action and an incorporated object.

(1) he'ih'ii-xoo-xook-bix-ohoe-koohuut-oo-no'
"Their hands would go right through them and appear on the other side."

A single verb can be a full clause conveying a full thought. Verbal prefixes code grammatical as well as many semantic features, inhibiting the dependency analysis since this framework only considers the relations between individual words.

2.1.2 Transitivity

The category of verbal transitivity is both syntactic and semantic (Cowell and Moss, 2008). To understand how many arguments are allowed in a verb's frame, one must examine both the morphological and the semantic structure of a verb. So, while semantically a verb *to'oo3ei* "to hit things" may appear transitive, grammatically it is intransitive, requiring only one argument, the subject, as in *too'oo3einoo* "I am hitting (unspecified) things." The transitivity of a verb is expressed in its inflection which must agree in person and number with its arguments. Truly transitive verbs carry inflections agreeing with both of its arguments:

(2) Nih-to'ow-oo-t nuhu' **hinen-ino**
PST-hit-3/4-3S this man-OBV.PL
"He hit these men"

Even though only one of the two arguments appears in the sentence, the verb *nihto'owoot* "s/he hit him/her" is marked to agree both with the semantic agent and undergoer of the verb. This semantic distinction in the arguments is not observed in intransitive and semi-transitive verbs. Because such verbs demonstrate morphological agreement only with one nominal[2], other nominals are considered outside of the argument structure of a verb even if they specify the semantic patient or theme.

(3) nih'ii-koo-ko'uyei-3i' **biino**
PST.IMPF-REDUP-pick things-3PL **chokecherries**
"They were picking chokecherries."

So in the example (3), the noun *biino* "chokecherries" is not reflected in verbal morphology, but corresponds with its semantics by specifying the object of picking. Being outside of the argument structure of this verb, syntactically the noun is better understood as a verbal adjunct specifying the manner of action, while semantically it is still the patient. So the designation of the relationship between such arguments and verbs as *dobj* of the universal dependencies is wrong because it does not consider verbal morphology, whereas the label of *nmod* would not account for its semantic role.

2.1.3 Obviation

Unlike many languages, Arapaho does not rely on word order or case markers to disambiguate between overt nominals; rather it uses a system of obviation that incorporates a distinction based on animacy along with the combination of verbal morphosyntax and pragmatics to mark particular grammatical roles. This system clearly distinguishes between two third person referents by marking one of them (a less salient one in the discourse) as obviative and leaving the other referent unmarked (proximate). In Algonquian languages, the obviation is argued to be a pragmatic feature structuring discourse outside of a single clause (Goddard, 1984). Verbal morphology also shows agreement with these categories: the transitive verb inflection clearly marks which argument is acting on the other. So, instead of the usual three persons, Arapaho has four, with the fourth person being the obviative argument. In the example below, the obviative argument is the noun *hiinoon* "his mother" which corresponds with the verbal subjunctive inflection *-eihok* "4th person acting on 3rd singular."

[2]We use phrases "nominal" and "nominal expression" to refer to nouns, noun phrases and nominalized verbs that function as noun phrases.

(4) Hohou, hee3**eihok** **hiinoon**
thank you say to s.o.-4/3S.SUBJ his/her mother
3eeyokooxuu.
Tipi-pole Child
"Thank you," his mother said to Under-the-Tipi-Pole Child.

As it is observed in this example, obviation does not correspond with the semantic or the syntactic role of an argument. Neither it depends on the transitivity of a verb. Rather, obviative status lines up with the semantic role of an obviative coded in verbal morphology. Based on this feature of transitivity and obviation, the current paper suggests employing the semantic labels in marking the syntactic relations.

2.2 Annotation procedures

We are not aware of previous attempts at dependency annotations with other Algonquian languages; however, dependency grammar has been one of the theoretical approaches in Algonquian syntax. The guidelines discussed below were created based on the annotations of a small set of Arapaho narratives. In the first phase of the project, the dependency relations were outlined based on annotations of a sample of several traditional narratives, totaling at about two thousand lines[3]. The annotators, one fluent non-native speaker and three graduate students in Linguistics well familiar with Arapaho language structure, were given a protocol established without the considerations of the UD framework but based purely on the Algonquian syntax patterns. Several problems using these syntax patterns clarified and specified the dependency relations, leading to the creation of a new set of labels.

In the second phase of the project, these new labels were further standardized based on the principles of the Stanford Dependencies (de Marneffe and Manning, 2008). Using this new set of relations, the annotations of the previous phase were converted and a total of 3616 lines of elicited personal and traditional oral narratives as well as 593 lines of conversational data were newly annotated. The disfluency of the conversational data indicated major issues with this annotation scheme which prompted us to turn to the UD-based system. The guidelines presented here have been used to remark the previous annotations of the data used in the second phase. No special software to perform the annotations has been used thus far, and all of the annotations are stored in a spreadsheet format.

Because the language is critically endangered, the resources available for this type of work are extremely limited. Importantly, it is not just that there are fewer recorded texts and conversations, but there are also fewer trained individuals able to perform any type of language annotation. So, during this particular project, most of the annotations were done by the first two authors of the paper with Andrew Cowell being the language expert due to his experience and acquired proficiency in the language. Over the course of six months, authors met regularly to discuss the annotations, solve the occurring issues, introduce and update labels. As a result, all of the current annotations are single annotated. The next part of the project includes more manual annotations using the guidelines proposed here as well as double annotations of at least a portion of the data to establish the inter annotator agreement. Having already annotated a few thousand lines of narratives, the focus of the following work will be on conversational data followed by machine learning.

3 Mapping the UD scheme

Out of the forty dependencies proposed by the UD, thirty Arapaho dependencies have one-to-one correspondence. Additional seventeen specifications and relations have been added to describe language-specific instances. The final scheme of Arapaho's nominal argument dependencies is presented in Table 1. Some of the dependencies were not used in the Arapaho scheme because such dependencies merely do not exist in this language. So, for example, the language does not have a grammatical category of an adjective; therefore, the dependency *amod* has not been used; instead descriptive verbs are analyzed as relative clauses, *acl*. Example (5) demonstrates the relative clause dependency where verb modifies the noun in the same manner that an adjective would.

(5)
acl
niibe'ei'i siikoocei'ikuu3oo nihnohkokoo'ohuni'i.
VII NI VII

nii-be'ei-'i siikoocei'ikuu3oo
IMPF-red-0PL rubber item
nih-nohk-okoo'ohuni-'i.
PST-INSTR-sealed with stiff object-0PL
"They would be sealed with the red rubber gasket."

In addition, there are no relative pronouns in the language, so the dependency relation *marker* is

[3]What we call "lines" here refers to a ToolBox line which represent a single clause, or a complete thought.

also obsolete in the current scheme. Similarly, there is no category of a number or numeral; instead the number can be expressed by a verb or a particle, at which instance it is analyzed just like other particles with the dependency of *advmod* to the word that it modifies. In sum, omitted UD relations are the ones that are either expressed by some other dependency or non-existent in the Arapaho language.

Several UD dependencies perfectly line up with the Arapaho scheme. So such relations as noun modifiers, adverbial modifiers, adverbial clauses, determiners, appositives, relative clauses, case markers, and a few more have a direct correspondence. For example, an adverbial clause in Arapaho is very similar, if not the same, as adverbial clauses described for other languages in the UD. Arapaho adverbial clauses, as it is seen in the example below, lack a distinct word introducing it; instead, the head of an adverbial clause exhibits particular morphological markers indicating its dependency. So in the example (6) this distinction is made by the subjunctive mode indicating that the verb *bih'iyoohok* "when it is dark" is a dependent of the main verb of the sentence.

(6)

advcl

Bih'iyoohok ce'no'useeni'.
VII VAI

Bih'iyoo-hok ce'-no'usee-ni'.
dark-SUBJUNCT back-arrive-1PL

"When it's dark, we'll come back."

In general, dependencies between function words and content words mirror the same dependencies in the UD framework, and most of these dependency labels are used.

The most complicated dependency relations tend to be between the content words, and especially the relations between the verb and its arguments. From the UD scheme, only one of such relations matches the Arapaho scheme with some modifications: *nsubj* and *csubj* correspond to subjects of intransitive verbs and transitive inanimate verbs. Similarly, subjects of passive verbs also correspond to the *nsubjpass* and *csubjpass* dependencies. Additional provisions are made in Arapaho scheme to account for the obviation status. In the following section, we discuss all of the provisions and additions made to the argument dependencies.

3.1 Subjects

While there is some correspondence between the UD's *nsubj* and subjects in Arapaho, it is, nonetheless, problematic to analyze subjects based purely on syntax since there is no syntactic features that would index the particular verbal arguments. Because nominals can take any position in the sentence and because they are not marked by a case corresponding with its syntactic role, the only certain way of finding a subject is in the person and number verbal agreement. The proximate and obviative distinction also does not clarify the syntactic role of the nominal, so with transitive verbs, the proximate form can be either agent or undergoer, and thus roughly correspond to either subject or object in English. In other words, the distinction of subject is not really important in the Arapaho language, especially with transitive verbs, and a relationship that is based on obviation would mark the dependencies more clearly. In response to this, the current dependency scheme adopted the UD dependency of *nsubj* and *csubj* with the additional marker *:obv* to index the obviative arguments of intransitive verbs expressed in the verbal morphology. The proximate counterparts are not marked. In the example (7), the obviative noun agreeing with the verb is such subject.

(7)

nsubj:obv

no'useeni3 nuhu' koo'ohwuu.
VAI DET NA

no'usee-ni3 nuhu' **koo'ohw-uu**.
arrive-4S this coyote-obv.
"This coyote came."

Similarly, the *nsubj* and *csubj* dependency is also used for animate arguments of transitive inanimate verbs (VTI) and inanimate arguments of intransitive inanimate verbs (VII). However, transitive verbs exhibit a double marker on indicating both the proximate and obviative participants, as well as the direction of action (agential relationship) between the two. The proximate participant can be either agent or patient, as can the obviative participant. So, an additional label employing the semantic distinction, *nagent* (nominal agent) is introduced.

(8)

nagent:obv

hiniisonoon heenei'itowuuneit.
NA VTA

hi-niisonoon heen-ei'itowuun-eit.
3S-father.obv REDUP-tell s.o.-4/3S

His father tells him.

UD	Arapaho Dependencies	Notes
nsubj	nsubj(:obv)	Nominal subjects of VII, VAI, and VTI verbs.
csubj	csubj(:obv)	Clausal subjects of VII, VAI, and VTI verbs.
nsubjpass	nusubjpass(:obv)	✓
csubjpass	csubjpass(:obv)	✓
	agent	Proximate agent of VTA expressed by a noun.
✗	nagent:obv	Obviative agent of VTA expressed by a clause.
	nagent:oblique(:obv)	Oblique agents of passive verbs
	cagent	Proximate agent of VTA expressed by a clause.
✗	cagent:obv	Obviative agent of VTA expressed by a clause.
	cagent:oblique(:obv)	Oblique agents of passive verbs
	dobj	Inanimate nominals as objects of VTI
dobj	dobj:under	Animate proximate nominals, undergoers of VTA
	dobj:under:obv	Animate obviative undergoers of VTA
iobj	iobj	Secondary objects of VTA not expressed in the verb
ccomp	ccomp	Additional specification of dependency (e.g., dobj, dobj:under, iobj, nmod) is required
xcomp	✗	
nmod	nmod	Adjuncts of verbs
	nmod:impobj	Implied objects of VAI.O, VAI.T, and incorporated verbs
	nmod:objad	Objects of adverbial particles and some verbal prefixes
	nmod:instr	Objects of instrumental particles and instrumental verbal prefixes

Table 1: Mapping of the UD argument labels and Arapaho nominal argument labels.

The following example further demonstrates the mismatch between subject and agent in Arapaho. Here, the verb is in passive voice, and the "subject" of the verb is "my grandfathers." However, this "subject' is obviative, and it is the oblique agent ("my father") which is proximate.

(9)

ne-isonoo nih-cih-won-biin-**eihi-ni3i**
1s-father PST-to here-ALLAT-give-PASS-4PL
ne-besiiwoho'
1S-grandfathers.obv

"My grandfathers were given (sth) by my father"

Since the verb is passivized and thus intransitive, only one argument is reflected in its morphology, the obviative subject *nebesiiwoho'* "my grandfathers." The label of *nagent* is kept with an additional marker *:oblique* to indicate that the argument *neisonoo* "my father" is not expressed in verbal morphology. Importantly, such oblique agents are different from noun modifiers, which are discussed further in the paper, because they specify the actor of the verb rather than its manner.

The subject relationship is not clearly defined in the Arapaho language. Instead, it is possible to talk about nominal expressions that are indexed by verbal morphology either as sole arguments of (syntactically) intransitive verbs or agential arguments (proximate or obviative) of the transitive animate verbs. We propose to account for this distinction as well as the distinction in obviation, which is clearly marked in nominal and verbal morphology.

3.2 Objects

The prototypical objects of transitive verbs do not easily fit the *dobj* relation in Arapaho. This is primarily because Arapaho verbs commonly undergo complex secondary derivation to produce verb stems which allow one to promote an animate argument to a core argument, marked inflectionally on the verb disregarding its semantic role. Thus, benefactives, recipients, goals, and even themes are typically the "object" marked inflectionally on the verb. Conversely, other arguments that would be classic "direct" objects in English are demoted, and not marked inflectionally on the verb. On the other hand, because the promoted animate argument is marked inflectionally, it can also easily be dropped from overt mention in the sentence, while unmarked items are much more likely to be mentioned explicitly.

Thus, when the manual for universal dependencies notes that *dobj* is the most patient-like argument of a verb, this is in direct tension with the tendencies of Arapaho transitive verb dependencies.

Additionally, when it notes that "if there is just one object, it should be labeled *dobj*, regardless of the morphological case or semantic role that it bears" (UniversalDependencies.org, 2014), this raises additional problems, since the actual 'object' marked on the Arapaho verb is highly likely not to appear in the sentence. The only exception and full correspondence to the UD's definition of the direct object is the inanimate object of an inanimate transitive verb (VTI):

(10)

dobj
niico'ontonounowoo nuhu' niinen.
VTI DET NI

nii-co'on-tonoun-owoo nuhu' **niinen**.
IMPF-always-use-1S this piece of fat

"I always use this fat."

Because the verb is transitive inanimate, it requires two arguments, only one of which (the animate agent) is marked inflectionally. The second argument can only be expressed by an inanimate noun and can either precede or follow the verb. So the overt nominal in the example above represents a prototypical direct object for transitive inanimate verbs. Meanwhile, transitive animate verbs can have up to three arguments (e.g., ditransitive verbs), with the two animate arguments being expressed inflectionally on the verb. So technically, ditransitive constructions may have only one overt nominal not corresponding to either of the person markers in verbal inflection. According to the UD definition cited above, such a nominal should be considered a direct object. In the following example, the true "object" of the Arapaho verb is "you," (since it is in imperative form) while "your eyes" is not marked on the verb, and is thus from the perspective of Arapaho grammar an oblique form.

(11)

dobj
Cihneeneeciihi hesiiseii.
VTA NI

Cih-nee-neeciih-i **he-siiseii**
EMPH.IMPER-REDUP-lend-1S.IMPER 2S-eyes

"Lend me your eyes."

There is no direct agreement between the secondary object *hesiiseii* "your eyes" and the verb. Ideally, this should be represented by *iobj* relation which emphasizes the indirect syntactic relation between the verb and the nominal.

Furthermore, objects of a transitive animate verb (VTA) and transitive inanimate verb (VTI) are different from the point of view of the grammar[4] and their respective part of speech designation[5]. Hence, a further specification of the *dobj* is necessary for transitive verbs. To stay consistent with the labels proposed for the *nagent* and *cagent* relations, the additional labels employed are *:under* and *:obv*.

(12)

nsubj:agent dobj:under:obv
Neisonoo nihcihwonbiinoot nebesiiwoho'.
NA VTA NA

ne-isonoo nih-cih-won-biin-oot
1S-father PST-to here-ALLAT-give-3S/4
ne-besiiwoho'
1S-grandfathers.obv

"My father came to give [me] to my grandfather."

In the example (12), the object clearly marked on the verb is the fourth person, or the obviative. Specifying this dependency relation disambiguates between the nominals and enables the correct translation of the sentence.

So, in the current scheme the distinction between different types of objects is further clarified. The *iobj* is reserved only for the secondary objects of the ditransitive verbs which show no verbal agreement. Meanwhile, the *dobj* is used to mark the dependency relation between the transitive inanimate verb and its object, which is also not specified in the verbal morphology. Label *dobj:under* with the additional specification of obviation indicates the dependency relation between transitive animate verbs and the undergoers specified in the verbal morphology.

3.3 Noun Modifiers

The dependency relation of noun modifier corresponds rather well to the noun modifiers in Arapaho. It is primarily used for the disambiguation between direct or indirect objects of transitive verbs and the implied, incorporated objects, or otherwise, adjuncts.

Having argued that some overt nominals of transitive animate nouns play a role of a secondary, or indirect object, we now also argue that such label in the same context can be inappropriate as well. Using the UD rules for distinguishing the dependency in the example below would lead to analyzing the nominal *koxouhtiit* "handgame" as a direct object of the main verb. But as one can see from

[4] VTI objects are not reflected in verbal morphology.

[5] Only the animate nominal expressions (NA) can be the objects of VTA.

the translation, it would also lead to a wrong analysis. Similarly, the indirect object analysis would also be incorrect. Indeed, annotating this noun as an oblique or an adjunct, *nmod*, is the only way of ensuring the correct analysis and translation.

(13)

nmod

Ceebe'eiheinoo koxouhtiit
VTA NI

ceebe'eih-einoo **koxouhtiit**.
IC.beat-3S/1S handgame

"He beats me in handgame."

When adjuncts are used with semi-transitive verbs, the *nmod* relation is further suffixed with *:objim* to note that the noun modifier further specifies the under-specified objects of semi-transitive verbs. Essentially, while these nominals are analyzed and marked as noun modifiers, for a successful translation they need to be marked as direct objects, which we have argued against in the previous section. In order to avoid the incorrect translation as well as incorrect analysis, the label *nmod:objim* is used. In the following example, the noun *bei'ci3ei'i* "money" semantically is the object of the semi-transitive verb. However, as we argue, marking it as direct or indirect object would violate the principles of Arapaho syntax.

(14)

nmod:objim

neeyeih'oonotooneenou'u bei'ci3ei'i.
VAI.O NI

neeyeih-'oonotoonee-nou'u **bei'ci3ei'i**.
IC.try-REDUP-borrow things-12.ITER money

"Whenever we try to borrow money."

In addition, some of these implied or incorporated objects with overt nominal expressions can be modified by an adverbial particle similar to a preposition in English.

(15)

nmod:objad case

nih'iinou'oo3i' neci' hi3oobei'i'
VAI NA PART

nih-'iinou'oo-3i' **nec-i'** **hi3oobei'-i'**
PST-float around-3PL **water-LOC under sth-LOC**

"They were floating around under the water"

In the example above, particle *hi3oobei'i'* "under" is a dependent of the adjunct *neci'* "water-LOC." This relation is reflected in the locative case marker on the noun showing a direct dependency with the particle. The Arapaho dependency scheme additionally distinguishes the instrumental case since there are special case markers defined by an adverbial or an adverbial prefix. So where the prefixes *hi'-*, *nohk-*, and *nii3-* are present or where the corresponding adverbial particles appear, the nominal adjunct is considered to be instrumental (*nmod:instr*). So in example (5), the relation between the head of the relative clause *siikoocei'iikuu3oo* "rubber item" and the main verb is *nmod:instr*.

Finally, an additional dependency *poss*, possessor modifier, is being used for possessive constructions with an overt possessor. Similar to Finnish (Tsarfaty, 2013; Haverinen et al., 2014), in Arapaho, it is possible to distinguish between the subject and the object of a possession. However, unlike in other languages, no special genitive construction exists to mark this type of relation. Instead, the possessor and possessed appear side-by-side. The possessed in such constructions has a third (or fourth) person possessive marker. So in a phrase *nii'ehihi' hi-siiseii* "little bird his-eyes" the possessor is "little bird" since the possessive prefix *hi-* "his" directly references this third person. The dependency relation marked here is possessor nominal modifying another nominal.

The examples above demonstrate that not all of the arguments that may semantically appear similar to the dependencies established in UD are the same in Arapaho. While under-specification of the semantic relationships can be beneficial in establishing some commonalities cross-linguistically, it can also result in misrepresentation of some of the relations and lowered efficiency in machine learning (Lipenkova and Souček, 2014). The major underspecification for the Arapaho language is the omission of proximate-obviative distinction: while we realize that it could potentially be problematic in cross-linguistic applicability, omitting this distinction disregards one of the main features of Algonquian syntax, and renders automatic translation of English transitive verbs into Arapaho effectively impossible.

4 Non-verbal roots

Adopting the relation of a root as the independent word in a clause or sentence allows us to avoid issues arising from securing the root node with verbs. So, like in the UD scheme, our annotations do not attach the node of a root to a particular part of speech even though they are usually represented by verbs. The main reason for doing this is avoiding the potential analysis of what is not there (Nivre, 2015; Hajicova et al., 2015; Osborne and Liang, 2015). In our annotations, the *root* often represents a pragmatically independent word, as for example in predicative type constructions (Cowell and Moss, 2008). Such constructions are used to topicalize one of the verbal arguments or the manner of action (i.e., verbal particles) similar to existential constructions in other languages. However, instead of marking the predicate as a root of the sentence as it is done in the Russian TreeBank (de Marneffe et al., 2014), the topicalized nominal or the particle is the root in Arapaho. The relation between the root and the predicate is *backreference*:

root backref

Ni'ook he'ne'nih'iisih'it.
NAME VAI.PASS

(16)
Ni'ook he'ne'-nih-'iisih'i-t
Puffy Eyes that-PST-how named-3S
"Puffy Eyes, that is how he is named."

In example (16), the argument of the verb *he'ne'nih'iisih'it* "that is how he is named" is not realized overtly, and the verbal prefix *ne'*- "that is" references back to the topical argument, making the verb actually a dependent of it. Were we to analyze distinct morphological elements, this prefix would act as a copula between the two. Overall, the reasoning for treating such topicalized elements (which sometimes may take other than the clause-initial position) comes from the combination of the pragmatics and morphology: nearly all of the verbal clauses with prefixes *ne'*- "that" and *nee'ees*- "that is how" are backreference dependents of such roots.

5 Conclusion

In this paper we demonstrate the use of Universal Dependency scheme with a language typologically different from the ones often included in machine-learning technologies. In using the UD framework, several unmentioned issues stemming from the reliance on the word order were noticed. For example, in the current annotation scheme, we reanalyzed the relationship of *parataxis* to account for verbs of citations, so that dependency would be traced from such a verb to the root of the whole clause. Similarly, the discourse marker dependencies were modified to include and analyze interjections. Unfortunately, it is outside of the scope of the paper to discuss these issues, but we hope that expanding this project to annotating conversational data and applying the annotated data to machine learning methods will further reveal some additional insights on analysis of discontinuous constituency.

In critiquing the UD, we, nonetheless, want to stress the eloquence of such an approach. Unlike the phrase structure annotations, UD allows us to account for the inconsistent phrase structures and dislocated tokens so often encountered in the Arapaho language. At the same time, however, we argue that to adequately account for the many linguistic nuances in annotations of such a morphologically and syntactically complex language like Arapaho, it is often necessary to include the semantic and pragmatic levels of analysis.

Acknowledgments

This research is funded by the National Endowment for the Humanities grant, project number 1551671 "Arapaho Lexical Database and Dictionary." We are especially thankful to the Northern Arapaho tribe for allowing us to conduct the work with their language.

References

Andrew Cowell and Alonzo Moss. 2008. *The Arapaho Language*. Westview Press, Boulder.

Marie-Catherine de Marneffe and Christopher D. Manning. 2008. Stanford typed dependencies manual. Revised: April 2015:1–22.

Marie-Catherine de Marneffe, Timothy Dozat, Natalia Silveira, Katri Haverinen, Filip Ginter, Joakim Nivre, and Christopher D. Manning. 2014. Universal Stanford Dependencies: A cross-linguistic typology. *In Proceedings of the Ninth International Conference on Language Resources and Evaluation (LREC'14)*, pages 4585–4592.

Ives Goddard. 1984. The obviative in Fox narrative discourse. In William Cowan, editor, *Papers of the Fifteenth Algonquian Conference*, pages 273–286. Carleton University Ottawa.

Eva Hajicova, Marie Mikulova, and Jarmila Panevova. 2015. Reconstructions of Deletions in a Dependency-based Description of Czech: Selected Issues. In *Proceedings of the Third International Conference on Dependency Linguistics (Depling 2015)*, pages 131–140, Uppsala, Sweden.

Katri Haverinen, Jenna Nyblom, Timo Viljanen, Veronika Laippala, Samuel Kohonen, Anna Missilä, Stina Ojala, Tapio Salakoski, and Filip Ginter. 2014.

Building the essential resources for Finnish: the Turku Dependency Treebank. *Language Resources and Evaluation*, pages 1–39.

Janna Lipenkova and Milan Souček. 2014. Converting Russian Dependency Treebank to Stanford Typed Dependencies Representation. In *Proceedings of the 14th Conference of the European Chapter of the Association for Computational Linguistics*, pages 143–147, Gothenburg, Sweden. Association for Computational Linguistics.

Ryan McDonald, Joakim Nivre, Yvonne Quirmbach-Brundage, Yoav Goldberg, Dipanjan Das, Kuzman Ganchev, Keith Hall, Slav Petrov, Hao Zhang, Oscar Täckström, Claudia Bedini, Núria Bertomeu Castelló, and Jungmee Lee. 2013. Universal Dependency Annotation for Multilingual Parsing Ryan. In *ACL 2013 - 51st Annual Meeting of the Association for Computational Linguistics, Proceedings of the Conference*, pages 92–97, Sofia, Bulgaria.

Joakim Nivre. 2015. Towards a universal grammar for natural language processing. *Lecture Notes in Computer Science (including subseries Lecture Notes in Artificial Intelligence and Lecture Notes in Bioinformatics)*, 9041:3–16.

Timothy Osborne and Junying Liang. 2015. A Survey of Ellipsis in Chinese. In *Proceedings of the Third International Conference on Dependency Linguistics (Depling 2015)*, pages 271–280, Uppsala, Sweden.

Reut Tsarfaty. 2013. A Unified Morpho-Syntactic Scheme of Stanford Dependencies. *Proceedings of the 51st Annual Meeting of the Association for Computational Linguistics (Volume 2: Short Papers)*, pages 578–584.

UniversalDependencies.org. 2014. Universal dependency relations (single document). `http://universaldependencies.org/u/dep/all.html`.

Appendix: Abbreviations

0PL	inanimate plural
12	first person plural inclusive
3S/4 or 1PL/2PL	the first number indicates the person and number acting on the following person and number (he to him; we to you.pl)
ALLAT	allative
DET	determiner
DETACH	detached adverbial prefix
DIM	diminutive
EMPH	emphatic
FUT	future tense
IC	phonological initial change
IMPER	imperative
IMPF	imperfect
ITER	iterative
LOC	locative
NA	animate noun
NAME	name
NARRPAST	narrative past tense
NI	inanimate noun
PART	particle
PASS	passive voice
PL	plural
PST	past tense
REDUP	reduplication
REL	relative prefix
S	singular
SELFBEN	self-benefactive
VAI	animate intransitive verb
VAI.O	animate intransitive verb with an implied object
VAI.PASS	animate intranstive passive verb
VAI.T	animate intransitive verb with a specific implied object
VII	inanimate intransitive verb
VTA	transitive verb with animate object
VTI	transitive verb with inanimate object

Annotating the discourse and dialogue structure of SMS message conversations

Nianwen Xue, Qishen Su, Sooyoung Jeong
Brandeis University
Computer Science Department
{xuen,qsu,jeong}@brandeis.edu

Abstract

In this paper we present a framework for annotating the discourse and dialogue structure of SMS message conversations. The annotation specifications integrate elements of coherence-based discourse relations and communicative acts in conversational speech. We present annotation experiments that show reliable annotation can be achieved with this annotation framework.

1 Introduction

With the pervasive use of mobile devices, Short Message Service (SMS) has been used widely in day-to-day communications. In many cases SMS messages have taken the place of traditional telephone conversations, and have become the preferred method for people to communicate with one another. SMS messages are by definition short, and due to its asynchronous nature, a participant does not have to wait to respond before another participant finishes. As a result, it is often the case that the conversation does not alternate in a rigid manner between participants.

The relations between the messages in an SMS conversation are in some ways very similar to those between utterances in conversational speech, where a conversant may agree or disagree with, respond to, or indicate understanding (or non-understanding) of an utterance by another speaker. To the extent that they are similar, the relations between SMS messages can be characterized in terms of the dialogue annotation framework described in (Core and Allen, 1997). The dialogue structure of the SMS "conversations" also tends to be more complex than that of speech conversations as a result of the more complex turn-taking patterns in SMS messages.

SMS message conversations are also different from conversational speech in that they are primarily in text form. Text within a single message also demonstrates the kind of discourse coherence that is typical of written text.

In this paper we describe a framework for annotating the discourse and dialogue structure of SMS message conversations. Based on the linguistic characteristics of SMS messages, we design an annotation framework that integrates elements of dialogue and discourse annotations, and report experiments that show reliable annotation with this framework.

The rest of the paper is organized as follows. In Section 2, we describe our annotation framework in detail. In Section 3 we report results on annotation experiments that show reliable annotation, and we will also discuss sources of disagreement. In Section 4 we discuss related work. We conclude our paper and describe future work in Section 5.

2 Annotation framework

In this section, we describe key elements of our annotation framework. We first describe basic units of our annotation, and then discuss how the basic units relate to each other to form a dialogue structure. Finally we present the set of relations we use in interpreting this structure.

2.1 Units of annotation

The basic units of annotation are individual text messages. The SMS messages are usually short, and most of the messages consist of single sentences, but there are a small and yet significant proportion of messages that consist of multiple sentences. In our current round of annotation, we do not analyze relations between the sentences inside one message, but we leave that possibility open for future rounds of annotation. Compared

Proceedings of LAW X – The 10th Linguistic Annotation Workshop, pages 180–187,
Berlin, Germany, August 11, 2016.

with discourse annotation of newswire text (Carlson et al., 2001; Prasad et al., 2008), determining the text units to perform annotation on is a relatively simple task, due to the fact that there is a natural boundary between text messages.

2.2 Structure of the SMS message conversations

Due to the asynchronous nature of SMS message conversations, individual messages are often "out of order", and determining which message relates to which is a substantial part of the annotation. This aspect of the annotation is different from the annotation of newswire texts or even conversational speech, where the "normal" order is generally maintained, although in conversation speech, there are often interruptions that break the normal pattern of turn-taking (Stolcke et al., 2000). Although there are some exceptions, in general, we assume that one message is only related to one previous message.[1] We call the message we are annotating the "anaphor", and the previous message that it relates to the "antecedent". Because the messages are "scrambled", the antecedent of a message is not always the immediately previous one, although it is in most cases. In addition, the antecedent of a message may not always be from a different participant. A participant may respond to a prior message by another participant, or continue his/her own line of thought without responding to an outstanding message from the other participant. A short snippet of an SMS message conversation is presented in Figure 1. On the left side of the figure is a graph that shows how the messages are connected. Each message is identified by a numerical number followed by a letter indicating the ID of the participant. For example, "7b" indicates message No 7 by participant "b". As should be clear from the graph, some messages (e.g., 7b,12b,14a, 15b,16a, 17b) are not linked to an immediately previous message, and some messages are connected to a previous message by the same participant. The graph shares many properties of a dependency tree in that there is a single root, and each anaphor is connected to one antecedent. It also more constrained than a dependency tree at the syntactic level in that the antecedent is always before the anaphor. The dependency tree is non-projective, since if all the arcs are drawn one one side, there will be crossing edges. These properties are important in fashioning a strategy for parsing this structure automatically, a topic that is out of the scope of this paper. Linking each message to its antecedent message is the first step of our annotation project.

[1]The assumption always holds except for a negligible number of cases where one message responds to multiple previous messages.

2.3 Relations between the messages

The second aspect of our annotation is to label the edges in graph, that is, to determine the relationship between each pair of connected messages. When annotating these relations, we make the distinction between same-participant message pairs and different-participant message pairs. The relations we use to label same-participant message pairs are drawn from the discourse relations defined in the Penn Discourse TreeBank (Prasad et al., 2008), but some PDTB relations are nonexistent in the SMS data. For example, we did not find cases of temporal relations in our SMS conversation data. This makes senses, since there is not much narrative text in SMS messages as there is in newswire such as Wall Street Journal articles in the PDTB and as a result, temporal relations are mostly unnecessary. On the other hand, there are also relations not covered in the PDTB. For example, there are cases where a participant uses another message to complete a previous message, presumably because s/he hit the "send" button in the middle of a message and later had to complete that message. There are also messages used to correct spelling mistakes of a previous message from the same participant. Such cases are not attested in carefully edited newswire text but they need to be accounted for in our annotation. The complete list of same-participant relations are presented in Table 3.

The different-participant relations are drawn from DAMSL (Core and Allen, 1997), a coding scheme for annotating communication acts in conversational speech. DAMSL is a multilayer annotation framework that annotates both forward and backward communicative functions. Since we focus on the relation between the current message and its antecedent, we limit ourselves to mostly annotating backward communicative functions. The set of different-participant relations are provided in Table 2. Two of our labels, *directives:request* and *directives:suggestion* may bear some resemblance to the forward communicative functions in DAMSL, but they are used to label

Figure 1: The SMS message as a dependency tree. The suffixes "a" and "b" on the tree nodes are the two participants. Messages in boxes have non-local (not immediately before) antecedents.

requests or suggestions in the context of a previous message. The following example is a case of *directive:suggestion*:

(1) A: I'm hungry.

B: let's go get some food!

It is important to note that unlike DAMSL, the targets of our annotation project are not individual utterances but are relations between pairs of messages. When labeling the backward communicative functions of an utterance in DAMSL, the antecedent of the utterance is assumed to be the immediately previous one, but we cannot make this assumption in our annotation.

There is a third group of labels that don't fit nicely into either group of same-participant or different-participant labels. Those labels are used to label messages that initiate a new topic, get attention, or fulfill a social obligation. These messages are explained in Table 4.

3 Annotation Experiments

The SMS data we performed our annotation experiments on are drawn from an LDC collection of SMS and Chat Messages collected under the DARPA BOLT program. Two annotators performed four rounds of annotation, working on the same documents so that inter-annotator agreement (IAA) statistics can be computed. We started with an initial set of guidelines. After each round of annotation, the annotators met and discussed cases of disagreement. If the differences are due to un-

Label	Description
Agreement:Acceptance	*Acceptance* refers to a positive response to proposals, requests, and suggestions, or agreement to assertions. Common key words of acceptance are "yes", "ok", "alright", etc.
Agreement:Rejection	*Rejection* indicates a negative response to proposals, requests, and suggestions, or disagreement to assertions. Rejection is often signaled by words like "no" or "nah".
Understanding:Acknowledgment	*Acknowledgment* signals a participant's understanding of a previous message. Cue words or phrases for *Acknowledgment* include "ok", "I understand", "yes", "I know", "I see", etc. *Acknowledgment* may also contain words or short phrases that express sentiment such as happiness, excitement, sadness, anger. These words or phrases can be laughing words (such as "haha" and "lol"), words that express surprise or excitement (such as "omg" or "yay") and appreciation (such as "awww"), profanity (such as "what the hell"), or emoticons.
Understanding:Non-Understanding	*Non-understanding* is used when a participant seeks clarification by asking clarification questions.
Directive:Request	This relation is used when a participant asks another participant to perform certain action. The immediate information or context of *Request*, as opposed to *Derivative Request*, comes from the other participant's message.
Directive:Suggestion	This relations is used when a participant offers another participant an idea or plan for consideration. The immediate information or context of *Suggestion*, as opposed to *Derivative Suggestion*, comes from the other participant's message.
Question	This relation is used to mark requests of information and clarification. Unlike the clarification questions mentioned previously, this type of question does not signal non-understanding. Instead it is a general request for additional information. The immediate information or context of *Question*, as opposed to *Derivative Question*, comes from the other participant's message.
Answer:Answer	An answer provides complete or partial information to a question in a previous text message.
Answer:Hold	A participant sometimes signals their acknowledgment of a question, but does not provide an answer to it. Moreover, if a participant responds to another participant's question with a question, such a response is considered as *Hold*
Feedback	This type of relation is used when a participant provides information in response to another participant's message that is neither a question nor a directive.

Figure 2: Dialogue Only Labels

clear instructions in the guidelines or unclear distinctions in the tagset, the guidelines are revised before the next round of annotation starts. We made sure that the document sizes and the number of messages that we annotate in each round stay constant so that we can observe the trend in the agreement statistics after each round of annotation. Before we discuss the IAA, we first present the distribution of the distances between each message and its antecedent in Table 5. The distance is computed by pooling the two sets of annotations by the two annotators. The results show that overall there is a distance of 1 for only 77.97% of the message pairs, meaning that the antecedent mes-

Label	Description
Contingency:Cause	*Cause* indicates that the situations in two text messages influence each other causally, and they are not in a conditional relation.(Group, 2008) This type of relation is used when the argument of the previous message is the result, and that of the following message is the cause.
Contingency:Result	Similar to the *Cause* relation, Result also indicates that the two arguments have a causal relation, and that they are not in a conditional relation. *Result* is used when the argument of a given message is the result caused by the situation of a previous message.
Contingency:Condition	Two text messages are in a conditional relation when the argument of one message is the condition and that of the other message is the consequence.
Expansion:Elaboration	A text message is considered as an elaboration of a previous one, when the current message clarifies or elaborates on the information that the previous message conveys. This relation can apply to two or more messages that are connected by conjunctions "and" and "but".
Expansion:Derivative Question	This type of relation concerns with requests of information and clarification, similar to *Question*. However, the immediate information or context of *Derivative Question*, as opposed to *Question*, derives from the same participant's own messages.
Expansion:Derivative Suggestion	This type of relation is used when a participant provides another participant an idea or plan for consideration of a future action, and its information or context derives immediately from the same participant's own messages.
Expansion:Derivative Request	This elation is used when a participant asks another participant to perform certain action, but its immediate information or context derives from the same participant's messages.
Expansion:Concession	This type of discourse relation is used to highlight prominent differences between two text messages. More specifically, "the highlighted differences are related to expectations raised by one argument which are then denied by the other"(Group, 2008).
Expansion:Alternative	This discourse relation is used when two text messages describe alternative situations. 'or", "instead" and "otherwise" are common cue words for this relation.
Expansion:Completion	Occasionally when a participant uses two or more messages to complete a sentence, and *Completion* is used to describe the relation between these messages.
Reflexive Feedback	This relation is used when a participant answers their own questions or responds to their own statements (such as laughing at their own joke).
Correction	*Correction* is generally concerned with correcting wrong information from a previous text message, such as typos.

Figure 3: Non-Dialogue Only Labels

sage is the immediately previous message in only 77.97% of the cases. For the remaining 22.03% of the cases, the antecedent is not the immediately previous message, indicating there is a significant proportion of messages that do not follow the "normal" order of turn-taking. The amount

Label	Description
Topic Introduction	It is used when a participant initiates a new topic in a new or existing conversation.
Attention Getter	An *Attention Getter* is a word or phrase used to attract the attention of another participant. It can be words like "Hey", "Oh", "Ah", etc., or the name of the other speaker.
Social Obligation	This type of discourse relation is used when a participant complies with certain social norms or obligations, such as apologies, acceptance or rejection of apologies, appreciation, greetings, farewell, etc. When a participant is signaling their desire for ending a conversation, that message is considered farewell, and is thus labeled as *Social Obligation*.
Other	Occasionally, a participant might send an empty message, and in that case, the relation of the empty message to its immediate previous message should be annotated as *Other*. *Other* is also used when a given message is nonsensical in relation to any previous message, or when the relation between two messages are not formalized in any of the categories above.

Figure 4: Dialogue and Non-Dialogue Labels

of "scrambling" is even higher between different-participant message pairs, where one participant is responding to a message of another participant.

The inter-annotator agreement statistics for the four rounds of annotation are presented in Table 1. Column 4 shows the agreement on connections only, which is computed as the percentage of messages that are linked to the same antecedent for both annotators. Column 5 shows the agreement on relations, which is computed as the proportion of message pairs that are annotated with the same relation, out of the total number of connections that both annotators agree on. So this calculation factors out connections that the two annotators have disagreements on. Column 6 shows the Cohen's $Kappa$ on relation agreement. The results show the agreement on connections stays relatively stable between rounds, indicating this aspect of the annotation is rather intuitive, and does not benefit from additional rounds of training. In contrast, there is significant improvement in the agreement on relations as guidelines are refined and the distinction between the relations are clarified. The final column shows the agreement on both connections and labels. The agreements statistics are lower, indicating a cumulative effect, but overall, it shows that reliable annotation can be achieved.

The inter-annotator agreement (IAA) statistics on connections are calculated with equation 3

$$P = \frac{N_a}{N_t}$$

where N_a is the total number of same connections, and N_t is the total number of connections. The inter-annotator agreement for connections with label is calculated similarly: N_a is the total number of same connections with the same label.

The Cohen's Kappa score for labels on the same connections is calculated as follows:

$$K = \frac{P_o - P_e}{1 - P_e}$$

where P_o is the sum of probabilities of choosing the same label, and P_e is the probability of choosing the same label by chance,

$$P_e = \sum P_i^a \times P_i^b$$

where P_i^a and P_i^b are the probabilities of annotator A and annotator B choosing label i, respectively. P_e is the sum of the products of P_i^a and P_i^b for all labels.

3.1 Examples of Inter-annotator Disagreement

There are two main types of disagreement between the annotators: disagreement on connections and disagreement on relations. Disagreement on connections happens when, given a message, the annotators disagree on which previous message is its antecedent. Disagreement on relations occurs when the annotators disagree on the relation between a given pair of messages.

Distance	1	2	3	4 and greater
Dialogue Links	73.30%	17.08%	5.72%	3.88%
Non-dialogue Links	84.22%	11.18%	3.22%	1.36%
Dialogue and Non-dialogue Combined	77.97%	14.56%	4.65%	2.80%

Figure 5: Distance Distributions

	Number of Files	Number of Messages	Agreement on connections	Agreement on relations	Kappa on relations	Agreement on both
Round 1	10	898	0.886	0.697	0.649	0.618
Round 2	14	873	0.886	0.722	0.680	0.640
Round 3	10	893	0.848	0.838	0.826	0.710
Round 4	10	890	0.867	0.881	0.875	0.764

Table 1: Inter-Annotator agreement statistics

Message ID	Timestamp	Participant ID	Content
m0007	2010-08-24 19:22:45 UTC	153902	Charming is the audience's subjective interpretation
m0008	2010-08-24 19:22:49 UTC	153901	so you can choose to be condescending?
m0009	2010-08-24 19:23:02 UTC	153902	Yes
m0010	2010-08-24 19:23:06 UTC	153901	but you cannot choose to be charming
m0011	2010-08-24 19:23:14 UTC	153902	You can attempt to be charming

Figure 6:

Disagreement on connections Although determining which message is connected to which previous message is intuitive for the most part, disagreement does happen when a message has more than one possible and meaningful connection. For instance, message m0010 in Figure 6 can be a response to message m0009 or an extension of message m0008. This is one of the cases on which the two annotators disagree.

Disagreement on Relations Certain words or phrases are generally ambiguous and prone to causing confusion and disagreement on labeling. For example, the word "yeah" or the phrase "I know" can either signal acknowledgment or express agreement. Disagreement on labeling often occurs when such words or phrases can be interpreted either way in a given context. Message m0053 in Figure 7 can be either acknowledgment or agreement of the assertion in their previous message, and either interpretation makes sense in this context.

4 Related work

There has been relatively little work on annotating the discourse and dialogue structure of SMS conversations. The work that is most similar to ours is that of (Perret, 2015), where they annotated the discourse structure of multi-party dialogues using a corpus collected from an on-line version of the *The Settlers of Catan* game. They argue that multi-party dialogues need to be modeled with a graph structure and adopted an annotation scheme in the SDRT framework (Asher and Lascarides, 2003). In our annotation, since we are dealing with SMS dialogues that involve two participants, we did not find a graph structure to be necessary. We opted for a simpler (non-projective) dependency structure that is easier to model algorithmically. In fact, (Perret, 2015) developed an automatic discourse parser based on the Maximum Spanning Tree, a tree-based dependency parsing algorithm (McDonald, 2006) instead of a graph-based algorithm. We also make a distinction be-

Message ID	Timestamp	Participant ID	Content
m0051	2015-02-27 13:45:13 UTC	152252	It's so stupid Sofie
m0052	2015-02-27 13:45:36 UTC	152252	I just feel like the general public should take an art class
m0053	2015-02-27 13:45:36 UTC	152212	i know

Figure 7: Disagreement on relations

tween same-participant and different-participant relations, and argue SMS message conversations need to be modeled with an annotation framework based on both discourse coherence and dialogue structures.

5 Conclusion and Future Work

In this paper we presented a framework for annotating the discourse and dialogue structure of SMS message conversations. The annotation specifications integrate elements of coherence-based discourse relations and dialogue structure in conversational speech. We conducted annotation experiments that show reliable annotation. Future work includes additional annotation based on this annotation framework and producing sufficient data that can be used to train a statistical parsing model.

Acknowledgment

We gratefully acknowledge a Faculty/Student Collaborative Research Grant from the Office of the Dean of College of Arts and Science Dean's at Brandeis University that has supported the first and third author of this paper. All errors and shortcomings are that of the authors of course.

References

Nicholas Asher and Alex Lascarides. 2003. *Logics of Conversation*. Cambridge University Press.

Lynn Carlson, Daniel Marcu, and Mary Ellen Okurowski. 2001. Building a discourse-tagged corpus in the framework of rhetorical structure theory. In *Proceedings of the Second SIGdial Workshop on Discourse and Dialogue - Volume 16*, SIGDIAL '01, pages 1–10, Stroudsburg, PA, USA. Association for Computational Linguistics.

Mark G Core and James Allen. 1997. Coding dialogs with the damsl annotation scheme. In *AAAI fall symposium on communicative action in humans and machines*, pages 28–35. Boston, MA.

The PDTB Research Group. 2008. The PDTB 2.0. annotation manual. *Technical Report IRCS-08-01*, page 28.

Ryan McDonald. 2006. *Discriminative Training and Spanning Tree Algorithms for Dependency Parsing*. Ph.D. thesis, University of Pennsylvania.

Stergos Afantenos Eric Kow Nicholas Asher Jérémy Perret. 2015. Discourse parsing for multi-party chat dialogues. In *Proceedings of the 2015 Conference on Empirical Methods in Natural Language Processing*, Lisbon, Portugal.

Rashmi Prasad, Nikhil Dinesh, Alan Lee, Eleni Miltsakaki, Livio Robaldo, Aravind Joshi, and Bonnie Webber. 2008. The Penn Discourse Treebank 2.0. In *Proceedings of the 6th International Conference on Language Resources and Evaluation (LREC 2008)*, Marrakech, Morocco.

Andreas Stolcke, Noah Coccaro, Rebecca Bates, Paul Taylor, Carol Van Ess-Dykema, Klaus Ries, Elizabeth Shriberg, Daniel Jurafsky, Rachel Martin, and Marie Meteer. 2000. Dialogue act modeling for automatic tagging and recognition of conversational speech. *Computational linguistics*, 26(3):339–373.

Creating a Novel Geolocation Corpus from Historical Texts

Grant DeLozier, Ben Wing**, Jason Baldridge*, Scott Nesbit†**
University of Texas at Austin*
University of Georgia†
grantdelozier@gmail.com, ben@benwing.com
jasonbaldridge@gmail.com, snesbit@uga.edu
* The first two authors contributed equally to the content of the paper.

Abstract

This paper describes the process of annotating a historical US civil war corpus with geographic reference. Reference annotations are given at two different textual scales: individual place names and documents. This is the first published corpus of its kind in document-level geolocation, and it has over 10,000 disambiguated toponyms, double the amount of any prior toponym corpus. We outline many challenges and considerations in creating such a corpus, and we evaluate baseline and benchmark toponym resolution and document geolocation systems on it. Aspects of the corpus suggest several recommendations for proper annotation procedure for the tasks.

1 Introduction

Geographic information is an important component of a number of areas including information retrieval (Daoud and Huang, 2013), social media analysis, and historical research (Nesbit, 2013; Grover et al., 2010; Smith and Crane, 2001). To date however, very few corpora exist for text geolocation tasks, and those which do exist have flaws or are very small in size. This is particularly true for tasks seeking to do geolocation work with historical texts. In the realm of document geolocation, there exist no historical corpora whatsoever; in the realm of toponym resolution historical corpora exist, but are flawed in important respects (Speriosu and Baldridge, 2013; DeLozier et al., 2015).

This paper describes the process of annotating a set of American Civil War archives commonly known as the *Official Records of the War of the Rebellion* (officially titled *The War of the Rebellion: a Compilation of the Official Records of the Union and Confederate Armies* and henceforth abbreviated as WOTR), arguably the most important and widely used corpus in this area of historical study[1].

	Docgeo subset	Topo subset	Full data
Total tokens	1,743,331	447,703	57,557,037
# volumes	118	15	126
# documents	7,533	1,644	254,744
Avg. tokens/document	231.43	272.32	225.94

Table 1: Statistics on WOTR, annotated subset and full data (using documents predicted based on a sequence model derived from the annotated data, as described in §3).

Document geolocation and toponym resolution enable work on the specific content of individual documents and themes contained within this corpus, revealing the ways in which content is distributed in the corpus over time and space (Ayers and Nesbit, 2011; Thomas III, 2011). Themes in this corpus pertinent to the study of Civil War literature include the rise of irregular warfare, the end of slavery in Confederate and Union states, the use of railroads by United States and Confederate armies in the war, and the destruction of the war-making capacity of the Confederate states. The annotation process and geolocation tools also enable historians to reexamine the process by which the archive was produced, an area which has recently seen growing interest (Sternhell, 2016).

We develop geolocation corpora for two related but separate tasks: document geolocation (docgeo) and toponym resolution (TR). Statistics on the full WOTR corpus and the annotated document geolocation and toponym subsets are shown in Table 1 and Table 2.

Geographic summaries of the annotations are given in Figure 1 (documents) and Figure 2 (toponyms). The docgeo annotations are concen-

[1] http://ehistory.osu.edu/books/official-records

Proceedings of LAW X – The 10th Linguistic Annotation Workshop, pages 188–198,
Berlin, Germany, August 11, 2016. ©2016 Association for Computational Linguistics

	Docgeo Subset
Documents	8,121
Documents with geometries	5,035 (62%)
Documents with only points	4,811 (59%)
Documents with polygons	224 (3%)

	Topo Subset
Avg. toponyms/document	7.17
Toponyms	11,795
Toponyms with geometries	10,380 (88%)
Toponyms with points	8,130 (69%)
Toponyms with polygons	2,296 (19%)
People	7,994
Organizations	2,591

Table 2: Statistics on WOTR, annotated subset (using documents predicted based on a sequence model derived from the annotated data, as described in §3).

trated in a number of areas that saw heavy fighting, such as in Virginia, South Carolina and Northern Georgia. The toponym annotations are more concentrated around the western theater of the Civil War. In both corpora, almost all US states are represented by at least some references. The toponym annotations contain more full-state polygons, while the docgeo annotations are primarily points, leading to the differing appearances of the two maps.

2 Geolocation tasks

Both toponym resolution and document geolocation involve assigning geographic reference, usually latitude-longitude coordinates, to spans of text, but differ as to the size of the span. Toponym resolution involves assigning such reference to individual, potentially ambiguous toponyms (e.g. *Springfield* or *Dallas*), while document geolocation assigns geographic reference to larger spans of text (documents, broadly construed).

Among the key difficulties associated with both tasks are ambiguity of reference, fluidity in the definition of the tasks, and lack of sufficient and/or appropriate training material. As an example of the issues surrounding ambiguity, consider the toponym *Springfield*. Dominant place name gazetteers indicate at least 236 unique senses of the term (and these underestimate the true total), with possible references spanning the globe. TR systems must choose referents in these highly ambiguous scenarios, even when correct referents are not listed in gazetteers. In document geolocation, the problem is even more acute, as a document can potentially be assigned a location anywhere on the globe.

Another issue affecting both domains is fluidity in how one defines the task itself. In toponym resolution, metonymy—the ability of a place name to refer to something closely related to a place (e.g. a government)—and demonymy—names for the people who inhabit an area (e.g. Americans)—are properties that must be considered. All existing TR corpora include metonymic uses of place names. The Local Global Lexicon (LGL) corpus (Lieberman and Samet, 2012) includes demonyms as toponyms and georeferences them, while all other corpora do not. An additional issue pertains to the range of entity types a system is expected to resolve. Many corpora limit their expectations to larger entities—e.g. TR-CoNLL (Leidner, 2008) is limited to cities, states, and countries), while others focus more on highly local entities (e.g. bus stops) (Matsuda et al., 2015). A final issue relates to whether systems ought to resolve places which are embedded inside other named entities. For example, the LGL corpus expects *New York* in the expression *New York Times* to be resolved to the state of New York. Many of the characteristics of existing TR corpora are summarized in Table 3.

In document geolocation, different researchers have interpreted the task differently, depending on the corpus: typically as either as the location of the document's author when the document was created, or as the geographic *theme* (i.e. topic) of the content of the document. The former interpretation has usually been used when working with social-media corpora such as Twitter (Han et al., 2014; Schulz et al., 2013) and Flickr (O'Hare and Murdock, 2013; Bolettieri et al., 2009), and the latter with encyclopedic corpora such as Wikipedia (van Laere et al., 2014) and historical corpora such as the unpublished Beadle Corpus (Wing, 2015). Another difficulty with using the geographic-theme interpretation is that this reference may not be easily identifiable for some texts. (For example, only about 10% of the articles in the English Wikipedia have document-level annotations assigned to them.)

An additional issue related to the definition of both tasks is the scope of the geographic reference. Smaller geographic entities, such as cities and neighborhoods, can be reasonably approximated as a point in latitude-longitude space, while

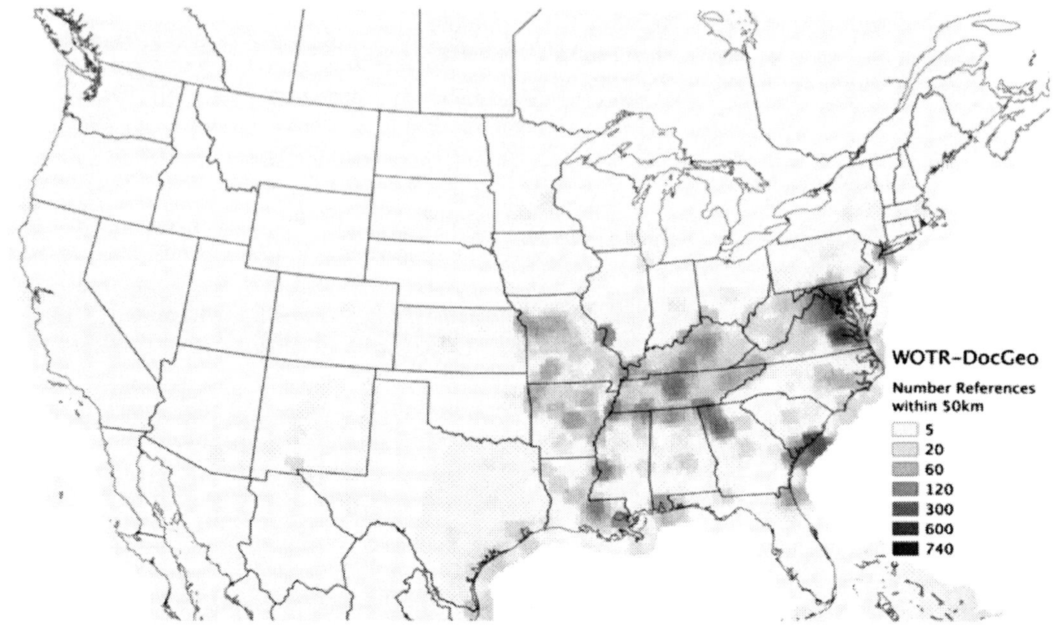

Figure 1: Distribution of References in WoTR-DocGeo

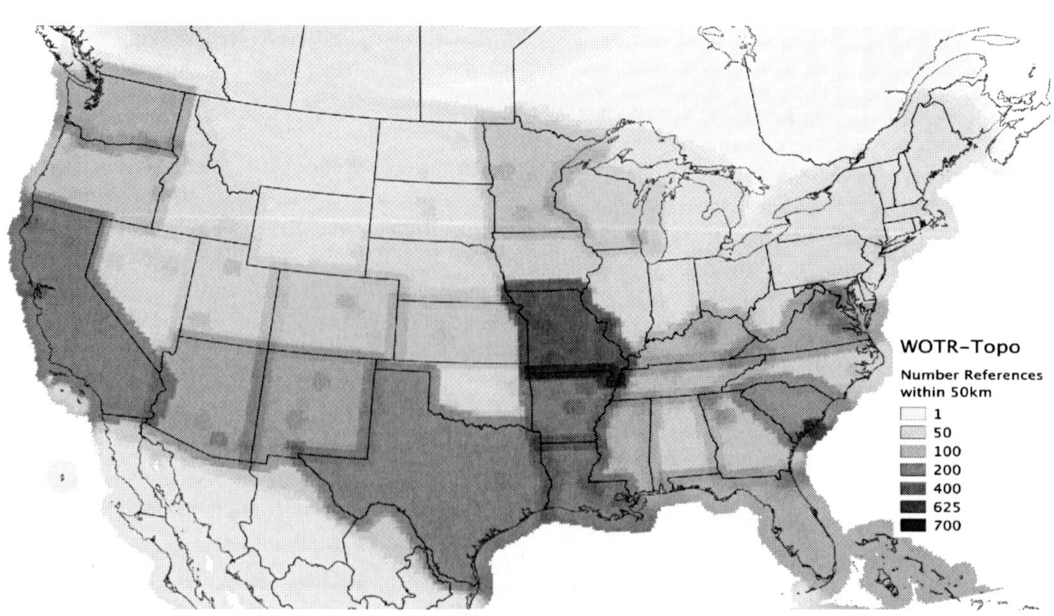

Figure 2: Distribution of Toponyms in WOTR-Topo

it is more difficult to do so for larger entities such as states or countries. Various solutions have been used for this problem, depending on the corpus. Wikipedia and most gazetteers take the simplest approach of assigning a point to all entities, regardless of size. However, for large entities such as countries, this necessitates choosing a single representative point (e.g. the geographic centroid or the capital city), which leads to many problems (e.g. the geographic centroid of the UK is a point in the Irish Sea).

Toponym resolution, especially, currently suffers from a lack of sufficient training material. Existing training corpora fixate around very narrow ranges of geographic entities. One major corpus used in toponym resolution, TR-CoNLL, has only 800 unique strings and 6259 toponyms, while gazetteers such as GeoNames list over 8 million unique places (which still greatly underestimates the true number of toponyms). Such mismatches do more than underscore the need for larger and more domain-diverse corpora; they point to fundamental issues associated with learning to resolve geographies from language. Geographic entities, like all named entities, are fiat objects; naming them dictates their existence (Kripke, 1980). Many systems have attempted to alleviate paucity problems by splicing corpora with latent annotations inferred from a more general resource like Wikipedia (Speriosu and Baldridge, 2013; Santos et al., 2014; DeLozier et al., 2015).

In document geolocation, the amount of training material available is crucially tied in with how the task is defined (as described above). Abundant training material is available from the various language-specific versions of Wikipedia and from social-media sites such as Twitter and Flickr, but the variations in language and task definition make the corpora highly domain-specific. This means that cross-corpus generalization is fraught with difficulty, particularly in domains where no previously-published corpora exist, such as historical documents. Nonetheless, researchers have achieved some success from docgeo domain adaptation, using Wikipedia as out-of-domain training material for historical documents under a co-training setup (Wing, 2015) and Flickr as a source of language-model data for geolocation of Wikipedia (De Rouck et al., 2011).

3 Data preparation

The source data available was in the form of text scanned directly from the published books using OCR (optical character recognition), and then hand-corrected. The digital form of the collection we accessed included page breaks which sometimes occur in the middle of a word, footnotes and headers undifferentiated from body text, and no formal delimiting of where particular records began and ended. Figure 3 is an example of part of the source text of a volume in the collection, after preprocessing to stitch up page breaks and remove footnotes, headers, footers, etc., but before splitting into individual documents.

To alleviate some of these issues in working with this form of the text, the following steps were taken to improve our annotated version of the corpus:

1. Remove page breaks and stitch up paragraphs divided across the breaks.

2. Create a GUI annotation tool to allow annotators to quickly note the extent of documents (which we term *spans*) and indicate the document locations on a map.

3. Create a sequence model to automatically split up the continuous text into documents, training it on the documents manually marked up by the annotators.

Stitching up page breaks As mentioned above, the source text is in the form of individual pages scanned from the published books, with page breaks, footnotes, stray headers, etc. often interrupting a paragraph in the middle of a word, frequently in an inconsistent fashion. A program was written that used various heuristics to do the majority of work, although several more steps and a good deal of hand editing were required to achieve satisfactory results.

Automatically locating document spans There is no indication in the source text where one document ends and another one begins. In a letter, for example, sometimes the destinee appears near the beginning of the letter, following a heading describing the location and date, while in other cases the destinee appears at the very end, after the salutation. Both examples can be seen in the text box in the annotation tool screen shot in Figure 4,

Table 3: Toponym Corpora

Corpus	Domain	Entity Types	Reference Types	Metonyms	Demonyms	Nested NE	Toponyms
TR-CoNLL	Contemporary International News	Cities,States, Countries	Point only	Yes	No	Most Encompassing NE	6259
LGL	Contemporary Local Newspapers	Few Locales, cities, states, countries	Point only	Yes	Yes	Annotates Embedded Places	5088
LRE	Tweets from Japan	Highly local 'facilities' and above	Point only	?	No	?	951
WOTR	US Civil War Letters + Reports	Locales, Cities, and States	Point and Polygon	No	No	Most Encompassing NE	10380

along with the way that successive documents directly abut each other. Because the unit of analysis is a single document, it is necessary to locate the beginning and end of each document, and this must be done automatically since only a fraction of the text was manually annotated.

To do this, a CRF (conditional random field) sequence model was created using MALLET (McCallum, 2002). Each successive paragraph was considered a unit in the sequence labeling task, and labeled with one of the following: *B* (beginning), *I* (inside), *L* (last), or *O* (outside), similar to how named entity recognition (NER) sequence labeling is normally handled. CRF's have the advantage over HMM's (hidden Markov models) that they can be conditioned on arbitrary features of the visible stream of paragraphs, including the neighbors of the actual paragraph being labeled. This allowed for various features to be engineered, such as (1) the presence of a date at the end of a line, possibly followed by a time; (2) the presence of certain place-related terms typically indicating a header line, such as *HEADQUARTERS*, *HDQRS* or *FORT*; (3) the presence of a rank-indicating word (e.g. *Brigadier*, *General* or *Commanding*) at the beginning of or within a line; (4) the presence of a line beginning with a string of capital letters, typically indicating a header line; (5) the presence of certain words (e.g. *obedient servant*) that typically indicate a salutation; (6) the combination of the above features with certain punctuation at the end of the line (comma, period, or colon); (7) the length of a line; (8) all of the above features for the actual paragraph in question as well as the previous, second-previous, next, second-next, and combinations thereof; and (9) the first and last words of the paragraph, after stripping out punctuation.

The resulting model performed well, but did not consistently handle the cases where the destinee is at the end of the letter, and so a postprocessing step was added to adjust the spans whenever such a situation was detected.

4 Annotation process

4.1 Annotation tool

A GUI annotation tool was written that allows document spans to be selected in a text box and points or polygons added on a map. Figure 4 shows a screen shot of the tool at work. Spans of text are indicated with inward-pointing red arrows at their edges and are colored yellow (a marked span without geometry), green (a span with geometry) or cyan (currently selected span for adding or changing the geometry). Points and polygons can be added by drawing directly on the map, by using the list of recent locations below the map, or (in the case of points) by entering a latitude/longitude coordinate into the text box and clicking **Set Lat/Long**.

The annotation tool is written in HTML and JavaScript using the OpenLayers[2] and Rangy libraries[3], with data stored using Parse, a *backend-as-a-service* which allows for free data storage within certain storage and bandwidth limits.

4.2 Document geolocation annotation

The docgeo annotation process took 280 hours over two months. Five annotators were hired, although in practice most of the work was done by a single annotator. 25-page subsections of 118 of 126 volumes were annotated with geographies. A few of the volumes had an additional 75 pages annotated.

4.2.1 Document annotator guidelines

Annotators were hired to note the individual documents within the archives and attach document-level geometries to them, which are intended to encode the geographic *theme* of the content of the

[2]http://openlayers.org/

[3]https://github.com/timdown/rangy

...

2. While congratulating the troops on their glorious success, the commanding general desires to impress upon all officers as well as men the necessity of greater discipline and order. These are as essential to the success as to the victorious; but with them we can march forward to new fields of honor and glory, till this wicked rebellion is completely crushed out and peace restored to our country.

3. Major-Generals Grant and Buell will retain the immediate command of their respective armies in the field.

By command of Major-General Halleck:

N. H. McLEAN,

Assistant Adjutant-General.

HEADQUARTERS DEPARTMENT OF THE MISSISSIPPI, Pittsburg, Tenn., April 14, 1862.

Major General U. S. GRANT,

Commanding District and Army in the Field:

Immediate and active measures must be taken to put your command in condition to resist another attack by the enemy. Fractions of batteries will be united temporarily under competent officers, supplied with ammunition, and placed in position for service. Divisions and brigades should, where necessary, be reorganized and put in position, and all stragglers returned to their companies and regiments. Your army is not now in condition to resist an attack. It must be made so without delay. Staff officers must be sent out to obtain returns from division commanders and assist in supplying all deficiencies.

H. W. HALLECK,

Major-General.

NEW MADRID, April 14, 1862.

J. C. KELTON:

General Pope received message about Van Dorn and Price. Do you want his army to join General Halleck's on the Tennessee? His men are all afloat. He can be at Pittsburg Landing in five days. Fort Pillow strongly fortified. Enemy will make a decided stand. May require two weeks to turn position and reduce the works. Answer immediately. I wait for reply.

THOMAS A. SCOTT,

Assistant Secretary of War.

SPECIAL ORDERS, HDQRS. DIST. OF WEST TENNESSEE,
No. 54. Pittsburg, Tenn., April 14, 1862.

II. Brigadier General Thomas A. Davies, having reported for duty to Major-General Grant, is hereby assigned to the command of the Second Division of the army in the field.

By order of Major-General Grant:

[JNumbers A. RAWLINS,]

Assistant Adjutant-General.

CAIRO, ILL., April 14, 1862.

H. A. WISE, Navy Department:

...

Figure 3: Example of WOTR source text, after stitching up text across page breaks, removing extraneous headers/footers/footnotes, etc.

document. The theme of a document is the primary location or locations that the document concerns. For example, if the document describes a battle, skirmish or other military action, the location of that action is the document's geography. Most correspondence is headed by the location at which it was written, which is often the same as the geographic theme, depending on what the content of the correspondence says. Annotators were allowed to mark multiple locations or to draw a polygon around an area of the map, which is useful when for example the geographic theme is logically a body of water or a section of a state rather than a single point. However, in the interests of achieving as many annotations as possible, annotators were encouraged to not overly make use of polygons or multiple points, preferring a single point when possible. In particular, the mere mention of a place name in a document is not sufficient for it to be included in the geographic theme; it must be of primary relevance to the subject of the document.

Annotators were encouraged to look up toponyms found within the text to retrieve their latitude/longitude coordinates, with helpful relevant keywords attached as necessary, such as *Civil War* or the region or commander mentioned in the larger document context. Annotators were shown how to retrieve the geocoordinate from Wikipedia pages, which was by far the most-frequently used resource, although Google Maps and niche US Civil War websites were used as well.

4.2.2 Document annotation challenges

Geographically diverse documents A large fraction of documents mention multiple places, and our annotators frequently struggled with determining the geographic theme of these documents, preferring to mark multiple points in questionable cases. These cases are common, with an average of 1.84 points per annotated document. The systems whose results are described in Table 5 are designed to work with documents annotated with a single point; to handle multiple-point documents, the centroid of the points was taken.

Difficult to geolocate documents The geographic theme of many documents is difficult to determine because they don't mention any easily identifiable locations. Some documents contain only ad-hoc names (e.g. *McCullan's Store* or temporary army camps named after individual com-

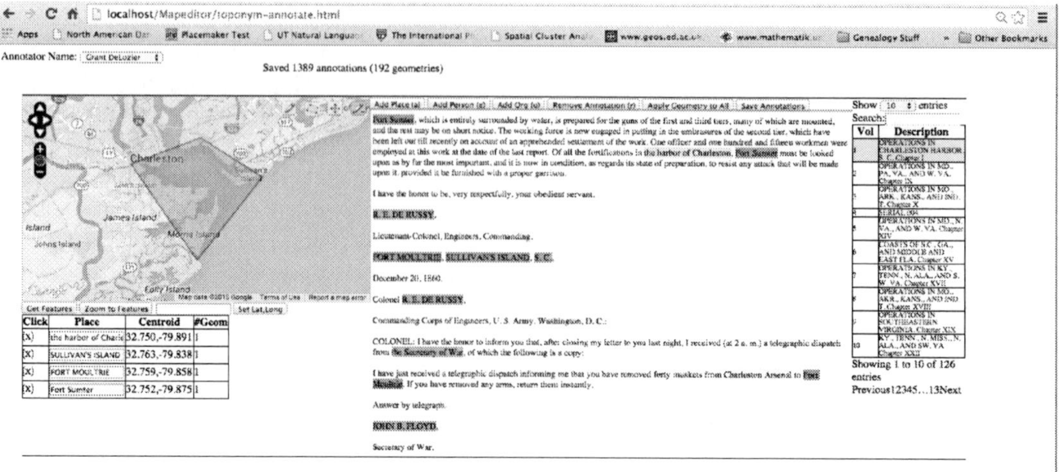

Figure 4: Screen shot of the toponym annotation tool. Place names highlighted in yellow, place names with geoemetries in green.

manders). Many documents mention only a location relative to a previously-specified location in a different document, making the theme discoverable only by looking at the whole series of correspondence. In some cases no clear geographic theme exists at all. In all such cases (amounting to about 38% of the total), the annotators assigned no geometry to the documents.

4.3 Toponym annotation

To begin the toponym annotation procedure, we identified a subset of the volumes which had been annotated with document geolocations (subsections of 15 volumes, selected in part for geographic and topic diversity). Stanford's Named Entity Recognizer (NER) was then run on the collection of documents, using the standard MUC, CoNLL trained models (Finkel et al., 2005). The place annotations that Stanford NER produced were used as a pre-annotated set, which annotators were then asked to correct and add geographic reference to.

The toponym annotation process, which spanned 4 months and occupied 290 hours, resulted in the annotation of 11,795 toponyms (10,389 with geometries) spanning 1,644 annotated documents across 100 page subsections of 15 volumes. Originally all toponym annotations were done by a single annotator. After this process all of the original annotations were reviewed by a second team of three annotators. These annotators were asked to correct a number of problems with the annotations that were not realized until after the initial annotation process had finalized. Corrections to the original annotation mostly focused on building consistent approaches to the challenges outlined in §4.3.2.

4.3.1 Toponym annotator guidelines

Annotators were asked to quickly scan the documents and look for place names. Place names which were not detected by Stanford NER should be added, and other entities incorrectly classified as places should be deleted. We directed annotators to include point, multi-point, polygon, and multi-polygon geometries where appropriate.

They key guidelines annotators were given for the task concerned three aspects of toponyms: metonymy, demonymy, and nested named entities. Annotators were asked to exclude metonymic and demonymic names from annotation. Named Entity Classification researchers have typically adopted the stance of annotating the most encompassing named entity (Finkel and Manning, 2009), though there are exceptions to this trend as is the case in the LGL corpus. Following the majority of related work, we ask annotators to only mark toponyms which constitute the most encompassing named entity (e.g. *44th Virginia Cavalry* is marked as an organization, and in this case the word *Virginia* would not be marked). Not included among nested named entities are toponym hierarchies, or disambiguators such as in the phrase *Richmond, VA, CSA*. In these cases each toponym is annotated with separate reference. To find the reference of places, annotators were allowed access to Internet search. As with document geolocation, annotators were encouraged to look up troublesome toponyms on the Internet, and mostly made use of Wikipedia.

4.3.2 Toponym annotation challenges

Conjunctive toponyms (toponyms that are joined by conjunctions) are a problem when they are in the form of *Varnell's and Lovejoy's Stations*. Here we assumed two toponyms should be added. However, due to how our GeoAnnotate tool worked, we could not annotate overlapping, discontinuous spanning place names. In these cases we asked annotators to mark *Varnell's* as a place separate from *Lovejoy's Stations*, including the *Stations* term only with the second toponym.

Possessive toponyms (toponyms partially consisting of a person's name) appeared in the corpus, e.g. *Widow Harrow's house*. Originally, we asked annotators to avoid annotating these as toponyms. We later amended our guidelines to ask annotators to mark these as toponyms only when the possessed entity was capitalized (e.g. Varnell's Station would be annotated).

Difficult Toponyms (toponyms that could not be geographically referenced) made up about 12% of the overall toponyms in Wotr-Topo. This was typical of toponyms that described the locations of ferries, bridges, railroads, and mills. These features usually no longer exist, so discovering their exact reference even with access to Google is very difficult.

Rivers, and physical features are difficult to reference geographically because their geometric definitions are often highly complex, vague, and poorly defined in gazetteers. Rather than ask annotators to annotate the full extent of rivers, we asked them to mark a point on the river that they felt was most relevant to the context. Annotators tended however to opt for whichever point the river's Wikipedia page indicated, though this was not always the case.

Geographically vague toponym regions appear in the texts. Some of the common examples appearing in the text are *the North*, *the South*, *the West*, and *Northern Mississippi*. We asked annotators to mark these as toponyms, and attempt to draw their reference given the context.

Referring Expressions (e.g. *the stone bridge*) are common. We originally asked annotators not to annotate them, yet we failed to anticipate referring expressions which were partially constituted of place names (e.g. *the Dalton road*). Given that these expressions contain proper place names, and are places themselves, we decided to ask annotators to try and reference the whole expression (i.e. the location of the road). Unfortunately though, discovering the georeference of such roads is very difficult, and annotators tended to mark the location as a point near one of the embedded city toponyms.

Embedded Named Entities : We gave our annotators a rule to only annotate the entity type of the *most-encompassing* named entity. Using this rule expressions like *44th Virginia Cavalry* became annotated as one single organization, rather than a place inside an organization. We did not anticipate however the range of semantically equivalent expressions such as *44th Cavalry of Virginia* or *44th Cavalry from Virginia*. The former form we tended to mark as an organization, while the latter we marked as an organization *44th Cavalry* plus a toponym *Virginia*.

5 Baseline and benchmark system evaluation

In order to gain an understanding of the difficulties of the corpus and encourage its adoption, we evaluate the performance of a number of baseline and benchmark systems on the dataset.

For docgeo, two methods are used for constructing grid cells: **Uniform** and adaptive (**KD**), which adjusts cell sizes to equalize the number of documents in each cell (Roller et al., 2012). **LR** uses flat logistic regression while **Hier** constructs a coarse-to-fine hierarchy of grids with a beam search (Wing and Baldridge, 2014)[4].

For TR, **Population** selects a matching gazetteer referent with the highest population. **WISTR** is a bag of words multinomial logistic regression model trained on Wikipedia (Speriosu and Baldridge, 2013). **SPIDER** is a weighted distance minimization approach that prefers selecting gazetteer referents that occupy minimal area (Speriosu and Baldridge, 2013). **TopoCluster** uses a geographic density estimation of the toponym and context words; **TopoClusterGaz**[5] additionally 'snaps' to the nearest gazetteer referent (DeLozier et al., 2015). All TR systems were

[4] https://github.com/utcompling/textgrounder

[5] https://github.com/grantdelozier/TopoCluster

Table 4: WoTR Toponym Resolution Results

System	A@161	Mean	P	R	F-1
Random	22.2	2216	14.8	6.4	8.9
Population	63.1	1483	42.2	18.2	25.4
SPIDER	67.1	482	37.8	16.3	22.7
WISTR	65.5	895	**54.9**	15.6	24.4
WISTR+SPIDER	67.0	489	37.9	16.4	22.9
TopoCluster	57.0	604	31.8	25.9	28.6
TopoClusterGaz	**71.5**	**468**	37.7	**30.7**	**33.8**

Table 5: Doc Geolocation Results

System	Acc@161km	Median	Mean
Random/Uniform	3.4	1009.5	865.6
Random/KD	8.3	828.8	753.2
NaiveBayes/Uniform	74.8	194.7	53.1
NaiveBayes/KD	72.2	204.4	80.2
LR/Uniform	**77.2**	189.8	53.6
LR/KD	74.4	182.1	59.8
Hier/Uniform	76.8	185.5	49.6
Hier/KD	76.2	**171.8**	**47.2**

trained using out of domain resources, but some weights and parameters (e.g. context window size) were optimized using the WOTR dev set.

Table 5 shows the results of a number of current text-only document geolocation systems (Wing, 2015) on WOTR. Compared with Naive Bayes, both flat (LR) and hierarchical logistic regression (Hier) produce additional benefits. Hier produces the best mean and median despite the fact that it is designed primarily for larger corpora than WOTR. Uniform grids do slightly better overall, a result we have seen before in similar-sized corpora, but adaptive (KD) grids do better with Hier, which is able to compensate somewhat for the larger adaptive grid cells found in low-density areas through its use of multiple grid levels.

Table 4 shows the resolution results of many state-of-the-art toponym resolution systems on the test split of WOTR. As can be seen, TopoClusterGaz outperforms all resolvers on all metrics when oracle NER is used, and outperforms others on Recall and F-1 Score when predictive NER is included in the evaluation. Key to the TopoClusterGaz's success is the ability to predict on both non-gazetteer and gazetteer matched entities, directly boosting Recall and F-1 Score by large margins. When evaluating on a development set of the data, we observed that most differences in system performance could be sourced to how the respective systems dealt with place names that do not have specific GeoNames entries, or are spelled differently than their GeoNames entry (e.g. *Camp Lapwai*, *Colo. Terr.*). TopoCluster often produced correct predictions on these entities, while the gazetteer dependent systems like Population, WISTR, and SPIDER were unable to make predictions. NER inclusive scores (P, R, F-1) are generally much lower for WoTR-Topo than other datasets because the NER systems utilized (Stanford-NER and openNLP-NER) are trained on very different domains. Nevertheless, strongly superior recall on the gazetteer-independent TopoCluster systems leads to higher F-1 scores on the dataset.

6 Conclusion

The War of the Rebellion corpus represents a unique domain for geolocation research. From the perspective of toponym resolution, the corpus is innovative in many respects: richness of geometric annotation (annotations with multi-point, polygon geometries), corpus size (with roughly twice the toponyms of other corpora), and place names not in gazetteers. Baseline system resolution results indicate that the corpus is the most difficult of the corpora surveyed, with A@161 km scores–and especially NER-inclusive scores–being significantly lower than the next most difficult corpus, LGL (DeLozier et al., 2015). The corpus is the first published document-geolocation corpus focusing on historical texts, the first based on running text, the first that was annotated specifically for the task of theme-based document geolocation, and the first annotated with multi-point and polygon geometries. Finally, the availability of text marked both with toponym and docgeo annotations presents new opportunities for joint inference.

7 Corpus availability

The corpus is freely available at our github page[6] under an MIT License. We hope others may expand and improve on the annotations.

8 Acknowledgements

We would like to thank David Staley and Ohio State University's Department of History for access to their high quality version of the War of the Rebellion corpus. This research was supported by a grant from the Morris Memorial Trust Fund of the New York Community Trust.

[6] https://github.com/utcompling/WarOfTheRebellion

References

Edward L. Ayers and Scott Nesbit. 2011. Seeing emancipation: Scale and freedom in the american south. *Journal of the Civil War Era*, 1(1):3–24.

Paolo Bolettieri, Andrea Esuli, Fabrizio Falchi, Claudio Lucchese, Raffaele Perego, Tommaso Piccioli, and Fausto Rabitti. 2009. CoPhIR: a test collection for content-based image retrieval. *CoRR*, abs/0905.4627.

Mariam Daoud and Jimmy Xiangji Huang. 2013. Mining query-driven contexts for geographic and temporal search. *International Journal of Geographical Information Science*, 27(8):1530–1549.

Chris De Rouck, Olivier Van Laere, Steven Schockaert, and Bart Dhoedt. 2011. Georeferencing wikipedia pages using language models from flickr. In *Semantic Web, 10th International conference, Proceedings*, page 8.

Grant DeLozier, Jason Baldridge, and Loretta London. 2015. Gazetteer-independent toponym resolution using geographic word profiles. In *Twenty-Ninth AAAI Conference on Artificial Intelligence*.

Jenny Rose Finkel and Christopher D Manning. 2009. Nested named entity recognition. In *Proceedings of the 2009 Conference on Empirical Methods in Natural Language Processing: Volume 1-Volume 1*, pages 141–150. Association for Computational Linguistics.

Jenny Rose Finkel, Trond Grenager, and Christopher Manning. 2005. Incorporating non-local information into information extraction systems by Gibbs sampling. In *Proceedings of the 43rd Annual Meeting on Association for Computational Linguistics*, pages 363–370. Association for Computational Linguistics.

Claire Grover, Richard Tobin, Kate Byrne, Matthew Woollard, James Reid, Stuart Dunn, and Julian Ball. 2010. Use of the Edinburgh geoparser for georeferencing digitized historical collections. *Philosophical Transactions of the Royal Society A: Mathematical, Physical and Engineering Sciences*, 368(1925):3875–3889.

Bo Han, Paul Cook, and Tim Baldwin. 2014. Text-based Twitter user geolocation prediction. *Journal of Artificial Intelligence Research*, 49(1):451–500.

Saul A. Kripke. 1980. *Naming and Necessity*. Harvard University Press.

Jochen L Leidner. 2008. *Toponym Resolution in Text : Annotation, Evaluation and Applications of Spatial Grounding of Place Names*. Universal Press, Boca Raton, FL, USA.

Michael D Lieberman and Hanan Samet. 2012. Adaptive context features for toponym resolution in streaming news. In *Proceedings of the 35th international ACM SIGIR conference on Research and development in information retrieval*, pages 731–740. ACM.

Koji Matsuda, Akira Sasaki, Naoaki Okazaki, and Kentaro Inui. 2015. Annotating geographical entities on microblog text. In *The 9th Linguistic Annotation Workshop held in conjuncion with NAACL 2015*, page 85.

Andrew Kachites McCallum. 2002. MALLET: A machine learning for language toolkit. http://mallet.cs.umass.edu.

Scott Nesbit. 2013. Visualizing emancipation: Mapping the end of slavery in the american civil war. In Justyna Zander and Pieter J. Mosterman, editors, *Computation for Humanity: Information Technology to Advance Society*, pages 427–435. New York: Taylor & Francis.

Neil O'Hare and Vanessa Murdock. 2013. Modeling locations with social media. *Information Retrieval*, 16(1):30–62.

Stephen Roller, Michael Speriosu, Sarat Rallapalli, Benjamin Wing, and Jason Baldridge. 2012. Supervised text-based geolocation using language models on an adaptive grid. In *Proceedings of the 2012 Joint Conference on Empirical Methods in Natural Language Processing and Computational Natural Language Learning*, EMNLP-CoNLL '12, pages 1500–1510, Stroudsburg, PA, USA. Association for Computational Linguistics.

João Santos, Ivo Anastácio, and Bruno Martins. 2014. Using machine learning methods for disambiguating place references in textual documents. *GeoJournal*, pages 1–18.

Axel Schulz, Aristotelis Hadjakos, Heiko Paulheim, Johannes Nachtwey, and Max Mühlhäuser. 2013. A multi-indicator approach for geolocalization of tweets. In Emre Kiciman, Nicole B. Ellison, Bernie Hogan, Paul Resnick, and Ian Soboroff, editors, *ICWSM'13: Proceedings of the 7th International AAAI Conference on Weblogs and Social Media*. The AAAI Press.

David A Smith and Gregory Crane. 2001. Disambiguating geographic names in a historical digital library. In *Research and Advanced Technology for Digital Libraries*, pages 127–136. Springer.

Michael Speriosu and Jason Baldridge. 2013. Text-driven toponym resolution using indirect supervision. In *ACL (1)*, pages 1466–1476.

Yael A. Sternhell. 2016. Afterlives of a confederate archive: Civil war documents and the making of sectional reconciliation. *Journal of American History*, 102(4):1025–1050.

William G. Thomas III. 2011. *The Iron Way: Railroads, the Civil War, and the Making of Modern America*. Yale University Press.

Olivier van Laere, Steven Schockaert, Vlad Tanasescu, Bart Dhoedt, and Christopher B. Jones. 2014. Georeferencing wikipedia documents using data from social media sources. *ACM Trans. Inf. Syst.*, 32(3):12:1–12:32, July.

Benjamin Wing and Jason Baldridge. 2014. Hierarchical discriminative classification for text-based geolocation. In *Proceedings of the 2014 Conference on Empirical Methods in Natural Language Processing (EMNLP)*, pages 336–348, Doha, Qatar, October. Association for Computational Linguistics.

Benjamin Wing. 2015. *Text-Based Document Geolocation and its Application to the Digital Humanities*. Ph.D. thesis, University of Texas at Austin.

Author Index

Association for Computational Linguistics
209 N. Eighth Street
Stroudsburg, Pennsylvania 18360

ISBN 978-1-5108-2777-6